Developments in the
Economics of Aging

A National Bureau
of Economic Research
Conference Report

Developments in the Economics of Aging

Edited by **David A. Wise**

The University of Chicago Press

Chicago and London

DAVID A. WISE is the John F. Stambaugh Professor of Political Economy at the John F. Kennedy School of Government, Harvard University, and director of the program on the Economics of Aging at the National Bureau of Economic Research.

The University of Chicago Press, Chicago 60637
The University of Chicago Press, Ltd., London
© 2009 by the National Bureau of Economic Research
All rights reserved. Published 2009
Printed in the United States of America

18 17 16 15 14 13 12 11 10 09   1 2 3 4 5
ISBN-13: 978-0-226-90335-4 (cloth)
ISBN-10: 0-226-90335-4 (cloth)

Library of Congress Cataloging-in-Publication Data

Developments in the economics of aging / edited by David A. Wise.
    p. cm.
    Papers presented at a conference held in Carefree, Ariz., in May 2005.
  Includes bibliographical references and index.
    ISBN-13: 978-0-226-90335-4 (cloth : alk. paper)
    ISBN-10: 0-226-90335-4 (cloth : alk. paper)
    1. Retirement—Economic aspects—Congresses. 2. Retirement income—Congresses. 3. Aging—Economic aspects—Congresses.
4. Older people—Economic conditions—Congresses. 5. Older people—Health and hygiene—Economic aspects—Congresses.
I. Wise, David A.
    HQ1062.D48 2009
    331.25′2—dc22
                                                      2008039077

Relation of the Directors to the
Work and Publications of the
National Bureau of Economic Research

1. The object of the NBER is to ascertain and present to the economics profession, and to the public more generally, important economic facts and their interpretation in a scientific manner without policy recommendations. The Board of Directors is charged with the responsibility of ensuring that the work of the NBER is carried on in strict conformity with this object.

2. The President shall establish an internal review process to ensure that book manuscripts proposed for publication DO NOT contain policy recommendations. This shall apply both to the proceedings of conferences and to manuscripts by a single author or by one or more co-authors but shall not apply to authors of comments at NBER conferences who are not NBER affiliates.

3. No book manuscript reporting research shall be published by the NBER until the President has sent to each member of the Board a notice that a manuscript is recommended for publication and that in the President's opinion it is suitable for publication in accordance with the above principles of the NBER. Such notification will include a table of contents and an abstract or summary of the manuscript's content, a list of contributors if applicable, and a response form for use by Directors who desire a copy of the manuscript for review. Each manuscript shall contain a summary drawing attention to the nature and treatment of the problem studied and the main conclusions reached.

4. No volume shall be published until forty-five days have elapsed from the above notification of intention to publish it. During this period a copy shall be sent to any Director requesting it, and if any Director objects to publication on the grounds that the manuscript contains policy recommendations, the objection will be presented to the author(s) or editor(s). In case of dispute, all members of the Board shall be notified, and the President shall appoint an ad hoc committee of the Board to decide the matter; thirty days additional shall be granted for this purpose.

5. The President shall present annually to the Board a report describing the internal manuscript review process, any objections made by Directors before publication or by anyone after publication, any disputes about such matters, and how they were handled.

6. Publications of the NBER issued for informational purposes concerning the work of the Bureau, or issued to inform the public of the activities at the Bureau, including but not limited to the NBER Digest and Reporter, shall be consistent with the object stated in paragraph 1. They shall contain a specific disclaimer noting that they have not passed through the review procedures required in this resolution. The Executive Committee of the Board is charged with the review of all such publications from time to time.

7. NBER working papers and manuscripts distributed on the Bureau's web site are not deemed to be publications for the purpose of this resolution, but they shall be consistent with the object stated in paragraph 1. Working papers shall contain a specific disclaimer noting that they have not passed through the review procedures required in this resolution. The NBER's web site shall contain a similar disclaimer. The President shall establish an internal review process to ensure that the working papers and the web site do not contain policy recommendations, and shall report annually to the Board on this process and any concerns raised in connection with it.

8. Unless otherwise determined by the Board or exempted by the terms of paragraphs 6 and 7, a copy of this resolution shall be printed in each NBER publication as described in paragraph 2 above.

Contents

Preface

This volume consists of papers presented at a conference held in Carefree, Arizona, in May 2005. Most of the research was conducted as part of the program on the Economics of Aging at the National Bureau of Economic Research and was sponsored by the U.S. Department of Health and Human Services, through National Institute on Aging grants P01-AG05842 and P30-AG12810 to the National Bureau of Economic Research. Any other funding sources are noted in the individual chapters.

Any opinions expressed in this volume are those of the respective authors and do not necessarily reflect the views of the National Bureau of Economic Research or the sponsoring organizations.

Introduction

David A. Wise

In 2008, the leading edge of the baby boom generation turns age sixty-two and becomes eligible to receive Social Security benefits. Projecting forward, the U.S. population age sixty-two and older will increase from forty-five million to nearly eighty million over a period of just twenty years. Compounding the impact of the aging baby boomers are trends in longevity. At age sixty-two, life expectancy is about twenty years for men and twenty-three years for women—and it is getting longer all the time. Whether this growing population of older Americans works or retires, how much they will have saved for their retirement, and what health care they will need—these are critical questions. Similar issues, questions, and challenges are being faced in countries around the world. What are the relationships between demographic trends, economic trends, health trends, and public policy, and what are the implications for individual health and wellbeing?

These questions motivate an ongoing research program at the NBER on the economics of aging. This is the eleventh in a series of NBER volumes that have emerged from that project effort. The previous ones were *The Economics of Aging, Issues in the Economics of Aging, Topics in the Economics of Aging, Studies in the Economics of Aging, Advances in the Economics of Aging, Inquiries in the Economics of Aging, Frontiers in the Economics of Aging, Themes in the Economics of Aging, Perspectives on the Economics of Aging* and *Analyses in the Economics of Aging.* Our aim is to understand more fully the relationships between age demographics, retirement and

David A. Wise is the John F. Stambaugh Professor of Political Economy at the John F. Kennedy School of Government, Harvard University, and director of the program on aging at the National Bureau of Economic Research.

health care policy, economic behavior, and the health and economic circumstances of people as they age.

Many of the topics addressed in this eleventh volume address emerging issues in the economics of aging, as our retirement systems evolve over time and adapt to an aging population demographic, both in the United States and around the world. The papers are organized into four topic areas: retirement saving, intergenerational transfers, retirement behavior, and health and economic circumstances. These four themes are among the largest organizational components of our larger research effort, and the chapters contained in each section build on a significant collection of prior research findings. They are incremental pieces of a larger whole. This introduction provides some context for the individual studies, and brief summaries that draw heavily on the authors' own language.

Retirement Saving

One of the most important aging-related trends in the United States is the growth of targeted retirement saving. Over the past twenty-five years, personal retirement accounts have replaced defined benefit pension plans as the primary means of retirement saving, and contributions to 401(k)-type plans have expanded dramatically. Retirement saving has become a substantively important component of postretirement support for a growing number of new retirees, and its importance increases every year. Recent projections, for example, show 401(k) asset levels by 2040 that are many times larger than the savings ever accumulated in traditional employer pension plans, and more important in retirement than Social Security for a growing number of households. This represents a fundamental transition in the composition of postretirement financial support in the United States.

The growing importance of targeted retirement saving in individual accounts has been a central theme in most of the prior volumes on the economics of aging, and it continues here. One aspect of these plans is that they shift responsibility for managing retirement assets from the professional money managers who oversee defined benefit plan investments to individual participants in defined contribution plans. The amount of assets that accumulate in individual retirement saving plans depends on decisions made by the workers themselves, such as whether to enroll in the plan, how much to contribute, and how to invest the assets. The first two chapters in the volume address issues that relate to 401(k) decisions: focusing first on the asset allocation decision among the investment options in a 401(k) plan, and second on the decision to initially enroll in a plan.

In chapter 1, "Lifecycle Asset Allocation Strategies and the Distribution of 401(k) Retirement Wealth," James Poterba, Joshua Rauh, Steven Venti, and I present evidence on the distribution of balances in 401(k)-type retirement saving accounts under various asset allocation strategies that investors might choose. In addition to a range of age-invariant strategies, such as an all-bond and an all-stock strategy, we consider several different lifecycle funds that automatically alter the investor's mix of assets as he or she ages. These funds offer investors a higher portfolio allocation to stocks at the beginning of a working career than as they approach retirement. We also consider a no lose allocation strategy, in which households purchase enough riskless bonds at each age to ensure that they will have no less than their nominal contribution when they reach retirement age, and then invest the balance in corporate stock. This strategy combines a riskless floor for retirement income with some upside investment potential.

Our results suggest several conclusions about the effect of investment strategy on retirement wealth. First, the distribution of retirement wealth associated with typical lifecycle investment strategies is similar to that from age-invariant asset allocation strategies that set the equity share of the portfolio equal to the average equity share in the lifecycle strategies. Second, the expected utility associated with different 401(k) asset allocation strategies, and the ranking of these strategies, is very sensitive to three parameters: the expected return on corporate stock, the relative risk aversion of the investing household, and the amount of non-401(k) wealth that the household will have available at retirement. At modest levels of risk aversion, or when the household has access to substantial non-401(k) wealth at retirement, the historical pattern of stock and bond returns implies that the expected utility of an all-stock investment allocation rule is greater than that from any of the more conservative strategies. When we reduce the expected return on stocks by 300 basis points relative to historical values, however, other strategies dominate the all-equity allocation for investors with high levels of relative risk aversion. The no lose plan yields an expected utility of wealth at retirement that is comparable to several of the lifecycle plans, but both the expected value of wealth and the expected utility level are slightly lower than the values associated with the lifecycle strategies.

In chapter 2, "Reducing the Complexity Costs of 401(k) Participation through Quick Enrollment," James Choi, David Laibson, and Brigitte Madrian focus on the decision to initially enroll in a 401(k) plan. Previous research has shown that 401(k) participation increases dramatically when companies switch from an opt-in to an opt-out (or automatic) enrollment regime. One reason that automatic enrollment increases 401(k) participation is that it allows workers to defer, temporarily or permanently, the complex decisions of how much to contribute and to allocate those contributions among investment alternatives. By creating a default contribution rate and investment allocation, and by making enrollment automatic, participation becomes easier, and more people participate sooner than they would do otherwise.

Chapter 2 considers another approach to simplifying enrollment, but in the context of an opt-in plan, rather than an automatic enrollment plan. What Quick Enrollment does is to establish a default contribution rate and a default asset allocation, just like the automatic enrollment plans, but without the automatic enrollment. So employees can opt into the 401(k) without being required to analyze the more complicated set of options available in the plan. The authors evaluate three different implementations of Quick Enrollment at two firms. Two of the implementations were short-term interventions that targeted nonparticipating employees who had previously been hired by the firms in the study. The third was an ongoing intervention for newly hired employees.

The authors find that Quick Enrollment tripled participation among new hires relative to a standard enrollment mechanism in which employees must actively select both a contribution rate and an asset allocation. When Quick Enrollment was made available to previously hired employees who were not participating in their 401(k) plan, 10 to 20 percent of these nonparticipants enrolled in the plan. The chapter goes on to consider possible modifications that would incorporate elements of an "active decision" approach without defeating the purpose of Quick Enrollment. For example, it compares the simplicity of alignable options, such as contribution rates, as compared with nonalignable options, such as investment allocation. Literature on the psychology of consumer choice suggests that increasing the number of alignable options (i.e., savings rates), will lead to increased Quick Enrollment utilization, whereas increasing the number of non-alignable options (i.e., asset allocation options), will lead to reduced participation.

Intergenerational Transfers

In all societies, intergenerational transfers are large and potentially have a strong influence on inequality and growth. The development of each generation of youth depends on the resources that older generations devote to their health, education, and sustenance. The direction of transfer, in this case, is from older to younger generations. At the same time, however, the well-being of the elderly depends on public programs that provide health care and income support and also on familial systems that dominate in many developing countries. These are transfers in the other direction, from younger to older generations. The importance of intergenerational transfers has not gone unnoticed by the research community. During the last two decades there have been important advances in measuring, modeling, and assessing the implications of intergenerational transfers at both the micro and the macro level. A comprehensive macro-level intergenerational transfer framework and accounting system, however, has not been developed, nor have there been efforts to model and measure familial transfers at the aggregate level.

In chapter 3, "Population Aging and Intergenerational Transfers: Introducing Age into National Accounts," Ronald Lee, Andrew Mason, An-Chi Tung, Mun-Sim Lai, and Tim Miller outline the key concepts and methods that are being used to construct National Transfer Accounts (NTAs). The goal of this accounting system is to measure intergenerational transfers at the aggregate level in a manner consistent with National Income and Product Accounts. Another critical objective of this research is to quantify both public and private transfers in a way that allows comparison and analysis. Although the research reported here is at an early stage, the authors believe that the development of the National Transfer Account system will prove useful in the same way that National Income and Product Accounts are useful despite their flaws, particularly as it becomes possible to follow the flow of intergenerational transfers of individual cohorts over their lifecycles.

A second aspect of the paper is to compare the lifecycles and support systems of Taiwan and the United States. The differences between these two countries are particularly interesting because of the relative importance of their familial support systems: strong in Taiwan and weak in the United States. The authors conclude that familial transfers from adult children to their parents in Taiwan are very large and comparable in magnitude to the transfers made in the United States through public programs, such as Social Security and Medicare. The results provide information about support systems that has not been previously available, including detailed information about the asset accumulation process and how it relates to variation in lifecycle needs.

Retirement Behavior

Another core theme of the NBER retirement program since its inception has been to better understand the determinants of retirement behavior, the effects on retirement of public and private retirement policies, and how they relate to retirement trends over time. In studies reported in previous volumes, we have explored the impact of pension plans on retirement at companies that offered traditional pension plans, documenting the powerful effect of plan provisions on retirement behavior. We have also looked at the influence of public retirement policies, particularly Social Security and Medicare, on retirement. Comprehensive modeling of retirement behavior, incorporating a diversity of influencing factors, has been a part of past NBER work as well.

Importantly, our ongoing analysis of retirement behavior has taken place at a time of historic transition in both public and private retirement policy. The significant transition from traditional pension plans, often with retiree health insurance benefits, to 401(k)-like programs without retiree health insurance, is one important change. Another is the reform of social security programs that have been implemented around the world in response to the financial pressures of population aging. The policy environment in which individual retirement decisions are being made is different from what it was even a decade ago. In this volume, retirement behavior remains a core component of our work, though with a focus on two more exploratory topics: one relating to asset accumulation and retirement, and the other to wellbeing or satisfaction in retirement.

In chapter 4, "The Effect of Large Capital Gains or Losses on Retirement," Michael Hurd, Monika Reti, and Susann Rohwedder consider the effect on retirement of unanticipated changes in wealth. Although it is natural to suppose that years in retirement are a normal good, so that increases in wealth would lead to earlier retirement, it has been difficult for researchers to disentangle the influence of wealth from the influence of other interrelated factors. For example, higher-paying jobs may have characteristics and amenities that make work more pleasant, thereby delaying retirement, relative to lower-paying jobs. Since higher-paying jobs also increase wealth, the result is a positive cross-sectional correlation between wealth and retirement age; just the opposite of what one might expect if one were analyzing the influence of wealth in isolation from these related factors. The stock market boom of the mid-1990s to 2000 and the subsequent bust between 2000 and 2002 provide an opportunity to study what was likely an unexpected wealth change for at least part of the population.

The researchers found no evidence that workers in households which had large gains retired earlier than they had anticipated, or that they revised their retirement expectations compared with workers in households that had no large gains. Going the other direction, however, there is some suggestion that the decline in the stock market led to an increase in the expected retirement age. The authors report that they have no good explanation for the asymmetry, but speculate that part of the answer may lie in expectations about future rates of return, and in the psychological adjustment of spending expectations, which may rise after a wealth increase, but not fall after a wealth decrease.

Chapter 5 also deals with retirement behavior, and also relates to the question of whether retirement should be considered a normal good. In "Early Retirement, Social Security and Well-Being in Germany," Axel Börsch-Supan and Hendrik Jürges look at the potential changes in subjective well-being or overall life satisfaction that may occur as individuals transition into retirement, comparing workers who retire early with those who retire later. Specifically, is the effect of retirement on well-being more favorable for those taking early retirement, as compared with those retiring at the normal retirement age? Several hypotheses are presented: (1) early retirees suffer from retirement, compared with later retirees, because they are more likely to have been forced out of jobs involuntarily, or by declining health, (2) early retirees benefit from retirement, compared with normal retirees, because they can make use of generous early retirement incentives not available to those who may retire later, or (3) there is no difference between early and normal retirement because both types of individuals have chosen retirement optimally.

The study finds that at ages younger than sixty, those who are retired are on average much less happy than those who are working. The difference is mainly due to a composition effect, as these early retirees are generally covered by disability pensions. Controlling for disability status, the well-being differential between early retirees and those still working vanishes. Thus, it is not retirement as such that reduces life satisfaction, but disability. The study also concludes that when workers develop functional disabilities, early retirement (because of disability) increases well-being significantly. Following over time the life satisfaction of individual workers who take early retirement, there is a marked drop in life satisfaction in preretirement years, and into retirement, but satisfaction returns to preretirement levels one or two years after retirement.

Health and Economic Circumstances

The remaining five chapters in the volume deal in some way with the relationship between health and economic circumstances. This, too, is a continuing theme of our research program more broadly. The pronounced gradient in health between people in different socioeconomic groups is well known. People who are richer or better educated live longer and have a higher quality of life than people in groups with lower socioeconomic status (SES). There are many reasons for this relationship, some of which result from the effects of poor health on economic outcomes, some of which result from the effects of economic circumstances and their long-term impact on health over the life course, and some of which relate to independent factors that affect both health and economic outcomes. Disentangling these interrelationships has been an important aspect of many recent investigations.

The diversity of methodological approaches we have applied in past research reflects the complexity of the topic. Interactions between health and work, childhood health and economic circumstances and those in adulthood, health events and out-of-pocket medical spending, demographics and health behavior, differential access to medical care, absolute economic circumstances versus relative circumstances, the impact of education on both economic and health outcomes, the role of extreme poverty, and the differences in both standards of living and social circumstances across countries—have all been explored as part of our ongoing NBER research effort. Five new directions are considered in this volume.

In chapter 6, "How Do the Better Educated Do It? Socioeconomic Status and the Ability to Cope With Underlying Impairment," David Cutler, Mary Beth Landrum, and Kate Stewart focus on how elderly people in different socioeconomic groups cope with disability in performing basic personal care activities, including dressing, bathing, and getting around inside the home, and activities required to live independently, such as preparing meals, grocery shopping, and managing money. The analysis considers two primary issues. The study evaluates first how much of the gradient in health is a result of underlying differences in functioning versus the ability to cope with impairments. The authors find that while the majority of socioeconomic differences in disability can be attributed to differences in underlying functioning—the better off have much less difficulty with these measures even in the absence of help—coping is important as well. In other words, the better educated are less likely to have functional disabilities in the first place, and cope with them better when they occur.

The second part of the study analyzes how people cope with impairments, how coping strategies vary by education, and whether the use of personal help and technological aids are important for successful coping. On these issues, the study finds that better-educated people use substantially more assistive technology and are more likely to use paid help than people with less education. They are less likely, however, to receive help from relatives, so that the overall use of personal care is actually lower among the better educated than among the less educated. The authors suggest that more work is needed on the complex interrelationships between underlying functional limitations, coping strategies, and the environment in which people live, in order to further understand how the better educated are better able to cope with their functional limitations.

In chapter 7, David Cutler and Edward Glaeser ask "Why Do Europeans Smoke More than Americans?" Americans have one of the lowest smoking rates in the developed world. The authors examine three potential explanations for the low level of smoking in the United States relative to other developed countries. One is the possibility that cigarette prices are higher in the United States, after accounting for taxes and other regulations on tobacco products. A second potential explanation is the higher income levels in the United States, compared with much of Europe, and the inverse relationship between income and smoking. The third potential explanation is that there are differences in beliefs across countries on the harmful health effects of smoking.

After analyzing the data, the authors firmly reject the first hypothesis, that differences in cigarette prices and regulations explain differences in smoking rates between Europe and the United States. If anything, tobacco consumption in the United States is less regulated than in most European countries, and controlling for regulation only makes the lower smoking rates in the United States more surprising. Moving on to the second hypothesis, the authors find that income differences explain no more than one quarter of the difference between European and American smoking rates. The most important factor appears to be differences in beliefs about the health consequences of smoking. While 91 percent of Americans think that cigarettes cause cancer, only 84 percent of Europeans share that view. Cutler and Glaeser estimate that this difference can explain between one quarter and one half of the total smoking difference between the United States and Europe. Moreover, the history of cigarettes within the United States suggests that American beliefs about smoking seemed to come about only after substantial information about the harms of smoking were presented—first by private researchers, then by the federal government. The authors refer to "soft paternalism" as a major factor in reducing smoking in the United States.

The study also speculates about why the United States, with its lower propensity toward regulation and paternalism generally, was more effective in changing beliefs about the health consequences of smoking. A review of smoking history suggests that entrepreneurial actions on the part of antismoking interest groups were quite important. According to this view, while greater U.S. entrepreneurship and economic openness led to more smoking during an earlier era (and still leads to more obesity today), it also led to faster changes in beliefs about smoking and ultimately less cigarette consumption.

In chapter 8, Jay Bhattacharya, Alan Garber, and Thomas MaCurdy explore "Trends in Prescription Drug Use by the Disabled Elderly." With the implementation of the Medicare Modernization Act in 2006, the federal government became responsible for the financing of prescription drugs for all Medicare recipients. Though there have been several attempts to forecast how much financial risk will be borne by the government in future years as a consequence of the introduction of Medicare Part D, no forecast has separately analyzed the effect of disability on Part D spending. This is unfortunate, because the disabled elderly are among the groups that might be most affected by pharmaceutical innovations and changes in the way prescription drugs are financed. This paper analyzes separately trends in the utilization of pharmaceuticals by disabled and nondisabled beneficiaries between 1992 and 2001. It examines trends for both the over-sixty-five population and the population under sixty-five that qualifies for Medicare by virtue of their disability.

The study finds that for those with and without functional limitations, and for both elderly and nonelderly Americans, expenditures on prescription drugs as a fraction of total medical expenditures grew sharply over this period. The most rapid growth was experienced by Medicare recipients covered by disability insurance (DI), a population that was also the fastest-growing segment of Medicare enrollees in the 1990s. The DI Medicare population had large increases in expenditures on all drug categories examined (psychotherapeutic, analgesic, antiarthritic, cardiovascular, and all other drugs), with especially large increases for psychotherapeutic drugs. Among the DI Medicare population with the highest pharmaceutical expenditures, the study finds particularly large increases in the prevalence of mental illness, with smaller increases in other chronic diseases.

Among the elderly Medicare population (as distinct from the DI Medicare population), there were also increases between 1992 and 2001 in pharmaceutical expenditures for all drug categories. Among the 10 percent of elderly Medicare enrollees with the highest expenditures, with and without functional limitations, there were moderate increases in the prevalence of several chronic diseases, including hypertension, arthritis, diabetes, and osteoporosis. Among those with functional limitations, the prevalence of mental illness also increased sharply. The authors suggest that if the trends indicated by these results continue, then Medicare's financial risk represented by the introduction of the new Part D drug benefit could be substantial.

In chapter 9, "Health and Well-being in Udaipur and South Africa," Anne Case and Angus Deaton present a descriptive account of health and economic status in India and South Africa, focusing on data from three research sites: one in rural Rajasthan, India; one in a shack township outside of Cape Town, South Africa; and one in a rural South African site that, until 1994, was part of a Bantustan. Income levels across the three sites are roughly in the ratio of 4:2:1, with urban South Africa richest and rural Rajasthan poorest. The paper emphasizes the lack of any simple and reliable relationship between health and wealth between and within these sites.

Among the comparative results reported in the study, South Africans were found to be taller and heavier than the Indians, though their children are no taller at the same age. South African self-assessed physical and mental health is no better, and South Africans are more likely to report that they have to miss meals for lack of money. In spite of differences in incomes across the three sites, South Africans and Indians report a very similar list of symptoms of ill health. Although they have much lower incomes, urban women in South Africa have fully caught up with black American women in the prevalence of obesity, and are catching up in terms of hypertension. These women have the misfortune to be experiencing many of the diseases of affluence without experiencing affluence itself.

Because health, like well-being, is multidimensional, and because the components of health do not correlate perfectly with one another, or with income-based measures, the study concludes that income on its own is likely to be misleading as a shortcut measure of international health. Even within places, such as those examined here, the links between health and wealth are far from universally strong. Where the "wealthier is healthier" hypothesis seems to work better is in comparisons between the three poor sites and much richer Americans. White Americans self-report better health than do black Americans, but both report substantially better physical and mental health than do South Africans and Indians in the three sites studied.

Finally in chapter 10, "The SES Gradient on both Sides of the Atlantic," James Banks, Michael Marmot, Zoe Oldfield, and James Smith present data on some of the most salient aspects of the SES-health gradient in England and the United States. There are several key findings. First, looking across a wide variety of diseases, average health status among men is much worse in America compared to England. Second, there exists a steep negative health gradient for men in both countries, where men at the bottom of the economic hierarchy are in much worse health than those at the top. This social health gradient exists whether education, income, or financial wealth is used as the marker of one's SES status. While the negative social gradient in male health is apparent in both countries, it appears to be steeper in the United States. These central conclusions are maintained even after controlling for a standard set of behavioral risk factors such as smoking, drinking, and obesity, and are equally true using either biological measures of disease or individual self-reports.

In contrast to these disease-based measures of health, the health of American men appears to be superior to the health of English men when self-reported general health status is used as the measure of health status. This apparent contradiction does not result from differences in comorbidity, emotional health, or ability to function, all of which still point to American men being less healthy than their English counterparts. The contradiction most likely stems instead from different thresholds used by American and English men when evaluating their health status on subjective scales. For the same objective health status, Americans are much more likely to say that their health is good than are the English.

While the ten chapters in this volume address somewhat diverse topics in the economics of aging, they contribute to an integrated research agenda that has focused on the health and economic circumstances of individuals as they age, and a worldwide population that is not only growing older, but experiencing fundamental changes across countries in terms of economic growth, age demographics, and population health.

I

Retirement Saving

1

Life-cycle Asset Allocation Strategies and the Distribution of 401(k) Retirement Wealth

James M. Poterba, Joshua Rauh, Steven F. Venti, and David A. Wise

The growing importance of defined contribution pension arrangements, such as 401(k) plans, is shifting the responsibility for managing retirement assets from the professional money managers who oversee defined benefit plan investments to individual participants in defined contribution plans. Retirement savers face the challenge of deciding how to allocate their retirement portfolios across broad asset classes and across many different financial products. Asset allocation decisions have important consequences for retirement wealth accumulation. Some policy analysts have voiced concerns that individual participants in defined contribution plans may not fully understand the risks associated with various investment options, and that they may consequently be exposed to greater risks of retirement income shortfall in defined contribution plans than in defined benefit plans.

Quantifying the risk associated with defined contribution pension plans and examining how individual choices affect this risk is an active topic of research. Samwick and Skinner (2004) compare the risks associated with

James M. Poterba is president and CEO of the National Bureau of Economic Research and the Mitsui Professor of Economics at the Massachusetts Institute of Technology. Joshua Rauh is an assistant professor of finance at the University of Chicago and a faculty research fellow of the National Bureau of Economic Research. Steven F. Venti is a professor of economics and holds the DeWalt H. Ankeny '21 and Marie Ankeny Professorship in Economic Policy at Dartmouth College, and is a research associate of the National Bureau of Economic Research. David A. Wise is the John F. Stambaugh Professor of Political Economy at the John F. Kennedy School of Government, Harvard University, and director of the program on aging at the National Bureau of Economic Research.

We are grateful to Tonja Bowen for outstanding research assistance, to John Campbell, Luis Viceira, and Robert Willis for helpful comments, to Morningstar for providing us with mutual fund data, and to the National Institute on Aging for research support under grant number P01 AG005842.

defined benefit and defined contribution plans for workers with a set of stylized wage and employment trajectories. Many other studies have examined the risk of different investment strategies in the context of lifetime saving programs that resemble defined contribution plans. Campbell and Viceira (2002) and Cocco, Gomes, and Maenhout (2005) explore the optimal asset allocation between stocks and bonds for life-cycle savers. Shiller (2005) tabulates the distribution of possible terminal wealth values when investors follow age-dependent asset allocation rules in a saving program that he models on a defined contribution Social Security system. Poterba, Rauh, Venti, and Wise (2005; hereafter PRVW [2005]), examine how different portfolio allocation strategies affect retirement wealth over the life cycle.

Previous findings about the level of retirement wealth associated with defined contribution saving programs, and about the risk of such wealth, are very sensitive to assumptions about the expected return on corporate stock. Stocks have offered substantially higher average returns than bonds over the eighty-year sample that is often used to calibrate the return distributions. PRVW (2005) find that this has an important effect on the distribution of retirement wealth for alternative asset allocation rules. Greater exposure to stocks leads to a higher average retirement account balance. For a risk-neutral retirement saver facing the historical return distribution, and choosing a fraction between zero and one hundred percent of her or his portfolio to allocate to stocks, this suggests that allocating the entire portfolio to stocks is optimal. As the risk aversion of a retirement saver increases, the optimal share of the retirement portfolio that is held in stocks declines.

Many commentators have raised questions about whether defined contribution plan participants are informed enough to make decisions about asset allocation and other dimensions of their retirement saving plan. Some plan sponsors have begun to offer participants investment options that permit them to avoid investment decision-making. One such innovation in the financial services marketplace is the life-cycle fund, which automatically varies the share of the saver's portfolio that is held in stocks and bonds as a function of the saver's age or years until retirement. These funds are one of the most rapidly growing financial products of the last decade. They offer investors the opportunity to exploit time-varying investment rules, typically reducing equity exposure as retirement approaches, without the need to make active investment management choices. In this chapter, we consider the effect of such life-cycle investment strategies on the distribution of retirement wealth.

This chapter extends previous research in two directions. First, we consider both the distribution of retirement assets and the expected utility of reaching retirement with a given asset stock. In contrast, a number of earlier studies focus only on the distribution of account balances, which does not capture the potential cost of an investment strategy with a high mean retirement balance but a small probability of a very poor outcome. We parameterize a utility-of-retirement wealth function as a power function of retirement wealth and recognize that wealth held outside the saver's defined contribution plan can have an important effect on utility at retirement. Second, we use actual Social Security earnings' histories to model household contribution flows to defined contribution plans. Several earlier studies have used simple stochastic processes to model labor income flows or have assumed that labor income follows a stylized path over the life cycle. Our results better capture the wide degree of heterogeneity in household earnings experiences.

The chapter is divided into five sections. The first summarizes theoretical research on the optimal pattern of age-related asset allocation. It then describes the life-cycle funds that have become increasingly popular in the retirement plan market. Section 1.2 describes the algorithm that we use to simulate the distribution of retirement plan assets under different asset allocation rules during the accumulation period. This discussion draws heavily on PRVW (2005). Section 1.3 describes our strategy for calibrating the simulation model, for selecting the sample of households for analysis, and for assigning distributions of returns to each of the assets in our study. The fourth section presents the various life-cycle asset allocation rules that we consider, including some that involve age-independent asset allocation rules. It then reports our central findings about the distribution of retirement account balances under these different rules as well as the expected lifetime utility at retirement under various rules. There is a brief conclusion in section 1.5.

1.1   Optimal Age-Dependent Asset Allocation Rules and the Rise of Life-cycle Funds

Financial economists have a long tradition of studying how a rational, risk-averse, long-lived consumer would choose to allocate her or his portfolio between risky and riskless assets at different ages. Samuelson (1969), in one of the first formal analyses, challenges the conventional wisdom that an investor with a long horizon should invest a larger fraction of her or his portfolio in risky assets because there is an opportunity to average returns over a longer period. This result is related to the earlier, more general observation by Samuelson (1963) that taking repeated identical uncorrelated risks augments the risk of the final outcome, rather than reducing it. In the context of the life-cycle portfolio selection problem, when returns on the risky asset are serially uncorrelated and there is no labor income, a rational investor should hold the same fraction of her or his portfolio in risky assets at all ages. This analytical result runs counter to the suggestion of many financial advisors, who suggest that investors reduce their equity exposure as they approach retirement. Merton (1969) derives similar results in the context of a lifetime dynamic optimization framework.

Perhaps in part because this result is inconsistent with much financial practice, subsequent research has tried to uncover reasons why an investor might choose to reduce her or his equity exposure as she or he ages. Bodie, Merton, and Samuelson (1988) argue that younger investors have greater flexibility in their subsequent labor supply decisions and that they should consequently be more tolerant of risk. They suggest that younger investors may rationally choose to hold a higher fraction of their portfolio in stock than older investors. Gollier (2001) and Gollier and Zeckhauser (2002) derive the conditions under which the option to rebalance a portfolio in the future affects portfolio choice. Their results suggest that under specific assumptions about the structure of utility functions, the optimal portfolio share devoted to equity will decline with age. Campbell et al. (2001) and Campbell and Viceira (2002) develop numerical solutions to dynamic models that can be used to study optimal portfolio structure over the life cycle if shocks to labor income follow specific stochastic processes and investors have power utility. Cocco, Gomes, and Maenhout (2005) solve such a model in the presence of nontradable labor income and borrowing constraints. They find that a life-cycle investment strategy that reduces the household's equity exposure as it ages may be optimal, depending on the shape of the labor income profile.

The empirical evidence on age-specific patterns in household asset allocation suggests, at best, weak reductions in equity exposure as households age. Gomes and Michaelides (2005) survey recent research on the correspondence between theoretical models of life-cycle asset allocation and empirical evidence on actual investment patterns. Ameriks and Zeldes (2004) and Poterba and Samwick (2001) present empirical evidence on how portfolio shares for stocks, bonds, and other assets vary over the life cycle. The general conclusion is that equity shares decline very little at older ages, although Ameriks and Zeldes (2004) find some evidence that some households cash out their equity holdings when they reach retirement or annuitize their accumulated holdings in defined contribution accounts.

To cater to the perceived desire of investors to reduce their equity exposure as they age, and to help investors overcome the problems of inertia in retirement asset allocation that are documented by Samuelson and Zeckhauser (1988), several financial institutions have created life-cycle funds. These funds are usually designed for an investor with a target retirement date. Life-cycle funds were available from Fidelity Investments as early as 1988, and there were at least 250 target-year life-cycle funds in the mutual fund marketplace in 2005. Several major mutual fund families now offer a sequence of different funds targeted to investors with different retirement dates. In some cases the life-cycle fund is a fund of funds that invests in a

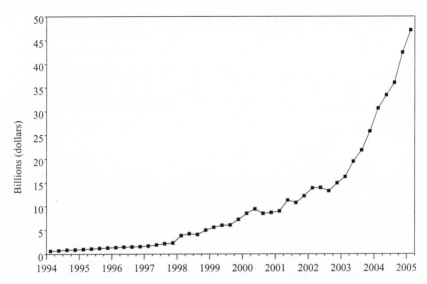

Fig. 1.1   Aggregate net assets of target-year life-cycle funds, March 1994–March 2005

Note: This figure shows quarterly net assets of all mutual funds categorized by Morningstar as retirement or life-cycle funds that also have a target-year rebalancing feature. As of March 2005, the $47.1 billion represents assets in the following families: Barclays Global Investors LifePath, Fidelity Freedom Funds, Fidelity Advisor Freedom, Intrust Bank NestEgg, Mass-Mutual Select Destination Retire, Principal Investors Lifetime, Putnam Retirement Ready, Scudder Target, State Farm Lifepath, TIAA-CREF Institutional Lifecycle, T. Rowe Price Retirement, Vanguard Target Retirement, Vantagepoint Milestone, and Wells Fargo Outlook. Net assets for life-cycle funds were assembled from fund reports and data provided by Morningstar.

mix of other mutual funds, while in other cases the fund manager holds a specific pool of assets and alters the asset mix as the fund ages.

Figure 1.1 shows the rapid growth in life-cycle fund assets during the last eleven years. The figure indicates that life-cycle funds held $5.5 billion in March 2000, and that their assets had grown to $47.1 billion by 2005. Many of these funds are offered in 401(k) plans. Marquez (2005) reports that Hewitt Associates estimates that 38 percent of all 401(k) plans offer life-cycle funds. At a time when Clements (2005) reports that the proliferation of investment options 401(k) plans has come under fire, life-cycle funds offer a way to combine both stock and fixed-income options into a single fund, and to offer investors a time-varying asset allocation mix. Life-cycle funds are sometimes suggested as a natural choice for the default investment option in automatic enrollment 401(k) programs.

The life-cycle funds offered at different fund families follow different age-phased asset allocation rules. Table 1.1 reports summary information on the life-cycle funds offered at leading mutual fund companies, which we define as the set of mutual fund companies tracked by Morningstar. The

Table 1.1   Target-year life-cycle mutual fund characteristics, March 2005

Retirement year	Years to retirement	Net assets ($ billion)	Weighted average expense ratio (%)	Number of fund families	Number of funds	2005Q1 weighted average asset allocation		
						Stocks (%)	Bonds (%)	Cash (%)
2005	0	4.1	0.6	10	40	30.0	42.0	28.0
2010	5	11.2	0.8	13	45	49.4	35.4	15.3
2015	10	2.9	0.6	8	22	58.2	35.7	6.1
2020	15	14.5	0.8	13	45	69.7	24.6	5.7
2025	20	1.9	0.6	8	22	79.2	17.2	3.6
2030	25	8.3	0.8	12	39	81.7	13.8	4.5
2035	30	0.6	0.8	6	15	85.2	10.4	4.4
2040	35	3.3	0.8	11	38	88.0	8.4	3.5

Note: Funds used in this analysis consist of all mutual funds categorized by Morningstar as retirement or life-cycle funds that also have a target-year rebalancing feature. Net assets for these funds as of 3/31/2005 were collected from fund reports and from Morningstar.com. The number of funds differs from the number of fund families for a given retirement year because funds have multiple classes of shares and "number of funds" counts each share class as a separate fund. The weighted average expense ratio is the average expense ratio including subfund expenses weighted by fund net asset value. Asset allocations are also averaged with fund net asset value weighting. One fund family also offers funds with retirement years 2011, 2012, 2013, 2014, 2045, and 2050. The information on these funds is not used in constructing this table.

table shows the average mix of stocks and bonds currently held by funds targeting different retirement years. None of the funds publish the specific asset allocation rule that they will follow going forward as retirement dates draw nearer, but many fund prospectuses indicate the mix of various asset categories that will be held for an investor at specific ages. We have interpolated between ages, when necessary, to estimate the asset mix at a standardized set of ages.

The table also shows the net asset holdings and weighted average expense ratios of funds with different retirement years. The expenses paid by investors in these funds, which typically range between sixty and eighty basis points per year, are substantially larger than what could be paid if an investor selected mutual funds from a company offering no-load index funds with low expense ratios and then rebalanced among them over time. For example, equity index funds, government bond index funds, and money market mutual funds can be obtained from Fidelity or Vanguard with no-load fees and expense ratios of ten to twenty basis points. However, if investors find it difficult to conduct such rebalancing on their own, or suffer from psychological biases that would lead them to neglect planned rebalancing, they might be willing to pay the additional expenses associated with target-year life-cycle funds in which the rebalancing happens automatically. A careful analysis of the expenses associated with life-cycle funds and of the services provided by these funds lies beyond the current study.

1.2   Modeling Retirement Wealth Accumulation in Self-Directed Retirement Plans

To analyze the distribution of 401(k) wealth at retirement that is induced by different asset allocation strategies, we need to model the path of plan contributions over an individual's working life and to combine these contributions with information on the potential returns to holding 401(k) assets in different investment vehicles. Rather than using information on household earnings patterns to estimate a stochastic model for the earnings process, and then using that model to simulate earnings paths for our analysis, we draw actual lifetime earnings histories from a large sample of households and carry out simulations by combining the contribution paths for various earnings histories with simulated patterns of asset returns. We focus our analysis on married couples because they are financially more homogeneous than nonmarried individuals, some of whom never married and others of whom have lost a spouse. About 70 percent of the individuals reaching retirement age are in married couples.

We assume that 9 percent of the household's earnings are contributed to a defined contribution plan each year. We further assume that the couple begins to participate in a 401(k) plan when the husband is twenty-eight, and that they contribute in every year in which the household has Social Security earnings until the husband is sixty-three. Households do not make contributions when they are unemployed or when both members of the couple are retired or otherwise not in the labor force. We assume that both members of the household retire when the husband is sixty-three, if they have not done so already, and that they do not contribute to a retirement plan after that age.

To formalize our calculations, we denote a household by subscript i and denote their 401(k) contribution at age a by $C_i(a) = .09*E_i(a)$ for $E_i(a)$, the household's Social Security-covered earnings at age a. The restriction to covered earnings is an important limitation that we later discuss further. We express this contribution in year 2000 dollars. To find the 401(k) balance for the couple at age sixty-three ($a = 63$), we need to cumulate contributions over the course of the working life, with appropriate allowance for asset returns. Let $R_i(a)$ denote the return earned on 401(k) assets that were held at the beginning of the year when the husband in couple i attained age a. The value of the couple's 401(k) assets when the husband is sixty-three is then given by:

$$(1) \qquad W_i(63) = \sum_{t=0}^{35} \left\{ \prod_{j=0}^{t} [1 + R_i(63 - j)] \right\} C_i(63 - t).$$

$R_i(a)$ depends on the year-specific returns on stocks and bonds and on the mix of stocks and bonds that the household owned when the husband was a years old. If the couple holds an all-stock portfolio, then $R_i(a) = R_{stock}(a)$.

If the couple holds all bonds, $R_i(a) = R_{bond}(a)$. A mixture of the two is, of course, possible. If the couple invests in a life-cycle mutual fund, the asset return at age a will be $R_{lifecycle}(a)$, which corresponds to the return on the mix of bonds and stocks that will be held by the life-cycle fund on behalf of an investor of age a.

We use simulation methods to estimate the distribution of $W_i(63)$, averaged over the households in our sample, for various asset allocation strategies. By comparing the distributions of retirement plan assets under each of these strategies, we can learn how these strategies affect retirement resources. The distribution of outcomes is of substantial interest, but it does not capture the household's valuation of different levels of retirement resources. In particular, while it can provide information on the potential frequency of low-wealth outcomes, it does not provide a metric for comparing these outcomes with more favorable retirement wealth values.

To allow for differential valuation of wealth in different states of nature, we evaluate the wealth in the 401(k) account using a utility-of-terminal wealth approach. We assume that all households have identical preferences over wealth at retirement. We drop the household subscript i and assume that the utility of wealth is described by a constant relative risk aversion (CRRA) utility function

$$(2) \qquad U(W) = \frac{W^{1-\alpha}}{1 - \alpha}$$

where α is the household's coefficient of relative risk aversion. The utility of household wealth at retirement is likely to depend on both 401(k) and non-401(k) wealth, so we modify (2) to recognize this wealth:

$$(3) \qquad U(W_{401(k)}, W_{non-401(k)}) = \frac{(W_{401(k)} + W_{non-401(k)})^{1-\alpha}}{1 - \alpha}.$$

Since the effect of a change in 401(k) wealth on household utility is sensitive to the household's other wealth holdings, we consider other assets on the household balance sheet in our empirical analysis.

For a given household, each return history, denoted by h, generates a level of 401(k) wealth at age sixty-three, $W_{401(k),h}$, and a corresponding utility level, U_h, where

$$(4) \qquad U_h = \frac{(W_{401(k),h} + W_{non-401(k)})^{1-\alpha}}{1 - \alpha}.$$

We evaluate the expected utility of each portfolio strategy by the probability-weighted average of the utility outcomes associated with that strategy. These utility levels can be compared directly for a given degree of risk tolerance, and they can be translated into certainty equivalent wealth levels (Z) by asking what certain wealth level would provide a utility level equal to the expected utility of the retirement wealth distribution. The certainty equivalent of an all-equity portfolio, for example, denoted by the subscript *SP*500, is given by:

(5) $Z_{SP500} = [EU_{SP500}(1 - \alpha)]^{1/(1-\alpha)} - W_{non-401(k)}.$

When a household has non-401(k) wealth, the certainty equivalent of the 401(k) wealth is the amount of 401(k) wealth that is needed, *in addition to the non-401(k) wealth,* to achieve a given utility level. We treat non-401(k) wealth as nonstochastic throughout our analysis.

Our approach to computing defined contribution (DC) plan balances at retirement resembles a strategy developed in Samwick and Skinner (2004). Part of their empirical analysis considers the pension benefits that a sample of workers would earn under several stylized defined benefit and defined contribution plans. It considers the benefits experience of a sample of actual workers, with actual earnings histories, under each plan. It does not, however, explore the sensitivity of retirement wealth to alternative investment strategies.

Our approach exploits the rich cross-sectional variation in household earnings trajectories. We use a large sample of Health and Retirement Survey (HRS) households to compute contribution paths for a 401(k) plan, and we then randomly assign return histories to these contribution paths. The result is a distribution of retirement balances for each household in the HRS sample. We combine the wealth outcomes by aggregating households into three broad educational categories to report our findings, but each entry in table 1.2 represents an average over the outcomes for many individuals. Our strategy can be thought of as drawing an HRS household at age twenty-seven and giving it two independent draws: first, a wage trajectory, which could be the actual wage trajectory for any of our sample households who have a particular education level, and then a lifetime vector of asset returns, which could be any of 200,000 draws. The return trajectory will determine the household's retirement wealth, conditional on the contribution flow.

One of the most important shortcomings of our analysis is our restriction to top-coded Social Security earnings records, rather than actual earnings histories. The real value of the taxable maximum earnings level for Social Security has varied over time, and so has the dispersion of earnings, so the fraction of earnings that are not captured on Social Security records varies from year to year. Higher-income workers have a higher likelihood of contributing to 401(k) plans, and they tend to contribute a higher share of earnings when they contribute, so the top-coding constraint is likely to bias our findings toward understating defined contribution plan accumulations. This is likely to be a particularly important concern when we present results for college-educated households, whose members' earnings are more likely to exceed the Social Security maximum than are the

Table 1.2   **Sample composition, HRS households**

	All households, head 59–72	Households 59–72, with SS earnings	Couples 59–72, with SS earnings	Couples 63–72, with SS earnings
Household head education less than high school				
Survey households	1,579	1,086	540	374
Population counterpart	3,769.3	2,653.4	1,324.2	938.3
Household head high school education and/or some college				
Survey households	2,793	1,954	1,076	689
Population counterpart	7,669.2	5,453.6	3,013.2	1,949.3
Household head at least college degree				
Survey households	1,132	793	526	337
Population counterpart	3,411.6	2,390.6	1,611.8	1,013.6
Total				
Survey households	5,504	3,833	2,142	1,400
Population counterpart	14,850.1	10,497.6	5,949.2	3,901.1

Source: Authors' tabulations based on the 2000 wave of the HRS and the Social Security earnings histories available for a subsample of HRS respondents. Population counterparts are calculated using the household weights provided in the HRS.

earnings from households with lower levels of education. There are several potential strategies for addressing top-coding problems such as those in the Social Security earnings records, and we hope to pursue them in future research.

1.3   Calibration of 401(k) Wealth Simulations

We select a subsample of married HRS households for analysis, construct their earnings trajectories, and measure their non-401(k) wealth at retirement. We then simulate retirement wealth based on these households' Social Security earnings records. Our sample of households is larger than that in PRVW (2005). We include all HRS couples headed by men aged sixty-three to seventy-two in 2000 for which Social Security earnings histories are available. Table 1.2 shows the effects of conditioning the sample on married couples in this age range. There are 3,833 HRS households with Social Security earnings histories. The restriction to couples eliminates approximately 44 percent of that sample, and the age restriction removes an additional 19 percent, leaving a sample of 1,400 households. The age restriction removes couples with heads between the ages of fifty-nine and sixty-two. Including this group would involve forecasting earnings beyond the time period of the data.

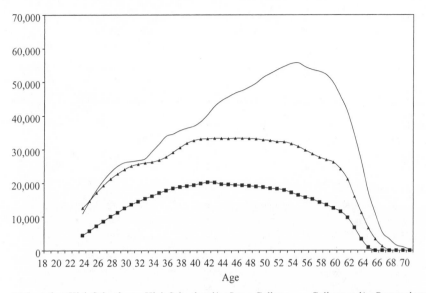

Fig. 1.2   Median household wage income in the HRS
Source: Authors' calculations from Social Security earnings histories of HRS respondents.

Our data restrictions make our subsample different from the HRS universe. This can be seen by comparing household earnings trajectories for the full HRS sample and our subsample, which we do in figures 1.2 through 1.4. Figure 1.2 shows earnings histories for all of the households in the HRS with earnings records. Figure 1.3 shows earnings histories for couples in which the husband is aged fifty-nine to seventy-two, which represents essentially all couples in the HRS. Figure 1.4 shows earnings histories for our primary sample of 1,400 married households headed by men aged sixty-three to seventy-two. In each figure, the sample is divided by educational attainment of the husband. Husbands are generally the primary earners in HRS households.

Two findings emerge from these figures. First, since we are focusing on couples, the total level of household earnings is higher than in the broad HRS universe for all educational levels. Second, the premium for the primary earner's education is smaller at all age ranges, but particularly in the early part of the earners' lifetime in our sample relative to the entire HRS population. This reduction in the education premium is primarily a function of our restriction to couples. Since the education levels of members of a married couple are not perfectly correlated, by focusing on couples we pool, to some extent, individuals with different levels of educational attainment.

We consider our sample households as reaching retirement age when the

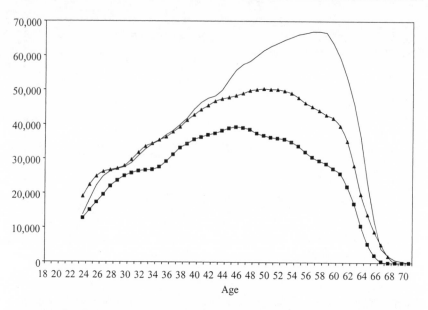

- Less than High School   - High School and/or Some College   — College and/or Postgraduate

Fig. 1.3   Median household wage income in the HRS for couples with male aged 59–72

Source: Authors' calculations from Social Security earnings histories of HRS respondents.

husband is sixty-three or sixty-four years old, and we need to determine non-401(k) wealth at this age. Our procedure for doing this varies according to the household's age. First, we consider wealth measurement for the nearly three-quarters of the sample with a household head who was either sixty-three or sixty-four in 1996, 1998, or 2000. For these households, a breakdown of nonpension wealth is available on a consistent basis in HRS waves 3, 4, and 5. We scale all household non-401(k) asset values to the 2000 base year, so that for each household we have an estimate of what their non-401(k) wealth would have been had they turned age sixty-three to sixty-four in the year 2000. We implement this scaling by replacing the nominal returns on asset holdings for the two years prior to the year in which the head of household was sixty-three or sixty-four, that is 1994 to 1995 for the 1996 households and 1996 to 1997 for the 1998 households, with nominal returns on assets in 1998 and 1999. We focus on returns in three broad categories of nonannuitized wealth: financial wealth, housing equity, and other wealth. Returns on housing equity are approximated by the growth rate of the Commerce Department's constant-quality house price index. Financial wealth, both within and outside of retirement accounts, is assumed to grow at a composite rate based on the national average allocation of tax-deferred financial assets between stocks, bonds, and

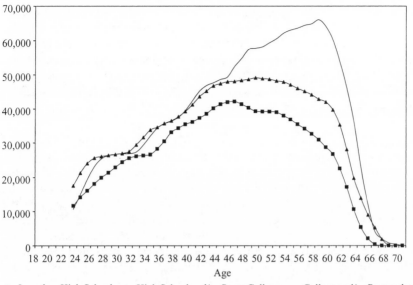

Fig. 1.4   Median household wage income in the HRS for couples with male aged 63–72
Source: Authors' calculations from Social Security earnings histories of HRS respondents.

deposits, as reported in the 2001 Survey of Consumer Finances. Other household wealth, which consists largely of jewelry and vehicles, is assumed to grow with the overall price level as measured by the CPI.

Second, we consider wealth measurement for the one quarter of the sample that reached the ages of sixty-three or sixty-four prior to 1996. We do not use the earlier waves of the HRS because the wealth questionnaire for waves 1 and 2 was different from that for later waves. Wealth values for these HRS households are imputed for each asset class based on the median measured asset growth for households between the ages of sixty-three and sixty-five, or sixty-three and sixty-seven, in the same educational category in later waves of the HRS.

To estimate defined benefit (DB) and defined contribution (DC) pension wealth for HRS households we use HRS pension wealth imputations, version 1.0, March 2005. This new research component of the HRS allows for more precise estimation of pension wealth than was previously possible, since it estimates imputed defined contribution wealth at all ages. For defined benefit wealth at age sixty-three to sixty-four we use the imputed present discounted value of pension wealth, assuming retirement at age sixty-two and gross up by one year at the intermediate-scenario Social Security Administration rate of 3 percent. For Social Security wealth (SSW) we follow the procedure from PRVW (2005), using cohort mortality tables and the Social Security Administration's intermediate-cost scenario discount rates to calculate the present discounted value of the current or projected Social Security benefits when the husband is age sixty-three to sixty-four. We normalize the value of the wife's Social Security to be the value when the husband is age sixty-three to sixty-four, assuming that Social Security payments start for the wife at age sixty-two if they have not started already. The present value of Social Security is determined as a joint survivor annuity.

Table 1.3 presents summary statistics on our estimates of household balance sheets normalized to age sixty-three to sixty-four. We report seven categories of wealth: the present discounted value (PDV) of Social Security payments, the PDV of defined benefit pensions, the PDV of other annuities, the current value of retirement accounts, the value of all other financial wealth net of debt, housing equity net of debt, and all other wealth. The top panel in table 1.3 shows medians while the bottom panel shows means. The restriction to couples clearly raises the mean and median of the distribution. The restriction to households in the age range sixty-three to seventy-two, with full earnings histories to age sixty-three, lowers the wealth distribution somewhat by removing a group that has not yet begun to spend down their assets. The final sample of couples aged sixty-three to seventy-two has median wealth of $536,800 and mean wealth of $783,400. The median high-school-educated household has 44 percent more total wealth than the median household with less than a high-school education, and the median college educated household has 61 percent more total wealth than the median high-school-educated household. The differences in means are even more dramatic.

Table 1.3 also shows the distribution of several wealth aggregates. One such aggregate is annuitized wealth, which is defined as the sum of the present discounted values of Social Security, defined benefit pensions, and other annuities. We also present the sum of annuitized wealth and all other financial wealth, as well as aggregates reflecting all wealth and all wealth excluding retirement account assets. When we calibrate our simulations with households' non-401(k) wealth, we focus on two wealth components: annuitized wealth and all wealth excluding retirement account assets. We do not include retirement account assets in the calibration of non-401(k) wealth, since these emerge from our simulation. By using the observed values of these wealth components from the HRS, and treating them as nonrandom when we evaluate the expected utility of 401(k) retirement balances, we are implicitly assuming that changes in 401(k) wealth values do not affect other components of wealth. We hope to eventually extend our analysis to allow for correlation between the returns on assets in 401(k) accounts and the returns on other household assets.

Table 1.4 disaggregates the household balance sheet aggregates by education level. The table underscores the substantial differences across

Table 1.3 Summary statistics on household balance sheet at age 63/64, HRS households

	All HRS households				HRS Couples with husband aged 63–72			
	Household head 59–72	Household Head 59–72 and with SS earnings	Couples 59–72, with SS earnings	Couples 63–72, with SS earnings	All	Less than high school degree	High school and/or some college	College and/or post-graduate
Medians								
Social Security	176.1	167.2	258.0	262.5	262.5	247.4	260.9	285.5
DB pension	0.0	0.0	0.0	0.0	0.0	0.0	0.0	0.0
Other annuity	0.0	0.0	0.0	0.0	0.0	0.0	0.0	0.0
Retirement accounts	15.0	15.0	35.7	22.7	22.7	0.0	20.4	81.7
IRA	8.1	8.4	22.0	12.0	12.0	0.0	11.5	49.6
DC pension	0.0	0.0	0.0	0.0	0.0	0.0	0.0	0.0
Other financial wealth	34.6	35.2	69.6	58.0	58.0	6.4	55.7	170.5
Housing equity	76.2	72.0	90.9	92.6	92.6	60.2	90.9	125.0
Other wealth	11.5	11.0	17.7	18.1	18.1	11.0	20.0	21.9
SS + DB + annuity	204.6	203.5	280.3	276.9	276.9	250.5	277.2	301.8
Total excluding retirement accounts	399.9	397.3	526.7	489.4	489.4	360.3	484.0	749.7
Total	439.1	435.6	587.5	536.8	536.8	370.1	531.1	856.3
Means								
Social Security	179.9	181.9	235.9	246.5	246.5	229.1	243.6	268.1
DB pension	62.4	63.1	85.2	47.7	47.7	33.9	44.4	66.6
Other annuity	4.9	5.0	5.2	5.0	5.0	0.8	7.3	4.6
Retirement accounts	107.8	113.2	154.7	136.4	136.4	36.8	83.1	330.9
IRA	73.2	72.8	95.2	77.3	77.3	29.4	67.4	140.6
DC pension	32.4	37.0	55.7	59.0	59.0	7.4	15.7	190.3

(continued)

Table 1.3 (continued)

	All HRS households				HRS Couples with husband aged 63–72			
	Household head 59–72	Household Head 59–72 and with SS earnings	Couples 59–72, with SS earnings	Couples 63–72, with SS earnings	All	Less than high school degree	High school and/or some college	College and/or post-graduate
Other financial wealth	177.4	179.3	223.1	199.7	199.7	69.6	138.7	437.3
Housing equity	113.2	103.1	125.3	115.3	115.3	78.7	106.6	165.7
Other wealth	26.2	26.5	32.8	33.0	33.0	19.2	30.1	51.3
SS + DB + annuity	247.2	250.0	326.3	299.2	299.2	263.8	295.3	339.3
Total excluding retirement accounts	587.3	583.8	727.3	647.0	647.0	431.3	570.6	993.6
Total	694.2	695.8	881.5	783.4	783.4	468.1	653.7	1324.5
Sample size								
Number of households	5504	3833	2142	1400	1400	374	689	337
Weighted size (000's)	14,850	10,498	5,949	3,901	3,901	938	1,949	1,013

Source: Authors' tabulations based on the 2000 HRS. All entries are normalized to calendar year 2000. To estimate DB and DC pension wealth for HRS households we use the pension wealth imputations from the HRS (March 2005 version). Other financial wealth includes stocks, equity mutual funds, bonds, fixed income mutual funds, checking and saving accounts, money market mutual funds, and certificates of deposit held outside of retirement accounts. Social security wealth is calculated as in PRVW (2005).

Table 1.4   Distribution of household balance sheet for HRS couples with husbands age 63–72, normalized to age 63/64 in year 2000

Net worth concept	All education levels	Less than high school degree	High school and/or some college	College and/or postgraduate
20th percentile				
SS + DB + annuity	189.8	169.4	198.8	204.6
Total excluding retirement accounts	292.2	216.8	312.2	387.8
Total	302.0	220.9	315.1	448.1
40th percentile				
SS + DB + annuity	257.0	230.7	257.3	281.2
Total excluding retirement accounts	419.1	314.1	423.6	607.8
Total	450.1	323.2	450.4	707.9
60th percentile				
SS + DB + annuity	295.6	265.7	296.1	338.0
Total excluding retirement accounts	575.3	413.6	549.8	878.6
Total	637.4	441.3	622.1	1,051.1
80th percentile				
SS + DB + annuity	362.8	313.7	354.3	449.3
Total excluding retirement accounts	830.4	575.4	745.2	1,229.6
Total	994.5	644.1	866.4	1,598.6

Source: Authors' tabulations from the 2000 HRS. DB pension wealth was calculated from the pension wealth imputations from the HRS (March 2005 version). Social Security and annuity wealth were computed as in PRVW (2005).

households, both within education categories and across such categories. The difference at most percentiles between the wealth of a household that did not complete high school and one that completed college is a factor of 2. These differences are of the same magnitude as the differences between the twentieth and sixtieth percentiles of the distribution for a given education level. The eightieth percentile of the distribution for all three education levels that we consider has wealth holdings that are at close to three times as great as those of households in the twentieth percentile for the same education level.

One difficult problem in constructing the non-401(k) wealth measure that enters equation (5) concerns the role of housing equity. Venti and Wise (2001) and other studies suggest that retired households do not typically draw down their housing wealth to finance nonhousing consumption. This implies that we should consider only financial resources as a source of wealth to support retirement spending, a strategy that could be justified by assuming that the utility from housing consumption is additively separable from all other consumption in the household's utility function, and that owner-occupied housing generates only housing consumption. The difficulty with this approach is that it is possible that households view their housing equity as a reserve asset that can be tapped to support other consumption in the event of financial difficulty. In this case, housing equity should be combined with financial assets in calculating the household's assets outside defined contribution plans. To allow for this possibility, we present results in which we consider housing as well as other financial assets as the household's non-401(k) wealth at retirement. We treat the non-401(k) components of the household balance sheet at retirement as nonstochastic, and use whatever value we calculate for the household in all of the simulations with various 401(k) balances.

We assume that the three primary assets that households may hold in their 401(k) accounts are corporate stock, nominal long-term government bonds, and inflation-indexed long-term bonds (TIPS). Calibrating the returns on these investment alternatives is a critical step in our simulation algorithm. We assume that 401(k) investors hold corporate stocks through portfolios of large-capitalization U.S. stocks. We do not address the possibility of poorly diversified portfolios—for example, with concentrated holdings in a single stock, as described in Munnell and Sunden (2004) and Poterba (2003). We assume that the distribution of returns on each of these asset classes is given by Ibbotson Associates' (2003) empirical distribution of returns during the 1926 to 2002 period. Large-capitalization U.S. equities have an annual average real return of 9 percent and a standard deviation of 20.7 percent, whereas long-term U.S. government bonds have an annual average real return of 3.2 percent and a standard deviation of 10 percent.

We assume that TIPS offer a certain real return of 2 percent per year, approximately the current TIPS yield. Index bonds deliver a net-of-inflation certain return only if the investor holds the bonds to maturity, and selling the bonds before maturity exposes the investors to asset price risk. We nevertheless treat these bonds as riskless long-term investment vehicles. In our simulations, when we draw returns from the stock and bond return distributions for a given iteration, we draw returns for the same year from both distributions. This preserves the historical contemporary correlation structure between stock and bond returns in our simulations.

Several analysts suggest that recent historical equity returns may correspond to a particularly favorable time period, and that these returns should not be extrapolated to the future. The academic literature on the equity premium puzzle, summarized, for example, in Mehra and Prescott (2002), raises the possibility that ex post returns exceeded ex ante expected returns over this period. To allow for such a possibility, we perform some simulations in which the distribution of returns from which we draw is the actual distribution, except that equity returns are reduced by 300 basis points in each year. Comparing these simulations with those in our baseline indicate the sensitivity of our findings to the future pattern of equity returns.

For each iteration of our simulation algorithm, we draw a sequence of thirty-five real stock and bond returns from the empirical return distribution. The draws are done with replacement and we assume that there is no serial correlation in returns. We then use this return sequence to calculate the real value of each household's retirement account balance at age sixty-three under the different asset allocation strategies. For each of the 1,400 households in our sample, we simulate their 401(k) balance at age sixty-three 200,000 times. We then summarize these 200,000 outcomes either with a distribution of wealth values at retirement, or by calculating the expected utility associated with this distribution of outcomes. We found in PRVW (2005) that roughly this number of iterations was needed to obtain robust findings, particularly at lower percentiles of the retirement wealth distribution.

1.4   Discussion of Results

We simulate nine different asset allocation strategies for the household's 401(k) account. The first three involve investing in only one asset: (i) a portfolio that is fully invested in TIPS; (ii) a portfolio that is fully invested in long-term government bonds, and (iii) a portfolio that is fully invested in corporate stock. The next two portfolios are heuristic portfolios that use simple rules for lifecycle asset allocation. Portfolio (iv) holds (110–age of household head) percent of the portfolio in stock, with the remaining balance in TIPS. Portfolio (v) is similar to (iv) except that nominal government bonds replace TIPS for the component of the portfolio that is not held in equity. Both of these portfolios are rebalanced at the end of each period. The next two are life-cycle portfolios consisting of stocks and TIPS, stocks, and government bonds, respectively. The equity weight for each of these funds is computed based on the average of the age-specific allocations in the life-cycle funds at Fidelity, Vanguard, T. Rowe Price, TIAA-CREF, Principal, Barclays, and Wells Fargo. The life-cycle funds from these fund families are weighted equally in this calculation, and the resulting equity allocation is similar to that in table 1.1. Portfolio (vi) invests the life-cycle fund average in equities and the balance in TIPS, while fund (vii) holds equities and nominal government bonds in the life-cycle mix. The next strategy that we consider, portfolio (viii), holds an age-independent mix of stocks and nominal government bonds. The equity share for this fund is 53 percent, which is the lifetime weighted average stock allocation in the life-cycle funds, where the weight assigned to the equity allocation in each year equals the household's 401(k) wealth at the beginning of that year, divided by the sum of beginning-of-year 401(k) wealth in all years.

The final investment strategy we consider, strategy (ix), is the "no lose" strategy that Feldstein (2005) proposes in his analysis of individual account Social Security reforms. At each age, we calculate the share of the household's 401(k) contribution that would have to be invested in TIPS to guarantee at least the contributed amount in nominal terms at retirement age. The required TIPS investment is $(1 + R_{TIPS})^{-(63-a)}$, where $63 - a$ is the number of years to retirement. This strategy is fundamentally different from the other life-cycle strategies because it does not involve portfolio rebalancing at each age. Instead, the equity share of the portfolio depends on the historical pattern of TIPS yields, which in turn determine the amount available for stock investment in past years, and on the historical returns on equity assets.

1.4.1   The Distribution of Retirement Wealth

Table 1.5 shows the distribution of 401(k) balances in thousands of year 2000 dollars averaged across the 1,400 households in our sample. There are two vertical panels in the table. In the leftmost panel, the simulations use the historical distribution of returns. The panel on the right reduces equity returns by 300 basis points. Households are stratified by education group within each panel. The table reports the mean wealth at retirement for each strategy, as well as four points in the distribution of returns. Since our interest is the comparison of wealth outcomes across different strategies, most of our discussion that follows focuses on a single education group, namely households headed by someone with a high school degree but not a college degree. The relative ranking of different strategies is similar for other education groups.

The first row of table 1.5 provides a point of reference for all of the subsequent calculations. It shows the certain wealth at retirement associated with strategy (i), holding only TIPS. For those with a high school degree and/or some college, this leads to a retirement balance of $162,600. The next panels show the results from strategy (ii), holding only nominal government bonds, and strategy (iii), holding only corporate stocks. Both of these strategies, as well as all of the subsequent strategies that we consider, involve risk, so we report information on the distribution of outcomes.

The second panel shows that holding only government bonds leads to a higher average retirement wealth, $192,700, than holding TIPS. The average wealth at retirement is nearly 20 percent greater than the value with TIPS, but the median wealth of $175,000 is less than 10 percent above the TIPS outcome. Moreover, there are many outcomes with retirement wealth values below the TIPS case. The tenth percentile outcome is $106,300 and the first percentile is $36,300.

When the 401(k) is invested in corporate stock, the average retirement balance is much higher than that with either TIPS or nominal government bonds: $812,000. This value is roughly four times greater than the outcome

Table 1.5   Simulated distribution of 401(k) balances at retirement ($2000)

Investment strategy/percentile	Empirical stock returns			Empirical returns reduced 300 basis points		
	Less than high school degree	High school and/or some college	College and/or postgraduate	Less than high school degree	High school and/or some college	College and/or postgraduate
100% TIPS	137.6	162.6	174.4	137.6	162.6	174.4
100% government bonds						
1	31.0	36.3	41.3	31.0	36.3	41.3
10	90.1	106.3	115.5	90.1	106.3	115.5
50	148.0	175.0	187.2	148.0	175.0	187.2
90	253.2	300.2	316.2	253.2	300.2	316.2
Mean	162.9	192.7	205.2	162.9	192.7	205.2
100% stocks						
1	11.1	12.8	14.5	6.4	7.3	8.5
10	151.4	179.9	190.1	79.9	94.3	102.4
50	460.5	549.8	564.9	234.8	278.8	293.5
90	1420.6	1704.9	1710.3	705.0	841.1	860.4
Mean	677.7	812.0	821.8	339.9	404.8	418.6
(110–age)% stocks, (age + 10)% TIPS						
1	46.4	54.3	59.2	35.9	41.9	46.2
10	150.5	178.1	189.2	115.9	137.0	146.9
50	240.5	285.2	300.0	185.2	219.3	232.8
90	380.9	452.3	471.7	293.3	347.7	365.6
Mean	256.0	303.6	318.7	197.1	233.5	247.2
(110–age)% stocks, (age + 10)% bonds						
1	32.2	38.0	42.1	25.2	29.6	33.1
10	138.7	164.1	175.0	107.0	126.4	136.1
50	253.7	301.0	316.1	195.1	231.2	244.9
90	466.4	554.6	574.2	357.7	424.7	443.3
Mean	284.2	337.4	352.6	218.4	258.9	272.8

(*continued*)

Table 1.5 (continued)

Investment strategy/percentile	Empirical stock returns			Empirical returns reduced 300 basis points		
	Less than high school degree	High school and/or some college	College and/or postgraduate	Less than high school degree	High school and/or some college	College and/or postgraduate
Empirical life cycle, stocks, and TIPS						
1	55.1	64.3	72.0	40.5	47.1	53.4
10	164.0	194.6	206.4	114.7	135.5	146.4
50	299.8	357.2	369.9	204.4	242.4	255.5
90	561.8	672.6	682.6	373.8	445.6	459.2
Mean	339.5	405.3	416.8	229.5	272.7	285.1
Empirical life cycle, stocks, and bonds						
1	31.9	37.3	41.9	23.6	27.6	31.5
10	155.2	184.2	195.1	108.3	128.0	138.1
50	311.6	371.3	384.3	212.1	251.7	265.1
90	642.7	769.4	779.9	427.8	509.7	524.6
Mean	367.0	438.2	449.7	247.5	294.3	307.0
Equivalent fixed-proportion stocks (53% baseline, 61.5% with reduced returns)						
1	30.8	35.9	40.1	18.8	21.8	25.0
10	150.5	178.4	189.2	104.3	123.2	132.7
50	294.7	350.6	364.9	215.5	255.7	269.5
90	582.9	695.5	711.7	450.2	535.9	553.6
Mean	340.0	404.9	418.6	254.5	302.4	316.0
Feldstein (2005) "no-lose" plan						
1	96.6	113.8	124.3	95.3	112.2	122.7
10	143.8	170.4	181.8	117.9	139.2	150.7
50	260.4	310.7	320.6	172.7	204.8	216.6
90	645.5	777.0	775.6	352.6	421.3	430.1
Mean	350.6	420.3	426.8	214.8	255.6	266.2

Source: Authors' tabulations of simulation results. See text for further details.

with nominal government bonds. Because the mean return on stocks is so much higher than that on either nominal or inflation-indexed bonds, even the low outcomes are often above the mean outcomes with bonds. The tenth percentile retirement wealth value with the all-stocks portfolio exceeds the average outcome with a nominal government bond portfolio. The first-percentile outcome, however, $12,800, is below the correspondingly low outcomes for the nominal bonds strategy.

The next two portfolios we consider, (iv) and (v), are heuristic lifecycle investment strategies with a mix of stocks and TIPS, or stocks and long-term nominal government bonds. In both cases the average value of retirement wealth falls between the value with an all-stock investment and that with an all-bond portfolio. When the nominal government bond share of the portfolio is (age + 10) percent, the average value of retirement wealth using historical equity returns is $303,600 for a household with a high school education. The proportional dispersion in the retirement wealth value is smaller than that for an all-equity portfolio, and greater than that for the bond portfolio. The difference between the ninetieth percentile and the tenth percentile retirement wealth value with an all-stock strategy is 1.88 times the mean value, and the corresponding measure for the all-bond portfolio is 1.01. With the nominal bond-stock heuristic lifecycle portfolio, the 90-10 spread is 1.16 times the mean outcome. The results for the heuristic portfolio that includes stocks and TIPS are broadly similar, although the ratio of the 90-10 spread to the mean retirement wealth in this case is 0.90. The first percentile outcomes with the two heuristic life-cycle portfolios are $54,300 and $38,000, respectively. Both are larger than first percentile outcomes with either the all-stock or all-bond portfolios.

The next two portfolios that we consider, (vi) and (vii), are the life-cycle portfolios that correspond to the average of the portfolios from various mutual fund complexes. While the age-specific equity allocation is somewhat different from the foregoing heuristic portfolios, the distribution of 401(k) wealth at retirement is similar. In particular, the mean value of retirement wealth is $405,300 when we combine TIPS and stocks, and $438,200 when we combine nominal long-term government bonds and stocks. The difference is due to TIPS offering a lower real yield than the historical average real return on nominal bonds during our sample period. The first-percentile outcome when we combine TIPS with stocks is higher than that for either of the heuristic strategies, reflecting greater weight on the bond investment in this case than for those strategies.

The next portfolio strategy, (viii), is the age-invariant strategy that holds an equity share equal to the weighted average equity share in the life-cycle funds across the whole life cycle. That share is 53 percent. One of the issues that our simulations can address is how the risk and retirement wealth of this strategy compare with the corresponding measures from the life-cycle portfolios. The mean wealth from this age-invariant allocation is very similar to that from the life-cycle portfolios: $404,900. The risk, as measured by the 90-10 spread relative to the mean, is also very similar. The very low realizations from the life-cycle strategies are somewhat higher than the very low realizations from the fixed allocation, with first-percentile outcomes of $35,900 for strategy (viii), compared with $64,300 and $48,800 for the two life-cycle strategies. Through most of the distribution, however, it seems that the two strategies yield similar results.

The similarity of the retirement wealth distributions from the life-cycle portfolios, and from strategies that allocate a constant portfolio share to equities, is one of the central findings of our analysis. This result calls for further work to evaluate the extent to which life-cycle strategies offer unique opportunities for risk reduction relative to simpler strategies that allocate a constant fraction of portfolio assets to equities at all ages.

The last strategy we consider is the Feldstein (2005) "no lose" plan. This strategy offers a mean return that is broadly similar to the mean returns on the life-cycle strategies. The mean retirement wealth for a high school-educated household is $420,300, which is between the mean wealth values with a life-cycle fund that holds TIPS and one that holds nominal government bonds. The important difference between this strategy and the life-cycle strategies and the all-stocks and all-nominal bonds strategies is found in the lower tail of the wealth outcomes. Because the no lose strategy holds TIPS, the first-percentile wealth value is $113,800, compared with values between $38,000 and $64,300 in the actual and heuristic life-cycle strategies.

The assumption that the equity return is drawn from its historical distribution is important for the absolute level of retirement wealth under most of the strategies that we consider, and also for the magnitude of the differences across strategies. The fourth, fifth, and sixth columns in table 1.5 present results that assume that equity returns are reduced by 300 basis points. The all-stock strategy is the one that is most affected by this change. The average wealth at retirement for this strategy falls from $812,000 to $404,800. The tenth-percentile wealth value drops from $179,900 to $94,300 in this case, and the first-percentile value drops to $7,300 from $12,800. This very low outcome emphasizes the risk associated with holding stocks: a very small chance of a very poor outcome. The average retirement wealth values for the various heuristic and empirical life-cycle funds decline when we reduce the value of the mean equity return. The mean wealth value for the no lose strategy falls relative to the life-cycle strategies, because the no-lose strategy has relatively more equity exposure than any of the life-cycle plans.

The distribution of retirement balances shown in table 1.5 is conceptually similar to the distribution reported in Shiller's (2005) analysis of personal accounts Social Security reform, although there are differences in the simulation procedure that affect the results. The most important difference is that Shiller (2005) uses data on stock and bond returns from a longer time period than we consider. This means he assumes a distribution of equity returns with a lower mean value than the one that we consider. Our results, when the average return on stocks is set at 300 basis points below the historical mean in our sample, are closer to those in Shiller (2005) than our results that assume that returns are drawn from the actual return distribution for 1926 to 2002.

1.4.2   Expected Utility of Retirement Wealth

Results like those in table 1.5 do not provide any information on the household utility associated with a particular retirement wealth outcome. To address this issue, we now evaluate the expected utility associated with various wealth outcomes from our simulation runs, using the procedure described in table 1.5.

Table 1.6 shows the expected utility generated by the distribution of retirement resources for each portfolio strategy using a certainty equivalent wealth measure to value the potential outcomes of the different portfolio strategies. In this table, we assume that the 401(k) balance is the household's only wealth. The values in the first horizontal panel in Table 1.6 are based on linear utility ($\alpha = 0$) and thus are the expected values of each investment choice. These results are identical to the average household retirement wealth calculations in Table 1.5, since a risk-neutral household cares only about the expected value of retirement wealth. In this case, the higher mean wealth of the all-stock strategy implies that it is the most preferred investment strategy. This is true both with the actual historical distribution of stock returns and with the distribution, which reduces the mean return by 300 basis points. It is also true for all education groups.

The next horizontal panel in table 1.6 presents results for households whose utility of retirement wealth is logarithmic. This level of risk aversion reduces the certainty equivalent value of the all-stock portfolio strategy relative to other strategies, but this strategy continues to generate the highest expected utility for all education groups. This outcome obtains when the expected stock return is set equal to its historical average and when it is reduced by 300 basis points. The empirical life-cycle fund that combines stocks with nominal government bonds generates the highest expected utility among the four life-cycle fund strategies, and the two empirical life-cycle strategies, (vi) and (vii), yield expected utilities substantially greater than either of the heuristic life-cycle funds. The expected utility of the fixed-proportions strategy continues to be close to the expected utility of the two empirical life-cycle strategies, although it now falls below both of the life-cycle strategies. This result is sensitive to the assumed rate of return on stocks; the fixed proportion strategy (viii) dominates the two empirical life-cycle strategies when equity returns are reduced by 300 basis points.

The third and fourth horizontal panels in table 1.6 consider households

Table 1.6 Certainty equivalent wealth ($2,000) for different asset allocation rules and different expected stock returns, no other wealth

Risk aversion/investment strategy	Empirical stock returns			Empirical stock returns, reduced 300 basis points		
	Less than high school degree	High school and/or some college	College or post-graduate	Less than high school degree	High school and/or some college	College or post-graduate
α = 0						
100% TIPS	137.6	162.6	174.4			
100% government bonds	162.9	192.7	205.2			
100% stocks	677.7	812.0	821.8	339.9	404.8	418.6
(110–age)% stocks, (age + 10)% TIPS	256.0	303.6	318.7	197.1	233.5	247.2
(110–age)% stocks, (age + 10)% bonds	284.2	337.4	352.6	218.4	258.9	272.8
Empirical life cycle, stocks and TIPS	339.6	405.3	416.8	229.5	272.7	285.2
Empirical life cycle, stocks and bonds	367.0	438.2	449.7	247.5	294.3	307.0
Equivalent fixed proportion stocks	340.0	404.9	418.6	254.5	302.4	316.0
"No-lose" plan	350.6	420.3	426.8	214.8	255.6	266.2
α = 1						
100% TIPS	137.6	162.6	174.4			
100% government bonds	149.7	177.1	189.4			
100% stocks	461.8	551.4	567.1	235.8	279.9	294.8
(110–age)% stocks, (age + 10)% TIPS	239.8	284.3	299.2	184.7	218.6	232.1
(110–age)% stocks, (age + 10)% bonds	253.9	301.3	316.5	195.4	231.4	245.2
Empirical life cycle, stocks and TIPS	301.9	359.7	372.7	205.8	244.2	257.4
Empirical life cycle, stocks and bonds	313.9	374.0	387.3	213.8	253.7	267.2
Equivalent fixed-proportion stocks	295.4	351.4	365.8	216.0	256.2	270.1
"No-lose" plan	285.1	340.4	351.0	190.1	225.6	237.7

α = 2						
100% TIPS	137.6	162.6	174.4			
100% government bonds	138.2	163.3	175.5			
100% stocks	316.5	376.5	394.1	164.9	194.9	209.3
(110−age)% stocks, (age + 10)% TIPS	224.5	266.1	280.6	172.9	204.6	217.8
(110−age)% stocks, (age + 10)% bonds	227.1	269.2	284.2	174.9	207.0	220.5
Empirical life cycle, stocks and TIPS	269.3	320.4	334.5	185.2	219.5	233.1
Empirical life cycle, stocks and bonds	269.7	320.8	335.2	185.5	219.7	233.6
Equivalent fixed-proportion stocks	257.1	305.4	320.3	183.7	217.5	231.3
"No-lose" plan	245.2	291.9	304.6	174.5	206.8	219.6
α = 4						
100% TIPS	137.6	162.6	174.4			
100% government bonds	119.1	140.5	152.3			
100% stocks	154.0	181.5	197.0	83.5	97.6	108.8
(110−age)% stocks, (age + 10)% TIPS	196.4	232.6	246.6	151.3	178.9	191.4
(110−age)% stocks, (age + 10)% bonds	182.2	215.5	229.9	140.6	166.0	178.8
Empirical life cycle, stocks and TIPS	216.6	256.9	272.3	151.5	179.0	193.0
Empirical life cycle, stocks and bonds	202.3	239.8	255.1	141.8	167.4	181.2
Equivalent fixed-proportion stocks	196.0	232.1	247.0	133.9	157.9	171.0
"No-lose" plan	201.7	239.3	253.4	156.2	184.7	197.9

Source: Authors' tabulations from simulation analysis. See text for further discussion.

with relative risk aversion coefficients of 2 and 4, respectively. As risk aversion rises, the life-cycle portfolios become more attractive relative to the all-stocks portfolio, and the "no lose" portfolio also becomes more attractive. This is illustrated most clearly by considering the bottom panel in table 1.6. The high volatility of stock returns and the associated risk of a low retirement wealth outcome reduces expected utility in this case relative to the earlier, less risk-averse cases. The certainty equivalent of the all-stock strategy is now \$181,500, which is still greater than the all-bond base (\$140,500), but the disparity is far smaller than at lower risk-aversion values. The various life-cycle allocation strategies dominate the all-stock strategy with a relative risk aversion of 4. The certainty equivalent of the four heuristic and empirical life-cycle strategies now ranges from \$215,500 to \$256,900. The empirical life-cycle strategies generate higher expected utility than either of the heuristic strategies, and they also generate higher expected utility than the strategy that holds the lifetime average equity share that corresponds to these strategies, but does so at all ages. With relative risk aversion of 4, the "no lose" plan also generates a higher expected utility than the all-stock strategy.

Three additional features of the results with a relative risk aversion of 4 warrant comment. First, when the average return on stocks is reduced by 300 basis points, the certainty equivalent of the all-stock strategy declines sharply, while the corresponding values for the life-cycle funds and the no-lose strategy do not decline as much. Feldstein's (2005) no-lose strategy is the preferred strategy in this setting, with the empirical life-cycle strategy blending stocks and TIPS taking the second rank.

Second, the no-lose strategy becomes more attractive as the level of risk aversion increases. With a risk aversion of 2, the no-lose plan yields an expected utility that falls below either of the empirical life-cycle allocation strategies, either with historical equity returns or with reduced average returns. In the case with relative risk aversion of 4, the certainty equivalent of the no-lose plan is roughly equal to the nominal bonds and stocks life-cycle strategy, and somewhat below that of the stocks-TIPS lifecycle strategy when equity returns have their historical values. When equity returns are reduced by 300 basis points, the certainty equivalent of the no-lose plan exceeds that of either of the life-cycle strategies.

Third, the expected utility associated with either heuristic life-cycle funds or empirical life-cycle funds rises relative to the expected utility of an all-stock investment strategy as risk aversion increases. For a relative risk aversion of 1, the certainty equivalent of an empirical life-cycle strategy that holds stocks and government bonds is roughly two-thirds of the certainty equivalent of an all-stock strategy, and it is roughly twice the certainty equivalent of an all-bond strategy. For a relative risk aversion of 4, however, the empirical life-cycle strategy's certainty equivalent is about one-third greater than that of an all-stock portfolio, and 60 percent greater than an all-bond portfolio. These findings suggest that the relative attraction of life-cycle funds and other asset allocation strategies is likely to be highly dependent upon household circumstances.

Table 1.6 considers the certainty equivalent of different investment strategies when retirement wealth from a 401(k) plan is the only source of utility at retirement. By assuming that the household is solely dependent on 401(k) wealth, these calculations exaggerate the level of retirement income risk faced by the household. Holding constant the household's relative risk coefficient, when the household has other sources of wealth, it will behave as though it was less risk averse.

Tables 1.7 and 1.8 present results with two alternative assumptions about non-401(k) wealth at retirement. The results in table 1.7 set non-401(k) wealth equal to other financial wealth in the HRS, while those in table 1.8 set non-401(k) wealth equal to all other wealth, adding together both financial wealth and housing wealth. The households in both cases are less averse to holding high fractions of their wealth in stocks. For a relative risk aversion of 2, for example, the certainty equivalent value of contributing to a 401(k) that is invested in the empirical life-cycle fund with stocks and TIPS is $320,400 when households have no wealth at retirement other than their retirement wealth. This value can be found in table 1.6. When other financial wealth is combined with retirement account wealth in determining the utility of retirement wealth, the certainty equivalent of the same strategy rises to $353,000. With housing equity added to the total, the certainty equivalent rises to $366,100. In each case these values represent the certainty equivalent of just the 401(k) account balance. This is the amount in addition to other wealth that would be needed to generate the expected utility associated with the uncertain retirement wealth distribution. The average value of retirement wealth associated with this strategy is $405,300, so the reduction in certainty equivalent value associated with the risk of unfavorable outcomes is smaller as non-401(k) wealth rises.

Allowing for nonretirement account wealth raises the attraction of stocks relative to other financial investments. In both tables 1.7 and 1.8, for all the risk aversion parameters that we consider, the expected utility of holding an all-stock portfolio is greater than that from holding any of the other portfolios that we consider. These results underscore the importance of recognizing and calibrating non-401(k) wealth as part of the valuation process.

1.5 Conclusions

This paper presents evidence on the distribution of balances in 401(k)-type retirement saving accounts under various assumptions about the asset allocation strategies that investors choose. In addition to a range of age-invariant strategies, such as an all-bond and an all-stock strategy, we

Table 1.7 Certainty equivalent wealth ($2,000) for different asset allocation rules and different expected stock returns, other wealth equal to other financial wealth in HRS

Risk aversion/investment strategy	Empirical stock returns			Empirical stock returns, reduced 300 basis points		
	Less than high school degree	High school and/or some college	College or post-graduate	Less than high school degree	High school and/or some college	College or post-graduate
$\alpha = 0$						
100% TIPS	137.6	162.6	174.4			
100% government bonds	162.9	192.7	205.2			
100% stocks	677.7	812.0	821.8	339.9	404.8	418.6
(110–age)% stocks, (age + 10)% TIPS	256.0	303.6	318.7	197.1	233.5	247.2
(110–age)% stocks, (age + 10)% bonds	284.2	337.4	352.6	218.4	258.9	272.8
Empirical life cycle, stocks and TIPS	339.6	405.3	416.8	229.5	272.7	285.2
Empirical life cycle, stocks and bonds	367.0	438.2	449.7	247.5	294.3	307.0
Equivalent fixed-proportion stocks	340.0	404.9	418.6	254.5	302.4	316.0
"No-lose" plan	350.6	420.3	426.8	214.8	255.6	266.2
$\alpha = 1$						
100% TIPS	137.6	162.6	174.4			
100% government bonds	156.9	185.5	198.1			
100% stocks	518.1	618.4	636.5	275.6	326.9	343.3
(110–age)% stocks, (age + 10)% TIPS	247.2	293.1	308.3	191.1	226.2	240.0
(110–age)% stocks, (age + 10)% bonds	266.9	316.6	332.4	206.6	244.7	258.9
Empirical life cycle, stocks and TIPS	316.4	377.1	390.2	217.0	257.5	270.7
Empirical life cycle, stocks and bonds	333.4	397.4	411.1	229.1	271.8	285.6
Equivalent fixed-proportion stocks	312.8	371.9	387.0	233.4	276.8	291.2
"No-lose" plan	306.1	365.6	376.2	200.3	237.8	249.7

$\alpha = 2$

100% TIPS	137.6	162.6	174.4			
100% government bonds	151.7	179.1	191.8			
100% stocks	416.5	495.4	517.1	233.1	275.6	292.9
(110−age)% stocks, (age + 10)% TIPS	239.1	283.3	298.6	185.6	219.5	233.3
(110−age)% stocks, (age + 10)% bonds	252.0	298.5	314.6	196.3	232.2	246.6
Empirical life cycle, stocks and TIPS	296.7	353.0	367.4	206.2	244.3	258.1
Empirical life cycle, stocks and bonds	306.2	364.2	379.4	213.8	253.3	267.6
Equivalent fixed-proportion stocks	290.0	344.3	360.3	216.0	255.7	270.6
"No-lose" plan	277.0	330.0	342.8	190.0	225.3	238.0

$\alpha = 4$

100% TIPS	137.6	162.6	174.4			
100% government bonds	142.6	168.2	180.9			
100% stocks	301.2	356.3	379.2	181.5	213.6	230.6
(110−age)% stocks, (age + 10)% TIPS	224.5	265.6	281.1	175.5	207.3	221.1
(110−age)% stocks, (age + 10)% bonds	227.2	268.7	285.1	179.1	211.4	226.0
Empirical life cycle, stocks and TIPS	265.0	314.5	330.6	188.4	222.7	237.2
Empirical life cycle, stocks and bonds	264.8	314.0	330.8	189.9	224.4	239.4
Equivalent fixed-proportion stocks	254.1	300.9	317.8	189.2	223.3	238.6
"No-lose" plan	241.1	286.4	301.2	176.1	208.5	221.9

Table 1.8   Certainty equivalent wealth ($2,000) for different asset allocation rules and different expected stock returns, other wealth equal to all HRS nonretirement plan wealth

Risk aversion/investment strategy	Empirical stock returns			Empirical stock returns, reduced 300 basis points		
	Less than high school degree	High school and/or some college	College or post-graduate	Less than high school degree	High school and/or some college	College or post-graduate
α = 0						
100% TIPS	137.8	164.9	178.0			
100% government bonds	163.0	194.9	208.6			
100% stocks	677.8	812.3	817.5	340.0	406.3	418.9
(110−age)% stocks, (age + 10)% TIPS	256.1	305.5	321.4	197.3	235.6	250.4
(110−age)% stocks, (age + 10)% bonds	284.3	339.2	355.1	218.5	260.9	275.8
Empirical life cycle, stocks and TIPS	339.7	406.9	418.7	229.7	274.7	288.0
Empirical life cycle, stocks and bonds	367.1	439.7	451.4	247.7	296.2	309.7
Equivalent fixed-proportion stocks	340.1	406.4	420.6	254.7	304.3	318.7
"No-lose" plan	350.7	421.8	428.4	214.9	257.6	269.1
α = 1						
100% TIPS	137.8	164.9	178.0			
100% government bonds	158.3	189.9	204.4			
100% stocks	534.1	647.6	677.0	284.5	344.3	366.8
(110−age)% stocks, (age + 10)% TIPS	248.9	297.7	314.9	192.5	230.4	246.0
(110−age)% stocks, (age + 10)% bonds	269.9	323.5	341.9	208.9	250.5	267.1
Empirical life cycle, stocks and TIPS	320.1	385.0	400.9	219.4	263.5	278.9
Empirical life cycle, stocks and bonds	338.4	407.6	425.0	232.4	279.4	296.0
Equivalent fixed-proportion stocks	317.0	380.9	399.4	237.1	285.0	302.7
"No-lose" plan	311.9	377.4	392.4	202.7	244.0	258.2

α = 2

100% TIPS	137.8	164.9	178.0	247.0	302.1	330.1
100% government bonds	154.0	185.3	200.5	188.0	225.6	241.9
100% stocks	441.7	541.3	583.5	200.4	241.3	259.3
(110−age)% stocks, (age + 10)% TIPS	242.2	290.4	308.7	210.4	253.6	270.8
(110−age)% stocks, (age + 10)% bonds	257.3	309.7	330.2	219.5	265.2	284.1
Empirical life cycle, stocks and TIPS	303.2	366.1	385.3	222.5	268.9	289.0
Empirical life cycle, stocks and bonds	314.8	381.1	402.8	193.8	233.9	249.9
Equivalent fixed-proportion stocks	297.5	359.2	381.0			
"No-lose" plan	285.7	347.3	367.0			

α = 4

100% TIPS	137.8	164.9	178.0	199.9	248.2	281.0
100% government bonds	146.6	177.3	193.7	179.8	216.8	234.3
100% stocks	333.7	415.8	468.1	186.0	225.6	245.7
(110−age)% stocks, (age + 10)% TIPS	230.1	277.2	297.4	195.4	237.1	256.9
(110−age)% stocks, (age + 10)% bonds	236.3	286.4	310.1	199.0	242.5	264.6
Empirical life cycle, stocks and TIPS	275.7	335.3	359.3	199.4	243.4	266.4
Empirical life cycle, stocks and bonds	278.5	340.1	367.5	181.3	219.6	237.7
Equivalent fixed-proportion stocks	266.4	324.4	350.9			
"No-lose" plan	252.3	308.3	332.9			

consider several different life-cycle funds that automatically alter the investor's mix of assets as he or she ages. These funds offer investors a higher portfolio allocation to stocks at the beginning of a working career than as they approach retirement. We also consider a no-lose allocation strategy for retirement saving, in which households purchase enough riskless bonds at each age to ensure that they will have no less than their nominal contribution when they reach retirement age, and then invest the balance in corporate stock. This strategy combines a riskless floor for retirement income with some upside investment potential.

Our results suggest several conclusions about the effect of investment strategy on retirement wealth. First, the distribution of retirement wealth associated with typical life-cycle investment strategies is similar to that from age-invariant asset allocation strategies that set the equity share of the portfolio equal to the average equity share in the life-cycle strategies. Second, the expected utility associated with different 401(k) asset allocation strategies, and the ranking of these strategies, is very sensitive to three parameters: the expected return on corporate stock, the relative risk aversion of the investing household, and the amount of non-401(k) wealth that the household will have available at retirement. At modest levels of risk aversion, or when the household has access to substantial non-401(k) wealth at retirement, the historical pattern of stock and bond returns implies that the expected utility of an all-stock investment allocation rule is greater than that from any of the more conservative strategies. When we reduce the expected return on stocks by 300 basis points relative to historical values, however, other strategies dominate the all-equity allocation for investors with high levels of relative risk aversion. The no-lose plan yields an expected utility of wealth at retirement that is comparable to several of the life-cycle plans, but both the expected value of wealth and the expected utility level are slightly lower than the values associated with the life-cycle strategies that we consider.

Our analysis of life-cycle funds suggests a number of issues that may warrant future research. First, it is possible that life-cycle funds should be different for single individuals and for married couples. The focus in these funds, so far, has been on accumulating wealth for retirement, and the conceptual justification for age-phased equity exposure would be age-related variation in household risk aversion. Single individuals may have fewer opportunities to respond to an adverse economic shock than married couples, so their tolerance of equity-market risk in their retirement accounts may be different from that for married couples.

Second, we have focused on only a limited set of outcome measures associated with different asset allocation strategies. While we consider various percentiles of the retirement wealth distribution as well as the mean value of wealth at retirement and the expected utility associated with this wealth value, other metrics may also deserve consideration. One possibility is the risk of shortfall associated with one strategy relative to another. The Feldstein (2005) no-lose strategy eliminates the shortfall risk associated with a defined contribution investment strategy relative to investing all contributions to a defined contribution plan in a zero-yield cash account. Shortfall risk measures could be computed for a range of other strategies.

Third, our analysis has not reduced participant returns in 401(k) plans for the expense ratios associated with asset management. Actual returns are reduced by these fees, and a potentially important issue in the comparison of life-cycle funds and other investment vehicles is the differential in fees across these investment options. We are currently exploring the effect of introducing investment management fees to a simulation algorithm like that developed here.

Finally, our analysis has considered several stylized life-cycle funds, but it has not tried to determine the optimal age-related allocation between stocks and bonds for households like the ones we examine. Several previous studies, including Campbell and Viceira (2002), Campbell, Cocco, Gomes, and Maenhout (2001), and Cocco, Gomes and Maenhout (2005) have evaluated optimal life-cycle portfolios under stylized assumptions about labor market risk and the distribution of financial market returns. It would be useful to compare the expected utility from the optimal life-cycle fund with the expected utility either from existing life-cycle funds or from age-invariant asset allocation rules.

References

Ameriks, John, and Stephen Zeldes. 2004. Do household portfolio shares vary with age? Working paper, Columbia University Graduate School of Business.

Bodie, Zvi, Robert C. Merton, and William Samuelson. 1991. Labor supply flexibility and portfolio choice in a lifecycle model. *Journal of Economic Dynamics and Control* 16:427–49.

Campbell, John Y., João Cocco, Francisco Gomes, and Pascal Maenhout. 2001. Investing retirement wealth: A life-cycle model. In *Risk aspects of investment-based Social Security reform,* ed. John Y. Campbell and Martin Feldstein, 439–82. Chicago: University of Chicago Press.

Campbell, John Y., and Luis M. Viceira. 2002. *Strategic asset allocation: Portfolio choice for long-term investors.* New York: Oxford University Press.

Clements, Jonathan. 2005. Plan paralysis: Why a wealth of choices in 401(k)s may not make investors rich. *Wall Street Journal* May 4, C1.

Cocco, João, Francisco Gomes, and Pascal Maenhout. 2005. Consumption and portfolio choice over the life cycle. *Review of Financial Studies* 18 (2): 491–533.

Feldstein, Martin. 2005. Reducing the risk of investment-based Social Security reform. NBER Working Paper no. 11084. Cambridge, MA: National Bureau of Economic Research.

Gollier, Christian. 2001. *The economics of risk and time.* Cambridge, MA: MIT Press.

Gollier, Christian, and Richard J. Zeckhauser. 2002. Horizon length and portfolio risk, *Journal of Risk and Uncertainty* 24:195–212.

Gomes, Francisco, and Alexander Michaelides. 2005. Optimal life cycle asset allocation: Understanding the empirical evidence. *Journal of Finance* 60:869–904.
Ibbotson Associates. 2003. *Stocks, bonds, bills, and inflation: 2003 yearbook: Market results for 1926–2002*. Chicago: Ibbotson Associates.
Marquez, Jessica. 2005. Lifecycle funds can help companies mitigate risk and boost employee savings. *Workforce Management* April:65–67.
Mehra, Rajneesh, and Edward Prescott. 2002. The equity premium puzzle in retrospect. In *Handbook of economics of finance* ed. G. Constantinides, M. Harris, and R. Stulz, 889–938. Amsterdam: North Holland.
Merton, Robert C. 1969. Lifetime portfolio selection under uncertainty: The continuous time case. *Review of Economics and Statistics* 51:247–57.
Munnell, Alicia, and Annika Sunden. 2004. *Coming up short: The challenge of 401(k) plans*. Washington, DC: The Brookings Institution.
Poterba, James. 2003. Employer stock and 401(k) plans. *American Economic Review* 93 (May): 398–404.
Poterba, James, Joshua Rauh, Steven Venti, and David Wise. 2005. Utility evaluation of risk in retirement savings accounts. In *Analyses in the economics of aging,* Vol. 10, ed. David Wise, 13–58. Chicago: University of Chicago Press.
Poterba, James, and Andrew Samwick. 2001. Household portfolio allocations over the lifecycle, In *Aging issues in the U.S. and Japan,* ed. S. Ogura, T. Tachibanaki, and D. Wise, 65–103. Chicago: University of Chicago Press.
Samuelson, Paul. 1963. Risk and uncertainty: The fallacy of the law of large numbers. *Scientia* 98:108–13.
———. 1969. Lifetime portfolio selection by dynamic stochastic programming. *Review of Economics and Statistics* 51:239–46.
———. 1989. The judgement of economic science on rational portfolio management: Indexing, timing, and long-horizon effects. *Journal of Portfolio Management* (Fall): 3–12.
Samuelson, William, and Richard J. Zeckhauser. 1988. Status quo bias in decision making. *Journal of Risk and Uncertainty* 1:7–59.
Samwick, Andrew, and Jonathan Skinner. 2004. How will 401(k) plans affect retirement income? *American Economic Review* 94:329–43.
Shiller, Robert. 2005. The life cycle personal accounts proposal for Social Security: A review. NBER Working Paper no. 11300. Cambridge, MA: National Bureau of Economic Research.
Venti, Steven F., and David A. Wise. 2001. Aging and housing equity: Another look. In *Analyses in the economics of aging,* Vol. 9, ed. David A. Wise, 213–37. Chicago: University of Chicago Press.

Comment   Robert J. Willis

In a previous paper in this series, these authors (hereafter denoted as PRVW), developed a simulation methodology to calculate probability distributions of retirement wealth that would be available to a couple who

Robert J. Willis is a professor of economics at the University of Michigan, where he is also a research scientist at the Institute for Social Research and a research associate of the Population Studies Center.

participated in a 401(k) plan over their labor market careers under alternative allocations of their contributions between bonds and stocks (PRVW 2005). Their findings confirmed, in the main, earlier findings by MaCurdy and Shoven (1992) that a household that allocates its 401(k) contributions to stocks will not only have much higher wealth, on average, when it reaches retirement, than a household that invests in bonds, but that such a household faces almost no chance of having lower wealth despite the greater riskiness of stocks. The reason, of course, is rooted in the "equity premium puzzle" (Mehra and Prescott 2002) where the puzzle is that historical rates of return on stocks in the United States substantially exceed what would be required to compensate people with plausible degrees of risk aversion for this excess risk. In my comments on their paper (Willis 2005), I suggested that their findings, together with the fact that many people fail to hold significant stocks either with direct ownership or indirectly in retirement accounts, creates a related "retirement portfolio puzzle."

PRVW (2005) improved on the previous literature in two important ways. First, the methodology they used to calculate probability distributions of retirement wealth associated with alternative portfolio allocation strategies allows them to calculate the tail probability of very poor outcomes with considerable precision under two assumptions. One is that the processes that determined the distribution of historical U.S. stock returns will continue to operate in the same way in the future. The other is that the pattern of household life-cycle earnings will remain the same for future cohorts as it was for the HRS cohorts used in their simulations. Second, they explicitly recognize that, because people are risk averse, the simulated real dollar value of terminal retirement wealth does not directly provide the correct metric for evaluating alternative investment strategies. To obtain such a metric, they calculate the certainty-equivalent amount of terminal wealth for households with varying degrees of risk tolerance. While they found that all-stock portfolios do have a positive, but very small, probability of doing worse than an all-bond portfolio, asset allocation strategies with a large share of equities tend to have higher expected utility than more conservative ones, except for households with very low risk tolerance. Moreover, if the household has significant background income from Social Security, a DB pension, or labor earnings, all stock strategies tend to dominate, even for these very risk-averse households.

In the current paper—PRVW (2006)—the authors build on their previous analysis to examine the implications of a number of alternative investment allocation strategies that differ from the simpler strategies studied in PRVW (2005). In their previous paper, they considered alternative asset allocation strategies in which fixed fractions of contributions are allocated to stocks and a riskless asset. These strategies were in the spirit of the classic Samuelson-Merton model, in which it is optimal to maintain a constant share of risky assets in the portfolio over the entire life cycle, although their simulations did not allow for the continuous portfolio rebalancing required by the optimal policy. More recent theories as well as popular financial advice suggest that older households should move to more conservative portfolios as they age, to compensate for the loss of flexibility in labor earnings following retirement, and perhaps for other reasons.

In PRVW (2006), the authors evaluate nine alternative portfolio strategies to determine how much such considerations matter for the expected utility of retirement wealth. These include three portfolios, each containing 100 percent of one of the pure asset types (TIPS, government bonds, corporate stock), several life-cycles strategies in which the portfolio shifts away from stocks as retirement approaches and, finally, a "no-lose" strategy that guarantees at least a zero real rate of return. Except for the final strategy, each portfolio is rebalanced at each age. As in their earlier paper, the authors draw random sequences of returns from a distribution of historical real returns for stocks and government bonds that are applied to an age-specific contribution sequence based on earnings histories of married HRS households in order to calculate the probability distribution of retirement wealth for each household. They find that the probability distribution of wealth does not vary dramatically among the alternative life-cycle strategies, nor does it vary much from the distribution associated with an age-invariant strategy with asset allocation shares equal to the average of the life-cycle plans. However, they do find that ranking of the alternatives in terms of expected utility is highly sensitive to parametric variations in the degree of risk aversion and expected rate of return to bonds. While households with a low degree of risk aversion or significant wealth from other sources gain from all-stock portfolios, people who are more risk averse, who have more pessimistic expectations about the future of stock returns and who will mainly rely on their 401(k) for retirement consumption may prefer a life-cycle strategy with some portfolio diversification. Interestingly, these rankings do not vary across education groups.

In my view, this is an excellent chapter, which demonstrates how the methodology developed in the previous PRVW paper can be used to address important practical questions about portfolio allocations to 401(k) plans. Like their previous paper, it offers the kind of advice that I would have liked to receive from a financial planner when I was young and, given its emphasis on life-cycle factors, is also useful to me now. I am grateful, too, to learn that my uninformed strategy may not have been too far from optimal, even though I, like a number of my economist friends, have never rebalanced my TIAA-CREF portfolio, even after reading Samuelson and Merton. As they point out in their conclusion, there is still more work to be done along these lines. In my comments, I will discuss one of these lines for future research—the analysis of portfolio choices by single people—a little more thoroughly. In addition, I want to suggest two other directions in which the PRVW analysis might be extended. One is to utilize their approach in models of actual portfolio decisions that people make. The other is to consider what their analysis suggests for political economy.

So far, PRVW have deliberately restricted their analysis to stably married couples whose earnings histories and non-401(k) wealth can be drawn from the HRS. They speculate that the rankings of the alternative strategies might differ for single people because one person has less flexibility to respond to economic or health shocks than do two people. While I agree with their intuition, I think that portfolio choices by people who are not stably married may involve more subtle theoretical and empirical analysis than could be done by simply applying their current techniques to single people.

It is important to distinguish three types of people who end up as singles: the never-married, the divorced, and the widowed. The easiest case is widowing, because it is an insurable risk. It seems to me, therefore, that one could simply include the earnings histories of married people who end up widowed in the simulation model used by PRVW (with an imputed earnings history for the spouse who dies) because this is a possible outcome from the ex ante viewpoint of a newly married couple. This modification would require one important change. In their current model, PRVW use the household as a unit of analysis and assume a household utility function. In family economics, the assumption of a unitary model in which the preferences of a multiperson household is represented by a single utility function has been supplanted by collective models (Chiappori 1992) in which the utilities (and the separate interests and resources) of each individual within the household can be represented. To introduce widowing within a collective model, the PRVW model could be modified by specifying a separate CRRA utility function for the husband and wife together with a sharing rule (e.g., a fixed Pareto weight) to allow determination of each spouse's utility when both are alive. Note that this approach would also provide a natural way to integrate the PRVW analysis of preretirement savings with an analysis of mortality risk and the annuity value of postretirement consumption.

Introducing single and divorced people into the PRVW model is considerably more complicated, because marriage and divorce are subject to choice and are most decidedly not insurable risks. However, the divorce revolution that more than doubled divorce rates between 1965 and 1980, together with the delay of marriage and increasing levels of non marriage in the United States, imply that it is extremely important to bring marriage, divorce, and remarriage into the analysis if the PRVW model is going to be used to provide practical advice about the kinds of portfolio strategies that should be followed by young workers who are now signing up for 401(k) plans. For example, about a quarter of the early boomer cohort born in 1948–1953 who entered the HRS in 2004 were divorced or separated and many of those currently married were not in their first marriage. It may be possible to use the life histories of such people within a simulation model of the type that PRVW have developed, but thought would need to be given about how to model the probabilities of marriage and divorce and the division of wealth between the partners. Collective models of marriage, divorce, and household allocations between spouses have been developed (see Browning, Chiappori, and Weiss, in progress) and applied to dynamic life cycle models consumption and saving by couples with endogenous divorce risk (Attanasio and Mazzocco 2002; Licht-Tyler 2002). Theoretical models of this sort might provide a useful theoretical framework to guide construction of a simulation model.

In their papers, PRVW assume that the relevant measures of the risk of future retirement portfolios is based on the history of stock returns. In this chapter, they consider expected rates of return of 6 percent and 9 percent, which represent historical averages for series of different length for the United States. This approach seems quite sensible for purposes of advising someone about the risks he or she might face in making portfolio decisions, although an advisor might well add the caveat that the range of expected returns would be considerably wider and would have a lower mean if historical data from other countries were also considered. The historical data need not, however, reflect an individual's beliefs about risks and returns in the stock market.

In work in progress, Gabor Kézdi and I have been examining expected stock returns based on probability questions in the HRS. It is clear from these data that there is great heterogeneity subjective to expected returns. In particular, it appears that many people believe that there is a greater-than-even chance that the stock market will fall during 2009. Had they based their expectations on the historical data, this probability would be substantially less than 50 percent. It appears, therefore, that many individuals believe that the expected return on stocks is lower than even the lowest of the historical average returns used by PRVW. This suggests that one possible resolution of the retirement portfolio paradox associated with the absence of stock in the retirement wealth of many people is that these people think that stocks are both riskier and have lower returns than alternative investments. In addition, holding the expected return constant, we show that increased subjective uncertainty leads people to behave in a more risk-averse manner. If respondents' subjective beliefs about stock returns can be elicited from surveys, the methods developed by PRVW could be used to study actual 401(k) allocations as well as to examine the welfare implications of hypothetical strategies.

It is interesting to ask how much people's beliefs would be influenced by more knowledge of historical returns. To the extent that broader participation in 401(k) plans leads people to acquire more knowledge about the historical patterns and change their beliefs accordingly, more people may choose portfolios containing substantial amounts of stock, similar to those that PRVW find promise the greatest expected utility. Alternatively, it might be the case that ordinary people and experts will continue to have divergent beliefs about equity returns. As defined-benefit pensions are replaced by defined contribution plans, such divergent beliefs will contribute to growing inequality in wealth and income among retired people who had similar earnings histories. Even with homogeneous beliefs, PRVW show that alternative portfolios that produce similar expected utility may yield very different levels of wealth and income from an ex post point of view. Moreover, the value of wealth at a given retirement age of adjacent cohorts is subject to considerable variation because of year-to-year variations in the stock market. For example, between March 24, 2000, and July 1, 2001, the value of stocks fell by 50 percent, implying that otherwise identical brothers with all-stock portfolios who purchased retirement annuities on those two dates would have radically different retirement incomes. Based on the historical returns data, there is about a 5 percent chance of a difference this large between adjacent years. As defined contribution retirement plans and private savings become the dominant source of retiree incomes, one may speculate that social and political judgments about horizontal inequity among retirees will create pressures to offset inequalities in outcomes through taxes and transfers. In that sense, the fundamental idea of defined benefit pensions may not be as dead as it now seems.

References

Attanasio, Orazio, and Maurizio Mazzocco. 2002. Intrahousehold allocation with limited commitment: An empirical characterization. Unpublished manuscript, Department of Economics, University of Wisconsin.

Browning, Martin, Pierre-Andre Chiappori, and Yoram Weiss. 2007. *Family economics.* Cambridge: Cambridge University Press.

Chiappori, Pierre-Andre. 1992. Collective labor supply and welfare. *Journal of Political Economy* 89:798–812.

Licht-Tyler, Stephen. 2002. Negotiations and love songs: The dynamics of bargained household decisions. Unpublished manuscript, Department of Economics, University of Michigan.

MaCurdy, Thomas E., and John B. Shoven. 1992. Stocks, bonds and pension wealth. In *Topics in the economics of aging,* ed. David A. Wise, 61–78. Chicago: University of Chicago Press.

Mehra, Rajneesh, and Edward Prescott. 2002. The equity premium puzzle in retrospect. In *Handbook of economics of finance,* ed. G. Constantinides, M. Harris, and R. Stulz, 888–936. Amsterdam: North Holland.

Poterba, James, Joshua Rauh, Steven Venti, and David Wise. 2005. Utility evaluation of risk in retirement savings accounts. In *Analyses in the economics of aging,* ed. David A. Wise, 13–58. Chicago: University of Chicago Press.

———. 2006. Lifecycle asset allocation strategies and the distribution of 401(k) retirement wealth NBER Working Paper no. 11974. Cambridge, MA: National Bureau of Economic Research.

Willis, Robert J. 2005. Discussion of James Poterba, Joshua Rauh, Steven Venti, and David Wise, "Utility evaluation of risk in retirement savings accounts." In *Analyses in the economics of aging,* ed. David A. Wise, 53–57. Chicago: University of Chicago Press.

2

Reducing the Complexity Costs of 401(k) Participation through Quick Enrollment

James J. Choi, David Laibson, and Brigitte C. Madrian

Previous research has shown that 401(k) participation increases dramatically when companies switch from an opt-in to an opt-out (or automatic) enrollment regime (Madrian and Shea 2001; Choi et al. 2004; Choi et al. 2006). Although automatic enrollment has been widely touted as an effective tool for encouraging saving, it has its detractors. Some libertarians dislike automatic enrollment because they view it as coercing individuals into the company-chosen default contribution rate and asset allocation. Indeed, the vast majority of automatically enrolled employees passively accept all of the defaults in the short run, and many remain at those defaults for years (Choi et al. 2004; Choi et al. 2006). Paternalists, in contrast, like the fact that automatic enrollment increases 401(k) participation but object to companies choosing default contribution rates that they perceive as

James J. Choi is an assistant professor of finance at the Yale School of Management and a faculty research fellow of the National Bureau of Economic Research. David Laibson is a professor of economics at Harvard University and a research associate at the National Bureau of Economic Research. Brigitte C. Madrian is the Aetna Professor of Public Policy and Corporate Management at the John F. Kennedy School of Government, Harvard University, and a research associate at the National Bureau of Economic Research.

We thank Hewitt Associates for their help in providing the data. We are particularly grateful to Lori Lucas and Yan Xu, two of our many contacts at Hewitt Associates, and to Greg Stoner and other employees at the two companies studied in the paper. We thank Jonathan Skinner and participants at the 2005 NBER Aging Conference for helpful comments and Hongyi Li for excellent research assistance. Choi acknowledges financial support from the Mustard Seed Foundation. Choi, Laibson, and Madrian acknowledge individual and collective financial support from the National Institute on Aging (grants R01-AG021650 and T32-AG00186). The opinions and conclusions expressed are solely those of the authors and do not represent the opinions or policy of NIA, the federal government, or the NBER. Laibson also acknowledges financial support from the Sloan Foundation.

too low and asset allocations that are too conservative.[1] Firms, however, have been reluctant to adopt more aggressive defaults for fear of participant lawsuits should the default investments decline in value.

One reason that automatic enrollment increases 401(k) participation is that it reduces the complexity of the decision-making task. Rather than evaluating all possible contribution rate and asset allocation options, employees need only compare the automatic enrollment default with nonparticipation. Relative to plans with automatic enrollment, opt-in plans impose a much greater decision-making burden on enrollees. But a high level of complexity in an opt-in plan is not necessary. There are ways to reduce complexity that are not as extreme as adopting automatic enrollment.

In this chapter, we analyze one such alternative, called Quick Enrollment, developed by Hewitt Associates.[2] Quick Enrollment gives employees the option of enrolling in the savings plan by opting into a default contribution rate and asset allocation preselected by the employer. If Quick Enrollment succeeds in reducing complexity by allowing employees to focus on evaluating a smaller subset of options (e.g., nonenrollment and the default), savings plan participation should increase relative to a standard opt-in enrollment regime. The fact that all Quick Enrollment elections are affirmative also addresses both the libertarian and paternalist objections to automatic enrollment. For libertarians, there is no coercion into the default. For paternalists, affirmative elections reduce the legal risks from choosing a less conservative default asset allocation. The implementations studied in this chapter may also motivate increased 401(k) participation by giving employees a deadline for using Quick Enrollment to join the 401(k) plan, akin to the "active decision" approach to 401(k) enrollment analyzed in Choi et al. (2005).

We evaluate three different implementations of Quick Enrollment at two firms. Two of the implementations were short-term interventions that targeted nonparticipating employees who had previously been hired by the firms we study. The third was an ongoing intervention for newly hired employees. For all three implementations, we find that Quick Enrollment resulted in substantial 401(k) participation increases, although these increases are not nearly as large as those obtained through automatic enrollment in other firms. We also document the importance of the Quick Enrollment default for contribution rate and asset allocation outcomes.

The chapter proceeds as follows. Section 2.1 describes the implementation of Quick Enrollment at the two firms we study and the data that we use to analyze its effect. Section 2.2 presents the results of our empirical analysis at the first company. Section 2.3 presents the results of our empirical

---

1. See Hewitt (2005), Profit Sharing/401(k) Council of America (2001), and Vanguard (2001) for a description of the empirical distribution of automatic enrollment defaults.
2. Hewitt Associates provided the data analyzed in this paper.

analysis at the second company. We conclude in section 2.4 by comparing Quick Enrollment with other mechanisms for influencing 401(k) savings outcomes.

2.1 Quick Enrollment Implementation at Two Firms

The first Quick Enrollment implementation we study was at a large health services company—hereafter referred to as Company A—with approximately 40,000 employees at more than twenty locations. Table 2.1 gives demographic characteristics for the active employees at this firm on December 31, 2003, along with characteristics of all private sector employees in the March 2003 Current Population Survey (CPS) as a basis for comparison. Relative to the U.S. population, Company A workers are slightly older, earn a little more, and are much more likely to be female.

Table 2.2 presents features of the 401(k) plan at Company A. Virtually all Company A employees in our data are immediately eligible for the 401(k) plan. At most locations, employees who are at least twenty-one years old and have attained 1,000 hours of service are eligible for a 50 percent matching contribution from the company on the first 4 percent or 6 percent of pay contributed to the plan. Employees may contribute up to 100 percent of their pay (provided their contributions do not exceed the IRS dollar contribution limits) to eleven different investment options. There is no employer stock in the fund menu.

Figure 2.1 shows the Quick Enrollment timeline at Company A. Prior to July 2003, the company used a standard opt-in enrollment process: employees were not enrolled in the 401(k) plan unless they made an affirmative

Table 2.1   **Employee characteristics**

	Company A active employees on Dec. 31, 2003	Company B active employees on Dec. 31, 2003	Private sector employees March 2003 CPS
Average age (years)	41.9	45.3	39.0
Percent male	26.5	76.2	53.4
Compensation			
Avg. annual income	$38,321		$36,782
Median annual income	$28,523		$27,000
Ethnic composition			
White (%)	84.3		83.1
Black (%)	12.7		10.5
Other (%)	3.0		6.3
Number of employees	~40,000	~20,000	

Source: Authors' calculations. Information on ethnicity and income is not available for Company B. Private household workers are excluded from our sample for the U.S. private sector (column 3).

Table 2.2   401(k) plan features

	Company A	Company B
Eligibility		
Eligible employees	Some small groups of employees not eligible (e.g., independent contractors, union employees)	U.S. employee
First eligible	Immediately upon hire	Immediately upon hire
Employer match eligible	Age 21 + 1,000 hours of service	Immediately upon hire
Enrollment	Daily	Daily
Employee contributions	Up to 100% of compensation	Up to 25% of compensation
Employer matching contributions		
Match rate and threshold	Depending on location and pay group, most employees receive a 50% match on the first 4% or 6% of pay contributed	Between 55% and 125% on the first 6% of pay contributed, depending on company profitability
Investment restrictions	No restrictions on employer match	Matching contributions invested 100% in employer stock. May diversify 25% of balances at age 45, up to 100% at age 55
Vesting of employer match	Vests 100% in 3 years	Immediate
Other		
Loans	Available	Available
Hardship withdrawals	Available	Available
Investment choices	11 options (no employer stock)	9 options, including employer stock

Source: Plan documents.

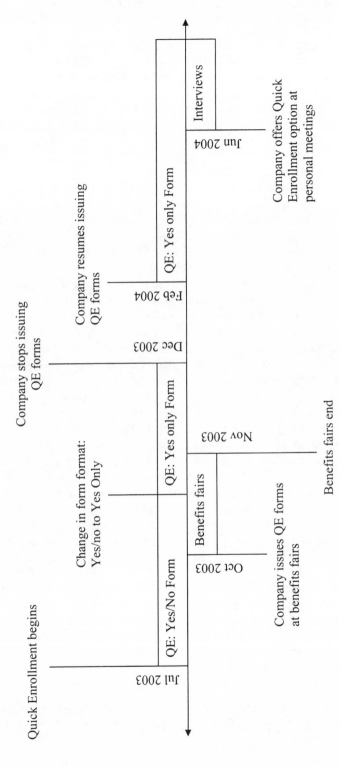

Fig. 2.1   Timeline of enrollment mechanisms at Company A

election through a toll-free phone call to the firm's benefits administrator or through visiting the benefits administration Web site. Changes in the 401(k) participation, contribution rate, and investment allocation could be made at any time.

In July 2003, Company A adopted Quick Enrollment on a trial basis at its main location. New employees attending orientation were given Quick Enrollment cards that gave them the choice of checking a box to initiate 401(k) participation at a contribution rate of 2 percent of salary (before tax) and a preselected asset allocation (50 percent in a money market fund and 50 percent in a balanced fund). Returning the Quick Enrollment card was not mandatory and was not described to employees as mandatory. However, the cards did note a deadline of two weeks after orientation for submitting the card if the employees wished to use the Quick Enrollment process (the deadline on the card was a specific date that changed according to when the new-employee orientation was held).[3]

From July through September, the Quick Enrollment form gave employees two options: "Yes! I want to enroll . . . and begin saving in the [Company A] Savings Plan," and "No. I don't want to enroll at this time." From October to December, the "No" option was eliminated from the Quick Enrollment form to investigate whether making nonparticipation salient through the "No" option affected enrollment. Failure to return either version of the form was treated as a negative 401(k) participation election. Employees also had the option to initiate participation on their own at any contribution rate and with any investment allocation through the standard channels (phone or Internet) throughout this time. In February 2004, Company A adopted Quick Enrollment as a permanent feature of its new employee orientation, with continued use of the yes-only form.

The second Quick Enrollment implementation took place at Company A from mid-June through early fall 2004 for nonparticipating employees who were already at the firm. This implementation occurred in conjunction with the adoption of a new Web-based benefits management system for all employees. As part of the transition to this new system, the company had employees meet individually with representatives of an outside vendor to help them register on the new system. These meetings were not designed to be individual financial planning sessions, but representatives answered questions about company benefits—in particular, the firm's life insurance products and savings plan. Nonparticipating employees were given the opportunity to enroll in the 401(k) plan using a Web-based Quick Enrollment interface. This implementation offered the same asset allocation as the new hire implementation, but employees could choose any pretax contribution

---

3. The company reports that many of the Quick Enrollment cards were handed in during the orientation rather than taken home and mailed in. The deadline was not actually binding, although employees probably did not know this.

rate. Employees did not have the option to use the Web-based Quick Enrollment option after the meeting.

The third Quick Enrollment implementation that we study is at Company B, a firm in the manufacturing industry. This company employs approximately 20,000 individuals. Table 2.1 gives demographic characteristics for the active employees at this firm on December 31, 2003. Company
B employees are significantly older than the U.S. average and much more
likely to be male. Other demographic data (e.g., race/ethnicity and pay) are
not available for this company.

Table 2.2 describes the 401(k) plan features at Company B. Employees
are immediately eligible for the 401(k) plan, which provides a variable
matching contribution between 55 percent and 125 percent, depending on
company profitability, on the first 6 percent of pay contributed to the plan.
The employer match is invested in employer stock. Employees may contribute up to 25 percent of pay (subject to the IRS dollar contribution limits) and choose among nine investment options, including employer stock.

Quick Enrollment at Company B was implemented as a one-time mailing to nonparticipating employees already at the firm in the latter half of
January 2003. Employees were given the option to check a box to enroll in
the 401(k) plan at a 3 percent (before-tax) contribution rate invested entirely in a money market fund. Figure 2.2 shows the Quick Enrollment
timeline at Company B. Although employees at Company B were given a
two-week deadline for returning the Quick Enrollment cards, this deadline
was not binding in practice. Cards returned after the deadline were held
and processed in May 2003.

The data we use to analyze Quick Enrollment at these two firms come
from Hewitt Associates, a large benefits administration and consulting
firm. The data are a series of year-end cross-sections of all employees at
Companies A and B. For Company A, we have cross-sections from year-

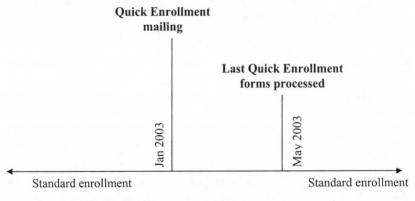

Fig. 2.2   Timeline of enrollment mechanisms at Company B

end 2002, year-end 2003, and September 1, 2004. For Company B, we have cross-sections from year-ends 2002 and 2003. These cross-sections contain demographic information such as birth date, hire date, gender, state of residence, and compensation.[4] They also contain point-in-time information on 401(k) savings outcomes, including participation status in the plan, date of first participation, the contribution rate, asset allocation, and total balances. In addition, we have ethnicity data for Company A employees active at year-end 2003 and September 1, 2004.

2.2   Quick Enrollment and 401(k) Outcomes at Company A

In designing the Quick Enrollment implementation at Company A, our initial intent was to compare participation under three enrollment mechanisms: the yes/no Quick Enrollment card, the yes-only Quick Enrollment card, and the standard opt-in enrollment protocol without Quick Enrollment. The empirical methodology to do this would have been straightforward: we would have three different treatment regimes and treated and untreated locations (the main location versus everywhere else). The untreated locations would allow us to control for time effects that might otherwise confound comparisons of the different enrollment regimes at the treated location.

Our ability to carry out this methodology in a completely convincing fashion has been limited by three factors. First, although Quick Enrollment forms were only distributed at the main location's orientation sessions, employees do not necessarily attend orientation at the location where they work. Therefore, a nontrivial number of employees at the untreated locations actually had the opportunity to use Quick Enrollment. This contamination of the control locations will cause a comparison of the main location against other locations to underestimate the Quick Enrollment effect. Second, after seeing Quick Enrollment's success at the new-employee orientations from July to September 2003, the benefits office decided to distribute Quick Enrollment forms at the firm's annual benefits fairs in October and November 2003. These benefits fairs were held at many locations, providing additional exposure to Quick Enrollment for employees at locations that would otherwise serve as controls. Third, the coincident timing of the benefits fairs with the yes-only Quick Enrollment form precludes a clean comparison of the yes-no and yes-only forms, since new employees also potentially attended the benefits fairs.

However, the permanent adoption of the yes-only Quick Enrollment form in February 2004 at the main location orientation sessions allows us to compare 401(k) outcomes at the main location from February 2004 onward to outcomes at the main location prior to Quick Enrollment's initial implementation in July 2003.

---

4. Compensation data are not available for Company B.

Table 2.3   Employee characteristics by hire cohort: Company A (main location)

	Feb.–May 2002 cohort in June 2002	Feb.–May 2003 cohort in June 2003	Feb.–May 2004 cohort in June 2004
Average age (years)	31.4	32.0	32.7
Percent male	27.6	28.6	28.9
Compensation			
Avg. annual income ($)	19,510	20,928	22,918
Median annual income ($)	16,619	17,282	17,581
Ethnic composition			
White (%)	77.1	79.1	75.6
Black (%)	20.6	17.9	21.6
Other (%)	2.3	3.0	2.8
Number of employees	455	407	733

Source: Authors' calculations.

Recall that the firm offered Quick Enrollment in a different fashion to nonparticipating employees from June to August 2004 in conjunction with its Web-based benefits management program rollout. Because of this, we restrict our initial Quick Enrollment analysis to employees hired from February to May 2004, and we do not examine these employees' 401(k) outcomes beyond mid-June 2004. We use as our control group employees hired from February to May 2003 and February to May 2002. Table 2.3 shows that the demographic characteristics of employees at the company's main location who were hired from February to May of 2002, 2003, and 2004 appear very similar.

Figure 2.3 plots the 401(k) participation rate against tenure for employees hired at the company's main location before and after Quick Enrollment. For employees hired from February to May of 2002 and 2003, the 401(k) participation paths track each other quite closely, suggesting no dramatic changes in employee characteristics or other factors influencing 401(k) participation. The participation rates for newly hired employees are extremely low: about 5 percent after the first month of employment and 15 percent after twelve months. The participation rates under Quick Enrollment are dramatically higher: 19 percent after the first month of employment and 35 percent in the third month. We do not calculate Quick Enrollment participation rates at higher tenure levels because they would be potentially contaminated by the June-to-August intervention described previously.

Figure 2.4 shows the one-month and three-month participation rates at the company's main location by hire month. Although there is some participation rate variability across hire months both before and after Quick Enrollment, this variation is dwarfed by the large participation increases generated by Quick Enrollment.

To control for potential differences in the demographic composition of

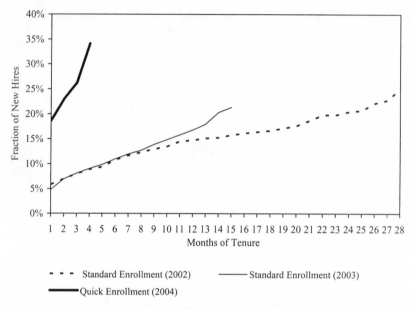

Fig. 2.3   401(k) participation by tenure (Company A, main location)

employees hired before and after Quick Enrollment, we run probit regressions of one-month and three-month participation in the 401(k) plan on age, gender, race, compensation, and a Quick Enrollment dummy, which is set to 1 for employees hired from February to May 2004. The sample in these regressions is employees hired from February to May of 2002, 2003, and 2004, with the employees hired in 2002 and 2003 serving as a pre-Quick Enrollment control group.[5] The first two columns of table 2.4 list the marginal effects at the sample means from the probit regressions for employees at the firm's main location where Quick Enrollment was used. The only statistically significant demographic characteristics are compensation and age: higher-paid and older employees are much more likely to enroll. The Quick Enrollment effect is large and statistically significant, increasing the one-month participation rate by fourteen percentage points and the three-month participation rate by sixteen percentage points. This represents a tripling of the one- and three-month participation rates prior to Quick Enrollment.[6]

5. In the three-month participation regressions, the sample is restricted to employees hired during February and March, since we do not observe three-month participation rates for employees hired in April and May of 2004 prior to the individual meetings that started in June 2004. For the sake of comparability, we also restrict the sample of employees hired in 2002 and 2003 to those hired in February and March. The results are qualitatively similar when employees hired in April and May of 2002 and 2003 are not excluded from the three-month participation regressions.

6. Ordinary least square (OLS) results, while not reported, yield qualitatively similar estimates.

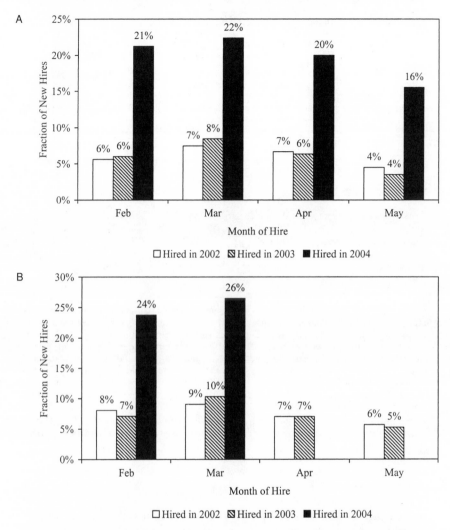

Fig. 2.4   *A:* **401(k) participation one month after hire, by hire month (Company A, main location);** *B:* **401(k) participation three months after hire, by hire month (Company A, main location)**

Note: 2004 three-month participation rates for April and May hires are not reported due to potential contamination with the June to August 2004 Quick Enrollment intervention for all employees.

Because Quick Enrollment was only distributed at the main location orientations, a useful specification check is to see whether there is a Quick Enrollment effect at other locations. The last two columns of table 2.4 present regression results for employees working at other locations. The Quick Enrollment coefficients are small in magnitude and statistically insignificant. These results suggest that the estimated Quick Enrollment effect at the

Table 2.4   Probit regressions of 401(k) enrollment at Company A: new hires

	Main location		Other locations	
	Enrolled in 1 month	Enrolled in 3 months	Enrolled in 1 month	Enrolled in 3 months
Age (years)	0.0013*	0.0031*	–0.0003	0.0006
	(0.0006)	(0.0013)	(0.0008)	(0.0013)
Female	0.0034	0.0191	0.0436*	0.0109
	(0.0147)	(0.0300)	(0.0152)	(0.0320)
Black	0.0048	–0.0544	–0.0241	–0.0525
	(0.0178)	(0.0329)	(0.0211)	(0.0305)
Other/unknown race	–0.0118	–0.0137	—[a]	—[a]
	(0.0367)	(0.0721)		
Pay ($1000's)	0.0031**	0.0036**	0.0028**	0.0032**
	(0.0004)	(0.0006)	(0.0004)	(0.0007)
Quick Enrollment cohort	0.1398**	0.1630**	0.0265	–0.0192
	(0.0174)	(0.0367)	(0.0189)	(0.0286)
Sample size	$N = 1613$	$N = 610$	$N = 776$	$N = 307$
Pseudo R^2	0.1667	0.1468	0.1515	0.1787

Source: Authors' calculations. The table reports marginal effects at sample means from a probit regression where the dependent variable is whether the employee has enrolled in the 401(k) either one or three months after hire. The sample in the one-month regressions is employees hired from February to May of 2002, 2003, and 2004. The sample in the three-month regressions is employees hired in February and March of 2002, 2003, and 2004. Female, Black, and Other/unknown race are dummy variables. Quick Enrollment cohort is a dummy for employees hired from February to May 2004 in the one-month regression and in February and March 2004 in the three-month regression. Standard errors are in parentheses under the point estimates.

[a]None of the sample of other/unknown race enrolled within three months of hire. Consequently, all of these employees as well as the Other/unknown race variable were dropped from this regression.

*denotes significance at the 5% level.
**denotes significance at the 1% level.

main location is indeed caused by Quick Enrollment and not spurious correlation with other factors.

Table 2.5 examines which employees are most affected by Quick Enrollment. In the first two columns, we break down the one-month participation rate by various demographic characteristics for employees hired prior to Quick Enrollment (February to May of 2002 and 2003) and after Quick Enrollment (February to May 2004).[7] The last two columns of table 2.5 divide the post-Quick Enrollment participants into two subgroups: those who enrolled using a non-Quick Enrollment channel, and those who en-

7. The results in table 2.5 are qualitatively similar for three-month rather than one-month enrollment rates. We report one-month enrollment rates in table 2.5 because the sample sizes for some of the demographic subgroups are quite small if three-month enrollment rates are used.

Table 2.5   **Enrollment rates by employee characteristics: new hires at Company A's main location at one month of tenure**

	Before Quick Enrollment	After Quick Enrollment		
	Fraction enrolling at any allocation	Fraction enrolling at any allocation	Fraction enrolling at nondefault allocation	Fraction enrolling at QE default allocation
Age				
< 30 (%)	4.4	12.2	3.4	8.8
	(528)	(319)	(319)	(319)
30–50 (%)	7.4	29.3	7.7	21.6
	(394)	(222)	(222)	(222)
> 50 (%)	8.1	26.5	6.3	20.3
	(86)	(64)	(64)	(64)
Gender				
Female (%)	5.9	18.5	4.5	14.1
	(716)	(426)	(426)	(426)
Male (%)	5.8	23.5	7.3	16.2
	(292)	(179)	(179)	(179)
Race/Ethnicity				
Black (%)	3.9	18.0	3.0	15.0
	(205)	(133)	(133)	(133)
White (%)	6.1	21.4	6.2	15.2
	(776)	(454)	(454)	(454)
Other/unknown (%)	14.8	0	0	0
	(27)	(18)	(18)	(18)
Compensation				
< $25K (%)	2.7	13.0	2.4	10.7
	(734)	(460)	(460)	(460)
$25K–$50K (%)	10.0	35.5	11.2	24.3
	(211)	(107)	(107)	(107)
>$50K (%)	28.6	60.5	23.6	36.8
	(63)	(38)	(38)	(38)

Source: Authors' calculations. The sample in column 1 is employees hired from February to May of 2002 and 2003. The sample in the remaining columns is employees hired from February to May of 2004. Sample sizes for each cell reported in parentheses.

rolled using Quick Enrollment. Because we do not have data on who actually used Quick Enrollment, we attribute Quick Enrollment utilization to those employees who have the Quick Enrollment default asset allocation. Although this approach may generate some classification error, the magnitude is likely to be quite small given that *none* of the new hires from January to June 2003 (before Quick Enrollment) who enrolled within their first month of employment elected the default asset allocation.[8]

8. Employees could have enrolled using Quick Enrollment and then subsequently changed their asset allocation, which would also cause us to misclassify them. There are not likely to be many such employees, given the frequency of our asset allocation observations.

For all of the demographic groups listed in table 2.5, 401(k) participation rates are substantially higher under Quick Enrollment (column 1 versus column 2). The absolute size of the participation increase is largest among those who are ages thirty to fifty (twenty-two percentage points) and earning more than $25,000 (twenty-six percentage points for those earning between $25,000 and $50,000, and thirty-two percentage points for those earning more than $50,000). The proportional increase relative to pre-Quick Enrollment participation rates is largest among blacks (385 percent), those earning less than $25,000 (396 percent), and those men age thirty to fifty (292 percent). Across all demographic groups, over 75 percent of all new-hire enrollments in the post-Quick Enrollment period occur through Quick Enrollment. Quick Enrollment is especially popular among blacks (83 percent) and those earning less than $25,000 (82 percent).

As discussed previously, Company A's second Quick Enrollment implementation occurred from mid-June to early fall of 2004, in conjunction with the new benefits management Web-site rollout. The aggregate participation impact of this extension of Quick Enrollment extension to all nonparticipating employees is striking (fig. 2.5). During a two-and-a-half month period, the firm's overall participation rate increased from 50 percent to 60 percent, converting 20 percent of nonparticipants into participants. The effects are similar for employees at both the main location and at other locations, which is not surprising, given that in this intervention, Quick Enrollment was made available to all nonparticipating employees, regardless of location.

Table 2.6, which is analogous to table 2.5, examines the impact of Quick

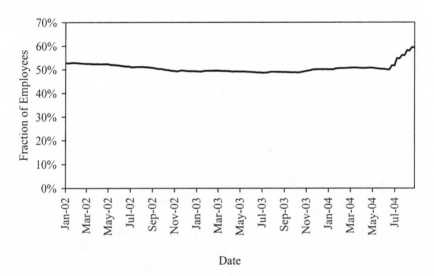

Fig. 2.5   401(k) participation rate (Company A, all employees at all locations)

Table 2.6   **Enrollment rates by employee characteristics: previously nonparticipating employees at Company A**

	Before Quick Enrollment	After Quick Enrollment		
	Fraction enrolling at any allocation	Fraction enrolling at any allocation	Fraction enrolling at nondefault allocation	Fraction enrolling at QE default allocation
Age				
< 30 (%)	3.2	24.8	2.3	22.5
	(5,103)	(2,560)	(2,560)	(2,560)
30–50 (%)	3.0	26.5	1.7	24.7
	(4,001)	(1,871)	(1,871)	(1,871)
> 50 (%)	5.1	17.7	1.1	16.6
	(686)	(367)	(367)	(367)
Gender				
Female (%)	3.2	26.7	1.9	24.7
	(7,092)	(3,489)	(3,489)	(3,489)
Male (%)	3.3	20.2	2.1	18.1
	(2,698)	(1,309)	(1,309)	(1,309)
Race/Ethnicity				
Black (%)	1.4	25.8	1.1	24.7
	(2,369)	(1,206)	(1,206)	(1,206)
White (%)	3.8	24.7	2.3	22.4
	(7,246)	(3,500)	(3,500)	(3,500)
Other/unknown (%)	5.7	21.7	2.2	19.6
	(175)	(92)	(92)	(92)
Compensation				
< $25K (%)	1.7	17.5	1.6	15.9
	(5,174)	(2,451)	(2,451)	(2,451)
$25K–$50K (%)	4.5	30.4	2.2	28.2
	(3,677)	(1,806)	(1,806)	(1,806)
>$50K (%)	6.9	40.1	3.0	37.2
	(939)	(541)	(541)	(541)
Tenure				
< 2 years (%)	4.3	20.1	2.3	17.8
	(4,053)	(1,795)	(1,795)	(1,795)
2–5 years (%)	2.8	27.6	2.1	25.5
	(2,507)	(1,488)	(1,488)	(1,488)
> 5 years (%)	2.2	27.9	1.5	26.4
	(3,230)	(1,515)	(1,515)	(1,515)

Source: Authors' calculations. The sample in column 1 is nonparticipants in June 2002 and June 2003 (some individuals will be included in the sample twice if nonparticipants in both 2002 and 2003). The time frame over which enrollment is calculated is June through August 2002 and 2003 for column 1, and June through August 2004 for the remaining columns. The sample in the remaining columns is nonparticipants in June 2004. Sample sizes for each cell reported in parentheses.

Enrollment on different demographic groups. The first column is the fraction of previously nonparticipating employees who enrolled from June to August of 2002 and 2003, prior to the adoption of Quick Enrollment.[9] The second column gives the fraction of nonparticipating employees enrolling from June to August of 2003 during the second Quick Enrollment implement at Company A. This is disaggregated in the last two columns according to whether the enrollment occurred through Quick Enrollment or not. Again, we identify Quick Enrollment usage through the presence of the default asset allocation, which was elected by virtually none of the employees who initiated plan participation prior to Quick Enrollment.

For all demographic groups, 401(k) enrollment rates are much higher under Quick Enrollment, and the vast majority of enrollments (92 percent across the entire population) are submitted through Quick Enrollment. Absolute enrollment changes are largest for women (twenty-four percentage points), blacks (twenty-four percentage points), those earning more than $25,000 (twenty-six percentage points for those earning between $25,000 and $50,000, and thirty-three percentage points for those earning more than $50,000), those aged thirty to fifty (twenty-four percentage points), and those who have been at the company more than five years (twenty-six percentage points). Relative increases are largest for those between ages thirty and fifty (823 percent), women (771 percent), blacks (1,764 percent), those making less than $25,000 a year (935 percent), and those who have been at the company for more than five years (1,200 percent).

Given the evidence from previous research on the impact of defaults on 401(k) contribution rates and asset allocation, it is natural to ask how Quick Enrollment, which can be viewed as a default that is opted into, affects these same outcomes. We have already noted that virtually no participants enrolling in the 401(k) plan prior to Quick Enrollment selected the default asset allocation (indeed, we identified Quick Enrollment usage by whether the participant's asset allocation matched the Quick Enrollment default.) In contrast, 73 percent of newly hired participants (table 2.5) and 92 percent of new participants among existing employees (table 2.6) had the Quick Enrollment default asset allocation in the post-Quick Enrollment period. Clearly, Quick Enrollment has an important effect on asset allocation outcomes.

Not surprisingly, Quick Enrollment has similar effects on contribution

9. Employees attending new-hire orientation at the main location in July and August 2003 were exposed to the Quick Enrollment intervention, thus attenuating the difference between the Quick Enrollment population and the comparison population. These employees are a small fraction of the total nonparticipating population, so their presence should not have a significant impact. Note also that employees who were nonparticipants in 2002 and again in 2003 are included in the sample more than once (and, if nonparticipants again in 2004, are also in the sample for the last three columns of table 2.6).

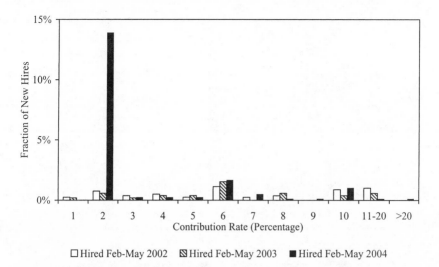

Fig. 2.6   Contribution rate distribution of new hires enrolling within thirty days (Company A, main location)

Note: Employees who did not enroll in the 401(k) plan within thirty days of hire are classified as having a zero contribution rate and are included in calculating the fraction of new hires at a given contribution rate, although we do not show the fraction of new hires with a zero contribution rate in this figure.

rates as well. Figure 2.6 shows the effect of Quick Enrollment on the distribution of contribution rates for new employees thirty days after hire.[10] As is typical in companies with an employer match, the modal contribution rate prior to Quick Enrollment is the employer match threshold of 6 percent; approximately 1 percent of new hires or 25 percent of newly hired participants contribute at this rate. Under Quick Enrollment, however, the modal contribution rate shifts to 2 percent, the Quick Enrollment default. The fraction of employees contributing 2 percent increases more than twenty-fold, from less than 1 percent of employees to 14 percent of employees. This represents an increase from 13 percent of participants to 75 percent of participants. We find no evidence for the type of contribution rate displacement that has been observed with automatic enrollment. Indeed, the increase in the fraction of employees contributing 2 percent of pay to the 401(k) plan at one month of tenure is approximately equal to the

10. We only observe contribution rates periodically, as described in section 2.1. In order to approximate the contribution rate distribution thirty days after hire, we use the contribution rate effective in the data extract closest to the employees' hire date and assign a zero contribution rate to those who did not enroll within thirty days of hire. Because our closest contribution rate observation is no more than eleven months after an employee's hire, this approximation should be very close to the actual distribution.

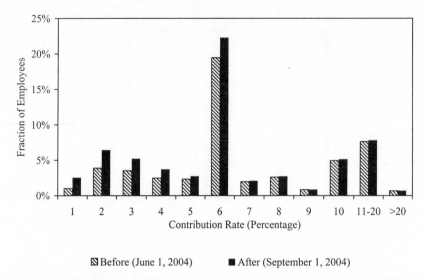

Fig. 2.7   Contribution rate distribution before and after individual meetings (Company A, all locations)

Note: Employees who had not enrolled in the 401(k) plan as of the snapshot date are classified as having a zero contribution rate and are included in calculating the fraction of total employees at a given contribution rate, although we do not show the fraction of employees with a zero contribution rate in this figure.

one-month participation increase attributable to Quick Enrollment from the probit regression in column 1 of table 2.1.

The second Quick Enrollment implementation, which occurred in conjunction with the individual Web-site registrations, gave employees the option to choose any contribution rate in conjunction with the Quick Enrollment default asset allocation. We would therefore expect less clustering at any particular contribution rate. Figure 2.7 shows the distribution of contribution rates for employees hired prior to June 2003, before Quick Enrollment was adopted in any form at Company A, at two points in time. The first distribution is from June 1, 2004, three weeks before the registration period Quick Enrollment implementation began, and the second is from September 1, 2004, which is our last data snapshot after this second Quick Enrollment implementation. As in fig. 2.6, the modal contribution rate before Quick Enrollment is the match threshold of 6 percent. Under Quick Enrollment, the fraction of employees with contribution rates between 1 percent and 6 percent increases noticeably, while there is little effect above 6 percent. Because Quick Enrollment participants are spread across several contribution rates, the match threshold remains the modal contribution rate.

2.3   Quick Enrollment and 401(k) Outcomes at Company B

We now turn to the Quick Enrollment implement at Company B which, similar to the second implement at Company A, also targeted previously hired nonparticipating employees.[11] As mentioned in section 2.1, this company executed a one-time mailing in late January 2003 to nonparticipating employees. Those returning the reply card were enrolled in the 401(k) plan at a 3 percent contribution rate, and all these contributions were invested in a money market fund. Cards returned by the deadline were processed in February 2003; late-reply cards were processed in May 2003.

In the case of Company B, our data identifies the employees who were mailed the Quick Enrollment cards. To measure the effect of Quick Enrollment, we need to identify what these recipients would have done in the absence of Quick Enrollment. We use two control groups for this purpose. The first is employees who were not participating on February 1, 2002, a year prior to Quick Enrollment. The second is the 16 percent of nonparticipants on February 1, 2003, who did not receive the Quick Enrollment mailing. We are not certain why the company did not send these employees Quick Enrollment cards.[12] Because selection into this group is unlikely to be random, comparisons with the Quick Enrollment recipients must be interpreted with caution.

Figure 2.8 shows the 401(k) participation time series for four groups of Company B employees: all nonparticipating employees as of February 1, 2002; all Quick Enrollment recipients; nonparticipants as of February 1, 2003, who received the Quick Enrollment mailing; and nonparticipants as of February 1, 2003, who did not receive the Quick Enrollment mailing. The x-axis in fig. 2.8, labeled "time since baseline," is the number of months since February 1, 2002, for nonparticipants as of that date, and number of months since February 1, 2003, for the other three groups. Quick Enrollment forms are first processed between months 0 and 1 (February and March of 2003); the final processing of forms takes place between months 3 and 4 (May and June of 2003). Our time series for the February 2002 nonparticipants begins at February 2002, when our contribution rate data begin, and ends before the January 2003 Quick Enrollment mailing, to avoid contamination with the Quick Enrollment mailing to some members of this group.

The February 2002 nonparticipants show a slow and steady increase in

11. The Quick Enrollment implementation at Company B used a yes/no reply card. The vast majority (88 percent) of cards returned had an affirmative election to participate in the 401(k) plan.

12. Seven percent of these individuals were hired in 2003, after the Quick Enrollment mailing list was formed. Another 9 percent were participating at the time the list was compiled. This leaves 84 percent unaccounted for.

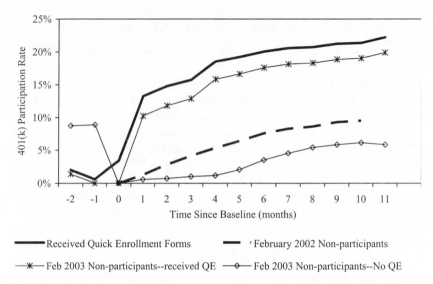

Fig. 2.8   401(k) participation of initial nonparticipants over time (Company B)

participation over time, with a participation rate of approximately 10 percent after ten months. The February 2003 nonparticipants who did not receive the Quick Enrollment mailing show a somewhat more sluggish increase in participation, with 6 percent of this group having enrolled after ten months (note the possible selection bias for this latter group). In contrast, the participation rate of Quick Enrollment recipients increases markedly between months 0 and 1, and again between months 3 and 4, which are exactly when the Quick Enrollment forms were processed. The group of all Quick Enrollment recipients participates at a slightly higher rate (about three percentage points) than February 2003 nonparticipants who received Quick Enrollment. This difference, however, is completely accounted for by the fact that some Quick Enrollment recipients enrolled on their own in the lag between the time when the nonparticipant mailing list was drawn up and when these individuals actually received the mailing (that participation increase between time –1 and 0 for this group).

The patterns in fig. 2.8 suggest that a plausible measure of Quick Enrollment's impact is the participation difference between the February 2002 nonparticipants and the February 2003 nonparticipants who received Quick Enrollment. Averaging this difference over months 1 to 10 yields a ten-percentage point participation increase due to Quick Enrollment. At month 4, a few weeks after the last forms were processed, this represents a near tripling of the participation rate. However, companywide participation increased by only two percentage points from a baseline of 74 percent between February 1 and June 1 of 2003.

There are several potential reasons why the Quick Enrollment effect was smaller at Company B than at Company A. First, Company B's initial participation rate was much higher, so the potential scope for increasing participation was smaller. Second, Company B's Quick Enrollment options may have been less attractive. Respondents were limited to only one contribution rate (3 percent) rather than many, and the available asset allocation was a money market fund rather than a mix of a money market fund and a balanced fund. Third, Company A had been using Quick Enrollment for new hires for almost a year when they began targeting previously hired nonparticipants, so there may have been a greater initial awareness and acceptance of Quick Enrollment. Finally, Company B's Quick Enrollment forms were distributed through a mailing, whereas Company A's forms were presented to employees in person.

Table 2.7, which is analogous to tables 2.5 and 2.6, reports enrollment

Table 2.7.   **Quick Enrollment utilization by employee characteristics: previously nonparticipating employees at Company B**

	Before Quick Enrollment	After Quick Enrollment		
	Fraction enrolling at any allocation	Fraction enrolling at any allocation	Fraction enrolling at nondefault allocation	Fraction enrolling at QE default allocation
Age				
< 30 (%)	3.5	14.9	5.7	9.2
	(824)	(697)	(697)	(697)
30–50 (%)	4.9	19.3	3.8	15.5
	(1,460)	(1,385)	(1,385)	(1,385)
> 50 (%)	2.9	18.2	5.6	12.6
	(275)	(302)	(302)	(302)
Gender				
Female (%)	4.4	16.7	4.7	12.0
	(611)	(491)	(491)	(491)
Male (%)	4.2	18.2	4.5	13.6
	(1,948)	(1,893)	(1,893)	(1,893)
Tenure				
< 2 years (%)	6.8	23.0	7.4	15.6
	(1,341)	(979)	(979)	(979)
2–5 years (%)	1.9	18.2	3.5	14.7
	(755)	(898)	(898)	(898)
> 5 years (%)	0.6	7.5	1.2	6.3
	(463)	(507)	(507)	(507)

Source: Authors' calculations. The sample in column 1 is nonparticipants in February 2002. The sample in the remaining columns is nonparticipants in February 2003. The time frame over which enrollment is calculated is February through May of 2002 for column 1, and February through May of 2003 for the remaining columns. Sample sizes for each cell reported in parentheses.

rates for various demographic groups at Company B. Enrollees under the Quick Enrollment regime are compared to employees who enrolled a year prior. As in table 2.5 and 2.6, we attribute Quick Enrollment utilization to those employees with the Quick Enrollment default asset allocation. Of Company B employees who enrolled between January 1, 2002, and February 18, 2003, (just prior to the initial Quick Enrollment processing), only 5.9 percent had the Quick Enrollment default asset allocation at the end of their initial participation year. In contrast, 75 percent of those enrolling between February and May 2003 chose the Quick Enrollment default asset allocation.

As in Company A, we find that enrollment rates are higher under Quick Enrollment for all demographic groups at Company B and that the majority of enrollees use Quick Enrollment rather than a traditional enrollment channel. The largest absolute changes are among those over age thirty (fourteen percentage points for those between ages thirty and fifty, and fifteen percentage points for those over age fifty) and those who have less than five years of tenure (sixteen percentage points). The largest relative changes are among those over age fifty (434 percent) and those with more than five years of tenure (1,050 percent).

Figure 2.9 shows the month 4 contribution rate distribution at Company B for the four employee groups in fig. 2.8. We do not show employees with a zero contribution rate, in order to highlight the differences across the other contribution rates. As in Company A, the impact of Quick Enroll-

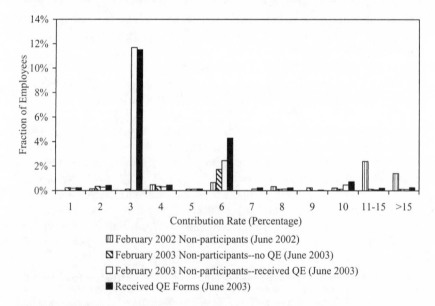

Fig. 2.9   Distribution of 401(k) contribution rates for new participants (Company B)

ment on contribution rates is readily apparent. Almost none of the employees who did not receive Quick Enrollment chose a 3 percent contribution rate. Instead, most enrollees chose rates at or above the 6 percent match threshold. In contrast, participants who received the Quick Enrollment mailing are largely enrolled at the 3 percent default contribution rate. In Company B we do find some evidence of contribution rate displacement. The 12 percent fraction of Quick Enrollment recipients at the default contribution rate exceeds the 10 percent impact of Quick Enrollment on participation. Quick Enrollment recipients at the 3 percent contribution rate thus appear to be composed both of employees brought into the plan because of Quick Enrollment and of employees who would have enrolled at a different—and likely higher—contribution rate in the absence of Quick Enrollment. The magnitude of the contribution rate displacement is similar to that estimated for automatic enrollment (Madrian and Shea 2001; Choi et al. 2004).

2.4   Conclusions

Madrian and Shea (2001), Iyengar and Jiang (2003), and Iyengar et al. (2004) have argued that the complexity of the 401(k) savings decision discourages employees from timely enrollment, even when they prefer participation to nonparticipation. Quick Enrollment is a low-cost manipulation that reduces this complexity by allowing employees to enroll at a default contribution rate and asset allocation preselected by the employer. We find that Quick Enrollment tripled participation among new hires relative to a standard enrollment mechanism in which employees must actively select both a contribution rate and an asset allocation. When Quick Enrollment was made available to previously hired employees who were not participating in their 401(k) plan, 10 percent to 20 percent of these nonparticipants enrolled in the plan.

Quick Enrollment has a much smaller participation effect than automatic enrollment, which typically induces near-universal participation. But relative to automatic enrollment, Quick Enrollment has the benefit of protecting employers from litigation if they pick defaults with equity exposure, since Quick Enrollment is an opt-in mechanism. Like automatic enrollment, Quick Enrollment causes clustering of enrollees at the employer-selected contribution rate and asset allocation. Those at the Quick Enrollment defaults include not only employees who would not have enrolled without Quick Enrollment, but also employees who would have otherwise enrolled with other elections. It is unlikely that this herding is first-best for employees. However, Quick Enrollment induces less herding than automatic enrollment.

The active decision approach to 401(k) participation—an alternative 401(k) enrollment mechanism studied by Choi et al. (2005)—requires employees to proactively make a retirement savings decision by a specific deadline without any employer guidance. The active decision participation effect lies well above the Quick Enrollment effect and below the automatic enrollment effect. The active decision approach's advantage is that there is no clustering of savings outcomes; the contribution rate distribution three *months* after hire under active decision is indistinguishable from the contribution rate distribution three *years* after hire under a standard opt-in enrollment regime. On the other hand, active decision forces employees to struggle with a difficult decision in a domain where they may have little expertise. A mechanism that gives employees a hard deadline with a Quick Enrollment option that has a small number of choices may be a fruitful hybrid approach.[13]

Another issue that should attract additional study is the optimal number of Quick Enrollment options. Quick Enrollment's primary goal is to increase 401(k) participation by reducing the complexity of enrolling in the 401(k) plan. However, employees who do not like the Quick Enrollment default will be unlikely to use it to enroll. Increasing the number of Quick Enrollment options makes Quick Enrollment attractive to a greater number of employees but also increases its complexity. An extremely large number of prebundled savings options would defeat the purpose of Quick Enrollment. However, increasing the number of options from one to two is unlikely to significantly increase Quick Enrollment's complexity.

Recent psychology research provides a framework for thinking about these issues. There are two potential sources of complexity in this 401(k) decision: choosing an appropriate contribution rate and choosing an appropriate asset allocation. Expanding the array of Quick Enrollment options could involve increasing either the number of contribution rate options (as in Company A's second Quick Enrollment implementation for nonparticipating employees), the number of asset allocation options, or both. One key difference between contribution rates and asset allocations is the extent to which the available options are easily comparable. Different contribution rates are alignable outcomes—they can be easily ordered from low to high—and this makes the different possible choices easier to compare (Gourville and Soman 2005). In contrast, different asset allocations are nonalignable outcomes: they vary in noncomparable dimensions like expected return, currency risk, inflation risk, business cycle risk, management fees, and so forth.

Gourville and Soman (2005) report results from brand choice experiments showing that increasing a brand's alignable options increases the probability that consumers purchase from that brand, whereas increasing

---

13. This might include giving employees the option of explicitly stating that they would rather make their own elections using the standard channels; there is no need to restrict sophisticated employees who have strong preferences about their retirement savings.

nonalignable options decreases purchase probability. Other papers that look only at the impact of increasing nonalignable options find that more options increase the likelihood of not choosing anything (Dhar and Nowlis 1999; Iyengar and Lepper 2000). Most importantly for this paper's results, Iyengar and Jiang (2003) and Iyengar, Huberman, and Jiang (2004) find a negative relationship between the number of funds in a 401(k) investment menu and 401(k) participation rates. This result holds even among firms with a relatively low number of funds.

In summary, the literature on the psychology of consumer choice suggests that increasing the number of alignable options (i.e., savings rates), will lead to increased Quick Enrollment utilization, whereas increasing the number of nonalignable options (i.e., asset allocation options), will lead to reduced Quick Enrollment utilization. The Quick Enrollment implementation for nonparticipating employees at Company A does not provide a direct test of this conjecture, as there was no variation in the number of contribution rate or asset allocation options. But it is worth noting that Quick Enrollment was very effective in increasing participation, even when employees were able to choose from the full array of (alignable) contribution rates. Further research on this front, where both the number of contribution rates and the number of asset allocation options were varied, would be informative for both the optimal design of Quick Enrollment-like interventions and for the literature on the psychology of choice more generally.

References

Choi, James, David Laibson, Brigitte Madrian, and Andrew Metrick. 2004. For better or for worse: Default effects and 401(k) savings behavior. In *Perspectives in the economics of aging,* ed. David A. Wise, 81–121. Chicago: University of Chicago Press.

———. 2005. Optimal defaults and active decisions. NBER Working Paper no. 11074. Cambridge, MA: National Bureau of Economic Research.

———. 2006. Saving for retirement on the path of least resistance. In *Behavioral public finance: Toward a new agenda,* ed. Ed McCaffrey and Joel Slemrod, 304–51. New York: Russell Sage Foundation.

Dhar, Ravi, and Stephen N. Nowlis. 1999. The effect of time pressure on consumer choice deferral. *Journal of Consumer Research* 25 (4): 369–84.

Gourville, John T., and Dilip Soman. 2005. Overchoice and assortment type: When and why variety backfires. *Marketing Science* 24 (3): 382–95.

Hewitt Associates. 2005. Survey findings: Trends and experiences in 401(k) plans 2005. Lincolnshire, IL: Hewitt Associates.

Iyengar, Sheena S., Wei Jiang, and Gur Huberman. 2004. How much choice is too much?: Contributions to 401(k) retirement plans. In *Pension design and structure: New lessons from behavioral finance,* ed. Olivia Mitchell and Stephen Utkus, 83–96. Oxford: Oxford University Press.

Iyengar, Sheena S., and Wei Jiang. 2003. Choosing not to choose: The effect of more choices on retirement savings decisions. Columbia University working paper.

Iyengar, Sheena S., and Mark Lepper. 2000. When choice is demotivating: Can one desire too much of a good thing? *Journal of Personality and Social Psychology* 79:995–1006.

Madrian, Brigitte, and Dennis Shea. 2001. The power of suggestion: Inertia in 401(k) participation and savings behavior. *Quarterly Journal of Economics* 116 (4): 1149–87.

Profit Sharing/401(k) Council of America. 2001. Automatic enrollment 2001: A study of automatic enrollment practices in 401(k) plans. Chicago: Profit Sharing/401(k) Council of America. Downloaded from http://www.pcsa.org/data/auto enroll2001.asp.

Vanguard Center for Retirement Research. 2001. Automatic enrollment: Vanguard client experience. Valley Forge, PA: The Vanguard Group. Downloaded from https://institutional2.vanguard.com/iip/pdf/CRR_automatic_enrollment _clientexp.pdf.

Comment   Jonathan Skinner

There is nothing like a powerful empirical randomized study to help clean old theories out of the attic and replace them with fresher and empirically more compelling ones. With this randomized study of the Quick Enrollment plan, the team of Choi, Laibson, and Madrian have added to their remarkable series of experiments on how 401(k) plan structures affect saving behavior. The experiment provides insights for two theoretical areas: the economics of savings and the economics of choice. I'll consider each in turn.

In the conventional model of lifecycle saving, individual agents maximize utility over their lifespan by smoothing consumption—or more precisely, by ensuring that all appropriate Euler-equation conditions are satisfied. Thus saving is simply a residual between earnings and optimally chosen consumption. In a series of papers, Madrian and colleagues have forced us to think quite differently about savings in optimizing models. First, in Madrian and Shea (2001), we found that the default matters; when new employees must opt out of a 401(k) saving plan, rather than having to opt into a 401(k) plan, they are far more likely to save more, at least within the 401(k). The result does not provide very strong support for our conventional models of saving: if something as trivial as a default rule could have a long-term impact on saving and hence on consumption, then we must conclude that these marginal savers aren't doing a very good job of

Jonathan Skinner is the John Sloan Dickey Third Century Professor in Economics at Dartmouth College and a research associate of the National Bureau of Economic Research.

optimizing. In Choi, Laibson, and Madrian (2004), they find more than just the default option matters; employee saving decisions are quite sensitive not just to default rules, but to a variety of other dimensions in the 401(k) plan.

And in this chapter, Choi, Laibson, and Madrian study an experiment in which workers are offered a quick enrollment option for the 401(k). Strictly speaking, it is not a default plan, because it requires an active choice to check the "yes" box, but it does constrain the worker into choosing a very conservative contribution rate (2 or 3 percent) and asset allocation (in one case, just money market accounts). Does this experiment by itself shed new light on saving behavior that we didn't know before? Yes, but not much. If workers were willing to be pushed into default saving plans, then it's not too surprising that the ease of checking a box on a form should have similarly long-term saving effects in perhaps a suboptimal long-term saving plan.[1]

Does this experiment tell us a great deal more about models of economic choice? Here the answer is yes. Economists have generally assumed that more choice is better in an almost tautological sense. But the burgeoning empirical evidence seems to suggest that too many options can actually discourage consumers from making choices even when those choices are probably beneficial. And this chapter provides another important piece of evidence against the notion that more choice is better. Indeed, too many 401(k) choices can result in no 401(k) at all.

While this is news to economists, sociologists and marketing experts have known this for years. One book by Steven Cristol and Peter Sealey gives away the punch line in the title: *Simplicity Marketing: End Brand Complexity, Clutter, and Confusion*. And in the famous 1970 book *Future Shock,* Alvin Toffler wrote:

> Today in the techno-societies there is an almost ironclad consensus about the future of freedom. Maximum individual choice is regarded as the democratic ideal. Yet most writers . . . conjure up a dark vision of the future, in which people appear as mindless consumer-creatures, surrounded by standardized goods, educated in standardized schools, fed a diet of standardized mass culture, and forced to adopt standardized styles of life. (p. 263)

> Ironically, the people of the future may suffer not from an absence of choice, but from a paralyzing surfeit of it. They may turn out to be victims of that peculiarly super-industrial dilemma: overchoice. (p. 264)

A more scientific test of this "paralyzing surfeit" is provided in Gourville and Soman (2006), who adopted Toffler's label of "overchoice" in their

---

1. This also presumes that workers are not offsetting 401(k) contributions by reducing saving in non-401(k) forms. Madrian and Shea (2001) found no evidence of substitution with perhaps their closest substitute: non-401(k) employee saving plans.

study of consumer choice behavior. They conducted several experiments on consumers at shopping malls. In one experiment, consumers were told: "Imagine that you are planning to buy a microwave oven. At the store, you will find the following alternatives." They would then provide subjects with a description of different microwaves as options, always with a "lone" brand (sometimes Panasonic, sometimes Sharp) matched with from one to five microwaves produced by the "alternative" brand (again either Sharp or Panasonic). The outcome variable was the percentage of times that one of the alternative brand choices was chosen.

There were two different classes of options, alignable and nonalignable. Alignable choices corresponded to different values along a given dimension, for example the size of the microwave. For the alignable choice, the power output, warranty, and features were held constant for both the target microwave and up to five alternatives. The alternatives varied only on the basis of capacity and price; ranging from 1.1 cubic feet (at a price of $140) to 1.9 cubic feet (at a price of $220), depending on the number of choices.

Nonalignable choices were options that were more difficult to compare. For these hypothetical microwaves, the options provided identical capacity (1.1 cubic feet) and power output, but the features differ across prices and the five alternative choices: on-line help, adjustable speed turntable, moisture sensor, hold warm features, and programmable menus.

The results were striking. When there were more alignable options, consumers were more likely to choose one of the offered options (rather than the lone brand). With one option, they chose the target brand slightly more than 50 percent; with four or five options they chose the target brand slightly less than 80 percent of the time. By contrast, offering more than two nonalignable options led to a decline in the likelihood that one of the alternative options would be chosen. When there were four to five nonalignable options, the choice of one of these target options dropped to just 40 percent.

These results make perfect intuitive sense. I can easily judge whether I want a bigger or smaller microwave based on past experiences of trying to fit plates or trays into them. But comparing adjustable speed with on-line help—I wouldn't have a clue. It's easiest to make no choice at all.

The analogy applies as well to the case of Quick Enrollment. With so many complex options, it's just easier to choose just one option, even if that option may not be perfectly suited to one's long-term saving plans. (The model is a little more complex here, because of the option to not contribute at all.) And the lessons from this research apply as well to the design of 401(k) programs. First, expanding the choice set along an alignable dimension, like the percentage of income to contribute, could actually increase the percentage of workers who sign up. Thus one could imagine three different subgroups for saving: Quick Enrollment Basic (2 percent of earnings) Quick Enrollment Saver (4 percent) and Quick Enrollment Supersaver (6 percent).

Second, there are inherent nonalignable choices that need to be made in making investments. How can one really compare Japanese stock funds, inflation-indexed bonds, or high-yield corporate bonds? Choosing a default of money market accounts may protect firms from legal suits in the event that the (say) Japanese stock market implodes, but it's not really the best approach to saving for retirement. Perhaps collapsing these non-alignable choices to something that sounds alignable—like "low growth/low risk," "middle growth/middle risk," and "high growth/high risk" would be one approach to strike a middle ground between a paralyzing surfeit of choice and the absence of any choice at all.

References

Choi, James, David Laibson, and Brigitte Madrian. 2004. Plan design and 401(k) savings outcomes. NBER Working Paper no. 10486. Cambridge, MA: National Bureau of Economic Research.

Cristol, Steven M., and Peter Sealy. 2000. *Simplicity marketing: End brand complexity, clutter, and confusion.* New York: Free Press.

Gourville, John, and Dilip Soman. Forthcoming. Overchoice and assortment type: When and why variety backfires. *Marketing Science.*

Madrian, Brigitte, and Dennis F. Shea. 2001. The power of suggestion: Inertia in 401(k) participation and savings behavior. *Quarterly Journal of Economics* 116 (4): 1149–87.

Toffler, Alvin. 1984. *Future Shock.* New York: Bantam.

II

Intergenerational Transfers

Population Aging and Intergenerational Transfers: Introducing Age into National Accounts

Andrew Mason, Ronald Lee, An-Chi Tung,
Mun-Sim Lai, and Tim Miller

3.1 Introduction

In all societies, intergenerational transfers are large and potentially have an important influence on inequality and economic growth. The development of each generation of youth depends on the resources that it receives from productive members of society for health, education, and sustenance. The well-being of the elderly depends on social programs that provide health care and income support and also on familial systems that dominate in many developing countries.

The importance of intergenerational transfers has not gone unnoticed by the research community. During the last two decades there have been important advances in measuring, modeling, and assessing the implications of intergenerational transfers at both the micro and the macro level.

Andrew Mason is a professor of economics at the University of Hawaii at Manoa and a senior fellow at the East-West Center. Ronald Lee is a professor of demography and of economics at the University of California, Berkeley, and a research associate of the National Bureau of Economic Research. An-Chi Tung is an associate research fellow at the Institute of Economics, Academia Sinica. Mun-Sim Lai is an assistant professor of economics at California State University at Bakersfield. Tim Miller is a Population Affairs Officer at the United Nations Economic Commission for Latin America and the Caribbean.

Developing the National Transfer Account System is a collaborative international effort supported by NIA, R01-AG025488, and NIA, R37-AG025247. The lead institutions are the Population and Health Studies Program, East-West Center, and the Center for the Economics and Demography of Aging, University of California at Berkeley. Collaborating institutions are the Nihon University Population Research Institute; the Statistics Bureau of Japan; Acadmia Sinica (Taipei); Lembaga Demografi, University of Indonesia; CEDEPLAR (Brazil), and the Economic Commission for Latin America and the Caribbean (ECLAC). Thanks to Alan Auerbach and other participants in the 2nd Meeting of the Working Group on Macroeconomic Aspects of Intergenerational Transfers, January 2005, University of California at Berkeley. Research assistance was provided by Comfort Sumida and Avi Ebenstein.

A comprehensive macro-level intergenerational transfer framework and accounting system, however, has not been developed. In particular, efforts to model and measure familial transfers at the aggregate level have lagged.

One purpose of this chapter is to outline key concepts and methods being used to construct National Transfer Accounts (NTAs), an accounting system for measuring intergenerational transfers at the aggregate level in a manner consistent with National Income and Product Accounts (NIPA). National Transfer Accounts provide estimates of economic flows across age groups that arise primarily because children and the elderly consume more than they produce, relying on reallocations from the working ages. (See Lee, Lee, and Mason 2008 for a more detailed analysis of the economic life cycle.) These flows can be cross-sectional—a transfer from parents to children, for example. Or the flows can be longitudinal—for example, accumulation of wealth during the working years and its disaccumulation during retirement. For want of a better term, we refer to these flows as "reallocations." When complete, NTA accounts will distinguish three forms of these flows: as the accumulation of capital, as transfers, and as credit transactions. Here we consider only two: transfers and asset transactions, combining capital and credit transactions. The accounts distinguish the institutions that mediate the transactions: governments, markets, and families. When complete, NTA accounts will provide estimates with sufficient historical depth to study the evolution of intergenerational transfer systems; the consequences of alternative approaches to age reallocations embodied in public policy with respect to pensions, health care, education, and social institutions (e.g., the extended family); and the social, political, and economic implications of population aging.

A second purpose of this chapter is to compare the life cycles and support systems of Taiwan and the United States. The differences between these two countries are particularly interesting because of the relative importance of their familial support systems—strong in Taiwan and weak in the United States. In the United States, private interhousehold transfers are small and, because few elderly live with their adult children, intrahousehold transfers are small, as well. In Taiwan, private interhousehold transfers are more important and, because many elderly live with their adult children, intrahousehold transfers are substantial. As a general proposition this is well known. The contribution here is to provide estimates of the economic flows that allow direct comparison of alternative forms of support. Our conclusion is that familial transfers from nonelderly adults to those sixty-five and older are large in Taiwan—exceeding U.S. public transfers measured as a percentage of consumption by those sixty-five and older.

There are other features of the reallocation systems in the United States and Taiwan that are explored. We show that income from assets is a very important source of income for the elderly in both countries, but particularly in the United States. This may come as a surprise, given the low saving rates in the United States and the relatively high saving rates in Taiwan. Asset income does play an important direct role in old-age support in Taiwan, but it also plays an indirect role by financing transfers from middle-aged adults to elderly parents.

The support systems for children are very similar in the United States and Taiwan. Almost all of the financial resources available to those under the age of twenty consist of transfers. In the United States, about 60 percent and in Taiwan about 75 percent of all transfers to children are familial transfers. The remainder consists largely of public transfers, of which support for public education is particularly important.

3.2 Background

Research on intergenerational transfers has laid a solid foundation for constructing the NTA system with the historical depth and cross-national perspective envisioned here. Following on the pioneering work of Samuelson (1958) and Willis (1988), a theoretical transfer framework has been developed by Lee and his collaborators (Lee 1994a; Lee 1994b; Bommier and Lee 2003). The Lee transfer framework has been applied to many different settings, but often under a restrictive set of assumptions (steady-state equilibrium and golden-rule growth). At the same time, generational accounting has been used to describe forward-looking public longitudinal data in various countries (Auerbach, Gokhale and Kotlikoff 1991; Auerbach, Kotlikoff and Leibfritz 1999).

Progress in modeling private and familial transfers at the aggregate level has been sporadic, but there have been important advances. The increased availability of surveys and micro-level studies has greatly improved our ability to measure familial transfers and to study why they occur (Lillard and Willis 1997; McGarry and Schoeni 1997; Altonji, Hayashi, and Kotlikoff 2000; Frankenberg, Lillard, and Willis 2002). Progress has been made in estimating and modeling bequests (Attanasio and Hoynes 2000; Poterba 2000; Poterba and Weisbenner 2001; Brown and Weisbenner 2002). There have been important advances in modeling the allocation of resources within households, a step critical to estimating intrahousehold intergenerational transfers (Lazear and Michael 1988; Bourguignon and Chiappori 1992; Deaton 1997; Bourguignon 1999). Innovative surveys provide new opportunities for analyzing intergenerational transfers (Chu 2000; Hermalin 2002). Building on the available theoretical framework and the extensive research on familial transfers, and utilizing the extensive household survey data that are available in many countries makes estimating familial intergenerational transfers and a complete set of National Transfer Accounts a feasible option.

Constructing estimates of familial transfers is important because they play such a key role around the world. Familial transfers are almost universally the primary source of resources for children. Familial transfers to the elderly can have a profound effect on intergenerational equity (Mason and Miller 2000). Outside the industrialized countries of the West, most elderly coreside with their adult children. In Japan and South Korea, the extent of coresidence has declined very rapidly in the last few decades, but roughly half of the elderly still live with children. In other Asian countries, the great majority of the elderly live with their children, and there is a surprising degree of stability in these arrangements. The situation in Latin America is less thoroughly documented, but data for six Latin American countries show that living in multigeneration households has been the norm there as well (Kinsella 1990).

Extended-living arrangements are less important in the West, but in some European countries the elderly are not living exclusively by themselves nor with their spouse. In Greece and Spain roughly 40 percent of those sixty-five and older were living in households with three or more persons in the early 1990s. At the other extreme, only about 5 percent of the elderly of Sweden and Denmark lived in households with two or more persons. France is in an intermediate position, with 16 percent of the elderly living in households with two or more persons (Kinsella and Velkoff 2001). In the United States, the great majority of elderly do not live with their children, but this has not always been the case. The percentage of sixty-five and older living with children in the United States declined from 64 percent in 1880 to 49 percent in 1940, 30 percent in 1960, and 18 percent in 1980 (Ruggles 1994).

A more comprehensive approach to intergenerational transfers is critical to resolving many important issues. The system of intergenerational transfers bears directly on current research on the demographic dividend. Increases in the share of the working-age population, particularly in East Asia, have contributed to rapid growth in per capita income (Kelley and Schmidt 1995; Bloom and Williamson 1998; Kelley and Schmidt 2001; Mason 2001; Bloom, Canning, and Sevilla 2002). The demographic dividend may dissipate, however, as the share of the elderly population rises and the share of the working-age population declines. If capital accumulation rather than familial or public transfer programs dominates the age reallocation systems for supporting the elderly, population aging may yield a second demographic dividend in the form of higher rates of saving and capital intensification of the economy (Mason 2005; Mason and Lee 2006). If aging is accompanied by a shift away from transfer systems, either public or private, the effects on capital accumulation may be especially pronounced (Lee, Mason, and Miller 2003).

A second area of research concerns an important factual issue—whether there are substantial generational inequities and whether they are changing over time (Preston 1984; Becker and Murphy 1988). One approach models intergenerational transfers as the outcome of political processes in which the magnitude and direction of transfers reflect the political power of the elderly relative to other demographic groups (Preston 1984; Razin, Sadka, and Swagel 2002). An alternative approach argues that intergenerational transfers are the outcome of cooperative private and social implicit contracts that are guided by altruism and efficiency concerns (Barro 1974; Becker and Tomes 1976; Becker and Murphy 1988).

A third area of research addresses the effects of intergenerational transfers on saving, economic growth, and equity (Feldstein 1974; Munnell 1974; Feldstein 1996; Gale 1998). These and similar studies inform efforts to evaluate existing transfer systems, to guide the development of new systems, and to anticipate the implications of alternative reform proposals. Social security reform, in particular, has been the subject of an enormous amount of research (Feldstein 1998; Feldstein and Samwick 2001; Krueger and Kubler 2002; Diamond 2006).

Operating in the background and providing the impetus for research and reform efforts is population aging. Low levels of fertility and continued improvements in life expectancy in many countries are leading to rapid population aging. The advanced industrialized countries—Japan, European countries, and the United States—are further along in the aging process. Many less developed countries, however, will soon have much older populations. Three aspects of population aging in the developing world are noteworthy. First, many countries are likely to experience population aging at a relatively low level of development. Not only will they have relatively low levels of income, but they may also have relatively underdeveloped political and financial institutions that are playing a prominent role in aging industrial societies. Second, familial support systems are more important in many developing societies than in the West. Third, we have found that population aging causes a large increase in the demand for life-cycle wealth relative to GDP. Population aging interacts with the transfer systems either to generate a major increase in the proportional implicit debt and transfer burden on the working population, or to generate a large deepening of the capital stock. Third World countries are at a crucial juncture, and depending on their policy choices, population aging will have one or the other effect. Hence, understanding how familial support systems operate, how they interact with alternative transfer systems, and how they are affected by population aging is critical.

3.2.1   National Transfer Accounts: An Overview

The purpose of National Transfer Accounts is to measure at the aggregate level the reallocations, across age, of economic resources. These reallocations occur because at some ages, individuals consume more than they produce.[1] At other ages individuals produce more than they consume. The reallocation system documents the means by which the young and the old—those with lifecycle deficits—draw on the surplus resources generated during the prime working ages.

Age profiles of consumption, production, and reallocations are viewed from an individual, rather than a household, perspective. In economies where formal sector employment dominates, measuring production (or earnings) for individuals is a relatively straightforward task. In traditional settings, where employment is informal and production is often organized within a family enterprise, estimating production by age for individuals is difficult. In any setting, allocating consumption to individuals is challenging, because most expenditure data are collected for households rather than individuals. Moreover, some goods are jointly consumed or involve increasing returns to scale, so that allocating consumption to individuals inevitably involves arbitrary rules.

From the household perspective, production and consumption are attributes of households, varying with age of the household head. Constructing production and consumption profiles is more straightforward, but there are tradeoffs involved. The first is that the effects of coresident children and elderly on household consumption and production profiles must be explicitly modeled or—as is often the case—neglected altogether. Indeed, a large share of all societal income redistribution occurs within households, and would therefore be invisible to accounting on a household basis. The second is the difficulty of translating changes in population-age structure into changes in the age structure of household heads and household membership.

Age reallocations are substantial relative to the economy. Consider the situation in Taiwan as represented in figure 3.1, panel A, which shows estimates of aggregate consumption and labor income by age in 1998. Total net reallocations to those twenty-three and younger, the young age group for which consumption exceeded labor income, amounted to 35 percent of total labor income. Total net reallocations to those who were fifty-seven or older, the old age group for which consumption exceeded labor income, amounted to 9 percent of total labor income. Thus, nearly half of all labor income was reallocated from the surplus ages to the dependent ages.[2]

The age profiles of aggregate consumption and labor income reflect the age distribution of the population (fig. 3.1, panel B), and per capita variation in labor income and consumption (fig. 3.1, panel C). In 1998, Taiwan's population was younger than the United States population. Thirty-one percent were under the age of twenty and 8 percent were sixty-five or older. Hence, the reallocations reflect that age structure—with more going to

1. Detailed methodology and other information can be found at www.ntaccounts.org.
2. Calculation details are discussed in the following.

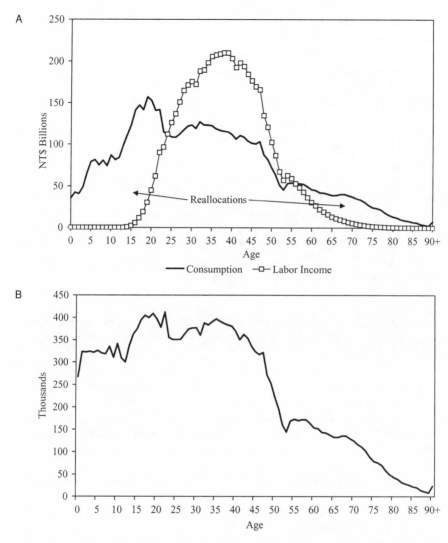

Fig. 3.1   *A,* **Aggregate consumption and labor income, Taiwan, 1998, nominal values;** *B,* **Population, Taiwan, 1998;** *C,* **Per capita consumption and labor income, Taiwan, 1998**

children and less going to seniors than in the United States. As will be seen in the following, Taiwan also has per capita profiles that are distinctive as compared with the United States. Taiwan's consumption profile is very flat and its labor income reaches a peak at a relatively young age as compared with the United States.

Reallocation systems, which bridge the gaps between consumption and labor income, vary along two important dimensions: the governing or me-

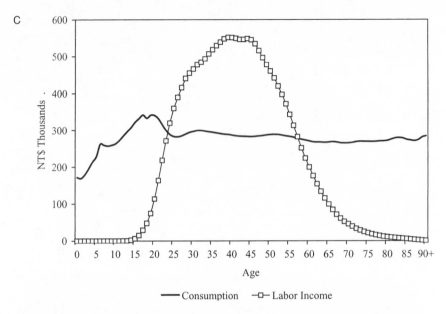

Fig. 3.1   (cont.) *A,* Aggregate consumption and labor income, Taiwan, 1998, nominal values; *B,* Population, Taiwan, 1998; *C,* Per capita consumption and labor income, Taiwan, 1998

diating institution and the economic form of the reallocation (Lee 1994a; 1994b). The public sector reallocates resources relying on social mandates embodied in law and regulation and implemented by local, regional, and national governments. Education, public pensions, and health care programs are important examples of public reallocation programs. Private-sector reallocations are governed by voluntary contracts, social conventions, and so on, that are mediated by households, families, charitable organizations, and other private institutions. Important examples of private reallocations are private saving and credit transactions and familial support to children and the elderly (table 3.1).

In this chapter we distinguish two economic forms that reallocations can take: asset-based reallocations and transfers.

Asset-based reallocations: Assets include capital, property, and credit. From the perspective of the individual (or household), these forms are close substitutes as reallocation mechanisms. They can be accumulated and disaccumulated. They yield income. They are used primarily to reallocate resources from the present to the future. From the perspective of the macro-economy, however, there are important differences between capital, property, and credit.

Capital-based reallocations: Transactions that increase future consumption by foregoing current consumption. They lead to a change in the

Table 3.1   **A classification of National Transfer Account reallocations.**

	Asset-based reallocations		Transfers
	Capital and property	Credit	Transfers
Public	Public infrastructure	Public debt Student loan programs Money	Public education Public health care Unfunded pension plans
Private	Housing Consumer durables Factories, farms Inventories Land	Consumer credit	Familial support of children and parents Bequests Charitable contributions

Source: Adapted from Lee 1994a.

stock of reproducible capital, including inventories. Only reallocations from younger ages to older ages are possible. Individuals can accumulate capital when young and dispose of it when old.

Property-based reallocations: Transactions that involve the trade of a nonreproducible asset; for example, land. They yield no change in aggregate wealth. Property acquired in one period can yield rental income in future periods or can be sold in future periods to finance consumption at older ages. At any point in time, property-based reallocations net to zero for all age groups combined. The purchase or rental of property produces an inflow for one individual that is matched by an outflow for another individual.

Credit-based reallocations: Intertemporal transactions based solely on a contractual obligation to trade economic resources in one period in return for compensation in one or more future periods. In a closed economy, credit-based reallocations do not lead to a change in aggregate wealth, because an increase in the wealth of one group is always balanced by the decline in wealth of another age group. The use of credit cards to finance consumption by individuals and the use of domestically held public debt, including the printing of money, to finance government programs are examples. Credit transactions can be used to reallocate resources in either direction.

Transfers: Reallocations from one group to another that involve no explicit quid pro quo.[3] Transfers can flow in either direction—from older to younger (parents and taxpayers to children) or from younger to older (adult children and taxpayers to the elderly).

3. Of course, important models of familial transfers emphasize implicit contracts; for example, risk sharing (Kotlikoff and Spivak 1981) or the exchange of money for time (Cox 1987).

The core of the NTA system consists of two accounts: the flow account and the wealth account. The flow account measures inflows and outflows between age groups that occur during the accounting period in question. The wealth account measures the value of the stock associated with each flow. This chapter emphasizes the flow account, and the wealth account is not discussed further.

3.2.2   The National Transfer Flow Account

The National Transfer Flow Account measures inter-age flows for a prescribed accounting period, typically a calendar or fiscal year. The NT Flow Account is governed by an accounting identity, which must be satisfied for any individual, household, age group, or economy, stating that for any period inflows are balanced by outflows.

$$(1) \qquad Y_L + Y_K + Y_M + \tau_g^+ + \tau_f^+ = C + I_K + I_M + \tau_g^- + \tau_f^-.$$

Inflows consist of labor income (Y_L), the returns to capital (Y_K) and land and credit (Y_M), and transfer inflows from the public sector (τ_g^+) and the private sector (τ_f^+). Outflows consist of consumption (C), investment in capital (I_K) or credit and land (I_M), and transfer outflows to the government (τ_g^-) and the private sector (τ_f^-). In this chapter, we do not distinguish capital from land and credit. Designating asset income by Y_A, assets by $A = K + M$ and saving by $S = I_K + I_M$, substituting into equation (1) and rearranging terms provides the key elements of the NT Flow Account. The difference between consumption and production, termed the *lifecycle deficit,* must be matched by *age reallocations,* consisting of *asset-based reallocations* and *net transfers:*

$$(2) \qquad C - Y_L \quad = \quad Y_A - S \quad + \quad \tau_g^+ - \tau_g^- \quad + \quad \tau_f^+ - \tau_f^-$$

$$\underset{\text{Life-cycle deficit}}{} \quad \underset{\text{Asset-based reallocations}}{} \quad \underset{\text{Net public transfers}}{} \quad \underset{\text{Net private transfers}}{}$$

$$\underset{\text{Net transfers}}{}$$

$$\underset{\text{Age reallocations}}{}$$

Transfers are further subdivided into *net public transfers* and *net private transfers,* consisting of bequests and inter vivos transfers.

The National Transfer Flow Account for Taiwan in 1998 is shown in summary form as table 3.2, to provide a concrete point of reference for further discussion. The totals in the table are based on National Income and Product Account values and thereby ensure consistency with NIPA. Briefly, consumption is equal to total final consumption expenditure.[4]

---

4. Private final consumption is adjusted to exclude indirect taxes that are assumed to be paid indirectly by consumers. In other words, the value of final consumption is calculated using basic prices that exclude indirect taxes.

Table 3.2   **National Transfer Flow Account, Taiwan, 1998, aggregate values, nominal, (NT$ billion)**

	Total	Domestic by age				
		0–19	20–29	30–49	50–64	65+
Lifecycle deficit	525	1,671	–13	–1,500	–25	391
Consumption	5,855	1,737	1,064	1,939	654	461
Public	1,549	590	246	419	161	133
Private	4,305	1,147	818	1,520	493	328
Less: Labor income	5,330	66	1,076	3,439	678	70
Age reallocations	525	1,671	–13	–1,500	–25	391
Asset-based reallocations	554	–21	–213	362	266	160
Public	–173	1	19	–103	–63	–27
Income on assets	0	0	–1	–5	3	4
Less: Public saving	173	–1	–20	97	66	31
Private	727	–22	–232	464	329	187
Income on assets	2,149	4	182	1,265	490	208
Less: Private saving	1,422	26	413	800	161	21
Transfers	–29	1,692	200	–1,862	–290	231
Public	2	436	–15	–463	–77	121
Private	–31	1,256	215	–1,399	–213	111
Inter vivos transfers	–31	1,256	146	–1,489	–130	186
Bequests	0	0	69	90	–84	–75

Private and public consumption correspond to private final consumption expenditure and government final consumption expenditure. Labor income has no exact NIPA counterpart, because the income of unincorporated firms includes returns to labor and to capital. We allocate two-thirds of this income to labor and one-third to capital, to obtain estimates of labor income and income on assets. Saving is defined as national saving net of depreciation. In a closed economy, net transfers and each of its components would sum to zero. In an open economy, international financial flows lead to net transfer totals that differ from zero. In Taiwan, for example, private transfers to abroad exceeded those received from abroad by NT$31 billion. More detailed information about adjustments is available from the authors.

All aggregates are allocated across age using methods that are briefly described in the following. The values are cumulated into broad age groups to facilitate presentation and discussion, but the underlying values were estimated by single-year of age, with an upper age group of ninety plus, as shown in figure 3.1.

The upper panel of the NT Flow Account (Table 3.2) reports the *lifecycle deficits,* the gaps between labor production and consumption. The lower panel reports the age reallocations and their components. As shown in the budget identity, equation (2), the lifecycle deficits and reallocations must be equal, in total and for each age group.

Life-Cycle Deficit

The life-cycle deficit is large and positive for children and the elderly, close to zero for young adults and those aged fifty to sixty-four, and large and negative only for adults aged thirty to forty-nine. Taiwan's life-cycle deficit for children was NT$1.7 trillion, 96 percent of their total consumption, and the life-cycle deficit for the elderly was NT$0.4 trillion, 85 percent of their total consumption. Thirty- to forty-nine-year-olds had a life-cycle surplus of $NT1.5 trillion. That those aged thirty to forty-nine had a large life-cycle surplus and that those aged fifty to sixty-four did not runs contrary to the conventional wisdom about the economic lifecycle; that fifty to sixty-four are ages conducive to high rates of saving. Note that the surplus was less than the total life-cycle deficit of the dependent age groups, leading to an overall deficit of NT$525 billion or 9 percent of total consumption. If the economy were on a golden rule steady-state growth path, the total life-cycle deficit would have been zero. A positive total life-cycle deficit occurs when consumption exceeds total labor income.[5]

The life-cycle deficit is a residual—calculated as the difference between consumption and labor income. All consumption—both public and private—is included in the NT Flow Account and all is allocated to individuals. Private consumption includes the rental value of owner-occupied housing. Public consumption includes goods and services that are consumed directly by individuals; for example, health care and education. Public consumption also includes the value of all other government consumption, such as spending on public safety, foreign diplomacy, public infrastructure, and so on.

All consumption is allocated to individuals based on their age, using allocation rules that vary with the type of good being allocated and the availability of data. Consider, first, public programs. The consumption of public education is allocated to students using age- and education-level-specific enrollment rates, assuming that the cost per student varies across education level (primary, secondary, tertiary) but does not vary by age within the educational level. Age profiles of publicly provided or financed health care in the United States (Medicare, Medicaid, and other public programs) are based on age estimates of the U.S. National Health Accounts for 1999 (Keehan et al. 2004). Control totals for these programs are taken from U.S. National Income and Product Account (NIPA) tables for 2000.[6] In

---

5. Dynamically efficient economies will have zero or positive total lifecycle deficits.
6. http://www.bea.doc.gov/bea/dn/nipaweb/index.asp. In Taiwan, public consumption of health is very small. A National Health Insurance program has been instituted that provides partial reimbursement of the cost of services of private health providers. This is classified as private health expenditure.

Taiwan, the shape of the age profile of consumption financed through National Health Insurance (NHI) is estimated using the variable "benefit income of NHI" reported in the Survey of Family Income and Expenditure (FIES). The aggregate control total is reported in *Health Trends and Vital Statistics Taiwan* (Department of Health, 1998). In the United States, the value of food stamps and public housing are assigned to members of households who report receipt of these benefits on the basis of equivalence scales. All other public consumption is allocated on a per capita basis.

Private consumption is estimated using household surveys that report the number and age of household members and total household consumption, but not the consumption of individual members. Allocation rules are used to distribute consumption to each household member. Per capita age profiles of consumption are then computed by averaging across the consumption estimates for all individuals of a given age in the survey.[7]

Age profiles of labor income are based on individual-level data on compensation and entrepreneurial income. We assume that two-thirds of entrepreneurial income is a return to labor and one-third is a return to capital.

Asset-Based Reallocations

Two broad economic forms by which resources are reallocated across age groups are presented in the lower panel of the NT Flow Account: asset-based reallocations and net transfers. Asset-based reallocation is the response to life-cycle problems captured in the classic life-cycle saving model. Suppose individuals relied exclusively on life-cycle saving to reallocate resources from the working years to old age. Sometime during the working years, individuals would begin to save. This would generate a net outflow in the NT Flow Account. As the individual accumulates assets, he or she would begin to receive asset income, an inflow. The net inflow from asset-based reallocations is measured by asset income less saving ($Y_A - S$). For a classic life-cycle saver, net asset-based reallocations would be negative during life-cycle surplus years. In his or her retirement years, the life-cycle saver generates inflows—positive net asset-based reallocations—sufficient to cover the life-cycle deficit. To do so the individual would rely on asset income (Y_A) and dissaving ($S < 0$).[8]

The NTA framework does not assume that individuals behave as life-cycle consumers, and other forms of behavior are captured by asset-based reallocations. For example, if young individuals go into debt to finance their

7. We have experimented with various methods for estimating the equivalence scales. We have found the Engels' and Rothbarth's methods to yield problematic results. At present, we first use regression methods to allocate expenditures on education and health care by age within households, and then allocate the remainder of household expenditures using equivalence scales. The equivalence scale is 0.4 for children under age five, increasing linearly from 0.5 at age five to 1.0 at age twenty, remaining constant for those older than twenty. See Deaton (1997) for a detailed discussion of allocation rules.

8. A pure lifecycle saver may not dis-save in the initial years of retirement.

education, this would be reflected as a positive asset-based reallocation during school years—as individuals incurred debt beyond necessary debt repayment—and as a negative asset-based reallocation later in life, as ex-students repaid their student loans. Alternatively, parents might accumulate assets in anticipation of the high costs of college. This would be reflected as negative asset-based reallocations for parents with precollege-age children and positive asset-based reallocations for parents with college-age children. If asset accumulation is driven by a bequest motive, we would see negative asset-based reallocations during working years and positive reallocations at the time of death.

Although the role of assets as a reallocation tool is most easily explained by describing the behavior of an individual or a cohort over time, the NT Flow Account reports the flows for a particular year for a cross-section of age groups. Asset-based reallocations at all ages may respond to short-term economic fluctuations. The asset income and disaccumulation of capital at older ages is not tied in any direct way to the accumulation at younger ages, as observed in the cross-section.

Assets are not assigned to individual members of the household. Rather, we assume that all assets are held by a single individual—the household head. Thus, results presented here are consistent with other analyses that report assets or saving by the age of the head. The results also suffer from the same difficulties of interpretation, particularly in societies where multi-generation extended households are common. The influence on our results of gender bias in the choice of head will depend on the age difference between husbands and wives. The mean age of age profiles tied to the age of the head will be greater if husbands are older than wives and more likely to be chosen as the head of the household.

In Taiwan, estimates of age profiles of net asset income are based on household-level data on entrepreneurial income, dividends, rent, and interest income and expense. For the United States, estimates are based on age profiles of net worth. In both countries, saving is estimated as a residual.

Transfers

The second form of reallocations is transfers. A transfer, as measured by the NTA system, is a transaction that transfers a good, service, or cash from an individual belonging to one age group to an individual belonging to another age group with no expectation of compensation or an explicit quid pro quo in any form. Transfers received are called *inflows* $[\tau^+(a)]$, transfer payments are called *outflows* $[\tau^-(a)]$, and *net transfers* are the difference between the two $[\tau(a) = \tau^+(a) - \tau^-(a)]$. Public transfers $[\tau_g(a)]$ are mediated by governments, which collect taxes from members of one set of age groups $[\tau_g^-(a)]$ and make transfers to members of other age groups $[\tau_g^+(a)]$. These two sets of age groups may well overlap. Private transfers are mediated by the family and nonprofit institutions serving households (NPISHs). Net private transfers are given by $\tau_f(a) = \tau_f^+(a) - \tau_f^-(a)$.

Public transfer inflows can be in the form of cash or in-kind. Cash public transfer inflows are typically targeted and the associated inflows often vary substantially with age. Welfare programs provide cash benefits to children and/or mothers. Unemployment benefits target those in the working ages. Pension benefits target the elderly.

The age pattern of the outflows depends on the mechanisms by which the programs are financed—the age variation of the economic resource being taxed and the age variation in the rate of taxation. The economic resource being taxed depends on the incidence of the tax. Our approach is to follow the methods employed in generational accounting (GA). With a few exceptions, GA assumes that the incidence of the tax falls on the entity that pays the tax: payroll taxes are paid by workers, sales taxes by consumers, property taxes by owners of property, and so forth (Auerbach and Kotlikoff 1999).

Private transfers largely consist of familial transfers. In virtually all societies, familial transfers are the dominant reallocation system through which children are supported. As previously noted, neither capital- nor property-based reallocations can be used to transfer resources in a downward direction; that is, from the working ages to the childhood ages. Credit plays a limited role for legal and institutional reasons. A few instances can be identified where supporting children is a community or a public responsibility rather than a familial responsibility. Examples include some African societies, the kibbutz in Israel, and limited experiments with the collectivization of child care in some Communist economies. But even where familial systems are primarily responsible for supporting children, public transfers can be substantial. In many countries, the public sector plays an important role in education. Also, many low-fertility countries have adopted or are considering policies that increase the importance of the public reallocation system vis-à-vis the familial system. These include family allowances, subsidization of child care, tax benefits, and so forth. Children are also the beneficiaries of a broad set of public goods and services that accrue to members of society at large.

Two forms of private transfers are distinguished in table 3.2 and the results discussed in the following. Inter vivos transfers consist of interhousehold transfer (transfers between two existing households) and intrahousehold transfers (transfers between individuals who belong to the same household). The second form, *bequests,* consists of transfers associated with the "death" of a household that may arise in several ways: the death of the household head, the merger of two preexisting households, or the intergenerational transition in headship as captured by a change in the individual designated as the household head.

Interhousehold Familial Transfers

Measuring interhousehold transfers is a relatively straightforward empirical task that relies directly on survey data from income and expenditure surveys or more specialized surveys of transfer behavior. Income and expenditure surveys typically report both gifts received and made, so that outflows and inflows can be calculated directly from the survey.

The most serious technical difficulty that arises is that transfers received may be seriously underreported in household surveys. Often, reported transfers made exceed reported transfers received. Part of the difference can be explained by remittances to and from abroad, but it is generally believed that differences due to reporting error can be substantial. According to one recent estimate, U.S. households reported giving $64 billion in 1997. They reported receiving $47 billion annually, on average, between 1993 and mid-1998 (Brown and Weisbenner 2002). In Taiwan the differences are smaller. In 1998, transfers received were NT$1.9 billion, while transfers given were NT$ 2.1 billion.

In a closed economy, aggregate outflows and inflows will be equal and should be adjusted to ensure aggregate consistency. In an open economy, outflows and inflows will no longer be equal. A further technical difficulty arises if inflows include capital transfers that arise from bequests. Transfers made by households that no longer exist at the time of the survey are not captured as outflows but may be captured as inflows.

NT Flow Accounts are estimated based on the assumption that all interhousehold transfers are between heads of households. With few exceptions, income and expenditure surveys do not provide information about transfers to and from individuals within households. One exception is the Taiwan FIES, which reports interhousehold transfer inflows to individuals and to the collective household. In 1998, 65.6 percent of the inflows were reported as to the household; 20.5 percent to the head, 1.0 percent to the spouse of the head, and only 1.9 percent to other household members.[9]

Intrahousehold Familial Transfers

Household members who consume more than their disposable income receive intrahousehold transfers from those who consume less than their disposable income. Disposable income is defined as labor income plus net public cash transfers (cash inflows less taxes) plus net interhousehold transfers. In some households, the disposable income of all members combined exceeds the total consumption of all members combined. The surplus is transferred to the household head and saved. In other households, total disposable income is less than total consumption, and they support some part of their consumption using asset income or, if necessary, by dis-

9. Calculated by authors.

saving. This portion of the deficit is financed by additional intrahousehold transfers from the household head to household members.

The consumption of durables, including the services from owner-occupied housing, are treated in a distinct fashion because, by assumption, the household head owns all household assets and thus all income generated by those assets flows to the head. The consumption of durables by any nonhead household member is financed by an intrahousehold transfer from the head to the member equal to the value of durable consumption.

Intrahousehold transfers to support current consumption (nondurable consumption) are financed by imposing a household-specific flat-rate tax on each member's surplus income. Within the household, each member is taxed at the same rate. The tax rate does not vary by age. Moreover, we assume that the household-specific tax rate for any sector (education, health, or other nondurable consumption) is identical for each household member.

Intrahousehold transfers are computed at the micro-level and aggregated to construct age profiles. To calculate the intrahousehold transfers requires estimates for each individual of consumption, labor income, net public cash transfers, and interhousehold transfers.

Bequests

Bequests capture all capital transfers that occur because of headship transitions. If a household head dies, if two independent households merge, or if the headship designation within an existing household shifts from one member to another, a capital transfer is generated. The estimates of bequests presented in table 3.2 are very preliminary and intended only to suggest magnitudes.

The estimates were obtained in the following way. First, the rate of return to assets was assumed to be independent of age. Thus, wealth by age has the same age distribution as asset income by age. Second, the survival rate of heads is assumed to be independent of wealth. If wealthy heads have a higher survival rate—a likely possibility—the mean age of bequests would be greater than those reported in table 3.2. Preliminary analysis suggests that the covariance between wealth and survival in Taiwan is relatively small, however. Third, we assumed that all capital transfers were to direct descendants, assumed to be thirty years younger than the household head. Thirty years is the mean generation length in Taiwan. If there is a parity bias in bequests—that is, if older children receive a larger share of bequests, the inflow would be to older individuals, on average, than assumed here. Given the low fertility and decline in parity bias in Taiwan, this is not likely to have a substantial effect. The use of a single age—thirty—rather than a distribution, also has an effect on the distribution of bequest inflows. In the United States, unlike Taiwan, if a decedent was married, the widower/widow is assumed to inherit the estate. Otherwise, the estate is inherited by the children of the decedent, whose ages are estimated using the average age shape of U.S. fertility over the last forty years. Future efforts will improve these estimates, and they are not emphasized here.

3.2.3   Estimation and Data Sources

National Transfer Flow Accounts are estimated relying on a variety of sources of information. National Income and Product Accounts are used to construct aggregate controls on public and private consumption, labor income (compensation of employees plus a portion of household entrepreneurial income), saving, asset income, public and private transfers, and its components.

Aggregates are allocated across age groups, relying on a variety of data sources, with extensive use made of administrative records and nationally representative income and expenditure surveys. For Taiwan, we make extensive use of the 1998 Family Income and Expenditure Survey of Taiwan (DGBAS various). For the United States, we make extensive use of the Current Population Survey (1998, 1999, and 2000), the Consumer Expenditure Survey (1998, 1999, 2000), the Survey of Consumer Finances (1998 and 2001), and the U.S. National Health Accounts (1999). More information about data sources and methods is available on www.ntaccounts.org.

3.2.4   Preliminary Results

The results presented in the remainder of the paper are snapshots—National Transfer Accounts for a single year in Taiwan (1998) and the United States (2000). The full value of the accounts will be realized only when we have constructed estimates for many years. That work is underway, but the estimates will not be available for some time. In the absence of these more extensive data, we cannot, for example, track cohorts over time. The inability to do so limits the extent to which we can explain the cross-sectional patterns that we observe. In particular, we often can only speculate about the extent to which the results reflect distinctive features of the years for which the accounts were constructed, possibly substantial cohort effects, or the effects of age. Before discussing the results, it is worthwhile to point out some of the key features of Taiwan and the United States that may bear on the results.

First, the fiscal crisis began to strike East Asia beginning in 1997, and Taiwan's economic growth was atypically slow in 1998. The crisis in Taiwan was much less severe than in many other East Asian countries, however. The year 2000 was an interesting year in the United States; the stock market peaked in 2000, and the economy began to slow after an extended period of strong economic growth.

Second, the current demographic situation in Taiwan and the United States is similar in important respects. The total fertility rate is much lower in Taiwan than in the United States. Life expectancy is about one and a-half to two years higher in the United States than Taiwan. Taiwan's population is younger, with 8.6 percent of its population aged sixty-five or older in 2000 as compared with 12.4 percent in the United States. Both countries experienced very substantial demographic change during the post-World War II era. The total fertility rate (TFR) was much higher and life expectancy at birth was much lower in Taiwan than in the United States in the 1950s, but changed very rapidly. The United States experienced its baby boom from 1946 to 1964. These experiences may bear in important ways on the behavior of those who are now in their sixties and seventies. Migration patterns are also different between the two countries. The United States, of course, has had relatively high rates of net immigration during recent decades. Taiwan has not, but it did experience a huge influx of young adults—heavily male—from the Chinese mainland in 1949 to 1950.

Third, the economies of Taiwan and the United States are very different. Taiwan is a middle-income country with a per capita GDP of a little less than $12,600 in 2001. In the United States, per capita GDP was $35,700 in 2001. But in 1960, real GNP per capita was only $1,000 in Taiwan (in 2001 prices) as compared with over $14,000 in the United States. Between 1960 and 2001, Taiwan's real rate of growth of per capita GNP exceeded 6 percent per annum! This implies extraordinary differences between the lifetime earnings of successive generations. Given a mean generation length of thirty years and an annual growth rate of 6 percent, per capita income increases by six-fold each generation. In contrast, real per capita GNP in the United States grew at an annual rate of 2.2 percent between 1960 and 2001, yielding roughly a doubling of per capita income per generation.

The Lifecycle Deficit

The individual lifecycles in Taiwan and the United States are broadly similar, but with some important differences (Fig. 3.2). In both settings, children and the elderly consume substantially more than they produce. In Taiwan, young adults begin to produce as much as they consume at age twenty-four; in the United States at age twenty-six. In Taiwan, adults no longer produce as much as they consume at age fifty-seven; in the United States, at age fifty-nine. The span of years during which there is a lifecycle surplus is surprisingly short in both countries—thirty-three years both in Taiwan and in the United States.

The shape of the production (labor income) age profiles for Taiwan and the United States are strikingly similar until adults reach their early forties. To facilitate comparison of the United States with Taiwan, the profiles in fig. 3.2 have been scaled by dividing by the simple average of per capita production from ages thirty to forty-nine. Both the level and slope of the age profiles are sensitive to the particular scaling factor chosen. However, the percentage change in labor income associated with an additional year of

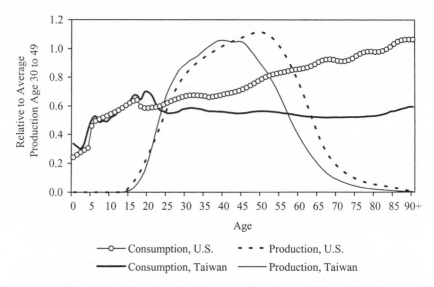

Fig. 3.2   Lifecycle of production and consumption, per capita, United States, 2000 and Taiwan, 1998

age is unaffected by scaling. In the late teens and early twenties, labor income grows somewhat faster in Taiwan, while between the early twenties and early forties, labor income grows somewhat faster in the United States. Between the mid-forties and late fifties, however, the income profiles diverge by as much as 5 percent per single year of age. The gap between the United States and Taiwan persists into the older ages. The differences in per capita labor income reflect differences in labor force participation—a particularly rapid drop in participation rates with age in Taiwan—due entirely to differences in female participation rates.

There are important similarities in the consumption patterns at young ages in Taiwan and the United States. Consumption by children, *relative to consumption by adults in their thirties and forties,* is similar in Taiwan and the United States. In both countries, consumption by young children is substantially less than consumption by older children and prime-age adults. In both settings, consumption by children increases in a large and discrete fashion as children enter school. The subsequent decline is associated with the decline in spending on education as children depart high school in the United States and college in Taiwan.

The differences in the consumption profiles for those in their thirties and older are quite striking, however. In the United States, the consumption profile rises very steadily with age. In Taiwan, the consumption profile is relatively flat, but declines gradually with age. The simple average of per capita consumption by those sixty-five to ninety-plus was 134 percent in

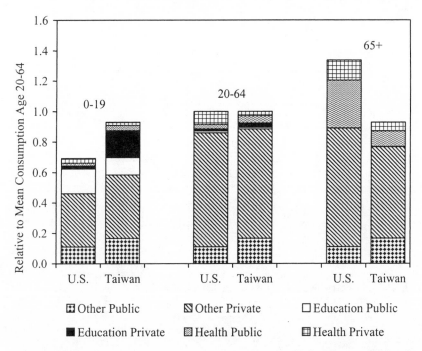

Fig. 3.3   Per capita consumption by age and components, United States, 2000 and Taiwan, 1998

the United States and 96 percent in Taiwan of per capita consumption of those age twenty to sixty-four. A substantial part of the difference can be attributed to the consumption of health (fig. 3.3). If we consider just non-health consumption, elderly and nonelderly adults in the United States had virtually identical consumption, while Taiwan elderly had nonhealth consumption equal to about 85 percent of the nonhealth consumption of adults between the ages of twenty and sixty-four. Thus, even controlling for health consumption, U.S. elderly were consuming at a much high rate relative to nonelderly adults than were the elderly in Taiwan.

The differences in consumption are most pronounced for the elderly, but they are not confined to them. In Taiwan, the average consumption by those age fifty to sixty-four was 95 percent of the average consumption of those age twenty to forty-nine, while in the United States the figure was 124 percent.

Why health consumption increased so much more steeply with age in the United States than in Taiwan and why nonhealth consumption declined with age in Taiwan are interesting questions, about which we can only speculate at this point. One possibility is that the lower consumption among older ages in Taiwan is a response to their lower relative current labor in-

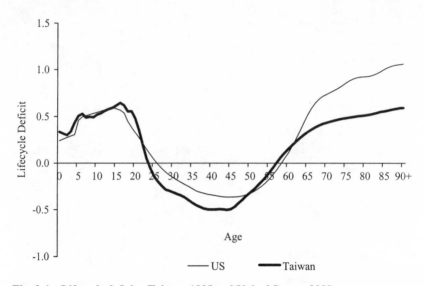

Fig. 3.4   Lifecycle deficits, Taiwan, 1998 and United States, 2000

Note: The lifecycle deficit is expressed relative to the simple mean of average production for those 30 to 49.

come. Another possibility is that the lower consumption of the elderly is a response to their relatively low lifetime labor income. Perhaps institutional differences are playing a role, with U.S. consumption patterns reflecting greater reliance on public transfer programs and Taiwan's greater reliance on familial transfer programs. Familial transfer programs internalize costs of excess consumption to the family.

The per capita deficits (fig. 3.4) are closer than their constituent elements—consumption and labor income. Taiwan's surplus is greater for young working-age adults—those under the age of fifty; the surplus values are similar for adults in their fifties and early sixties. The most striking difference between the two series is the substantially larger lifecycle deficit for U.S. elderly. Given the age distribution of the population, the lifecycle reallocation system of the United States shifts a larger share of resources to older ages than does the Taiwan reallocation system. That the U.S. population is older than the Taiwan population only serves to reinforce this feature of the U.S. reallocation system.

The Reallocation System

The broad features of the reallocation system are presented in figure 3.5 for Taiwan in 1998 and in figure 3.6 for the United States in 2000. Panel A reports the aggregate flows to and from each age group. Panel B reports the per capita flows. Four economic forms used to reallocate resources are distinguished: asset-based reallocations, public transfers, private transfers,

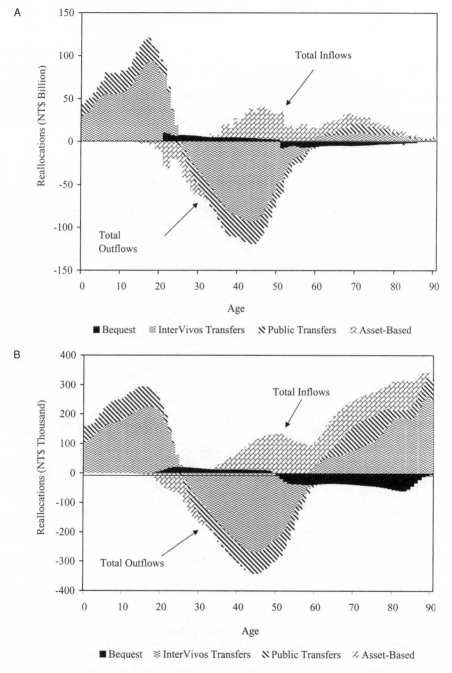

Fig. 3.5 *A*, Components of age reallocations aggregate values, Taiwan, 1998; *B*, Components of age reallocations per capita values, Taiwan, 1998

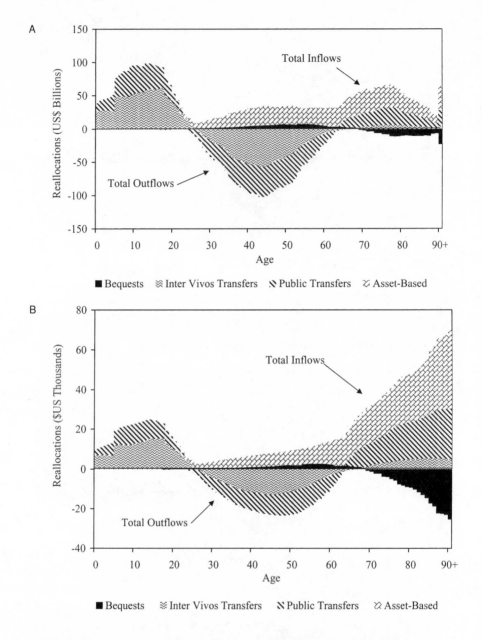

Fig. 3.6 *A,* Components of age reallocations, aggregate values, United States, 2000; *B,* Components of age reallocations per capita values, United States, 2000

and bequests. Negative values represent outflows and positive values represent inflows. The values are stacked in the figures. For example, teenagers in Taiwan received net transfers of about $NT 100 billion, of which about one-fourth was public and three-fourths was private. At many ages there are simultaneously inflows from one system and outflows from another system. In both the United States and Taiwan, asset-based reallocations are producing inflows to most working ages while public and private transfers are producing outflows at the same ages. The outflows less the inflows equal the lifecycle deficits for Taiwan and the United States.

The reallocation systems that support children are similar in Taiwan and the United States. In both, transfers dominate the reallocation system for children, with total transfers nearly equal to total reallocations. Familial transfers are particularly important. Private, intrahousehold transfers accounted for 74 percent of all transfers in Taiwan and 57 percent in the United States.[10] The importance of familial transfers should not come as any great surprise. We know that asset-based reallocations are infrequently used to support the consumption of children. Of asset-based reallocations, only credit can be used to support consumption by children. Creditors have limited recourse if children default on their debt, limiting the extent to which children can borrow. Thus, transfers dominate the child reallocation system in both Taiwan and the United States—and no doubt elsewhere.

Public transfers to children are also quite substantial. In Taiwan, 24 percent of all transfers were public transfers, as compared with 38 percent in the United States. As can be seen in figure 3.3, a significant portion of these transfers is public education spending. Of roughly equal importance is children's pro rata share of pure public goods and other goods that cannot be assigned to specific individuals.

In Taiwan and the United States, the old-age reallocation systems are very different than the child reallocation systems. The elderly rely both on asset-based reallocations and transfers to generate inflows. The elderly can, in principle, generate asset-based reallocation inflows in two ways: first, by earning asset income on their accumulated wealth and, second, by dissaving or liquidating their assets. There are many ways in which this can be accomplished. The elderly can sell off financial assets or a family business or farm, take out a reverse mortgage on a home, or sell their home and rent or buy a less expensive residence.

For U.S. elderly, asset reallocations are very important, constituting 65.3 percent of life-cycle reallocations. Of this total, 65.1 percent of total reallocations was net asset income and 0.2 percent was dissaving. At first

---

10. Dependent children do not receive interhousehold transfers in the accounting system, by assumption.

glance this seems to provide strong support for the life-cycle saving hypothesis and runs contrary to previous empirical research—that U.S. elderly save. However, the saving reported here includes the dissaving that occurs because the death of households generates downward transfers of assets. For the cohort, this is dissaving but is not undertaken for life-cycle purposes. If we confine our attention to surviving households, about half of reallocations were asset reallocations and half were transfers. Income on assets amounted to 65.1 percent of reallocations as before, but 16.9 percent of reallocations were saved and the remainder (48.2 percent) was devoted to the life-cycle deficit. Thus, our estimates imply that the elderly did save, but they also relied heavily on the income generated by assets accumulated during their working years. This provides support in a different form for the life-cycle hypothesis.

For Taiwan's elderly, asset-based reallocations were also important but less so than in the United States. Asset-based reallocations were 40.9 percent of total reallocations; asset income amounted to 54.2 percent of total reallocations, but 13.3 percent of that was saved. Given that bequests were equal to 19.2 percent of total reallocations, total saving by survivors was 32.5 percent of total reallocations. Considering only surviving households, asset-based reallocations were 21.7 percent of total reallocations (54.2 percent in asset income less 32.5 percent that was saved). The surviving elderly in Taiwan had less asset income and saved more than their U.S. counterparts. Asset reallocations were thus less important to surviving elderly households in Taiwan than in the United States.

Transfers were important components of the reallocation systems for the elderly in both countries but, again, a clear picture requires careful attention to the role of bequests. In the United States, public transfers are particularly important. If we ignore bequests, public transfers constituted 37.0 percent and private transfers 7.3 percent of total reallocations to the elderly. Transfers are almost as important as asset-based reallocations, and public transfers dominate. Private transfers to the elderly are small in the United States. Note, however, that private transfers are greater than one would think, based solely on interhousehold transfers, even in the United States. Once bequests are taken into account, however, we see that the direction of the private transfer is from the old to the young rather than the reverse. Bequests were more than twice private transfers to the elderly in 2000.

In Taiwan, public transfers were less important than in the United States, but private transfers far more than compensated for the lower level of public transfers. Public transfers were 31.0 percent of total reallocations for the elderly; private inter vivos transfers were 47.6 percent of life-cycle reallocations. Combined transfers excluding bequests were over three-fourths of life-cycle reallocations, with private transfers playing a particularly important role. Unlike the United States, private transfers are still in an upward direction—from adult children to elderly parents—even after taking bequests into consideration.

In important respects the reallocations for those with life-cycle surpluses are just the counterpart for the reallocations for children and elderly, as just described. This is true by definition for transfers, because inflows and outflows must match, ignoring the relatively modest amounts of international flows. The large public transfer inflows to U.S. elderly must be matched by large public transfer outflows from those in the working ages. Likewise, the large private transfer inflows to Taiwan elderly must be matched by large private transfer outflows from those in the working ages. Exactly which working ages experience the public sector outflows depends on the tax systems, their incidence, and the age distribution of the economic resources being taxed. Exactly which working ages experience the private sector outflows depends to a great extent on the coresidence patterns that, in turn, govern intrahousehold transfers.

In Taiwan, the burden of financing public transfers falls a little more heavily on those age thirty to forty-nine, for whom net public transfers are –13.5 percent of labor income, than on those age fifty to sixty-four, for whom net public transfers are –11.4 percent of labor income. In the United States, the opposite is true: the burden falls slightly more heavily on those age fifty to sixty-four, for whom net public transfers are –22.7 percent of labor income, than on those age thirty to forty-nine, for whom net public transfers are –21.6 percent of labor income. Private transfers in Taiwan, however, are a much heavier burden for those age thirty to forty-nine. Their net private transfers are –40.7 percent of their labor income. Inter vivos transfers are –43.3 percent of labor income. Net private transfers for those age fifty to sixty-four are –31.4 percent of their labor income and inter vivos transfers are only –19.2 percent of labor income. It is tempting to argue that those below fifty are heavily burdened because they are paying for the high consumption of children. The net transfers from those age 30 to 49 are more or less equal in absolute value to the net transfers to those under age thirty. The generation length in Taiwan is about thirty years, however, and it is likely that children are being supported by those over age fifty, and the elderly are being supported by those under age fifty. In the United States, net private transfers are smaller than in Taiwan, at –24.8 percent of labor income for those age thirty to forty-nine and –17.0 percent for those age fifty to sixty-four.

Unlike transfers, asset-based reallocations need not balance.[11] In both Taiwan and the United States, total asset income substantially exceeded total saving. As can be seen in figs. 3.5 and 3.6, asset-based reallocations are positive at most adult ages, not just at old age. In Taiwan, we see some

---

11. In golden rule steady-state growth, all asset income is saved and total net asset-based reallocations are equal to zero.

negative asset-based reallocations at young adult ages, but these are small. We see even less negative asset-based reallocations for the United States.

This is a puzzling pattern, and not what we would expect to see if workers are accumulating pension assets. Suppose workers contributed a fixed percentage of their income to a pension fund during their working years, and any interest generated by the fund was allowed to accumulate within the fund—a normal practice. Saving by the workers would exceed interest income by the portion of labor income that was contributed to the fund each year. Asset-based reallocations would be negative during the working years and would turn positive only after retirement. Even under very general conditions, as cohorts begin to accumulate wealth, saving must exceed asset income. Judging from the substantial asset income of older cohorts, it is clear that they enter old age with a substantial amount of wealth. The key question is "Why is saving so much less than asset income among working adults?"

First, these are cross-sectional data, not longitudinal data. There may be particular features of the years in question—1998 in Taiwan and 2000 in the United States—that led to high consumption and low saving during the working ages. The financial crisis hit East Asia beginning in 1997. Taiwan was influenced less than many other East Asian countries, but economic growth did slow in 1998. The United States experienced an enormous run-up in the stock market, which peaked in 2000. Housing prices also increased very substantially in the United States. Perhaps working-age Americans responded to the significant increases in their real wealth by increasing their consumption and reducing their saving.[12]

Second, the cross-sectional patterns may reflect longer-run trends. In Taiwan, saving rates declined substantially between the late 1980s and the late 1990s. The United States has experienced a long-run secular decline in saving rates over the last three to four decades. It may be that in both countries, asset-based reallocations are becoming less important than they were in the past. Hence, we observe relatively little saving at young ages, but relatively large, asset-based reallocation inflows at older ages.

A third point to consider is that the asset-based age reallocations are serving a life-cycle purpose other than the accumulation of pension wealth as envisioned in the standard life-cycle saving model. We think it is plausibly the case in Taiwan, where asset-based reallocation inflows are substantial for those in their forties and early fifties. At these ages, people in Taiwan are doubly burdened by dependent children and dependent elderly. This is reflected in the very substantial inter vivos transfer outflows at these ages. In a sense, life cycle saving is indirectly financing the consumption of

---

12. Net saving rates increased during the 1990s in the United States, but whether this is true at all ages is unknown.

the elderly by financing transfers from middle-aged adults to their elderly parents.

A final point is that the asset-based reallocation pattern will vary, depending on the importance of bequests and behavior regarding bequests.

Sources of Support

Sources of income are a standard and useful descriptive measure in reports on the economics of aging. The NTA system yields a more complete measure of the sources of support for the dependent populations by including familial, intrahousehold transfers, and dissaving. In figs. 3.7 and 3.8 we compare the sources of support; that is, the methods by which consumption was financed, in Taiwan and the United States.

The methods by which the consumption of dependent children—defined as those under the age of twenty—are financed are very similar in Taiwan and the United States. In both countries, earnings by children are relatively unimportant. Virtually all consumption is financed by transfers. Private transfers dominate, totaling 57 percent of consumption in the

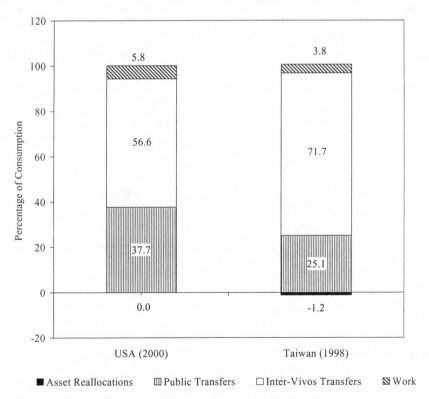

Fig. 3.7   Finance of consumption, young dependents age 0 to 19

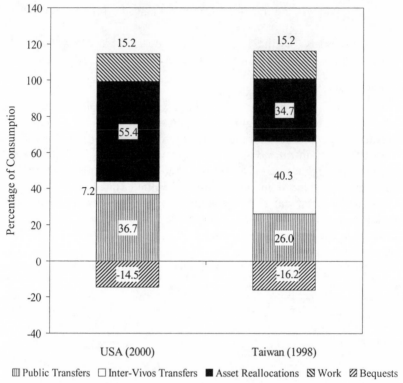

Fig. 3.8   Finance of consumption, persons 65 or older

United States and 72 percent of consumption in Taiwan. The remainder consists of public transfers.

The finance of consumption by the elderly is very different in Taiwan and the United States. Work plays a similar role in both—contributing about 15 percent of consumption in both the United States and Taiwan. Asset-based reallocations and public transfers are more important in the United States. Private, familial transfers are more important in Taiwan. The greater importance of public transfers in the United States and private transfers in Taiwan are consistent with what relatively casual observers might expect. The greater importance of asset-based reallocations in the United States may come as a surprise—perhaps to many. Saving rates are not as high in Taiwan as in other East Asian countries. Moreover, the current consumption by the elderly in Taiwan is very high relative to lifetime earnings. In an economy characterized by such rapid economic growth, the relatively flat consumption profile shown in fig. 3.1 would almost certainly be possible only if the reallocation system relied more on transfers and less on assets.

3.3   Conclusions

The reallocation of resources across age groups is an important feature of any economy, yet it goes largely unmeasured at the aggregate level. The objective of the research described here is to rectify that situation. By doing so we should increase our understanding of generational differences in the command over resources, the institutional mechanisms by which resources are redistributed across generations, and how population aging is likely to influence economic performance.

The research reported here, however, is in an early stage. The estimates are preliminary and many of the methodologies are still being refined. Moreover, there are a number of difficult issues that cannot be addressed in an entirely satisfactory way, given the data and analytic techniques that are currently available. Nonetheless, we believe that the development of the National Transfer Account system will prove useful in the same way that National Income and Product Accounts are useful, despite their flaws. The value will be enhanced, in particular, as estimates for additional years allow us to follow cohorts over their life cycles.

The results reported here provide information about support systems that has not been previously available. We provide detailed information about the asset accumulation process and how it relates to variation in life cycle needs. In both countries, asset income is important to those who are currently retired, but dissaving is not. In Taiwan, asset income indirectly supports the elderly by financing transfers from middle-aged adults to elderly parents. Somewhat surprisingly, the accumulation of assets by working-age adults is modest in both countries. Why this is so and whether it is a persistent or transitory feature is a question that cannot be answered with a single year of data.

One of the most important objectives of this research is to quantify both public and private transfers in a way that allows comparison and analysis. We find that private, familial transfers from adult children to their elderly parents are very important in Taiwan—similar in magnitude to public support to the elderly in the United States. Familial transfers are almost entirely intrahousehold transfers.

Public transfers are also important in Taiwan and, although not documented here, known to be growing. Further analysis will hopefully shed light on whether the growth of public transfers has served to crowd out private transfers or whether the elderly have gained in terms of consumption by being able to rely on a mix of assets, public programs, and familial transfers.

One of the most striking differences between Taiwan and the United States is the age pattern of consumption. In Taiwan, consumption appears to vary little by age. In the United States, however, consumption by the elderly is very high. A large portion of the extra consumption—but by no means all—is due to high consumption of health care goods and services. This will clearly have important implications for how population aging will influence the economies of Taiwan and the United States.

References

Altonji, J. G., F. Hayashi, and L. Kotlikoff. 2000. The effects of income and wealth on time and money transfers between parents and children. In *Sharing the wealth: Demographic change and economic transfers between generations,* ed. A. Mason and G. Tapinos, 306–57. Oxford: Oxford University Press.

Attanasio, O. P., and H. W. Hoynes. 2000. Differential mortality and wealth accumulation. *Journal of Human Resources* 35:1–29.

Auerbach, A. J., J. Gokhale, and L. J. Kotlikoff. 1991. Generational accounts: A meaningful alternative to deficit accounting. In *Tax policy and the economy,* ed. D. Bradford, 55–110. Cambridge, MA: MIT Press.

Auerbach, A. J., and L. J. Kotlikoff. 1999. The methodology of generational accounting. In *Generational accounting around the world,* ed. A. J. Auerbach, L. J. Kotlikoff, and W. Leibfritz, 31–41. Chicago: University of Chicago Press.

Auerbach, A. J., L. J. Kotlikoff, and W. Leibfritz, eds. 1999. *Generational accounting around the world.* Chicago: University of Chicago Press.

Barro, R. J. 1974. Are government bonds net worth? *Journal of Political Economy* 82 (6): 1095–117.

Becker, G. S., and K. M. Murphy. 1988. The family and the state. *Journal of Law and Economics* 31 (April): 1–18.

Becker, G. S., and N. Tomes. 1976. Child endowments and the quantity and quality of children. *Journal of Political Economy* 84 (4 pt. 2): S143–62.

Bloom, D. E., D. Canning, and J. Sevilla. 2002. *The demographic dividend: A new perspective on the economic consequences of population change.* Santa Monica, CA: RAND.

Bloom, D. E., and J. G. Williamson. 1998. Demographic transitions and economic miracles in emerging Asia. *World Bank Economic Review* 12 (3): 419–56.

Bommier, A., and R. D. Lee. 2003. Overlapping generations models with realistic demography. *Journal of Population Economics* 16:135–60.

Bourguignon, F. 1999. The cost of children: May the collective approach to household behavior help? *Journal of Population Economics* 12:503–21.

Bourguignon, F., and P.-A. Chiappori. 1992. Collective models of household behavior: An introduction. *European Economic Review* 36:355–64.

Brown, J. R., and S. J. Weisbenner. 2002. Is a bird in hand worth more than a bird in the bush? Intergenerational transfers and savings behavior. NBER Working Paper no. 8753. Cambridge, MA: National Bureau of Economic Research.

Chu, C. Y. C. 2000. *Panel study of family dynamics.* Taipei, Taiwan: Academia Sinica.

Cox, D. 1987. Motives for private income transfers. *Journal of Political Economy* 95:508–46.

Deaton, A. 1997. *The analysis of household surveys: A microeconometric approach to development policy.* Baltimore and London: World Bank.

Diamond, P. 2006. Pensions for an aging society. *NBER Working Paper* no. W11875. Cambridge, MA: National Bureau of Economic Research.

Feldstein, M. 1974. Social Security, induced retirement, and aggregate capital accumulation. *Journal of Political Economy* 82 (5): 905–26.

————. 1996. The missing piece in policy analysis: Social Security reform. *American Economic Review* 86 (2): 1–14.

————, ed. 1998. *Privatizing Social Security*. Chicago and London: University of Chicago Press.

Feldstein, M., and A. Samwick. 2001. Potential paths of Social Security reform. *NBER Working Paper* no. 8592. Cambridge, MA: National Bureau of Economic Research.

Frankenberg, E., L. A. Lillard, and R. J. Willis. 2002. Patterns of intergenerational transfers in Southeast Asia. *Journal of Marriage and the Family* 64 (August): 627–41.

Gale, W. G. 1998. The effects of pensions on household wealth: A reevaluation of theory and evidence. *Journal of Political Economy* 106 (4): 706–23.

Hermalin, A. I., ed. 2002. *The well-being of the elderly in Asia: A four-country comparative study*. Ann Arbor, MI: University of Michigan Press.

Keehan, S. P., H. C. Lazenby, M. A. Zezza, and A. C. Catlin. 2004. Age estimates in the National Health Accounts. *Health Care Financing Review* 1 (1): 1–16.

Kelley, A. C., and R. M. Schmidt 1995. Aggregate population and economic growth correlations: The role of the components of demographic change. *Demography* 32 (4): 543–55.

————. 2001. Economic and demographic change: A synthesis of models, findings, and perspectives. In *Population matters: Demographic change, economic growth, and poverty in the developing world,* ed. N. Birdsall, A. C. Kelley, and S. W. Sinding, 67–105. Oxford: Oxford University Press.

Kinsella, K. 1990. Living arrangements of the elderly and social policy: A cross-national perspective. *US Census Bureau/CIR Staff Paper no. 52*. Washington, DC: U.S. Bureau of the Census.

Kinsella, K., and V. A. Velkoff. 2001. An aging world: 2001, International Population Reports. Washington, DC: U.S. Bureau of the Census.

Kotlikoff, L. J., and A. Spivak. 1981. The family as an incomplete annuities market. *Journal of Political Economy* 89 (2): 372–91.

Krueger, D., and F. Kubler. 2002. Pareto improving Social Security reform when financial markets are incomplete? *NBER Working Paper* no. 9410. Cambridge, MA: National Bureau of Economic Research.

Lazear, E. P., and R. T. Michael. 1988. *Allocation of income within the household*. Chicago and London: University of Chicago Press.

Lee, R. D. 1994a. The formal demography of population aging, transfers, and the economic life cycle. In *Demography of aging,* ed. L. G. Martin and S. H. Preston, 8–49. Washington, DC: National Academy Press.

————. 1994b. Population, age structure, intergenerational transfers, and wealth: A new approach, with applications to the U.S. In *The family and intergenerational relations, Journal of Human Resources*, ed. P. Gertler. 29:1027–63.

Lee, R. D., S.-H. Lee, and A. Mason. 2008. Charting the economic lifecycle. In *Population aging, human capital accumulation, and productivity growth (suppl. to Population and Development Review 33)*, ed. A. Prskawetz, D. E. Bloom, and W. Lutz, 208–37. New York: Population Council.

Lee, R. D., A. Mason, and T. Miller. 2003. From transfers to individual responsibility: Implications for savings and capital accumulation in Taiwan and the United States. *Scandinavian Journal of Economics* 105 (3): 339–57.

Lillard, L. A., and R. J. Willis. 1997. Motives for intergenerational transfers: Evidence from Malaysia. *Demography* 34 (1): 115–34.

Mason, A. 2001. *Population change and economic development in East Asia: Challenges met, opportunities seized.* Stanford, CA: Stanford University Press.

———. 2005. *Demographic transition and demographic dividends in developed and developing countries.* United Nations Expert Group Meeting on Social and Economic Implications of Changing Population Age Structures, Mexico City. New York: United Nations.

Mason, A. and R. Lee. 2006. Reform and support systems for the elderly in developing countries: Capturing the second demographic dividend. *GENUS* 42 (2): 11:35.

Mason, A., and T. Miller. 2000. Dynasties, intergenerational transfers, and lifecycle income: A case study of Taiwan. In *Sharing the wealth: Demographic change and economic transfers between generations,* ed. A. Mason and G. Tapinos, 57–84. Oxford: Oxford University Press.

McGarry, K., and R. Schoeni. 1997. Transfer behavior within the family: Results from the asset and health dynamics (AHEAD) study. *Journals of Gerontology Series B: Psychological and Social Sciences* 52B (special issue): 82–92.

Munnell, A. H. 1974. *The effect of Social Security on personal savings.* Cambridge, MA: Ballinger.

Poterba, J. 2000. The estate tax and after-tax investment returns. In *Does Atlas shrug? The economic consequences of taxing the rich,* ed. J. Slemrod, 333–53. Cambridge, MA: Harvard University Press.

Poterba, J., and S. J. Weisbenner. 2001. The distribution burden of taxing estates and unrealized capital gains at the time of death. In *Rethinking estate and gift taxation,* ed. W. G. Gale and J. Slemrod, 422–449. Washington, DC, Brookings Institution.

Preston, S. H. 1984. Children and the elderly: Divergent paths for America's dependents. *Demography* 21 (4): 435–57.

Razin, A., E. Sadka, and P. Swagel. 2002. The aging population and the size of the welfare state. *Journal of Political Economy* 110 (4): 900–918.

Ruggles, S. 1994. The transformation of American family structure. *American Historical Review* 99 (1): 103–28.

Samuelson, P. 1958. An exact consumption loan model of interest with or without the social contrivance of money. *Journal of Political Economy* 66:467–82.

Willis, R. J. 1988. Life cycles, institutions and population growth: A theory of the equilibrium interest rate in an overlapping-generations model. In *Economics of changing age distributions in developed countries,* ed. R. D. Lee, W. B. Arthur, and G. Rodgers, 106–38. Oxford: Oxford University Press.

Comment   Andrew Samwick

This is a very interesting chapter that seeks to evaluate a methodology for apportioning the traditional National Income and Product Account (NIPA) aggregates to persons by age. This methodology allows us to better understand how demographic trends and fiscal policy interact to change lifecycle consumption and income profiles. It expands the usual

Andrew Samwick is a professor of economics at Dartmouth College and a research associate of the National Bureau of Economic Research.

generational account framework to include private as well as public transfers, and it illustrates the results for the United States and Taiwan.

The methodology is well summarized by equation (2), given at the household level as:

$$C - y^l = (rA - S) + (\tau_g^+ - \tau_g^-) + (\tau_f^+ - \tau_f^-).$$

The left side of the equation is the lifecycle deficit—the amount by which consumption exceeds labor income at a given age. Funding for consumption in excess of current labor income must come from some combination of sources on the right side of the equation: dissaving in excess of capital income, net transfers from the public sector, or net transfer from the private sector. Economists have focused to varying degrees on the first three of these terms. This chapter is the first I have seen to incorporate the last term (private transfers) into a comprehensive analysis by age.

The basis for this methodology is to use nationally representative household surveys to figure out the distribution of NIPA aggregates across the population, where, in most cases, the distribution is done by age. Unfortunately, most of that apportionment process is not discussed specifically in this chapter, and the interested reader must consult the authors' prior work. At one level, this exercise is analogous to benchmarking the survey total to the NIPA number that was gathered by a different means. In evaluating the methodology in light of the main results, the critical question is whether any of the methods for apportionment presuppose life cycle behavior (e.g., quadratic specifications in age).

The central results are shown in figs. 3.2, 3.5, and 3.6. They show the life-cycle patterns of consumption and production as well as the aggregate and per capita transfers by age in the two countries. The most novel result is that the period of lifecycle surplus is surprisingly short in both countries. Public and private transfers are particularly large during this period. The data also seem to show very little active saving in these years, despite large asset income in later years. (It is possible that this disparity reflects the influence of cohort effects—asset income may be lower in the future. Alternatively, the year 2000 was a very good one for capital appreciation in the United States. It may be that the asset reallocations were unusually large that year.) Private transfers to the elderly are substantially larger in Taiwan.

The prominence of private transfers in these accounts raises some questions about their economic interpretation. The first question is the extent to which they are voluntary, particularly the transfers to the elderly in Taiwan. Some portion may reflect social customs that impose a burden on the younger generation that they have little choice but to accept. In the traditional national income accounts, there is a similar problem. Some expenditures, like rebuilding after a natural disaster, count for gross domestic product but are a reflection of lower, not higher welfare. How should we change our interpretation of a large private transfer when we believe it to be involuntary?

The second question is the extent to which the private transfers substituting for the lifecycle behavior that we have come to expect but have not seen overwhelmingly in the micro data. For example, fig. 3.2 suggests that in the United States, consumption continues to rise even after lifecycle production has started to fall. However, fig. 3.6 does not admit much of a role for private transfers. The main components are asset reallocations and public transfers. I think that this reflects, in part, that the transfer accounts are calibrated to the mean, not the median. Because of the skewness of the wealth distribution, the median would reflect a greater importance of public transfers and a lesser importance of asset reallocations. What would it show for private transfers?

As this chapter is breaking new ground, it is tempting for a discussant to suggest avenues for further research on this topic. The first is to consider the next level of disaggregation beyond age. Gender seems to be the natural extension, and this would force the authors to think about other ways of allocating consumption and production within households. The second is to show the calculations in a few different ways. Specifically, health expenditures comprise a large component of the public transfers to the elderly, and education expenditures comprise a large component of both the public and private transfers to the young. It would be interesting to see how important those transfers are in this framework. The authors could show the calculations with and without these expenditures, distinguished by type.

Finally, it is worth noting that the variation in this analysis is entirely cross-sectional. The time-series properties of this methodology are still to be investigated, and extending the methodology to multiple years of data is an important direction for further research. There are three areas in which the time-series dimension may shed additional light on life-cycle behavior. First, with new data, the life-cycle deficits may change, as would the corresponding age reallocations. Second, the allocation rules estimated from micro data might change. Third, it might be possible to distinguish cohort or time effects, which may be important as well.

Retirement Behavior

The Effect of Large Capital Gains or Losses on Retirement

Michael D. Hurd, Monika Reti, and Susann Rohwedder

4.1 Introduction

Although it is natural to suppose that years of retirement are a normal good, so that increases in wealth would lead to earlier retirement, it has been difficult for research to estimate plausible wealth effects on retirement.[1] Part of the reason for the difficulty is that some of the cross-section variation in wealth is the result of taste variation: for example, people who are especially risk averse will tend to accumulate more wealth and to retire later than those who are less risk averse. Also, it is difficult to control for the quality of the job: higher paying jobs tend to have amenities that make work more pleasant, thus delaying retirement, and at the same time, higher incomes are associated with greater rates of wealth accumulation. Such positive cross-section correlations between wealth and retirement age are apparently large enough to offset negative correlations induced by a wealth effect on retirement.

In panel data, observed wealth change may not be related to a wealth effect on retirement. Economic models of wealth accumulation and retirement imply that individuals accumulate wealth so that they can retire at an optimal age. As long as there are no unforeseen changes in the environment

Michael D. Hurd is a senior economist and director of the RAND Center for the Study of Aging and a research associate of the National Bureau of Economic Research. Monika Reti is an independent researcher. Susann Rohwedder is an economist in the Labor and Population Program at RAND and at the RAND Center for the Study of Aging.

Financial support from the Department of Labor and the National Institute on Aging under grant P01 AG022481 is gratefully acknowledged.

1. Two examples are Gustman and Steinmeier (1986) and Samwick (1998). Both report small wealth effects on retirement.

or in other determinants of retirement, the optimal retirement age will not change over time. The constancy of the optimal anticipated retirement age holds, whether individuals save at a high rate (large wealth accumulation) or at a low rate. The result is that we should observe no relationship between wealth change and changes in anticipated retirement simply because the anticipated retirement age would not change. Only when there are unanticipated changes in the determinants of retirement would the optimal anticipated retirement age change.

The stock market boom of the mid-1990s to 2000, and the subsequent bust between 2000 and 2002, provide an opportunity to study what was likely an unexpected wealth change for at least part of the population. The boom produced wealth increases for some that were substantially similar to the thought experiment of giving large windfall wealth increases to the population that was approaching retirement, making it possible to avoid many of the difficulties associated with nonexperimental data. The purpose of this chapter is to study the associated change in actual retirement and in expected retirement of that population.

In 1992 the age-eligible respondents in the Health and Retirement Study (HRS) were approximately fifty-one to sixty-one years old (Juster and Suzman 1995). Their financial resources included private savings, part of which was invested in the stock market, part in the bond market, and part in checking and savings accounts and other miscellaneous assets. They also had claims to pensions, some of which were direct benefit (DB) plans and some direct contribution (DC) plans.

Between wave 1 in 1992 and wave 2 in 1994, the stock market increased in value by 14 percent as measured by the New York Stock Exchange Composite Index (NYSEI). However, beginning in 1994, stock prices increased at much greater rates than they had historically: between waves 2 and 4 in 1998 the NYSEI increased by 90 percent. Thus, between 1994 and 1998 many households had large gains in wealth. By historical projection, much of these gains would have been unanticipated and could reasonably be taken to be exogenous to previous decisions about saving and anticipated retirement. The stock market continued to rise until about August, 2000, and then dropped sharply until about August, 2002, when it was about 27 percent below its peak. Although the decline was not sustained for as long as the increase, in terms of deviations from expectations it likely was sharper.

Under the assumption that some of the gains and losses in the stock market were unanticipated, the increase and subsequent decline in wealth have aspects of a natural experiment in which some households had large changes in wealth in the years shortly before retirement and others did not. A number of households would have had similar economic positions in 1994 except that their portfolio mix differed: some held stocks and some did not. Some households had firm-directed DC plans that invested in stocks and some had plans that invested in bonds. These households would have had very different changes in the value of their private assets and in their DC plans, and the differential change would not have been expected and would have been only partially under their control. Thus, variation in tastes that makes the interpretation of nonexperimental data so difficult is likely to be much less important.

In summary, there were large changes in wealth for some of the respondents, and some of the wealth change can be assumed to be unanticipated. Their behavior in the waves following the large changes can be compared with the behavior of respondents who had no such wealth changes, and the difference can be attributed to a windfall wealth effect.

Our main research question is: how did the large increase and subsequent decline in wealth affect behavior? An obvious response for workers in the age range of the HRS is to buy more leisure by retiring earlier than anticipated or by delaying retirement following a loss in wealth. We will study actual retirement and anticipated retirement as measured by the subjective probability of working past age sixty-two, which is asked in every wave of HRS. We ask whether those with wealth gains retired earlier than those who did not have them, and whether anticipated retirement as measured by the subjective probability of working past age sixty-two changed in the panel in response to the wealth changes. The difference between actual and anticipated retirement should be particularly informative, as it will show whether those workers that had large gains in wealth actually retired earlier than their intentions as stated before any windfall gain in wealth. This will be a direct measure of the elasticity of retirement with respect to wealth that takes into account any individual propensity to retire.

By comparing changes in retirement or retirement intentions during the stock market boom period with changes in retirement or retirement intentions during the bust period, we will find whether there are asymmetries in responses to wealth gain compared with wealth loss.

4.1.1 Prior Research

Besides econometric estimations based on conventional household surveys, as in Gustman and Steinmeier (1986), there have been three approaches to estimating the effect on labor supply of unexpected wealth gains. Imbens, Rubin, and Sacerdote (1999, 2001) estimated the effect of windfall gains in wealth from the behavior of lottery winners. Their basic finding was that large gains induced a reduction in labor force participation, but the magnitude was small in the population, although larger among those of retirement age. The age difference is very plausible, in that many workers approaching retirement age may be on the margin of working or retiring, so that a positive wealth shock could induce retirement.

Younger workers are likely to be far from the margin. Furthermore, a given wealth shock would represent a greater increase in the fraction of the rest-of-lifetime resources of older workers, so the effect should be greater.

A second approach is based on inheritances. Holtz-Eakin, Joulfaian, and Rosen (1993) used 1982 and 1986 IRS tax records on inheritances and income to estimate the effect of large wealth gains on labor force participation. Based on their estimates, we calculate that a wealth gain of about $300,000 would reduce participation by about seven percentage points. Joulfaian and Wilhelm (1994) used the PSID to estimate the effects of inheritances on labor supply, but they found substantially smaller effects than Holtz-Eakin, Joulfaian, and Rosen.

Cheng and French (2000) used the estimates based on the lottery findings and on the Holtz-Eakin, Joulfaian, and Rosen findings on inheritances to calculate the effects of the stock market gains between December 31, 1994, and December 31, 1999. They estimated that about two-thirds of the gain in the stock market over that time period was unanticipated. From that estimate, along with the behavioral responses due to lotteries and inheritances, they calculated that labor force participation among those fifty-five to sixty-four years old was about 1.1 percentage points lower than it would have been in the absence of the stock market run-up. While this is a carefully done and useful study, it is based on many constructed variables and the samples in the underlying studies are small, especially for the lottery study.

The third approach for finding the effects of the stock market boom on retirement is based on HRS data on actual retirement or expected retirement.

Sevak (2002) compared the retirement rates of those with DC pension plans with those with DB pension plans in 1992 and again in 1998.[2] The thinking is that those with DC plans had windfall gains from the stock market run-up whereas those with DB plans did not have such gains, or at least did not within the plans. Indeed, Sevak reports substantial increases in the value of DC plans during the 1990s, as do Cheng and French. She found that in 1998, DC plan holders had retirement rates about seven percentage points higher than DB plan holders compared with the differential in 1992, and interpreted the difference to be due to the increase in value of DC holdings. While the results have plausibility and are in accord with the general aim of this chapter, we have some reservations based on the very substantial increase in the fraction of the population with DC plans: in 1992 about 38 percent of men in the HRS population in the relevant age range (fifty-five to sixty) had a DC plan, but in 1998 about 56 percent had a DC plan. Similarly, the percentage of men with a DB plan only fell from

---

2. The measure of retirement is a self-report about retirement, not actual labor force participation.

38 percent to 25 percent. Such a large compositional change means that there could be other factors in the higher retirement rates: for example, if those with a marginal attachment to the labor force were the same type of people who acquired DC pensions between 1992 and 1998, the compositional changes would be the correct explanation for the retirement difference, not the run-up in the values of DC plans.

Hurd and Reti (2001) conducted an analysis based on four waves of the HRS (1992, 1994, 1996, and 1998). Their measure of anticipated retirement is the subjective probability of working full time past age sixty-two, which we discuss at length later. They compared the change in anticipated retirement of stockholders versus nonstockholders. They found no difference in the change. Their study has a number of limitations, however. First, there may be a time lag between stock price changes and changes in retirement plans, because people often take time to adjust to new situations.[3] Perhaps such changes in retirement plans had not taken place by 1998. Second, the gains in the stock market accelerated after 1998, so possibly the gains observed by Hurd and Reti were not yet large enough to induce substantial changes in behavior. Third, Hurd and Reti imposed no structure on their estimation, yet theory suggests that people in differing economic circumstances or with differing characteristics would have been affected differently. For example, if most of the wealth gain is concentrated among the very well-to-do, there may be little change in average retirement behavior even though average wealth increased substantially. Fourth, Hurd and Reti only studied wealth change in posttax accounts and had no control for pension wealth. But wealth in pretax accounts such as DC plans is substantial, and for many may be a more important determinant of retirement than wealth in posttax accounts. Furthermore, some who do not have stocks in posttax accounts may have had gains in pretax accounts, which would blur the differences between the two groups.

Coronado and Perozek (2003) found an effect of stock market holdings, but they used a different measure of anticipated retirement than Hurd and Reti—the expected retirement age. They compared the expected retirement age as stated in 1992 with the actual retirement age as observed in 1998. This measure is more difficult to use than the subjective probability of working because of fairly high rates of nonresponse, because of right censoring when comparing it with actual retirement, and because some workers say they will never retire. Right censoring is particularly difficult: for example, by 1998 among those retired, 50 percent had retired earlier than their expected retirement age as stated in 1992 but just 18 percent had retired later. This difference indicates substantial censoring: many of them who eventually will retire later than expected had not yet retired by 1998.

---

3. For example, Imbens, Rubin, and Sacerdote report a lag of several years between winning the lottery and changes in labor supply.

A positive aspect of their paper is that Coronado and Perozek included measures of pension wealth, which perhaps was responsible for their finding an effect.

Khitatrakun (2004) based an analysis on the expected retirement age. He made an advance over previous studies based on expected retirement by controlling for right censoring and for stock market wealth and other important determinants of retirement that could mitigate a wealth effect. He found a significant reduction in expected retirement or actual retirement among those who had substantial stock market wealth and who did not have a defined benefits pension plan.[4] For example, those with stock holdings in the top 25 percent revised downward their expected retirement age or actually retired about eleven months earlier than anticipated.[5] These results are suggestive of a measurable effect in the part of the population that experienced an important gain in wealth.

Based on data from the HRS, the CPS, and the SCF, Coile and Levine (2004) conclude that few households have enough stock wealth that the variation in stock prices is likely to have a noticeable effect on average labor force participation rates. Indeed, they find no evidence that changes in the stock market had a measurable effect on participation.

In summary, there were large changes in wealth for part of the preretirement population, and at least some of the wealth change was likely unanticipated. Their behavior in the waves of the HRS following the large changes can be compared with the behavior of respondents who had no such wealth changes. Whether there will be differences and whether they can be attributed to a windfall wealth effect will depend on whether the wealth changes were anticipated. But there is a considerable literature that takes the gains to be at least partially unexpected. For example, Poterba (2000) states that "The evidence suggests that the rising stock market has surely contributed to rising consumer spending in the 1990s."[6] Were the increases fully anticipated, economic theory would not call for any change in consumption. If consumption responds to stock gains, the theory suggests that retirement would also respond.

4.2   Wealth in the HRS population

Our study population will be the original HRS cohorts born in 1931 to 1941 and observed in 1992 and every two years until 2002, and the

4. Restricting the sample to those lacking a DB plan for these estimations was done under the argument that DB plans restrict freedom about when to retire, so that a stock gain would have little effect on expected or actual retirement.

5. However, the result is mainly due to the 1992 to 1994 and 1994 to 1996 waves. These were not the waves of large stock market gains, which suggests that factors other than the stock market may have been responsible.

6. See also Juster, Lupton, Smith, and Stafford (1999) and Parker (1999).

Table 4.1   **Average income and wealth (thousands) of age-eligible respondents, cross-section.**

Wave	N	Total household income	Total wealth	Financial	Housing	Stock	Number stock owners	Percent stock owners
1	9,769	46.1	206.6	47.3	60.6	18.7	3281	33.6
2	8,844	50.5	238.9	60.4	67.4	25.6	3181	36.0
3	8,467	53.9	264.7	70.4	72.5	36.0	3071	36.3
4	11,191	60.5	301.3	85.2	83.8	49.0	4332	38.7
5	10,584	63.1	361.8	103.5	97.0	62.2	4244	40.1
6	10,284	61.3	374.0	97.3	110.0	49.2	3868	37.6

Source: Authors' calculations, based on HRS.

Note: Financial wealth, measured in nominal dollars, is the sum of the holdings of stocks, checking and savings accounts, bonds, certificates of deposit, and other, minus debt. See table 4.3 for detailed listings.

War Baby cohorts born in 1942 to 1947 and observed in 1998, 2000, and 2002.

Table 4.1 shows cross-section income, wealth, and some components of wealth, all measured at the household level. The unusual increase in income at wave 4 is due to the induction of the War Baby cohort into the HRS in 1998. They were fifty-one to fifty-six at the time and had higher average income than the original HRS cohort. Income reached a maximum in wave 5, when the average age of the HRS cohort was about sixty-two, and then began to decline as retirement accelerated. Wealth increased by 10 to 15 percent per wave until wave 5, when it increased by about 20 percent. There was a large increase in financial wealth and stock wealth between waves 4 and 5. The increase is partly the result of the boom in the stock market.

We define stock ownership either to be direct ownership outside the pension system or ownership in a defined contribution (DC) pension. In the HRS, respondents are asked whether they (or their spouse) own any stocks or mutual funds. Respondents with DC pensions are asked whether any of the DC balance is invested in stocks. Although there was an increase in the percentage of the cohort holding stocks, from about 34 percent in wave 1 to 40 percent in wave 4, the primary cause of the increase in stock wealth was gains in the value of stocks per household, not in the number of owners. Housing wealth increased at a rate somewhat higher than the rate of increase of consumer prices, which was about 2 percent per year over each two-year period.

The change from wave to wave in cross-section income and wealth is not necessarily the average change experienced by individuals in the cohort because of cohort effects, differential mortality, and differential sample attrition by socioeconomic stratum. Table 4.2 controls for cohort effects and changes in composition by following the same individuals over each two-year panel comparison. For example, we observe data on 8,805 age-eligible

Table 4.2   **Average income and wealth (thousands) of age-eligible respondents, panel.**

Wave	N	Total household income	Total wealth	Financial	Housing	Stock	Number stock owners	Percent stock owners
				All				
1	8,805	46.8	209.0	48.3	60.8	19.4	3061	34.8
2	8,805	50.5	238.9	60.6	67.5	25.7	3167	36.0
2	8,066	51.3	240.2	61.4	67.6	25.7	2986	37.0
3	8,066	54.1	266.0	70.9	72.2	36.1	2969	36.8
3	7,732	54.6	272.0	72.5	73.6	37.3	2874	37.2
4	7,732	54.9	314.3	90.8	87.1	51.1	2814	36.4
4	10,202	60.8	308.5	87.4	85.3	50.0	4044	39.6
5	10,202	63.2	365.5	104.5	97.5	62.9	4127	40.5
5	9,703	64.3	370.4	105.9	99.2	64.5	3985	41.1
6	9,703	61.6	373.2	98.4	111.1	49.8	3716	38.3
				Stock owners in both waves				
1	2,417	70.0	395.5	126.1	91.8	64.3	2417	100.0
2	2,417	81.0	473.9	156.0	111.7	81.7	2417	100.0
2	2,401	81.5	457.3	151.6	107.7	78.3	2401	100.0
3	2,401	85.6	520.0	185.4	111.7	112.2	2401	100.0
3	2,258	87.0	536.2	187.6	118.0	111.8	2258	100.0
4	2,258	89.6	651.4	242.4	149.0	156.7	2258	100.0
4	3,219	96.3	588.8	224.2	123.9	144.9	3219	100.0
5	3,219	103.4	704.1	260.0	148.6	178.7	3219	100.0
5	2,943	106.0	741.2	276.0	157.7	189.1	2943	100.0
6	2,943	101.3	734.9	246.4	177.5	148.6	2943	100.0
				Stock owners in neither wave				
1	4,994	32.2	106.3	11.8	42.1	0.0	0	0.0
2	4,994	32.7	110.5	14.9	45.5	0.0	0	0.0
2	4,512	33.4	111.5	14.2	42.7	0.0	0	0.0
3	4,512	34.8	118.9	13.0	47.9	0.0	0	0.0
3	4,302	34.1	118.9	12.7	48.0	0.0	0	0.0
4	4,302	34.0	122.6	13.5	52.8	0.0	0	0.0
4	5,250	37.9	123.7	11.7	51.7	0.0	0	0.0
5	5,250	37.0	142.3	16.4	57.9	0.0	0	0.0
5	4,945	37.0	143.0	15.9	58.5	0.0	0	0.0
6	4,945	36.6	154.3	19.5	67.4	0.0	0	0.0
				Entrants into stock owning				
1	750	53.9	215.9	27.1	74.7	0.0	0	0.0
2	750	59.3	312.2	73.2	80.8	38.0	750	100.0
2	568	61.0	264.3	49.6	82.7	0.0	0	0.0
3	568	66.7	345.6	82.0	94.3	37.9	568	100.0
3	556	65.0	291.7	35.9	83.6	0.0	0	0.0
4	556	73.3	447.2	128.1	97.2	73.7	556	100.0
4	908	59.3	274.2	33.6	87.4	0.0	0	0.0
5	908	74.6	444.2	123.5	114.4	72.7	908	100.0
5	773	64.6	374.0	37.5	135.7	0.0	0	0.0
6	773	68.6	444.9	114.7	127.0	60.0	773	100.0

Table 4.2   (continued)

Wave	N	Total household income	Total wealth	Financial	Housing	Stock	Number stock owners	Percent stock owners
				Exiters from stock owning				
1	644	64.4	297.1	63.6	73.9	23.6	644	100.0
2	644	64.2	266.9	42.6	56.7	0.0	0	0.0
2	585	55.8	318.1	66.4	80.5	33.6	585	100.0
3	585	61.3	281.0	36.7	76.4	0.0	0	0.0
3	616	70.1	354.9	100.8	79.9	58.7	616	100.0
4	616	56.2	296.8	41.6	90.1	0.0	0	0.0
4	825	69.8	428.9	94.8	146.3	52.9	825	100.0
5	825	60.8	378.6	37.8	131.1	0.0	0	0.0
5	1,042	76.0	399.5	103.4	100.2	66.2	1042	100.0
6	1,042	62.2	336.8	43.2	118.6	0.0	0	0.0

Source: Authors' calculations, based on HRS.

Note: Financial wealth, measured in nominal dollars, is the sum of the holdings of stocks, checking and savings accounts, bonds, certificates of deposit, and other, minus debt. See table 4.3 for detailed listings.

persons over the two-year period between waves 1 and 2. The income of the households of those respondents increased from about $46.8 thousand to $50.5 thousand, an increase of about 8 percent. This compares with a cross-section two-year change from $46.1 to $50.5 (table 4.1). Overall, the change in the panel is about the same as the change in the cross-section, which shows that differential mortality and differential sample attrition are not very important determinants of the characteristics of the HRS sample.[7] As far as the wealth components are concerned, they also changed in the panel in about the same way as in the cross-section.

The second panel of table 4.2 shows income and wealth of those who were owners of stocks in both of two consecutive waves. A comparison of income in wave 2 among the 2,417 who survived in the panel from wave 1 to wave 2 ($81.0) with the income in wave 2 of the 2,401 who survived from wave 2 to wave 3 ($81.5) shows that the panel aspects of the income data are not very important at the aggregate level. Similar comparisons across the other waves lead to the same conclusion.

The levels of total wealth and financial wealth of stockholders were much greater than average wealth. For example, in wave 1 stock owners had total wealth of about $395,500 whereas average wealth was just $209,000. Furthermore, the growth of wealth between the waves was much

7. Although differential morality is rather strong, the total number of deaths is too small to have much influence on the sample characteristics.

greater, especially between waves 3 and 4 and 4 and 5. Possibly more relevant than the rate is the absolute level of the wealth of stockholders: wealth increased by about $115,000 between waves 3 and 4, and by $116,000 between waves 4 and 5. Only a relatively small fraction of the increase could have come from saving out of income, because the two-year total income was only about $175,000 between waves 3 and 4 and $200,000 between waves 4 and 5. This relationship between wealth increase and income is in sharp contrast to the wealth change of the entire sample: for everyone, wealth increased by $42,000, yet total income was about $55,000 per year, or $110,000 over the two years between waves. Thus, for stockholders, the achieved saving rate out of pretax income between waves 3 and 4 including capital gains was about 65 percent, whereas for the entire sample it was about 39 percent.

Among stock owners, wealth in housing was considerably higher than average, and the growth rate was somewhat higher over the six waves, about 115 percent compared with 80 percent for everyone. Whether housing wealth increased by converting some of the stock gains to housing would require study of the detailed transactions. In any event, the gains are only modestly larger among stockholders: for example, between waves 3 and 4, the housing wealth of stockholders increased by 26 percent compared with a gain of 18 percent among nonstockholders.

Among stockholders in both waves, stock wealth increased between waves 3 and 4 by about $45,000, or 40 percent. Over this same approximate period the New York Stock Exchange Composite Index increased by 57 percent.[8] We do not know whether to attribute the difference in the rates of return to difference in portfolios or to a rebalancing of portfolios.

The third panel shows the financial situation of those who did not own stock in either of two successive waves. For example, 4,994 persons were in households that did not own stock either in wave 1 or wave 2. It is apparent that this group had much lower levels of income and of all types of assets, including housing, and that the rates of growth of assets were approximately zero. Furthermore, this is the largest group of those considered here, about 60 percent of the sample.

The next panel shows income and wealth of those who did not own stock in a baseline wave but did own stock in the succeeding wave. The average income in this group was mostly higher than of the entire sample, and considerably higher than the income of those who were not stock owners, but it was lower than the income of stock owners in both waves. This group had large wealth increases, especially between waves 3 and 4, and 4 and 5: about $160,000, even more than among stock owners in both waves. Even among this group, which had very large wealth gains, little if any was put

---

8. June 1, 1996 to June 1, 1998.

into housing. For example, even though total wealth increased by about 53 percent between waves 3 and 4, average housing wealth increased by about 16 percent. The gain is similar to those who do not hold stocks: their housing wealth gain was 10 percent.

The final panel of table 4.2 shows the financial information of those who owned stock in a baseline wave but not in the succeeding wave. Thus, 664 persons were in households that exited from the stock market between waves 1 and 2. The overall pattern is one of fairly high wealth levels at the baseline wave but substantially lower wealth at the next wave. Thus, ownership of stock predicts high wealth in cross-section, but eliminating stock from the portfolio predicts a fall in wealth. Furthermore, the decline in wealth was greater than the decline in the value of stockholdings. For example, between waves 1 and 2, stock wealth declined by about $24,000 but total wealth declined by about $30,000. Housing wealth declined particularly between waves 1 and 2. Overall, these figures suggest some financial distress, leading the households to sell off their stockholdings and even reduce their housing wealth.

In summary, table 4.2 shows very active wealth dynamics, with some groups gaining considerable wealth and some groups losing considerable wealth. From the point of view of wealth inequality, the groups with the highest initial wealth had the greatest wealth gains, both in absolute terms and relative terms. These results suggest increasing wealth inequality over time in the HRS cohort.

Because of the very large wealth changes between waves 4 and 5, we show in table 4.3 the detailed components of wealth in the panel over those waves. Among all households, the value of IRAs, housing, and stock wealth increased notably. The large increase in IRAs was probably at least partly due to the stock market boom, but the HRS does not have very good information about the composition of IRAs.[9] The other components of wealth were little changed.

Among those who owned stocks in both waves, the value of IRAs, stock wealth, and housing increased. Holdings of CDs, checking and saving and bonds changed very little, suggesting little rebalancing of portfolios in response to the stock market gains.

Among those who were not stock owners, average holdings of each type of wealth was small, with the exception of housing. Furthermore, except for a 37 percent increase in IRAs, none of the wealth components increased substantially. While this group, which constitutes about 60 percent of our sample, has rather low levels of financial assets, it includes many people who are still in their fifties and still have time to save before

---

9. From 1998 on HRS asks whether an IRA held stocks. If so, whether the IRA is held mostly in interest-bearing assets, mostly in stocks or about half in each.

Table 4.3   Wealth and wealth components, waves 4 and 5 (thousand)

	All $N = 10,202$			Stock owners both waves $N = 2,593$			Stock owners neither wave $N = 5,899$			Stock owners Wave 4 only $N = 877$			Stock owners Wave 3 only $N = 833$		
	Wave 4	Wave 5	Change	Wave 4	Wave 5	Change	Wave 4	Wave 5	Change	Wave 4	Wave 5	Change	Wave 4	Wave 5	Change
Bond	6.8	6.0	-0.7	20.9	17.2	-3.7	0.8	0.6	-0.1	5.8	11.8	6.0	6.1	3.4	-2.7
Business	32.2	37.7	5.5	57.3	68.1	10.8	17.5	16.3	-1.2	28.2	53.7	25.6	62.2	77.2	15.0
CD	7.4	9.2	1.8	14.3	18.0	3.7	3.7	5.2	1.5	8.1	10.7	2.6	10.5	8.3	-2.2
Check	16.9	19.3	2.5	33.2	35.7	2.4	8.7	10.8	2.1	18.9	25.7	6.8	21.5	22.3	0.8
Debt	4.4	3.6	-0.8	3.2	2.9	-0.3	4.5	3.9	-0.7	4.6	3.9	-0.7	7.2	4.1	-3.1
IRA	46.9	64.0	17.1	102.7	142.2	39.5	17.7	24.3	6.6	56.2	76.8	20.6	70.6	88.1	17.4
Nethouse	85.3	97.5	12.2	133.6	161.7	28.2	53.1	59.8	6.8	96.2	123.8	27.6	152.2	136.4	-15.8
Real estate	41.3	46.1	4.8	82.3	93.4	11.1	17.1	20.6	3.5	62.7	74.1	11.4	61.9	49.8	-12.1
Other	10.9	10.8	-0.1	27.5	23.6	-3.9	3.7	4.3	0.6	9.3	18.4	9.1	11.4	8.4	-3.0
Stock	50.0	62.9	12.9	173.5	216.2	42.7	0.0	0.0	0.0	0.0	91.9	91.9	72.3	0.0	-72.3
Transp	15.4	15.8	0.3	24.3	25.1	0.8	10.9	10.8	-0.1	17.1	19.5	2.3	18.5	17.9	-0.6
Total	308.5	365.5	57.0	666.3	798.4	132.1	128.6	148.9	20.3	298.0	502.6	204.6	480.1	407.7	-72.3

Source: Authors' calculations, based on HRS.

retirement. Furthermore, they are likely to be qualified for Social Security benefits, and some may anticipate pension income. However, because of the positive correlation between household wealth and pension eligibility, it is likely that many of the households in this group do not have rights to a pension.

Among new entrants to the stock market, there were very substantial gains in wealth. Aside from the increase in stock wealth, there were large increases in business wealth, IRAs, and housing.

Those who left the stock market between waves had large declines in housing and real estate as well as in stocks. The notable exception to the overall fall in wealth was an increase in IRAs. Apparently IRAs were shielded from the economic distress that is evident from the large wealth decline.

4.3   Labor Force Participation in the HRS

Work status is derived from a self-report: whether working for pay, hours worked, and a self-classification as to retired, partially retired, or not retired. From this, people are coded as working full-time, part-time, unemployed, partly retired, retired, or not in the labor force. A combination of the first four categories corresponds to the current population survey (CPS) definition of labor force participation.

Across the six waves of the HRS, we observe a decline in the percentage of people working full time and part time (table 4.4), with a small up-tick between waves 3 and 4 because of the inclusion of the younger War Baby cohort, which is reflected in the increase in sample size. The percentage of the sample retired increased across waves for both full and partial retirement. Labor force participation declined with age (fig. 4.1). When compared with the labor force participation rates from the CPS, the HRS indicates slightly higher participation rates, although the trend line is mirrored (not shown). Labor force participation at each age was relatively constant for all interview years of the HRS (not shown). An exception is labor force participation by those aged approximately sixty-two to sixty-seven, where participation increased especially between waves 4 and 5. At the gross level of population participation this increase is at odds with a substantial stock market wealth effect.

Table 4.5 shows transitions from full-time work. About 79 percent of full-time workers in wave 1 were working full time in wave 2. With the exception of 1998, when the War Baby cohort was added, in each successive wave the transition rate to full-time work decreased and the rates of retirement increased. There was some part-time work, but the dominant route to retirement among full-time workers was to complete withdrawal from the labor force.

Table 4.4   Labor force status

	1992		1994		1996		1998		2000		2002	
	N	Percent	N	Percent	N	Percent	N	Percent	N	Percent	N	Percent
Full time	5,394	55	4,333	49	3,592	42	4,856	43	3,921	37	3,070	30
Part time	989	10	832	9	612	7	861	8	754	7	659	6
Unemployed	254	3	216	2	134	2	141	1	127	1	135	1
Partly retired	330	3	444	5	621	7	794	7	865	8	950	9
Retired	1,308	13	1,861	21	2,273	27	2,870	26	3,305	31	3,997	39
Not in labor force, not retired	1,494	15	1,158	13	1,235	15	1,669	15	1,612	15	1,473	14
Total	9,769	100	8,844	100	8,467	100	11,191	100	10,584	100	10,284	100

Source: Authors' calculations, based on HRS.

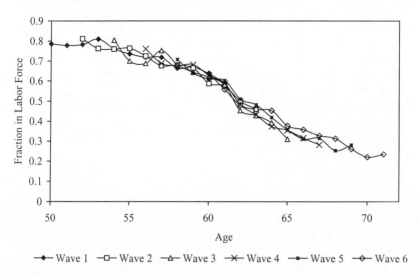

Fig. 4.1   Labor force participation rates, cross-section

Table 4.5   **Transition rates from full-time work**

		Employment status in following wave					
						All	
	Full	Part		Partly	Not in		
Baseline	time	time	Unemployed	retired	labor force	*N*	Percent
1992	79.3	5.4	1.9	3.0	10.4	4,903	100
1994	76.0	4.6	1.2	4.9	13.3	3,992	100
1996	74.0	4.5	1.2	5.7	14.6	3,302	100
1998	75.4	5.0	1.1	4.7	13.9	4,462	100
2000	70.1	5.8	1.9	6.0	16.3	3,644	100

Source: Authors' calculations, based on HRS.

4.4   Anticipated Retirement

A major strength of the HRS is that it asks about anticipated retirement. This is especially important for this research, as we can study the change in anticipated retirement and compare actual retirement with anticipated. We will base anticipated retirement on the subjective probability of working past age sixty-two. It was asked of all workers in the following way:

> Thinking about work generally and not just your present job, what do you think are the chances that you will be working full time after you reach age sixty-two?

The respondents had already been told to evaluate their chances "On a scale of 0 to 100 where 0 equals absolutely no chance and 100 equals absolutely certain . . ." If the chances of working after age sixty-two were positive, the worker was asked about the chances of working after age sixty-five. Because of the high rates of retirement at or near sixty-two, we will base our measure of anticipated retirement on the chances of working after age sixty-two, which we call P62.

In waves 2 to 6 the subjective probability question was asked on a 101-point schedule. In wave 1 scaling was on an eleven-point scale, 0–10. We have analyzed the change in P62 from waves 1 to 2 and found an unexplained decline in P62 among those who worked in both waves. We found no declines in other waves and the decline is not according to the laws of probability: among those who remain in the labor force, P62 should increase in panel as it does in other waves. Because of this unexplained decline we will not make comparisons between waves 1 and 2. For the purposes of this chapter, dropping this comparison is not important, because the stock market boom did not begin until approximately wave 3 in 1996.

As far as the validity of P62 is concerned, it has been shown to vary in cross-section with variables that induce retirement or are related to retirement. For example, eligibility for a DB benefit before age sixty-two is associated with actual retirement prior to age sixty-two, and it reduces P62 (Hurd and McGarry 1993). The implication is that P62 will predict actual retirement, and, indeed, it has considerable predictive power for retirement in the HRS panel (Hurd 1999). While these results indicate that P62 has validity in a qualitative sense, in this chapter we would like to establish the validity of P62 as a predictor of the quantity of full-time work at age sixty-two. To do that, we would like to answer two main questions: Does P62 predict continuation of workers in full-time work? Is it properly scaled; that is, does it predict the level of full-time work at or shortly after age sixty-two?

The first question, whether it predicts continuation in full-time work, can be addressed by finding whether those with lower subjective probabilities tend to leave full-time work before age sixty-two at a higher rate than those with higher subjective probabilities. Even if the subjective probability of working past sixty-two is not properly scaled, it could still be an adequate predictor of continuation in full-time work until age sixty-two.

Table 4.6 shows the average P62 as reported in earlier waves as a function of work status in later waves. For example, 193 respondents who were age sixty-two in wave 6 (2002) and working full time reported an average P62 of 58.2 percent in wave 2 when they were approximately age fifty-four. They can be compared with 291 respondents who were not working full time in wave 6: they reported an average P62 of 37.3 percent in wave 2. This and other similar comparisons show that P62 is a rather consistent predictor of working full time after age sixty-two, even when assessed up to eight years earlier.

The second question—whether P62 is properly scaled, could in principle

Table 4.6   *P62* as a qualitative predictor of labor force participation: mean *P62* by age and work status in 2002. Panel data, age-eligible cohort

Baseline wave	Age in 2002	Full time in 2002		Not working full time in 2002	
		Observations	Mean P62	Observations	Mean P62
Wave 2	61	252	55.8	239	36.0
	62	193	58.2	291	37.3
	63	140	61.9	294	37.7
	64	143	61.1	262	33.9
Wave 3	61	267	58.5	209	34.4
	62	187	57.1	257	36.3
	63	147	62.2	285	34.0
	64	147	63.7	245	40.6
Wave 4	61	263	57.1	191	35.4
	62	194	65.8	241	31.7
	63	140	67.4	250	38.1
	64	149	70.1	221	41.1
Wave 5	61	260	63.8	152	36.7
	62	191	74.7	188	40.2
	63	135	82.1	203	40.2
	64	34	75.6	29	47.9

Source: Authors' calculations, based on HRS.

be answered by comparing the average of P62 in some population with the average rate of full-time work when that population reaches sixty-two. This would be a valid comparison, because the expected participation rate of each individual at age sixty-two is just P62, so the average population participation rate would be approximately the average P62.[10] There are, however, several obstacles to carrying out this comparison. First, even if each individual correctly states his or her probability of working past sixty-two, intervening events, such as an unexpected change in health status, will cause a revision in P62. By itself, such a revision will not cause a divergence between the average of the subjective probabilities and the average population rate of working full time after age 62. If a population were fully informed of the probabilities of events that could influence retirement, these contingencies would be included in the calculation of P62. Thus, under rational expectations in a stationary environment, the average P62 should accurately predict the average rate of full-time work after age sixty-two. However, if there were unanticipated events that affect the entire population, the average of the subjective probability of working past sixty-two would

10. Actual participation at age sixty-two is a binomial random variable that takes the value of 1 with probability $P62$ and the value of 0 with probability $1-P62$. Then, the expected value of the average of the random variables will be the average of the $P62$.

no longer predict the average rate of working full time after sixty-two. Such events might be an unanticipated improvement in health in the population or an unanticipated increase or decrease in wealth, such as that which resulted from the stock market gains during the 1990s and subsequent losses.

We can test for proper scaling in two ways. First, we observe part of the population in, say, wave 2 that will reach age sixty-two in some future wave. The average P62 among workers in wave 2 should approximate the fraction of those same workers who are working full time at age sixty-two. Similar calculations can be made for other waves. Unfortunately, the query about P62 is somewhat ambiguous, and could be interpreted as working full time shortly after the sixty-second birthday or by the end of the year in which the person was sixty-two years old. Our response to the ambiguity will be to find the fraction of sixty-two-year-olds working full time and the fraction of sixty-three-year-olds working full-time.

Table 4.7 shows averages of P62 and actual rates of working full-time at ages sixty-two and sixty-three. The averages of P62 were calculated over workers in waves 2, 3, 4, or 5 who at the time of interview were less than age sixty-two; the actual rates of full-time work were calculated over data from

Table 4.7   P62 as a quantitative predictor of labor force participation. Panel data, age-eligible cohort

Baseline wave	Age in 1996		Age in 1998		Age in 2000		Age in 2002	
	62	63	62	63	62	63	62	63
Wave 2								
Observations	347	322	420	371	416	411	484	434
Mean P62	51.3	54.9	45.5	51.2	46.9	41.9	45.6	45.5
Percent working full time	45.8	42.2	41.7	38.8	43.3	37.7	39.9	32.3
Wave 3								
Observations			391	274	392	394	444	432
Mean P62			49.9	60.7	50.1	45.9	45.0	43.6
Percent working full time			46.3	47.4	45.7	40.9	42.1	34.0
Wave 4								
Observations					370	313	435	390
Mean P62					51.5	53.9	46.9	48.6
Percent working full time					48.4	46.0	44.6	35.9
Wave 5								
Observations							379	338
Mean P62							57.6	57.0
Percent working full time							50.4	39.9

Source: Authors' calculations, based on HRS.

later waves of workers who had passed their sixty-second birthday. For example, we identified 347 people who were age sixty-two in wave 3 and who were working in wave 2 when they would have been approximately age sixty. In wave 2, their average subjective probability of working past sixty-two was 51.3 percent, yet just 45.8 percent were observed working full time when they were age sixty-two in wave 3. Similarly, we identified 322 people who were age sixty-three in wave 3 and were working in wave 2 when they would have been approximately age sixty-one. Their average subjective probability of working past sixty-two was 54.9 percent, but just 42.2 percent were actually working full time in wave 3. The divergence between P62 and the percentage working full time is much greater in the second column than in the first column because some left full-time work while age sixty-two. A comparison in the other waves between the average subjective probability of working past sixty-two and the actual rate of full-time work shows similar discrepancies: the average of the subjective probability is about 4.2 percentage points higher than the actual rate of full-time work at age sixty-two and about 10.3 percentage points higher than the rate at age sixty-three. We conclude that the most plausible target age is age sixty-two, and that the main reason for the difference between P62 and the rate of full-time work among respondents who are sixty-two is due to retirement shortly after reaching age sixty-two. Even so, the differences are small enough that they do not raise serious questions about the validity of the P62 measure. Of course, it is plausible that unanticipated macro-events caused the entire population to leave the labor force earlier than anticipated.

A second method of studying P62 for proper scaling is based on the population properties of P62 and how they evolve in the panel. The population properties of P62 are broadly of two types: successive cross-sections and panel. To see how they evolve, consider two extreme situations: in the first retirement is a completely controlled process with no uncertainty. At wave 1 all workers know their retirement ages, and if it is less than sixty-two, P62 is zero; if it is greater than sixty-two, P62 is 1. Between waves 1 and 2 some workers reach their retirement ages and retire. Under the assumption that no one reenters the labor force, the probability that the leavers would work past sixty-two is zero, but because they correctly knew they would be leaving the labor force between waves 1 and 2, they would have reported P62 to be zero in wave 1. Thus were we to assign P62 to be zero in wave 2, it would be unchanging in the panel over this group.

Those who remained in the labor force from wave 1 to 2 continue to anticipate retiring at the same age as in wave 1, so P62 is either zero or 1, as it was in wave 1. In panel the average P62 would be constant over this group. Therefore, the average P62 would be constant in panel when averaged over the population of both workers and leavers and the cross-section average would be the same in both waves. The cross-section average calculated only over workers would of necessity increase, because in wave 2 that average excludes the leavers and they all reported P62 to be zero in wave 1.

Now consider the other extreme, where retirement is completely stochastic—caused by a random health event or a random layoff. Under the assumption of rationality (workers know the probabilities of all events), P62 at time t given that someone is in the labor force would be calculated as

$$(1) \quad (P62_t | LF_t) = (P62_{t+1} | not\ LF_{t+1})P(not\ LF_{t+1})$$
$$+ (P62_{t+1} | LF_{t+1})P(LF_{t+1}).$$

If

$$(P62_t | LF_t) < (P62_{t+1} | LF_{t+1})$$

then

$$(P62_{t+1} | not\ LF_{t+1}) < (P62_{t+1} | LF_{t+1}).$$

This relationship holds at the individual level, so that when P62 is averaged over those who are in the labor force both at t and at $t + 1$, P62 will increase in the panel.

The population average of P62 in wave $t + 1$ regardless of labor force status is

$$\frac{1}{n} \sum (P62_{t+1}) = \frac{1}{n} \sum [(P62_{t+1} | not\ LF_{t+1})P(not\ LF_{t+1})$$
$$+ (P62_{t+1} | LF_{t+1})P(LF_{t+1})]$$

But the terms on the right-hand side of this equation are the same as the right-hand side of (1), so that the average P62 is constant in panel when calculated over the population, regardless of labor force status in $t + 1$. This implies that the cross-section average over the whole population will be unchanging.[11]

The average P62 over workers in cross-section will increase from wave to wave provided the average P62 reported in wave 1 by the leavers is the same or smaller than the average reported by stayers. This condition will hold provided P62 has explanatory power for retirement.

We would expect the actual situation to lie somewhere between the two extremes: some workers are quite sure of their retirement age because of pension provisions or tastes. Others have only weakly defined retirement preferences and wait for random events to unfold. Nonetheless, the predictions are the same: in a stable environment, average P62 should remain constant as a cohort ages. Even though new information may arrive at the individual level, causing individuals to reassess their own subjective prob-

---

11. Assuming no entry into or exit from the population.

ability, the revisions should roughly sum to zero, because individuals will have correctly forecast the average probabilities of the new information and the resulting revisions.

Were the probability of reentry to the labor force zero, it would be rather easy to test for panel consistency of average P62. We would first find the average over workers in wave t. Under stationarity

$$\overline{P62_t} = \frac{1}{n_1} \sum P62_t = \frac{1}{n_t} \sum P62_{t+1},$$

where there are n_t workers at t. Then

$$\frac{1}{n_t} \sum P62_{t+1} = \frac{1}{n_t} \left[\sum (P62_{t+1} | LF_{t+1}) + \sum (P62_{t+1} | not\ LF_{t+1}) \right].$$

Under the assumption that

$$\sum (P62_{t+1} | not\ LF_{t+1}) = 0$$

the observed average over the working population would be

(2) $$\overline{P62_t} = \frac{n_{t+1}}{n_t} \frac{1}{n_{t+1}} \sum (P62_{t+1} | LF_{t+1}) = \frac{n_{t+1}}{n_t} \times \overline{P62_{t+1}}.$$

If $(n_{t+1})/(n_t)$, which is the retention rate in the labor force, is less than 1, as it would be among those in their fifties, the average P62 will increase with age. A test of stationarity (with rational expectations) is that the average of P62 among those in the labor force evolves according to (2).

It is likely, however, that some who leave the labor force will return; hence the probability of working past sixty-two among those who left the labor force between a baseline wave and the succeeding wave is not zero. Because P62 is only asked of those who are working, we have no respondent reports by those who left the labor force on the probability of working past sixty-two. The HRS does, however, ask nonworkers about reentry into the labor force (date not specified), which should be powerfully related to their probability of working at age sixty-two. Therefore we estimate P62 among those who are working at wave t but have left the labor force by wave $t + 1$ as follows.

We want P62$_t$ for the population that was working at t (and reported P62$_t$) but was not working at $t + 1$. Our method is to fit a predictive model of working at age sixty-two over the population that was working at age a but not working at age $a + 1$. The covariates in this model are age and the response to the following question:

P016 (On this same 0 to 100 scale), what are the chances that you will be working for pay at some time in the future?

The left-hand variable is an indicator variable for whether the person is observed to be working at age sixty-two. For example, someone age fifty-

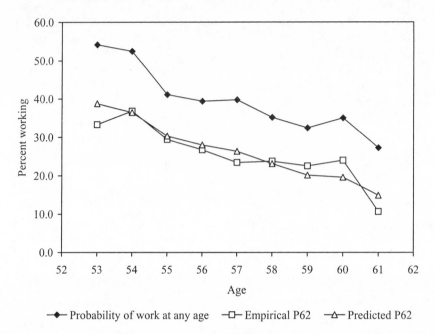

Fig. 4.2   Actual and fitted probability of working at 62

five and working in 1994 reported P62, but was not working in 1996. In the HRS such a person would be asked about the probability of working at some time in the future. In HRS 2002, when he was sixty-three, we observe whether this person was working in 2001 when he turned sixty-two. If so, the left-hand variable takes the value of 1, otherwise 0. The probability for working sometime in the future has high predictive power for working at age sixty-two: the estimated coefficient and standard error are 0.42 and 0.03, respectively. The interpretation is that a change in the subjective probability of working for pay from 0 to 100 will change the predicted probability of working full time after the age of sixty-two by 42 percentage points. We use this fitted equation to estimate $P62_{t+1}$ for the population that was working at t (and reported $P62_t$) but was not working at $t + 1$.

Figure 4.2 shows the fitted and actual probabilities of working at age sixty-two among those in the labor force at t but not in the labor force at $t + 1$, and the average values of P016.

Having calculated P62 for those who leave the labor force between wave t and $t + 1$, we can find the panel change in P62 for all who were in the labor force at wave t whether or not they remained in the labor force to wave $t + 1$.

Table 4.8 shows the results of our calculations of P62 in the panel. Among the 752 who were age fifty-four to fifty-five in wave 3, were work-

Table 4.8 Average subjective probability of working after age 62; panel among those working at time t

Age and labor force status in wave $t+1$	Wave 2 to 3			Wave 3 to 4			Wave 4 to 5			Wave 5 to 6		
	N	Wave t	Wave $t+1$	N	Wave t	Wave $t+1$	N	Wave t	Wave $t+1$	N	Wave t	Wave $t+1$
Age 52–53												
Not in labor force							43	34.3	39.2			
In labor force							509	48.5	46.5			
All							552	47.4	45.9			
Age 54–55												
Not in labor force	81	31.3	31.4	72	28.9	28.1	64	28.3	33.0	53	29.3	33.7
In labor force	671	47.4	46.6	688	48.0	48.2	490	45.9	47.1	416	47.8	48.9
All	752	45.7	45.0	760	46.2	46.3	554	43.9	45.4	469	45.7	47.2
Age 56–57												
Not in labor force	107	28.7	26.6	115	31.5	21.1	73	22.8	23.4	80	29.5	28.9
In labor force	900	46.0	45.7	787	46.9	47.7	596	47.9	49.1	445	48.7	49.5
All	1007	44.2	43.6	902	45.0	44.3	669	45.1	46.3	525	45.8	46.3
Age 58–59												
Not in labor force	109	32.0	22.0				118	30.0	25.1	102	33.3	20.5
In labor force	765	46.4	48.3				747	48.3	52.9	481	51.0	52.7
All	874	44.6	45.0				865	45.8	49.1	583	47.9	47.1
Age 60–61												
Not in labor force	143	28.2	17.4	112	25.8	14.6	128	27.3	18.0	123	36.4	18.9
In labor force	689	50.2	55.8	676	51.7	53.2	674	52.3	58.6	626	55.0	56.3
All	832	46.4	49.2	788	48.0	47.7	802	48.3	52.1	749	51.9	50.1
All ages												
Not in labor force	440	29.8	23.4	299	28.8	20.3	426	28.1	25.3	358	32.9	23.8
In labor force	3025	47.4	48.8	2151	48.8	49.6	3016	48.8	51.4	1968	51.1	52.3
All	3465	45.1	45.6	2450	46.3	46.0	3442	46.2	48.2	2326	48.3	47.9

Source: Authors' calculations, based on HRS.

Note: Wave t refers to one of waves 2–5; wave $t+1$ refers to one of waves 3–6. Subjective probability of working after age 62 in wave t and in wave $t+1$ is either reported by those still in the labor force or calculated for those not in the labor force.

ing in wave 2, and reported a value of P62 in that wave, the average value of P62 was 45.7 percent. This average is composed of 81 reports by those who left the labor force between wave 2 and 3 and of 671 by those who remained in the labor force. The average P62 of those who left was just 31.3 percent in wave 2. This shows again that P62 has considerable predictive power for labor force participation even at ages considerably less than sixty-two. Taking possible reentry into account, for that group we calculate P62 in wave 3 to be 31.4 percent. The average in wave 2 of those who remained in the labor force was 47.4 percent and the average in wave 3 was 46.6 percent. The overall average was 45.0 percent; therefore, the average probability of the cohort declined by 0.7 percentage points between the waves.

Because for this age group the predicted P62 in wave 3 among the leavers is about the same as their average in wave 2, stationarity in P62 requires that the average P62 of those who remained in the labor force also remain constant between the waves as it did.

Similar calculations for those who were fifty-six to fifty-seven in wave 3, and so forth show a sharply declining P62 by age among those who leave the labor force between the waves. This is mainly a consequence of the sharp decline in the probability of reentry, as shown in fig. 4.2. If workers knew the exact age at which they would retire, their reports of P62 would not change in the panel so that P62 would be constant among those who remained in the work force. If there are stochastic events that have positive probability of occurring and that can cause a worker to leave the labor force, the fact that a worker remained in the labor force should cause an upward revision in P62. Just as in a life table, survival for two years in the labor force increases the probability of survival in the labor force to any fixed age, such as sixty-two. We see this pattern in the age bands of fifty-eight to fifty-nine and sixty to sixty-one.

We cannot make similar calculations for those aged fifty-four to fifty-five in wave 4 because almost all of the age-eligibles were past that age by wave 4. For the other age groups, the patterns are similar, and for all ages taken together P62 was almost exactly constant across waves.

The War Babies were added to HRS in 1998 (wave 4). In most age bands the average P62 increased between waves 4 and 5.

At a broad level, the changes in P62 do not show any support for the hypothesis that the large capital gains, especially between waves 3 and 4, and 4 and 5 were used to finance early retirement or led to a reduction in P62. As shown in the last line of the table, the average change from wave 2 to 3 was 0.5, from wave 3 to 4 was –0.3, from wave 4 to 5 was 2.0, and from wave 5 to 6 was 0.4. The only substantial change was from wave 4 to 5, when the stock market increased sharply. A wealth effect would cause a reduction in P62 rather than an increase.

Table 4.9   Average wealth (thousands) of age-eligibles who are in the labor force at time *t* and report P62; panel

	N	Total household income	Total wealth	Financial	Housing	Stock	Number stock owners	Percent stock owners
Wave								
2	3,465	60.5	238.6	55.8	68.9	24.0	1,470	42.4
3	3,465	66.3	266.4	66.9	73.1	33.6	1,500	43.3
Wave								
3	2,450	69.7	268.8	63.8	74.8	32.7	1,092	44.6
4	2,450	72.5	339.9	96.5	100.1	54.2	1,101	44.9
Wave								
4	3,442	78.5	306.7	75.8	92.2	45.1	1,732	50.3
5	3,442	84.3	379.5	100.9	103.3	63.1	1,764	51.2
Wave								
5	2,326	89.8	380.2	103.5	103.9	68.7	1,288	55.4
6	2,326	88.5	381.0	96.9	118.6	54.3	1,203	51.7

Source: Authors' calculations, based on HRS.

4.5   Wealth Change and Retirement Probabilities

We can, of course, perform a much sharper test of our hypothesis by studying wealth change at a more disaggregated level. So, we divided the sample according to whether a household held stocks either directly or held them indirectly in DC pension plans.[12] Table 4.9 has financial information about our analytical sample. The sample is composed of those who were working and reported P62 in wave *t*, and either reported P62 in wave *t* + 1 or left the labor force, allowing us to calculate P62 as we described earlier.[13] The income levels of this group are considerably higher than for the entire HRS population as reported in table 4.2, especially in the later waves. For example, average incomes in table 4.9 in waves 3 and 4 were about $69.7 thousand and $72.5 thousand, whereas for the entire population they were $54.6 thousand and $54.9 thousand. The main reason for the difference is that everyone in table 4.9 was working at baseline.

Wealth increased very substantially between waves 3 and 4, and 4 and 5. As would be expected from the run-up in the stock market, wealth in stocks increased, with a corresponding increase in financial wealth. But the increase in financial wealth only accounted for about one-third to one-half

12. The HRS did not record stock ownership in IRAs prior to 1998, so we have not included such ownership.
13. The sample size varies across tables because of missing values and sample selection. For example, table 4.9 includes all age-eligibles, but table 4.8 includes only those in the specified age bands, which excludes some age-eligibles.

of the total increase; other important components were housing and business wealth (not shown separately). Between wave 5 and 6, stock wealth declined, and when contrasted with the growth in prior waves, the rate of decline was substantial: taking the average growth rate in stock wealth between waves 3 and 5 would predict wave 6 stock wealth of about $105,000 rather than the actual $54,300.

The rate of stock ownership is much higher than in table 4.2, partly a reflection of the higher wealth of workers and the strong positive correlation between wealth and the propensity to hold stocks. Also, the table includes stock ownership via DC plans.

In table 4.10 we show the changes in the probability of working past sixty-two that are associated with the large wealth changes. As discussed earlier, the relevant population in each baseline wave is the working population, selected to include those who report P62 and also selected to include those for whom we have a value (either reported by the respondent or calculated) of P62 in the succeeding wave. We call the baseline wave t and the succeeding wave $t + 1$. In waves 2 and 3 we observed 3,465 workers who satisfied these criteria (and for whom we had observations on household wealth, including their stock ownership status in both waves). Their average household wealth in wave t, which is wave 2 in this case, was $238,600, and their nominal wealth increased by 11.6% by wave $t + 1$ (wave 3). On average, P62 increased from 45.1 to 45.6. The average P62 in wave 3 is calculated over actual reports by those who remained in the labor force, and over our estimate of the probability of working past sixty-two among those who left the labor force between waves.

There were 1,206 respondents who were in households that owned stocks in both waves 2 and 3. These households had an average increase in wealth of 14.5 percent. Among the 1,701 respondents who did not own stocks in either wave, wealth increased by 5.2 percent. New entrants into stockholding had large wealth gains, and exiters from stockholding had almost constant nominal wealth.

In cross-section high wealth is associated with earlier expected retirement: those who owned stocks in both waves t and $t + 1$ had the most wealth in wave t, and also the lowest average P62; those who owned stock in neither wave had both the lowest wealth and the highest P62. However, in the panel there is no systematic relationship between wealth change and the change in P62: stockowners in both waves and new entrants into stockholding both had large gains in wealth; yet in one case P62 was almost constant and in the other case it increased. Those who did not own stocks or those who left stockholding both had small or little wealth increases, yet P62 increased in one case and declined in the other.

Averaged over all respondents, wealth increased by 26.5 percent between waves 3 and 4, and 23.7 percent between waves 4 and 5. Comparing the overall change in wealth and P62 from waves 2 to 3 with the overall

Table 4.10   Wealth (thousands) and the subjective probability of retirement; panel comparison

	Waves 2–3			Waves 3–4			Waves 4–5			Waves 5–6		
	N	Wealth	P62	N	Wealth	P62	N	Wealth	P62	N	Wealth	P62
All												
Wave t	3,465	238.6	45.1	2450	268.8	46.3	3442	306.7	46.2	2326	380.2	48.3
Wave t + 1	3,465	266.4	45.6	2450	339.9	46.0	3442	379.5	48.2	2326	381.0	47.9
Percentage change		11.6	1.0		26.5	−0.7		23.7	4.2		0.2	−0.8
Stock owners in both waves												
Wave t	1,206	404.6	43.5	890	449.7	44.6	1415	458.5	45.1	987	577.6	47.4
Wave t + 1	1,206	463.5	43.7	890	594.7	45.9	1415	584.5	47.7	987	576.6	49.1
Percentage change		14.5	0.5		32.2	2.8		27.5	5.8		−0.2	3.7
Stock owners in neither wave												
Wave t	1,701	120.5	46.0	1147	125.0	46.7	1361	137.1	46.3	822	148.0	48.5
Wave t + 1	1,701	126.8	46.5	1147	127.2	46.7	1361	161.3	47.9	822	161.0	47.0
Percentage change		5.2	1.1		1.7	−0.1		17.7	3.5		8.8	−3.2
Entrant to stockownership												
Wave tw	294	201.3	47.8	211	300.6	51.2	349	222.7	54.1	216	421.7	50.4
Wave t + 1	294	247.0	49.8	211	512.8	44.1	349	342.6	52.6	216	455.4	48.7
Percentage change		22.7	4.2		70.6	−13.8		53.8	−2.7		8.0	−3.4
Exiters from stockownership												
Wave t	264	283.3	44.2	202	254.3	46.5	317	449.9	42.5	301	337.5	49.0
Wave t + 1	264	287.1	43.7	202	244.7	44.8	317	441.7	46.3	301	286.9	46.0
Percentage change		1.3	−1.3		−3.8	−3.7		−1.8	9.1		−15.0	−6.3

Source: Authors' calculations, based on HRS.

Note: Wave t refers to either of waves 2–6 and wave t + 1 refers to either of waves 3–6. Sample is those in the labor force in wave t. In wave t P62 is reported; in wave t + 1 P62 is reported for those who remain in the labor force; P62 is calculated for those who have left the labor force. Age-eligible population.

change in wealth and P62 from waves 3 to 4 and 4 to 5 we find little support for the idea that large changes in wealth led to earlier retirement: in the normal period between waves 2 and 3 wealth increased by 12 percent and P62 increased slightly; in the two succeeding abnormal periods, when wealth increased by 24 to 27 percent, P62 was approximately constant or increased.

This conclusion is reinforced when we compare the wealth change of stock owners with the wealth change of those who owned in neither wave. Among those who owned in both waves 3 and 4, wealth increased by $145,000, or 32.2 percent, yet P62 increased by 1.3 percentage points. Among those who owned in neither wave, both wealth and P62 were approximately constant. If we consider those who owned stock in neither wave to be a control group that on average had its expectations realized with respect to health, earnings, and so forth, its lack of revision in P62 suggests stationarity. Under our hypothesis, stock owners should then have revised downward the probabilities of working past 62: instead they revised them upward. Similarly, between waves 4 and 5 those who did not own stocks had an increase in wealth of $24,000 and an increase in P62 of 1.6 percentage points. Stock owners had a much larger increase in wealth ($126,000) yet a larger increase in P62 (2.6 percentage points).

Only in waves 5 to 6 do we see a suggestion of a wealth effect: owners of stock had no wealth change, which was likely much below expectations, and an increase in P62 of 1.7 percentage points. Those who did not own stocks had an increase in wealth of $13,000 and a decline of P62 of 1.5 percentage points. Taking non-stock owners as the control group, we would calculate a stock market effect on P62 of 3.2 percentage points.

A possible explanation for the lack of a wealth effect on P62 is that we have not controlled for age. To do that we limit the presentation to a comparison between those who owned stocks in both waves and those who owned stock in neither wave. In that these two groups experienced the greatest difference in wealth change, we expect that they will have the greatest difference in the change in retirement expectations.

Table 4.11 shows these changes. As an example of the overall results, consider those who were fifty-eight to fifty-nine in wave 4. Between waves 3 and 4,323 stock owners had a remarkable wealth increase of about $190 thousand, or 45.7 percent, while 418 non-stock owners had approximately constant wealth. Stock owners increased P62 by 0.7 percentage points and non-stock owners increased P62 by 0.6 percentage points. This comparison is not consistent with the hypothesis that some of the large wealth gains will be used to finance earlier retirement. Similar comparisons in waves 4 to 5 show, if anything, greater increases in P62 among stock owners than among non-stock owners.

However, between waves 5 and 6 in every age band P62 increased among stock owners, but with one exception it decreased among nonowners. For

Table 4.11   Wealth (thousands) and subjective retirement probabilities: panel

	Waves 2–3						Waves 3–4						Waves 4–5						Waves 5–6					
	Stock owners			Nonstock owners			Stock owners			Nonstock owners			Stock owners			Nonstock owners			Stock owners			Nonstock owners		
Ages in wave t + 1	N	Wealth	P62	N	Wealth	P62	N	Wealth	P62	N	Wealth	P62	N	Wealth	P62	N	Wealth	P62	N	Wealth	P62	N	Wealth	P62
Ages 52–53																								
Wave t	285	387.3	43.9	337	110.2	48.5							268	354.4	42.8	191	115.5	48.9						
Wave t + 1	285	420.1	43.9	337	118.5	45.4							268	467.0	44.2	191	142.4	45.4						
Percentage change		8.5	0.0		7.5	-6.4								31.8	3.1		23.3	-7.2						
Ages 54–55																								
Wave t	335	357.8	41.3	502	124.4	45.4	286	397.3	43.1	342	137.7	46.9	253	378.0	44.8	191	169.7	41.5	216	431.8	44.1	153	149.1	46.9
Wave t + 1	335	414.6	41.2	502	133.7	45.2	286	563.8	43.8	342	142.4	47.6	253	511.4	47.1	191	187.8	41.9	216	457.1	46.4	153	142.0	47.5
Percentage change		15.9	-0.1		7.4	-0.5		41.9	1.7		3.4	1.5		35.3	5.0		10.7	0.8		5.9	5.1		-4.8	1.2
Ages 56–57																								
Wave t	304	445.0	41.8	444	129.0	46.4	323	415.2	43.9	418	131.4	44.3	287	449.5	43.1	248	138.6	48.1	234	495.7	44.9	172	178.3	46.6
Wave t + 1	304	512.8	43.3	444	124.0	46.1	323	604.9	44.2	418	136.4	44.9	287	590.5	44.9	248	149.4	47.7	234	484.8	47.3	172	180.4	44.5
Percentage change		15.2	3.5		-3.9	-0.6		45.7	0.7		3.8	1.3		31.4	4.0		7.9	-0.8		-2.2	5.3		1.2	-4.5
Ages 58–59																								
Wave t	282	434.1	47.5	418	115.0	44.4	281	542.8	47.0	387	107.0	49.2	316	542.8	45.1	364	138.5	45.3	246	569.7	48.1	208	148.8	47.4
Wave t + 1	282	512.1	46.9	418	128.1	49.5	281	614.4	49.9	387	103.7	47.9	316	682.0	47.6	364	170.8	49.3	246	600.9	49.4	208	161.3	46.6
Percentage change		18.0	-1.1		11.4	11.5		13.2	6.0		-3.1	-2.7		25.6	5.5		23.3	8.8		5.5	2.6		8.4	-1.6
Ages 60–61																								
Wave t													291	541.6	49.2	367	129.0	47.1	291	758.2	51.2	289	128.9	51.4
Wave t + 1													291	644.5	54.4	367	156.0	51.2	291	718.7	52.4	289	159.5	48.4
Percentage change														19.0	10.6		20.8	8.6		-5.2	2.4		23.7	-5.8
All																								
Wave t	1206	404.6	43.5	1701	120.5	46.0	890	449.7	44.6	1147	125.0	46.7	1415	458.5	45.1	1361	137.1	46.3	987	577.6	47.4	822	148.0	48.5
Wave t + 1	1206	463.5	43.7	1701	126.8	46.5	890	594.7	45.9	1147	127.2	46.7	1415	584.5	47.7	1361	161.3	47.9	987	576.6	49.1	822	161.0	47.0
Percentage change		14.5	0.5		5.2	1.1		32.2	2.8		1.7	-0.1		27.5	5.8		17.7	3.5		-0.2	3.7		8.8	-3.2

Source: Authors' calculations, based on HRS.

example, among sixty- to sixty-one-year-olds, P62 increased by 1.2 percentage points among owners but declined by 3.0 percentage points among nonowners. Over all age groups the average increase among owners was 1.7 percentage points and the average decrease among nonowners was 1.5 percentage points. Thus our estimate of the stock market effect between waves 5 and 6 would be 3.2 percentage points.

We will use a Cox proportional hazards model to estimate the effect on years of full-time work, which may be a more natural concept to quantify than P62.

Let f_t be the survival curve in full-time work, and let h_t be the hazard out of full-time work.

$$h_t = -\frac{d \ln f_t}{dt}$$

and

$$-\ln f_t = \int h_t dt + c.$$

At some beginning age (say, fifty-one) $f_t = 1$ so that $c = 0$.

Suppose that during a time of surprising stock market gains or losses

$$h_{t,s} = h_t e^{\alpha_t s}$$

where $s = 1$ if a stock owner and 0 otherwise. During an era when stock market gains are normal, $\alpha_t = 0$ and we can estimate h_t directly from data. The strategy will be to use panel data on the number working full time at time $t + 2$ and the number working full time at t. Because of reentry into the labor force they need not be the same people. Thus the hazard will be the net hazard. We would like one-year hazards h_t from t to $t + 1$, but the data panel span two years. Thus a two-year empirical hazard that spans ages t to $t + 2$ will include h_t and h_{t+1}. Our solution will be to use an average of the hazards from $t - 1$ to $t + 1$ and from t to $t + 2$ normalized to an annual hazard.

Let n_t be the number working full-time at age t. In panel we observe pairs (n_t, n_{t+2}) in adjacent waves. The average one-year hazard is

$$\frac{1}{2}\left(\frac{n_t - n_{t+2}}{n_t}\right).$$

Estimate h_t as

$$\frac{1}{2}\left[\frac{1}{2}\left(\frac{n_{t-1} - n_{t+1}}{n_{t-1}}\right) + \frac{1}{2}\left(\frac{n_t - n_{t+2}}{n_t}\right)\right],$$

which is the average of the one-year hazards centered on t. Then

$$f_t \approx e^{-\Sigma_{t=0}^{t} h_t}.$$

The area to the left of this curve is the expected years of full-time work:

$$E(\text{years full time}) = \Sigma f_t$$

In an era of unexpected losses in the stock market, we have estimated $f_{62,s} - f_{62} = k$ where $k \approx -0.032$.

According to the Cox proportional hazard model

$$f_{t,s} = e^{-e^{\alpha s}\int h_t dt} = (f_t)^{e^{\alpha s}}$$

then

$$\ln(f_{62,s}) = e^{\alpha s} \ln(f_{62}) = \ln(k + f_{62})$$

and

$$e^{\alpha s} = \frac{\ln(k + f_{62})}{\ln(f_{62})}.$$

For example, if $k = 0.032$ and $f_{62} = 0.45$, then $e^{\alpha s} = 0.913$ and

$$f_{t,s} = f_t^{0.913}.$$

Figure 4.3 shows a curve for estimated survival in full-time work beginning at age fifty-one, and a survival curve for those with an increased P62 due to stock market loss ($k = 0.032$). The vertical distance between the two curves at age sixty-two is 0.032. The effect of the stock market loss on expected full-time work is the area between the two curves. This area is approximately 0.38 year out of an estimated remaining life expectancy in full-time work of 8.7 years.

Although the results in table 4.11 for the change between waves 5 and 6

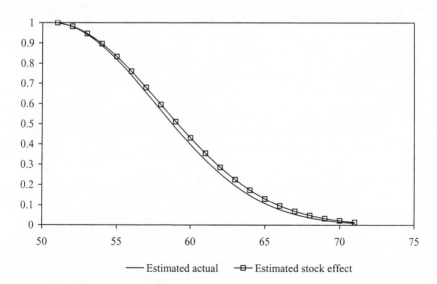

Fig. 4.3   Survival in full-time work

are suggestive, we would like a more formal statistical analysis. Therefore, we estimated the regression of the change in P62 at the individual level on categorical age indicators and on stock ownership indicators interacted with wave transition indicators. Table 4.12 shows the results from that regression for four wave transitions. The results broadly mirror what is in table 4.11. For example, between waves 5 and 6 the change in P62 among stock owners was 3.4 percentage points greater than the change in P62 among nonowners. However, the estimated standard error of that difference is 2.1, so the difference is not statistically significant. Furthermore, the differences in the waves 3 to 5 are positive, whereas the gain in the stock market suggests a downward adjustment to P62, which would lead to negative differences.

Thinking that noise in P62 may increase the standard errors substantially, we investigated the qualitative change in P62: whether the change in P62 is positive. We estimated the regression of an indicator variable for a positive change on age and ownership indicators, as in table 4.12. The results are in table 4.13. The pattern is identical to the pattern in table 4.12, but the scaling is different: table 4.12 refers to a change in P62 that is scaled 0 to 100, whereas table 4.13 refers to the probability of an increase in P62

Table 4.12   **Regression results: Change in P62 by wave. Stock owners and nonstock owners**

	Stock owners	Nonowners	Difference	Standard error of difference
Wave 2 to 3	−0.22	0.00	−0.22	1.38
Wave 3 to 4	0.45	−0.86	1.31	2.08
Wave 4 to 5	2.77	1.48	1.29	1.92
Wave 5 to 6	1.18	−2.22	3.41	2.13

Source: Authors' calculations, based on HRS.
Note: Pooled regression across four wave transitions.

Table 4.13   **Regression results: Probability of an increase in P62. Stock owners and nonstock owners**

	Stock owners	Nonowners	Difference	Standard error of difference
Wave 2 to 3	0.000	0.000	0.000	0.032
Wave 3 to 4	0.030	−0.004	0.034	0.048
Wave 4 to 5	0.082	0.042	0.039	0.044
Wave 5 to 6	0.051	−0.048	0.099	0.049

Source: Authors' calculations, based on HRS.
Note: The left-hand variable equals 1 if P62 increased between waves and equals 0 otherwise.

that is scaled 0 to 1.0. Thus, between waves 3 and 4 the probability is 0.034 greater among stockholders that the revision in P62 will be positive than among nonowners. The difference in the probability of a gain between waves 5 and 6 is 0.099, which is statistically significant; that is, stock owners were almost ten percentage points more likely to report an increase in P62 between waves 5 and 6 as nonowners. This difference is consistent with stock market losses causing an increase in retirement age.

We have been treating all stock owners as if they were the same, even though stock wealth is highly skewed. We imagine that the stock wealth increase would have to be substantial relative to total wealth to induce a detectable change in retirement behavior. Accordingly, we constructed indicator variables for total wealth and stock wealth quartiles and repeated the type of regression reported in table 4.12 but with interactions between total wealth and stock wealth quartiles all interacted with the wave transition. Table 4.14 shows the variation in the change in P62 as a function of the quartiles relative to nonowners. For example, in the top wealth and top stock wealth quartiles in wave 3, P62 increased by 4.6 percentage points more among owners than among nonowners. The table shows some suggestive patterns: during the boom times of waves 3 to 5, P62 declined among those in the top stock wealth quartile and the third wealth quartile relative to nonowners. During the bust times of waves 5 to 6, P62 increased among those in the same quartiles. These patterns would be expected according to a wealth change argument especially because the intersection of those quartiles contains those respondents with relatively great stock market exposure. However, other entries in the table do not follow any such easily interpretable pattern; furthermore, none of the entries is statistically significant.

Table 4.14   **Regression results: Change in P62 among stock owners relative to nonstock owners by stock wealth and total wealth quartiles**

	Wealth quartile	
Wave and stock wealth quartile	3	4
Wave 3 to 4		
3	4.46	2.99
4	−4.73	4.63
Wave 4 to 5		
3	2.58	3.67
4	−2.79	−0.29
Wave 5 to 6		
3	0.80	1.57
4	5.14	4.91

Source: Authors' calculations, based on HRS.
Note: Pooled regression across four wave transitions.

We have been using the interview wave to group observations because of the strong relationship between wave and stock market change. But within a wave the actual interview date varied by as much as a year, so that the stock market level varied a great deal even within a wave. Accordingly, the change in the stock index varied greatly from observation to observation, depending on interview date in both waves.

We addressed this problem by finding the level of the stock index during the month of interview so that we can construct the actual change in the stock index between interviews for each respondent. This provides additional variation in the change in stock prices and allows us to combine observations from different waves.

We imagine that the effect of stock price change on P62 could be nonlinear: variation in change within a normal range would have little effect; only large deviations from historical change would be interpreted by respondents as an unexpected wealth effect. Based on stock price change data over about thirty years, we calculated the two-year stock price change distribution. From this we generated individual indicator variables to show whether the interview-to-interview change in the stock price was in one of the percentile intervals 0 to 5, 5 to 10, 10 to 50, 50 to 90, 90 to 95, 95 to 100. For example, all the observations based on waves 5 to 6 fell in the first two intervals, which represent the bottom 10 percent of historical stock price changes.

Table 4.15 shows the results of the regression of the change in P62 on variables that indicate in which of the stock change bands the actual change in the stock index belonged. The coefficients for nonowners control for macro events so the difference is what is relevant. Thus stock owners who were interviewed when the change in the stock market was in the lowest 5 percent of historical stock changes revised upward P62 by 2.34 percentage points relative to nonowners who were interviewed at similar times. We see that, indeed, there is little difference between owners and

Table 4.15   Regression results: change in P62 according to stock index change since last interview: stock owners and nonstock owners

Percentile of stock index change	Owners	Not owners	Difference	Standard Error of difference
0–5	1.88	–0.46	2.34	3.02
5–10	–1.54	–2.14	0.60	3.05
10–50	1.26	1.84	–0.59	1.94
50–90				
90–95	–0.15	1.42	–1.57	2.61
95–100	–1.44	0.01	–1.44	2.61

Source: Authors' calculations, based on HRS.

nonowners when stock change was in the middle of the distribution. At the extremes, the differences are what would be expected from an unexpected wealth gain. However, as the standard errors show, none of the differences is statistically significant.[14]

A more direct way to estimate a wealth effect is from the regression of the change in P62 on the change in wealth. As noted in the introduction, however, changes in wealth that are induced by a shock to health and that simultaneously cause a change in retirement will lead to biased ordinary least squares (OLS) estimates of a wealth effect. In this example, we might see in panel a decline in wealth and a reduction in retirement age. Therefore, we use predicted change in stock market wealth since the last interview as an instrumental variable. That is, we specify

$$\Delta P62 = \alpha \Delta wealth + u$$

and

$$\Delta wealth = \beta \Delta stockindex \times stockwealth$$

We believe u and $\Delta wealth$ are likely to be correlated.

In actual estimation, our instrumental variable is highly predictive of the change in wealth. However, our estimates of α are not of a consistent sign and are not statistically significant, so we do not report them.

4.6   Conclusions

Between waves 3 and 5 of the HRS the stock market increased in value at substantially greater rates than in recent history, and, accordingly, we observe a large increase in the asset holdings of HRS households. We assumed that much of the increase in wealth was unanticipated, because of the very much greater rates of return than had been experienced in prior years. Our major question was to find whether households used this wealth gain to retire earlier than anticipated.

We found no evidence that workers in those households which had large gains retired earlier than they had anticipated or that they revised their retirement expectations compared with workers in households that had no large gains. We can compare these results with those of Imbens, Rubin, and Sacerdote (2001). They estimated the effect of windfall gains in wealth from the behavior of lottery winners. Their basic finding was that large gains induced a reduction in labor force participation. Based on a comparison of the change in labor force participation of winners with the

---

14. We repeated these regressions, but with linear splines with knots at the percentile points, as shown in table 4.15. The results are approximately the same and also lack statistical significance, so we do not show them.

change in labor force participation of losers (Imbens, Rubin, and Sacerdote, 2001, table 2) we calculate that a windfall gain of about $300,000, which is approximately the wealth gain between waves 3 and 4 of stockholders in both waves, would reduce labor force participation by about one percentage point. We interpret this to be a rather small effect, basically indistinguishable from our main finding.

Holtz-Eakin, Joulfaian, and Rosen (1993) used IRS data on inheritances to estimate the effect of large wealth gains on labor force participation. Based on their estimates we calculate that a wealth gain of about $300,000 would reduce participation by about seven percentage points. This is a substantially different magnitude from what we actually found.

We realize that in making these comparisons we have assumed that the entire gain in wealth by stockholders was unanticipated whereas in reality at least some of the gains would have been anticipated. We have no method of separating anticipated from unanticipated gains, but were we able to isolate unanticipated gains, the difference between our results and the results from Holtz-Eakin, Joulfaian, and Rosen would be reduced.

Guided by the life-cycle model, we began this research with the expectation that the large wealth gains would be at least partly spent on earlier retirement and that the losses would delay retirement. Our thinking was that the gains were analogous to the thought experiment of giving a relatively large group of older workers a windfall wealth shock. What actually happened was probably more complicated. There was, indeed, a large wealth gain that we believe was largely unanticipated. But most likely the gain was accompanied by a change in the expectation of the normal rate of return on the stock market. Evidence for this conjecture is partly anecdotal. In addition, however, without such a change in expectations it would be difficult to explain the increase in the rate of stockholding. For example, between waves 1 and 4 the rate of stock ownership in the HRS increased by about four percentage points, or about 15 percent. If indeed the anticipated rate of return from holding stocks increased substantially, the life-cycle model cannot make a prediction about a contemporaneous increase in consumption: the substitution toward saving induced by the large increase in the reward from saving could overcome the income effect resulting from the large gains to wealth.

We found some suggestion that the decline in the stock market led to an increase in the expected retirement age. Supposing that is the case, we have no good explanation about the asymmetry: why there should be no response to a stock gain and a possible response to a stock loss. Part of the answer undoubtedly lies in expectations about future rates of return. There may be, however, psychological explanations that are outside of the life-cycle model, such as an unwillingness to reduce spending or asymmetries with respect to gains and losses.

References

Cheng, Ing-Haw, and Eric French. 2000. The effect of the run-up in the stock market on labor supply. *Economic Perspectives* 24 (4): 48–65.

Coile, Courtney C., and Phillip B. Levine. 2004. Bulls, bears, and retirement behavior. NBER Working Paper no. 10779. Cambridge, MA: National Bureau of Economic Research.

Coronado, Julia L., and Maria Perozek. 2003. Wealth effects and the consumption of leisure: Retirement decisions during the stock market boom of the 1990s. Federal Reserve Board Working Paper no. 2003-20.

Gustman, Alan, and Thomas Steinmeier. 1986. A structural retirement model. *Econometrica* 54 (3): 555–84.

Holtz-Eakin, Douglas, David Joulfaian, and Harvey Rosen. 1993. The Carnegie conjecture: Some empirical evidence. *Quarterly Journal of Economics* 108 (2): 413–35.

Hurd, Michael D. 1999. Labor market transitions in the HRS: Effects of the subjective probability of retirement and of pension eligibility. In *Wealth, work and health: Innovations in measurement in the social sciences,* ed. James P. Smith and Robert Willis, 267–90. Ann Arbor: University of Michigan Press.

Hurd, Michael, and Kathleen McGarry. 1993. The relationship between job characteristics and retirement. NBER Working Paper no. 4558. Cambridge, MA: National Bureau of Economic Research.

Hurd, Michael D., and Monika Reti. 2001. The effects of large capital gains on work and consumption: Evidence from four waves of the HRS. RAND Working Paper 03-14.

Imbens, Guido W., Donald B. Rubin, and Bruce Sacerdote. 1999. Estimating the effect of unearned income on labor supply, earnings, savings, and consumption: Evidence from a survey of lottery winners. *NBER Working Paper* no. 7001. Cambridge, MA: National Bureau of Economic Research.

———. 2001. Estimating the effect of unearned income on labor earnings, savings, and consumption: Evidence from a survey of lottery players. *American Economic Review* 91 (4): 778–94.

Joulfaian, David, and Mark Wilhelm. 1994. Inheritances and labor supply. *Journal of Human Resources* 29 (4): 1205–34.

Juster, F. Thomas, Joseph Lupton, James P. Smith, and Frank Stafford. 1999. Savings and wealth: Then and now. EconWPA Working Paper 0403027.

Juster, F. Thomas, and Richard Suzman. 1995. An overview of the Health and Retirement Study. *Journal of Human Resources* 30 (Supplement): S7–S56.

Khitatrakun, Surachai. 2004. Wealth and the timing of retirement. Unpublished manuscript, Department of Economics, University of Wisconsin-Madison.

Parker, Jonathan. 1999. Spendthrift in America? On two decades of decline in the U.S. saving rate. In *NBER Macroeconomics Annual 1999,* ed. Ben Bernanke and Julio Rotemberg, 317–69. Cambridge, MA: MIT Press.

Poterba, James. 2000. Stock market wealth and consumption. *Journal of Economic Perspectives* 14 (2): 99–118.

Samwick, Andrew. 1998. New evidence on pensions, Social Security and the timing of retirement. *Journal of Public Economics* 70 (2): 207–23.

Sevak, Purvi. 2002. Wealth shocks and retirement timing: Evidence from the nineties. Michigan Retirement Research Center Working Paper 2002-027.

Comment   Courtney Coile

The stock market fluctuations of the past decade are unprecedented in recent U.S. economic history. Following five straight years of double-digit
growth, the major stock market indices lost at least half of their value over
a two-year period, starting in mid-2000. It was widely perceived that workers had accelerated their retirement during the boom and had been forced
to delay retirement during the bust. For example, in July 2002 the cover
story in Time magazine asked "Will You Ever Be Able to Retire?" Aggregate labor supply statistics seemed to provide some support for delayed retirement during the bust, as the labor force participation rate of men age
fifty-five to sixty-four jumped by two percentage points between 2000 and
2002.

The chapter by Hurd, Reti, and Rohwedder explores the link between recent stock market fluctuations and retirement behavior. Although others
have also examined this subject, including Coile and Levine (2006) and
Kezdi and Sevak (2004), this paper is the first to focus on the effect of the
market boom and bust on subjective retirement probabilities. This focus
has two advantages. First, it allows the authors to look for responses that
would not yet be reflected in behavior, such as a decision by a fifty-five-
year-old worker to retire at age sixty rather than age sixty-two as a result of
large capital gains in his or her 401(k) account. Second, it helps the author
surmount the identification problem that has plagued some of the earlier
literature: if there are unobservable differences between stockholders and
nonstockholders, such as in preferences for leisure, then any differences in
retirement behavior will confound the effect of these unobservable factors
with the effect of market fluctuations. By looking at the change in retirement probabilities, the authors can control for these unobservable differences.

In their analysis, the authors use the Health and Retirement Study
(HRS), a survey of the young elderly that began in 1992 and reinterviews
participants every other year. The authors begin by examining changes in
stock and other assets between waves of the survey. In table 4.2, they show
that stockholders, who constitute roughly one-third of households, experienced large increases in average stock assets during the market boom and
large decreases during the bust—for example, average stock assets rose by
$44,900 (40.2 percent) from 1996 to 1998 and by $33,800 (23.3 percent)
from 1998 to 2000, before falling by $40,500 (21.4 percent) from 2000 to
2002. These large changes in average stock assets are a necessary condition
for finding an effect of market fluctuations on retirement, but may not be

Courtney Coile is an associate professor of economics at Wellesley College and a faculty
research fellow of the National Bureau of Economic Research.

sufficient; since wealth data is notoriously skewed, one cannot tell how broadly these gains and losses were shared from these averages alone. Thus, it would be useful to see more of the distribution of changes in stock assets among stockholders.

Although not the central focus of this chapter, an interesting fact that can be gleaned from table 4.2 is that over any two-year period, about one-sixth of households change their stockholder status, half of them acquiring stocks and the other half selling them. Since this is a nontrivial share of households, it would be interesting to know more about these transitions—do they represent households opening or closing 401(k) or IRA accounts, households reallocating assets held outside of retirement accounts, or simply measurement error in asset reporting?

Next, the authors spend some time validating their dependent variable, the subjective probability of working past age sixty-two (P62); others, such as Hurd and McGarry (1995), have done similar validation exercises for other subjective probability measures in the HRS. The authors show that individuals who report a higher P62 are more likely to be in the labor force at the end of the sample period (2002) than other workers, and that the average value of P62 matches up well with the fraction of the sample that actually works past age sixty-two. They also provide a theoretical discussion of how P62 is expected to evolve over time, arguing that it should remain constant in the absence of unexpected, cohortwide shocks. In this analysis, they assume that individuals incorporate the probability of idiosyncratic shocks, such as negative health events, in their calculation of P62. It would be useful to extend this discussion to consider the case where people fail to fully incorporate the probability of negative shocks and explore how P62 would be expected to evolve over time in this case, since this is the key outcome measure of interest.

In their primary analysis, the authors compare the change in P62 over time for stockholders and nonstockholders. Although they do not use this specific language, in essence what they have is a double experiment resulting from the stock market boom and bust, where we expect the behavior of stockholders to differ from that of nonstockholders during the boom, and for this difference to reverse itself during the bust. Figure 4C.1 shows a stylized example of the expected change in P62 over time for the two groups. Based on the authors' theoretical discussion, the expected change in P62 is zero for nonstockholders, who experience no unexpected cohortwide shock. By contrast, for stockholders the expected change is zero between waves 2 and 3 when stock returns are fairly typical, negative between waves 3 and 4 and waves 4 and 5 when stock returns are higher than expected, and positive between waves 5 and 6 when stock returns are lower than expected. Figure 4C.2 shows the difference in the expected change in P62 for the two groups; since the line for the nonstockholders is flat at zero, this difference is simply the line for the stockholders group.

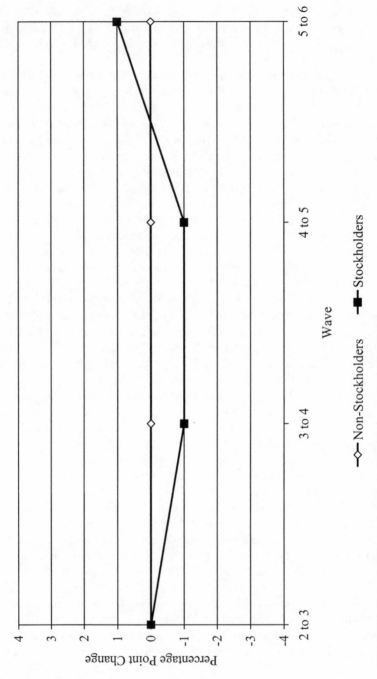

Fig. 4C.1   Expected change in P62, stockholders versus nonstockholders

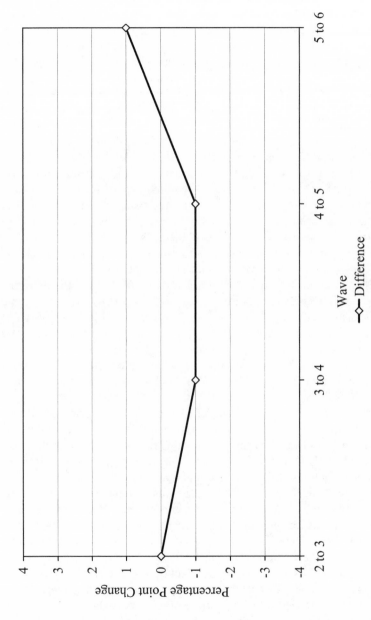

Fig. 4C.2   Expected change in P62, difference between stockholders and nonstockholders

The actual changes in P62 calculated by the authors (taken from their table 4.10) are shown in figures 4C.3 and 4C.4. The change in P62 over time for nonstockholders is essentially flat, as predicted, though it jumps up somewhat between waves 4 and 5 before returning to normal. The change in P62 for stockholders, however, does not have the expected pattern of falling in the middle waves while the market is booming and rising at the end when the market falls; indeed, the pattern is essentially the opposite of what was predicted. When one takes the difference between the two groups, the difference rises in the final period, as expected, but it does not fall in the middle periods.

What might explain the pattern observed in figure 4C.4? One possible explanation is that there is asymmetry in stockholders' response to unexpected wealth gains, so that they postpone retirement when the market crashes but do not accelerate it when the market soars. However, the data in figure 4.3 casts doubt on this theory, as the rising difference in the last period is driven primarily by nonstockholders lowering their assessment of P62 rather than by stockholders raising their assessment of P62. A second possibility is that nonstockholders are more likely to experience shocks like bad health news and layoffs, yet both groups believe they face the same risk. This situation would generate a positive difference in the expected change in P62 over time, because the nonstockholders would be incurring the shocks and reducing their probability of working past age sixty-two at a greater rate than stockholders. If the importance of unexpected shocks is rising with age, this could explain why the difference is rising over time, since the HRS sample ages over time. This is something the authors could account for in their analysis, by including such shocks as explanatory variables.

What can we conclude about the effect of market fluctuations on retirement behavior? The authors report that they find "no evidence that workers in those households that had large gains retired earlier than they had anticipated or that they revised their retirement expectations compared with workers in households that had no large gains." The same conclusion is reached by Coile and Levine (2006), looking at actual retirement behavior rather than the change in retirement expectations. There are two possible explanations for the lack of an effect. The first is that the number of people who experienced large unexpected wealth gains from market fluctuations is relatively small—indeed, Coile and Levine (2006) argue that this is the case. The second is that the effect of unexpected wealth on labor supply is fairly small. The authors are sympathetic to this argument, citing evidence from lotteries, and some of the other papers about stock market fluctuations seem to show this, too. For example, Coronado and Perozek (2003) find that being a stockholder is associated with retiring six months earlier than expected, but that each additional $100,000 of unexpected gains is associated with retiring only two weeks earlier than expected.

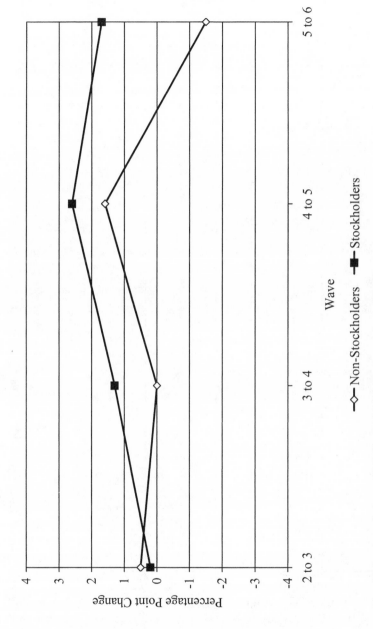

Fig. 4C.3   Actual change in P62, stockholders versus nonstockholders

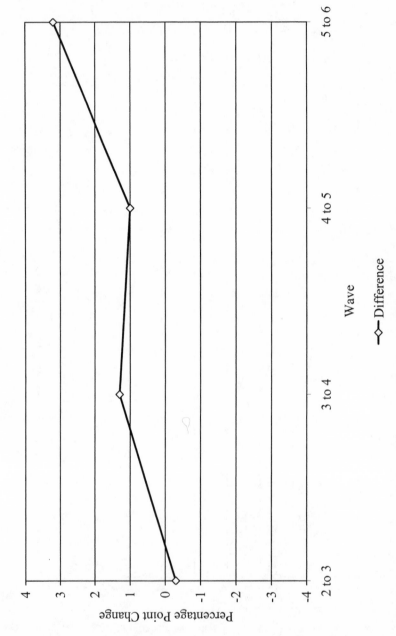

Fig. 4C.4   Actual change in P62, difference between stockholders and nonstockholders

While there is little evidence for a widespread labor market response to the recent market boom and bust, it is certainly possible that consumers have changed other behaviors in response to the market fluctuations. For example, households may have changed their consumption of goods and services or adjusted their plans to make a bequest. Households may also have adjusted their expectations about future market returns and may have altered savings or portfolio allocation decisions as a result. All of these questions are clearly fruitful areas for future research.

References

Coile, Courtney C., and Phillip B. Levine. 2006. Bulls, bears, and retirement behavior. *Industrial and Labor Relations Review* 59 (3): 406–29.

Hurd, Michael D., and Kathleen McGarry. 1995. Evaluation of the subjective probabilities of survival. *Journal of Human Resources* 30 (supplement): S268–S292.

Kezdi, Gabor, and Purvi Sevak. 2004. Economic adjustment of recent retirees to adverse wealth shocks. Michigan Retirement Research Center Working Paper no. 2004–75.

Early Retirement, Social Security, and Well-Being in Germany

Axel Börsch-Supan and Hendrik Jürges

5.1 Introduction

Germans retire early. While the statutory normal retirement age for men and women is age sixty-five, the actual average retirement age is much earlier. Only about 20 percent of all entrants use the normal pathway of an old-age pension at age sixty-five. The most popular retirement age is age sixty. The average retirement age in 1999 was 59.7 years for men and 60.7 years for women (these numbers refer to West Germany). In East Germany, retirement age was 57.9 years for men and 58.2 years for women.

Early retirement is popular. It is seen as a much-appreciated social achievement that especially increases the well-being of those workers who suffer from work-related health problems. The 1972 reform in Germany, which introduced early retirement without actuarial adjustment in the benefits, was a great political success.

However, times have changed. With an increasingly aging population and the precarious financial state of the public pension system, the costs of early retirement have received increased scrutiny. The German social security contribution rate, in 2003 at 19.5 percent of gross income, was projected in the mid-1980s to exceed 30 percent of gross income at the peak of

Axel Börsch-Supan is a professor of economics at the University of Mannheim, director of the Mannheim Research Institute for the Economics of Aging, and a research associate of the National Bureau of Economic Research. Hendrik Jürges is an assistant professor at the Mannheim Research Institute for the Economics of Aging, University of Mannheim.

This paper is part of phase 4 of the NBER's International Social Security Project. Financial support was provided by the National Institute on Aging through the NBER (Grant P01 AG05842) and by the DFG through Sonderforschungsbereich 504. We are also grateful for financial support by the State of Baden-Württemberg and the German Insurers Association (GDV).

population ageing in 2035 if the accustomed benefits (i.e., eligibility age and replacement rate) were maintained.[1] This led to a string of pension reforms since 1992, effectively bidding farewell to the pure pay-as-you-go system and introducing a multipillar pension system with two funded pillars of occupational and individual pensions in addition to the traditional unfunded retirement insurance.

These reforms, however, only timidly touched the early and not at all the normal retirement ages, which were age sixty and sixty-five, respectively. Bearing increasing life expectancy in mind, raising the age of retirement would appear to be an obvious reform option. The introduction of modest actuarial adjustments in the 1992 reform was delayed by almost ten years because of its unpopularity. Only recently, as part of the proposals of the "Rürup-Commission," the reform discussion has shifted once again to the pivotal normal retirement age as a means to reduce early retirement and shift the average retirement age a few years forward.

This chapter is the fourth paper in a string of studies on early retirement in Germany, which are accompanied by sister studies in other Organisation for Economic Co-operation and Development (OECD) countries as part of the International Social Security Project, coordinated by Jonathan Gruber and David Wise. In the first stage (Börsch-Supan and Schnabel 1998, 1999), we described and quantified the incentives to retire early in the form of implicit taxes on continued work.

The second stage (Börsch-Supan, Schnabel, Kohnz, and Mastrobuoni 2004; Berkel and Börsch-Supan 2004) provided econometric estimates of the strength of incentive effects on old-age labor supply, using several specifications of incentive variables. These highly significant and large estimates were used to simulate labor force participation responses to several policy changes. For instance, introducing (almost) actuarially fair adjustments (6 percent per year of delay) would increase the average retirement age of German men by about three years and two months. The effects are about half the size for women.

In the third stage, Börsch-Supan, Kohnz, and Schnabel (2004) used these estimates and converted them into budget effects on the German public pension system. They simulated the impact of several stylized reform plans on older workers' net fiscal contributions to the finances of the German public pension system, distinguishing between a direct effect by changing contributions and benefits for a given work history (a purely mechanical effect) and an indirect effect through labor supply responses to the reform (a behavioral effect). This chapter finds very large cost implications of early retirement. For instance, the unpopular introduction of a 6 percent per year actuarial adjustment would imply a reduction of pension expen-

---

1. See Börsch-Supan (1998, 2000) for a description of the problems plaguing the German public pension system.

ditures for a typical cohort by 18 percent in direct benefit reductions and by an additional 26 percent through labor supply responses.

This fourth stage changes the point of view and looks at the benefits of these large costs. The immediate benefit from early retirement is income support without the necessity to continue working. This should directly benefit those workers who feel strained, for example, due to work-impeding health problems, and should manifest itself in an improvement of well-being. This chapter therefore uses available measures of well-being and applies various difference-in-difference methods to elicit the response of well-being to early and normal retirement.

Research on these issues is difficult, since the measures of health that are commonly available in general-purpose surveys may suffer from the very same justification bias as measures of well-being do (Bound 1991). We therefore need exogenous variation separating the effects on health and well-being. Unfortunately, we cannot follow the same strategy as the other chapters in this volume, which are able to exploit institutional variation (changes in the generosity of the social security system) that affects different cohorts differently.

There are two reasons why this approach does not work well in Germany. First, the last observable major change in program generosity that affected cohorts differently was the 1972 reform, when several early retirement options were introduced. However, we don't have good data on most key variables before and during the 1970s. The recent string of pension reforms mentioned previously does also affect cohorts differentially, but the effects are too recent to be reflected in the currently available data.

Second, most program changes that have been happening in Germany between 1972 and 2001 (e.g., the switch from gross to net wage indexation in 1992) have affected everyone who is receiving benefits in equal proportion. Hence, there is no differential impact on cohorts. This can be most easily seen by looking at the German pension benefit formula, which defines the benefits of pensioner i in year t:

$$B_{t,i} = PV_t \cdot EP_i \cdot AA_i$$

Where

PV_t = Current pension value in year t,
EP_i = Number of individual earnings points collected by pensioner i until his or her retirement
AA_i = Actuarial adjustment, dependent on the retirement age of pensioner i.

Benefits therefore have a simple structure: an individual component $EP_i \cdot AA_i$, determined by each person's earnings history and retirement age, which stays fixed for the entire retirement period, and an aggregate component PV_t, which adjusts benefits over time equally for all pensioners. EP_i

represents the point system and AA_i is determined by actuarial accounting rules (see, e.g., Börsch-Supan and Wilke [2003]). A typical worker who works forty years and earns the average wage receives forty earnings points. If this worker retires at age sixty-five, no actuarial adjustments take place ($AA = 1$). In the second half of 2002, the current pension value, PV_t, was 25.86 euro. Hence this typical worker receives a pension of 1,034.40 euro per month.

Each year—currently at July 1—the current pension value PV_t is recalculated with the aid of the benefit indexation formula. Until recently, this benefit indexation formula was essentially a simple indexation rule to the average annual level of wages and salaries (before 1992, gross wages and salaries; after 1992, net wages and salaries). From the year 2005 on, it will also include an indexation to the system-dependency ratio (the number of full-time equivalent pensioners divided by the number of full-time equivalent employees who contribute to the system).

Since the current pension value PV_t has a direct influence on every individual pension, the benefit indexation formula is a critical determinant for the well-being of pensioners and the amount of money spent by the public pension scheme. However, it does not differentiate among cohorts. The individual component $EP_i \cdot AA_i$ is not affected by the recent string of reforms,[2] and the change in the current pension value, PV_t, is a pure time effect. As opposed to many other public pension systems, the German system so far does not differentiate between the existing stock of pensioners and new entrants.[3]

In this chapter, we therefore try to follow another route to identification, and study long-term development in subjective well-being or overall life satisfaction before and after retirement, conditional on retirement age. We try to answer whether early retirement is beneficial for the individual in terms of overall life satisfaction—that is, we ask if the effect of retirement on well-being is more favorable for those taking early retirement than for those retiring at the normal retirement age. Put differently, we attempt to compare the well-being of those collecting early retirement benefits versus those in some other status.

Retirement as such (independent of the age at which someone retires) might be beneficial, because individuals are able to enjoy more leisure. It might be harmful, however, because individuals who stop working may

---

2. There are subtle changes in the computation of earnings points, especially the extent to which higher education contributes to the points. They are too subtle to be reflected in the GSOEP data.

3. An exception is the recent change in early retirement rules. They will provide a potentially very helpful instrument to follow the approach taken in the other chapters in this volume. We will, however, have to wait for another few years to see the effect in micro data sets such as SHARE or GSOEP.

lose their purpose in life. In any case, the effects of early retirement can only be properly evaluated if compared with normal retirement.

Of course, an individual's retirement age is not endogenous. It depends on several factors—institutions, health, labor force, status of spouse, and so forth. When we study the effect of retirement on well-being, we thus face the usual task of disentangling cause and effect. For example, persons in bad health are likely to retire earlier but also to report worse life satisfaction. Those who hope or believe that life satisfaction will increase after retirement are more likely to retire at any age. So we are facing a typical evaluation problem. Clearly, in a situation where individuals can choose freely when to retire, we should expect individuals who gain most from early retirement to be those who are most likely to retire early.

The econometric problem is to find a counterfactual value for life satisfaction had a person not taken early retirement. Aggregated across all early retirees, we would then have an estimate of the intangible benefits of early retirement.

The common belief seems to be that early retirement is beneficial—at least to those who retire early, because individuals make use of what is mostly described as "generous" retirement incentives. This view assumes that early retirement is always voluntary, that it is the choice of the retiree. But of course, this need not be the case. Think of a fifty-eight-year-old worker who becomes unemployed. In Germany, reemployment chances at this age are bleak. The worker will probably stay unemployed and draw unemployment benefits until he or she turns sixty and then "retire," that is, receive social security payments instead of unemployment insurance.

It is a priori unclear whether early retirees should be better off than those retiring at the normal retirement age. We distinguish three kinds of arguments:

- Early retirees suffer from retirement (compared to normal retirees) because they are forced out of the labor force by employers; that is, early retirement is at least to some extent involuntary. If someone who retired early was given the opportunity to retire later, he or she would enjoy an increase in well-being. A normal retiree forced to retire earlier would suffer a well-being loss.
- Early retirees benefit from retirement (compared to normal retirees) because they can make use of generous early retirement incentives (somewhat limited; not available to everyone). As a consequence, they experience an increase in well-being that is larger than the corresponding increase of those who take normal retirement. If someone who retires early was forced to retire later, he or she would suffer a well-being loss. A normal retiree allowed to retire earlier would enjoy a well-being increase.
- There is no difference between early and normal retirement, because

both types of individuals have chosen retirement optimally. If someone who retired early was forced to retire later, he or she would suffer a well-being loss. A normal retiree forced to retire earlier would suffer a well-being loss, too.

We build our study on two strands of literature. One strand studies the relationship between labor market events and life satisfaction. Winkelmann and Winkelmann (1998) show that unemployment reduces well-being. They employ the German Socio-Economic Panel (GSOEP) such as this panel, and use conditional logit models. Clark et al. (2003) study the set point model of happiness: demographic events (marriage, divorce, birth of first child) and labor market events (unemployment, layoff, and quitting a job) with GSOEP data. The set point model assumes that individuals return to initial levels of well-being after some time. Their results are that the strongest life satisfaction effects often appear at the time that the events in question occur. However, there are both significant lag and lead effects. For some events, there is rapid return to baseline satisfaction, while others have a lasting effect. Their focus is on respondents age nineteen to fifty-nine, somewhat younger than our sample.

Another strand of the literature studies retirement, in particular the effect of retirement on mental health, depression, and so forth. Retirement—the end of working life—is a major change in everyone's life. Some studies have found psychological well-being increases after retirement, others have found that it drops. Charles (2002) studies the effect of retirement on depression, while Lindeboom, Portrait, and van den Berg (2002) study the effect of retirement, a significant decrease in income, death of the spouse, disability, and a move to a nursing home on the mental health of elderly individuals, using data from the Longitudinal Aging Study Amsterdam (LASA). Measures for the dependent variable are the mental health and depression scales MMSE and CES-D.

Convincing causal studies are rare. Psychologists have largely ignored the problem of causation. It is, in fact, difficult to find, for example instruments that can be useful in this context. For example, health status is a major factor in the retirement decision, but health certainly influences life satisfaction.

5.2   Early Retirement Incentives in Germany

The generosity of the German public pension system in terms of early retirement possibilities and financial incentives to retire early has changed quite a bit during the last thirty years (see table 5.1 for a list of major changes). Until 1972, the public pension system was very inflexible, and permitted retirement only at age sixty-five. The only exception was disabled workers, who, however, made up for roughly 50 percent of new re-

Table 5.1	Trends in program generosity
Year	Measures taken/changes
1972	Introduction of several generous early retirement options
	—Flexible retirement at 63
	—Old-age disability pensions at 62
1978	Gross wage indexation suspended for several years
1984	Eligibility requirements reduced from 15 to 5 contribution years
	Restrictions on disability pensions eligibility
1992	Change from gross to net wage indexation
	Several long-run changes not yet fully phased in
	—Actuarial fairness
	—Regular retirement age for women increases from 60 to 65
Since 2001	Add indexation to system dependency ratio and several other changes

tirement entries. The 1972 pension reform changed this dramatically by introducing the opportunity to retire at different ages (flexible retirement) during a window of retirement. This window began at age sixty for unemployed women and workers who could not appropriately be employed for health or labor market reasons. It began at age sixty-three for workers with a long service history (thirty-five years, including higher education, military service, a certain number of years for raising children, etc.). Normal retirement age was (and still is) age sixty-five. The 1972 reform did not introduce an actuarial adjustment. The reforms in the 1990s will shift the window of retirement for all workers to age sixty-two and will include an adjustment of benefits, although this adjustment will remain less than actuarially fair; see table 5.1.

The introduction of early retirement had a huge impact on retirement age. Within a few years, retirement age among men dropped by about three years (see Börsch-Supan and Schnabel [1998]). The average retirement age fell below age sixty.[4] The resulting distribution of retirement ages became marked by distinct spikes at ages sixty, sixty-three, and sixty-five (see Börsch-Supan and Schnabel [1999]). The retirement age of sixty-five now mostly applies to women with a very short earnings history, while the most popular retirement age among men has become age sixty. Since average life expectancy of a male worker at age sixty is about eighteen years, the earlier retirement age amounts to an increase in pension expenditures of about 15 percent. The effect is smaller, but still significant, for women.

Until recently, there was no adjustment of benefits to retirement age.[5]

---

4. Averaged over new recipients of old-age and disability pensions. Results for women are similar.

5. Curiously, the German system before 1992 provided a large increase in retirement benefits for postponing work at ages sixty-five and sixty-six. However, this incentive was ineffective, because the inducements to early retirement by far offset it.

However, because benefits are proportional to the years of service, a worker with fewer years of service would get lower benefits. With a constant income profile and forty years of service, each year of earlier retirement decreased pension benefits by 2.5 percent, and a postponement of retirement vice versa. The 1992 reform introduced retirement age-specific adjustment factors. These actuarial adjustments add 3.6 percent to the previously stated 2.5 percent, and are therefore lower than required for incentive neutrality (see Berkel and Börsch-Supan [2004]). The system before the 1992 reform was particularly distortive in rewarding early retirement. As opposed to workers, for example, in the United States, who have no incentive to retire before age sixty-five and only a small disincentive to retire later than at age sixty-five (see Diamond and Gruber 1997), the German social security system tilts the retirement decision heavily toward the earliest retirement age applicable. The 1992 pension reform in Germany has diminished but by no means abolished this incentive effect.

The failure to adjust benefits in an actuarially fair manner creates a loss in unfunded social security wealth when a worker postpones retirement. This loss has been computed by Börsch-Supan and Schnabel (1998). It is large relative to the labor income that could be earned when working longer. This loss can thus be interpreted as an implicit tax on earnings when postponing retirement. This implicit tax exceeded 50 percent before the 1992 pension reform and will still be in excess of 20 percent in 2004, when the 1992 reform will have been fully phased in.

Several formal econometric analyses have studied the incentive effects of the nonactuarial adjustment on early retirement. These studies employ variants of the microeconometric option value analysis developed by Stock and Wise (1990). Börsch-Supan, Schnabel, Kohnz, and Mastrobuoni (2004) derive from their estimates that the 1992 reform will increase the average retirement age only by about half a year, and reduce retirement before age sixty from 32 percent to about 28 percent, while a switch to a system with actuarially fair adjustment factors would shift the retirement age by about two years.

5.3 Trends in Program Generosity and the Well-being of the Elderly Population

In this section, we examine whether there is a direct relationship between the generosity of the social security system, measured as real total social security expenditures divided by the size of the population aged fifty-five and older, and the economic and psychological well-being of the elderly. Figure 5.1 shows the evolution of average social security expenditure since 1960, both in absolute terms and in its growth rate one year earlier. The graph shows a break in 1978, when the growth of the average public pensions virtually ceased. The average growth rate between 1960 and 1978 was

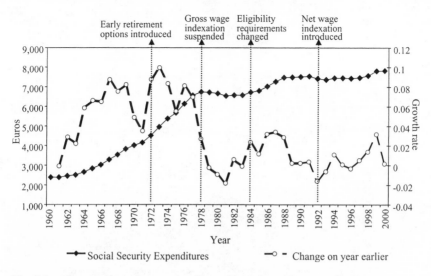

Fig. 5.1   Changes in program generosity and social security expenditures

Table 5.2   Data sources for key well-being dimensions

Dimension	Data source	Level	Available years	Type	Approximate sample size
Income	GSOEP	I, HH	1984–today	Panel	10,000 individuals
Expenditures	EVS	HH	1978, 1983, 1988, 1993, 1998	Cross-sections	40,000 head of household
Subjective Well-being	GSOEP	I	1984–today	Panel	10,000 individuals
	Welfare survey	I	1978, 1980, 1984, 1988, 1993, 1998	Cross-sections	2,000 individuals
	Eurobarometer	I	1973–today (with gaps)	Cross-sections	1,000 individuals
Self-reported health	GSOEP	I	1992–today	Panel	10,000 individuals
Mortality	StaBu life tables		1950–today	Aggregate	not applicable

6.1 percent—after 1978 the average went down to 0.8 percent. There are seven years in which real growth rates have been negative.

We study the effect of the program's generosity on the various key dimensions of well-being: income, expenditures, poverty rates, general life satisfaction, self-reported health, and mortality. Measures for these dimensions-dependent variables are derived from various data sources (see table 5.2 for an overview). Unfortunately, since the main data source is the GSOEP, we do not have much data before 1984. Our possibilities to study public pension reforms before 1984 are thus very limited.

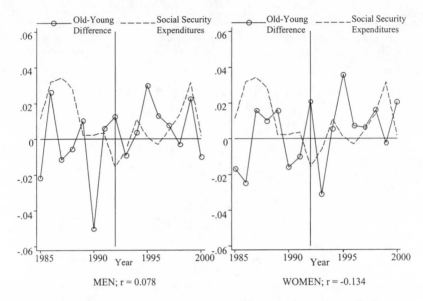

Fig. 5.2 **Social security expenditures growth and relative income growth of the elderly**

Our basic method to examine effects of program generosity is a variant of the difference-in-differences approach. We split our samples into two groups: old (age fifty-five-plus) and young (age twenty-five to forty-nine). For both groups we first calculate first differences (annual growth rates) in our key measures. Then we calculate the difference between first differences of the old and the young population, which gives us the relative change in well-being of the elderly. Finally, this measure is regressed on the change in program generosity—that is, the annual growth rate in average social security expenditures as shown in figure 5.1.

Figure 5.2 contains the relative income growth, separately for elderly men and women, together with annual growth rate in social security expenditures (dashed line). The first impression is that a couple of ups and downs of both measures coincide, so that there might indeed be some association between the two measures. However, the correlation coefficients are not significantly different from zero and they have different signs for men and women. On this rather descriptive level, it is not possible to find an effect of social security expenditures on the well-being of the elderly.

This also holds in figure 5.3, where we show the five-year growth rates in total household expenditures of old relative to young households. The correlation between this measure and the five-year growth rate in social security expenditures is actually negative. Figure 5.4 shows the development of the old population's poverty rate relative to the young population's poverty rate. The negative correlation coefficient indicates that social security ex-

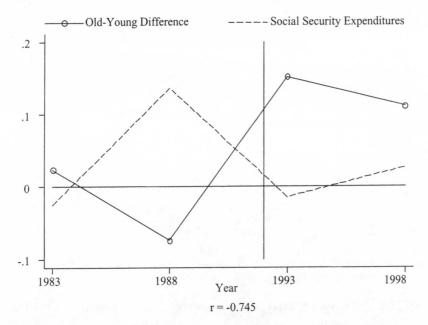

r = -0.745

Fig. 5.3 Social security expenditures growth and relative expenditure growth of the elderly

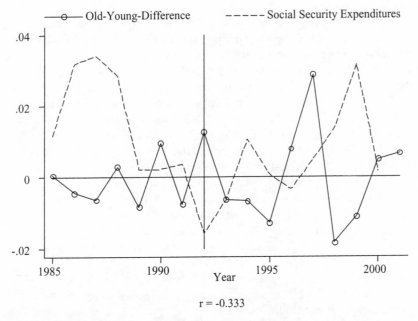

r = -0.333

Fig. 5.4 Social security expenditures growth and relative poverty rates of the elderly

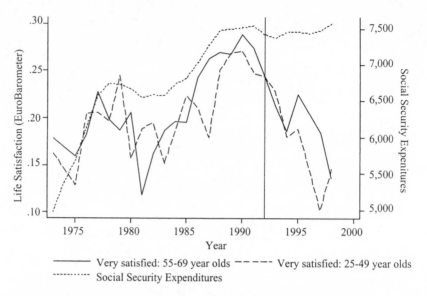

Fig. 5.5   **Social security expenditures and well-being (Eurobarometer)**

penditures decrease with old relative to young poverty. However, the relationship is not significant.

Figures 5.5 and 5.6 show the development of two different measures of overall subjective well-being or happiness. Figure 5.5 contains Eurobarometer results. The Eurobarometer life satisfaction scale is a four-point Likert scale with answer categories "very satisfied," "fairly satisfied," "not very satisfied," "not at all satisfied." Here we show the proportion of respondents who claim to be "very satisfied" with their lives. There seems to be an astonishingly close relationship between social security expenditures and the well-being of both young *and* old, at least until 1990. When we calculate the difference in well-being between the young and the old, or the difference in changes in well-being, the correlation between social security expenditures and the well-being of the elderly vanishes. Moreover, using the Welfare Survey and the GSOEP as alternative data sources on well-being, it is not possible to replicate the Eurobarometer results. Both surveys use the same eleven-point scale, from 0 (not at all satisfied) to 10 (completely satisfied) to elicit information on general life satisfaction. Figure 5.6 shows the proportion of a value of 9 or 10 on this scale. In contrast to the Eurobarometer results, life satisfaction decreases more or less continuously in both age groups since 1978. The reason for this difference is unclear. Possible reasons are differences in sampling, interview modes, question contexts, and so on, between the different surveys. It is clearly beyond the scope of the present chapter to provide an explanation for what is probably a survey artifact. In the following analysis, we will use GSOEP data only, that is, consistent data from a single source.

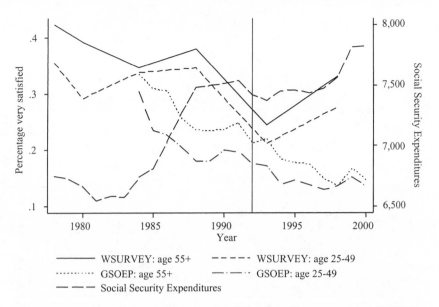

Fig. 5.6   Social security expenditures and well-being (welfare surveys and GSOEP)

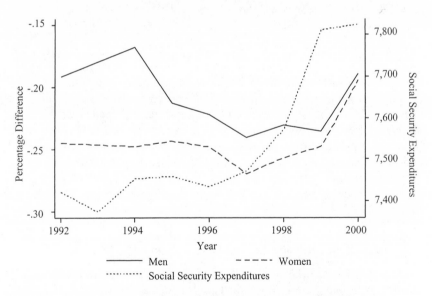

Fig. 5.7   Social security expenditures and self-reported general health

Our final measures of well-being are self-reported general health and life expectancy. Self-reported health is available in the GSOEP only since 1992, and it is measured on the World Health Organization (WHO)-format five-point Likert scale with values from "very good" to "very bad." Figure 5.7 shows the old-minus-young difference in the proportion of respondents

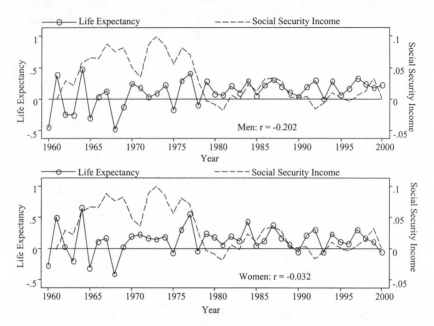

Fig. 5.8   Social security expenditures changes and life expectancy changes

who claim that their health is "very good," "good," or "fair," separately for men and women. For example, a value of –0.2 means that the proportion of individuals in fair or better health is twenty percentage points higher among the young than among the old. We observe no significant relationship between social security expenditures and self-reported health.

Figure 5.8 shows annual changes in life expectancy at age fifty-five, separately for men and women. Again, some ups and downs in life expectancy and social security expenditures seem to coincide. In particular, after 1980, there is a positive correlation (roughly 0.4 for both sexes). However, considering the entire period from 1960 to 2000, the correlation is slightly negative.

5.4   Early Retirement and the Well-being of Retirees

The data used in this and the following sections are drawn exclusively from the German Socio-Economic Panel and cover the years 1984 to 2002. Our subsample consists of all West German employees who retire during the observation period at an age of between fifty-five and sixty-five, where retirement is defined by the receipt of benefits and who are between fifty and sixty-nine years old. We have a reasonable number of observations (see table 5.3).

The GSOEP contains information on a large number of household and

Table 5.3   **Numbers of observations, by year, sex, and labor force status**

	Men		Women	
Year	Not retired	Retired	Not retired	Retired
1984	449	19	219	10
1985	442	70	242	19
1986	450	114	262	35
1987	473	154	282	50
1988	486	182	295	70
1989	498	208	295	92
1990	502	241	299	116
1991	465	292	297	135
1992	428	322	273	157
1993	398	342	256	168
1994	376	355	237	195
1995	341	352	193	214
1996	302	371	182	225
1997	249	373	152	240
1998	189	372	118	246
1999	143	401	99	252
2000	80	410	58	274
2001	38	406	25	281
2002	56	363	42	246

individual characteristics as well as the respondents' overall life satisfaction and satisfaction with aspects of their lives. The core of six aspects mentioned in each survey year consists of health, household income, job (if employed), housework (if respondent is looking after home or family), leisure time, and dwelling. Responses are all on a scale from zero to ten, where zero means "not satisfied at all" and ten means "completely satisfied." The satisfaction data in the GSOEP is unique in that it provides comparable data over a long period. It has been found to be very useful in a number of studies (e.g., Winkelmann and Winkelmann 1998, Clark et al. 2003, Jürges 2003)

Our main dependent variable—subjective well-being—is measured on an ordinal scale. Ideally, we would statistically account for this fact in an ordered response framework. In repeated cross-sections this would be straightforward. However, with panel data, it seems natural to take advantage of the possibility to account for unobserved individual heterogeneity such as individual reference levels for life satisfaction. Estimation of ordered probability models with random effects is straightforward, but the random-effects model is very restrictive, as it assumes zero correlation between the individual effect and observed characteristics. We have good reason to suspect that this assumption is violated in the present application, because the Hausman test, applied to the linear random and fixed-effects models, rejects the random-effects specification at a very high significance level. A fixed-effects model should therefore deserve more trust than a random-effects model. Greene (2001) recently showed how to avoid the computational difficulties associated with nonlinear fixed-effects models, so that estimation of a fixed-effects ordered probit model would be feasible. However, even with up to nineteen observations for each individual, the inconsistency of the individual effects (the incidental parameter problem) carries over to the slope parameters. This does not hold for the linear fixed-effects regression.

In the following analyses, we follow a different approach to account for the ordinal nature of the subjective well-being variable. We apply the "empirical normal transformation" to the life-satisfaction index (see van Praag and Baarsma [2001]). This transformation replaces the index values k on the life-satisfaction index from zero to ten by numbers.

$$k^* = N^{-1}[cum.p(k - 1) + 0.5p(k)]$$

where N denotes the standard normal distribution, $cum.p(k - 1)$ is the proportion of respondents with life satisfaction less than k, and $p(k)$ is the proportion of respondents with life satisfaction equal to k. Life satisfaction k^* has approximately a mean of 0 and standard deviation 1. Parameters can thus (again, approximately) be interpreted in terms of standard deviations.[6]

Figure 5.9 shows the development of subjective well-being over time for both men and women. It is more or less a replication of figure 5.6. Although there are some minor differences between genders, the overall pattern is the same: from 1984 to 1987, well-being declines sharply. Between 1990 and 1992, there is a characteristic reunification-hump. Well-being then falls until 1995 below the prereunification level and remains fairly constant, with some ups and downs afterward. While we also find the reunification hump in alternative sources that measure well-being over a longer period (e.g., the Eurobarometer; see fig. 5.5), it is unclear why we find the sharp decline in the first couple of years of the GSOEP. Part of this trend might be a panel artifact. Respondents seem to overstate satisfaction levels in the first waves of the GSOEP relative to later waves (see, e.g., Landua [1993], Schräpler [2001] or Jürges [2003]). Two reasons for this finding come into mind. First, respondents initially might not be willing to reveal their true level of dissatisfaction. In later waves, when the interviewer and the interview situation become familiar to the respondents, this kind of bias might vanish. Second, the satisfaction scales have endpoints. Respondents might learn that once they have stated the highest satisfaction level, they have no means to express improvements in satisfaction, and that it is only possible to convey equal or

---

6. The obtained results are similar to those without transformation (except, of course, for the different scaling), but the statistical fit is slightly better.

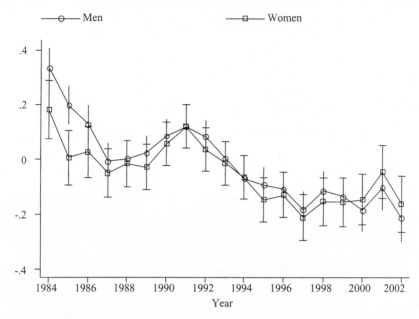

Fig. 5.9   Subjective well-being (by year and sex)

less satisfaction. Second- or third-time respondents could therefore adjust their answers downward in order to gain the flexibility to state improvements in life). Repeated measurement effects can also be found for health, income, and job satisfaction measured in GSOEP.

Since the aggregate movements of average life satisfaction in the GSOEP are quite strong, they potentially influence our results. For this reason, we use detrended satisfaction data whenever possible.[7] One potential drawback of detrending is that certain types of comparisons are no longer possible; for example, comparisons that exploit institutional variations over time. However, between 1984 and 2002, variations in the German public pension system have been minimal. As previously mentioned, the immediate effects of the 1992 reform (change from gross to net wage indexation) applied to everyone (independent of retirement age). The other changes are currently—that is, ten years after the reform—phased in slowly.

Figure 5.10 describes well-being by age for retired and nonretired individuals. While life satisfaction appears to be quite stable among males and females who are not retired, it shows a strong increase among the retired up to about age sixty. The initial gap (at age fifty-five) is between .5 standard deviations for males and 1 standard deviation for females, and de-

---

7. We detrend the data by subtracting the difference between the annual average and the overall average from each individual's value in the respective year.

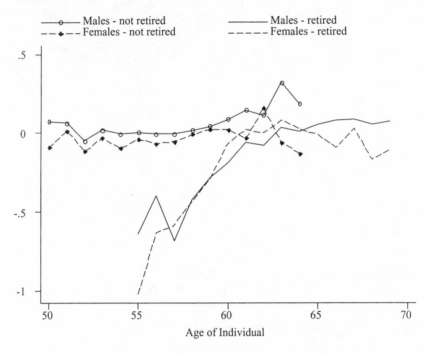

Fig. 5.10   Age trends in average life satisfaction (by sex and retirement status)

creases to about .1 standard deviations and zero, respectively. How can the result in figure 5.10 be interpreted? Are those who retire early becoming unhappy (the earlier the worse) or are those who are unhappy before age sixty more likely to retire?

To answer this question, it is instructive to compare the development of life satisfaction from age fifty to age sixty-nine for individuals who retire at different ages. For each gender, we will distinguish four different groups of retirees (see table 5.4). The first group consists of men or women retiring at age fifty-five to fifty-nine and who are legally disabled *in the year of retirement,* thus receiving disability pensions. Workers are defined as legally disabled if their capacity to work is reduced by at least 30 percent. The second group consists of all other men or women retiring at age fifty-five to fifty-nine. The third group of men consists of those who retire between age sixty and sixty-two. These are men who receive old-age pensions following unemployment or disability. The third group of men retires at age sixty-three or later, usually receiving normal old-age pensions. A large proportion of women retire at age sixty. This is the normal retirement age for women with an employment history of more than fifteen years. The third group of women are those retiring at age sixty-one or later: these are women with short employment histories.

Table 5.4   Retirement age and pension types for different subgroups (number of individuals in each group in parentheses)

	Men	Women
Disability pensions (DI)	Age 55–59	Age 55–59
	(N = 120)	(N = 40)
Other early retirement	Age 55–59	Age 55–59
	(N = 91)	(N = 51)
Old-age pensions after unemployment/disability	Age 60–62	
	(N = 384)	
Old-age pensions	Age 63–65	Age 60
	(N = 204)	(N = 207)
Old-age pensions (short employment history)		Age 61–65
		(N = 136)

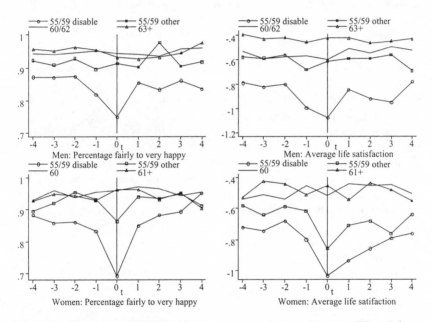

Fig. 5.11   Proportion of *fairly* to *very happy* respondents and *average life satisfaction* before and after retirement. Upper row men, lower row women

The following figures describe the development of some key well-being indicators from four years before retirement to four years after retirement, separately for men and women and for each of the four subgroups described in table 5.2. Figure 5.11 shows the proportion of respondents who are fairly to very happy (defined as having a value of between five and ten on the life-satisfaction index) and average life satisfaction. Even in this simple descriptive graph, there are a number of interesting findings. Early retirees are less happy than normal retirees, both before and after retirement. The most unhappy group are those who retire early and are disabled at retirement. It seems as if they are on a much lower life satisfaction level throughout the entire nine-year interval. For example, the proportion of men who retire on DI before they are sixty and who are at least fairly happy is, on average, somewhat more than 85 percent (see top left panel). The same proportion among those who retire between age sixty and sixty-five is about 95 percent. Put differently, the proportion of unhappy respondents is roughly three times as high among the disabled retiring before age sixty. Turning to average life satisfaction (top right panel), we see that those who retire at the normal age are the most happy throughout the entire nine-year period. Again, the least happy are early retirees who are legally disabled. Among females, the results are similar to men. The only difference is that women who retire before age sixty and who are not disabled at that time are continuously less happy than those retiring later.

Another interesting feature of figure 5.11 is the life-satisfaction trough in the year of retirement found for the DI retirees. Among men, this is the only group of retirees that shows systematic developments in well-being around retirement age. The proportion of unhappy respondents almost doubles in the retirement year. We also see some anticipation effect, as the well-being decrease already starts one year before retirement. But being unhappy does not seem to last long. One to two years after retirement, happiness among the disabled early retirees is back to the initial level. The results for women are basically similar to those for men. Happiness hits an all-time low in the year of retirement only among early retirees, but individuals mostly seem to recover quickly. To summarize, while leaving work as such does not increase the proportion of unhappy respondents, it is associated with lower well-being levels of early retirees. Of course, the causal direction of this relationship remains unclear.

Figure 5.12 describes the development of a number of disability status, self-reported general health, and per capita household income. Merely by definition, we find a large and increasing proportion of legally disabled respondents among those who retire early and are disabled at retirement. As with life satisfaction, we see a clear difference in health levels between those who retire early (presumably on disability pensions) and those who retire at the normal age. While more than 80 percent of those who retire at age sixty-three or later report being in fair or better health, the corresponding proportion among disabled early retirees is between 20 and 60 percent. Note that we do not control for age in the sense that individuals are compared at the same age. Early retirees are, in fact, younger, so that controlling for age would lead to even larger health differences.

What is even more striking than the differences in levels are health trends before and after retirement. The disabled early retirees experience gradu-

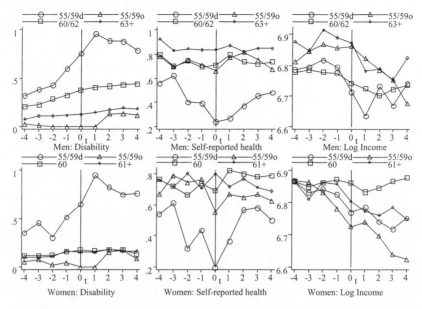

Fig. 5.12   Legal disability, self-reported health, and per capita household income before and after retirement

ally declining self-reported health until they retire. The proportion of respondents in "fair" to "very good" health declines from 60 percent three years before retirement to slightly more than 20 percent at retirement. However, after retirement, health gradually improves, and the proportion of those who are at least in "fair" health is back to nearly 50 percent. Among the other subgroups, self-reported health shows only small and probably unsystematic movements.

The right column of figure 5.12 shows log per capita household income before and after retirement. Income decreases after retirement in all subgroups except women who retire at age sixty.

5.5   Estimating the Effect of Early Retirement on Well-being

5.5.1   Estimation

As pointed out earlier, Germany has no good natural experiments that could be exploited for our purpose. We therefore start by simple before-and-after comparisons covering four years before and after retirement, separately for the eight different subgroups, and then follow with more elaborate difference-in-difference methods and their variants.

For simple before-and-after comparisons, we estimate

$$y_{it} = \sum_{t=-4}^{4} \delta_t + \gamma Z_{it} + c_i + \varepsilon_{it},$$

where $t = 0$ is the year of retirement, and we restrict $\delta_0 = 0$ to avoid dummy variable trap. Thus, δ_t measures the well-being differential between year t and the year of retirement. These estimates serve to illustrate how subjective well-being behaves around retirement age for different parts of the population. A lot of individual heterogeneity is captured by c_i; for example, a baseline satisfaction level. Others have explicitly modeled baseline satisfaction (Clark et al. 2003) by taking the average of life satisfaction before the observation period (i.e., seven to five years before the event under study). The disadvantage of this procedure for our study is obvious: all individuals that retire within the first four years of the GSOEP would drop out of the analysis. As previously mentioned, we use disability status and income as control variables Z.

We then continue by estimating differences-in-differences; that is, we compare the before-and-after estimates obtained in the first stage. For the sake of exposition let us assume there are only two types of individuals— early and normal retirees. We pool both types of individuals and estimate:

$$y_{it} = \sum_{t=-4}^{4} \delta_t + \sum_{t=-4}^{4} \beta_t R_i + \gamma Z_{it} + c_i + \varepsilon_{it},$$

where R_i indicates early retirement of individual i. We restrict $\delta_0 = \beta_0 = 0$, that is, all differences in well-being levels between early and normal retirees *at the age of retirement* are absorbed by c_i, the individual component. The double differences in well-being are measured by β_t:

$$\beta_t = [E(y_t | R, Z) - E(y_0 | R, Z)] - [E(y_t | R, Z) - E(y_0 | R, Z)]$$

5.5.2   Results

Figures 5.13 and 5.15 show the set of simple before-and-after comparisons of average life satisfaction (based on fixed-effects models). The graphs show average subjective well-being relative to $t = 0$, the year of retirement, together with the limits of a 90 percent confidence interval. The control variables used are log per capita household income and individual disability status as a measure of health.

Let us first consider figure 5.13, which contains the results for men. The top left panel shows that the life satisfaction of those who are younger than sixty and legally disabled at retirement increases by about .2 standard deviations after retirement and more or less also remains at that level in the following years. The increase is significant at the 10 percent level. Compared to the year of retirement, early retirement thus had a positive effect on the well-being of the retirees. However, it should be noted that well-being levels had already been on their post-retirement level two years be-

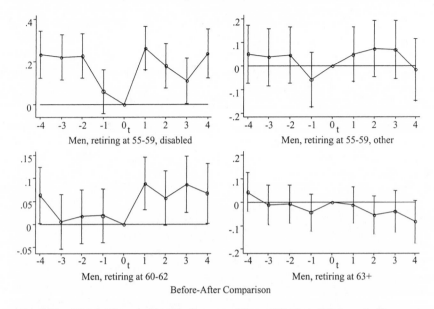

Fig. 5.13   Fixed-effects estimates of average life satisfaction, before and after retirement, men (by retirement age, with 90 percent confidence interval)

fore retirement. The graph suggests the existence of a two year preretirement dip in well-being among men who retire so early. Men who retire when they are younger than sixty (top right panel) but not disabled have only very small fluctuations in well-being, which are by no means statistically significant.

Male respondents who retire between age sixty and sixty-two also experience a significant increase in well-being in the years following retirement, although the size of the effect is only about half that of the first group (bottom left panel). There is also no preretirement dip in subjective well-being.

Finally, the bottom right panel of figure 5.13 contains the well-being development of normal retirees. Well-being levels remain largely the same before and after retirement. It seems as if normal retirement thus has no effect on individual well-being. The slight downward trend is not significant.

Figure 5.14 contains the results for women. The picture for female early retirees is similar to that for male early retirees: retirement proves to be beneficial for well-being if post-retirement years are compared to the year of retirement itself. But if we look back further to three or four years before retirement, we get the impression rather that early retirement is associated with a temporary drop in well-being. In contrast to men, the well-being increase after retirement is not statistically significant. However, this is mainly due to the smaller sample size. Another difference to men is that

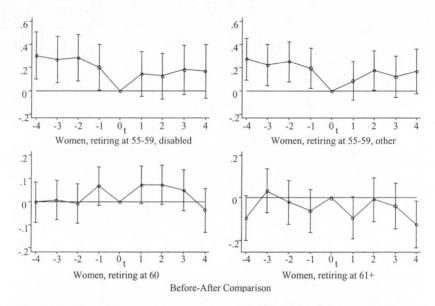

Women, retiring at 55-59, disabled

Women, retiring at 55-59, other

Women, retiring at 60

Women, retiring at 61+

Before-After Comparison

Fig. 5.14   Fixed-effects estimates of average life satisfaction, before and after re-tirement, women (by retirement age, with 90 percent confidence interval)

nondisabled early retirees show very much the same pattern as disabled early retirees. It seems as if these are not really different groups of individuals. We currently have no good explanation for that result.

For women who retire at or after the normal retirement age (sixty), well-being evolves in a similar fashion as for their male counterparts. There are a few ups and downs, but no systematic trends. If anything, retirement seems to be slightly beneficial in the first three years after retirement for those who retire at age sixty, but the effect is not significant.

We now compare early retirees with normal retirees and estimate differences-in-differences. The results are reported in the fig. 5.15 and 5.16, again together with their 90 percent confidence intervals. The male comparison group is those retiring at age sixty-three to sixty-five. The female comparison group is those who retire at age sixty. The differences-in-differences results are not much different than the simple before-and-after comparisons in the top rows. That was to be expected, given the relatively flat well-being profile of normal retirees. The added value is that we have standard errors (or confidence intervals, respectively) for the difference between early and normal retirees. Among men, all three groups of early re-tirees enjoy larger increases in levels of life satisfaction after retirement than normal retirees. The difference is not significant for nondisabled early retirees. Among women, there is a significant decrease in well-being before retirement, followed by a nonsignificant increase after retirement.

The general picture that emerges from our analysis is that early retire-

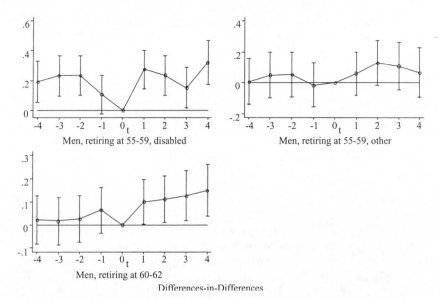

Fig. 5.15 **Difference-in-differences estimates of average life satisfaction, before and after retirement, men (by retirement age, with 90 percent confidence interval)**

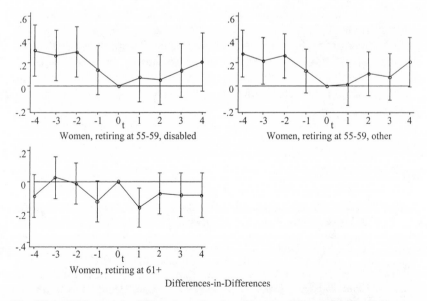

Fig. 5.16 **Difference-in-differences estimates of average life satisfaction, before and after retirement, women (by retirement age, with 90 percent confidence interval)**

ment, as such, seems to be related to subjective well-being—in fact, more so than normal retirement. Individuals are generally less happy in the year of retirement than in the years before and after retirement. Early retirement appears to be accompanied by a negative (most probably health-related) shock to well-being, but after a short while, things go back to normal—that is, the effect is negative and short-lived rather than positive and long.

5.6   Summary and Conclusion

The main results of this chapter can be summarized as follows: at ages younger than sixty, those who are currently retired are, on average, much less happy than those still working. The difference is mainly due to a composition effect. Early retirees are mostly people on disability pensions. If disability status is controlled for, the well-being differential between early retirees and those still working vanishes. Thus, it is not retirement as such that reduces life satisfaction, but disability.

Those who retire early are, on average, less happy than those who retire later. This holds at each age; that is, before, at, and after retirement. In other words: the unhappy retire earlier but they never catch up with the happier ones.

Early retirement (because of disability) increases well-being significantly. Early retirement is more beneficial than normal retirement, but only if post-retirement years are compared to the year of retirement itself. Looking further back reveals that there is a marked drop in life satisfaction in preretirement years.

Our conclusion, therefore, is: early retirement most probably is a reaction to a health shock. Retirement helps those affected because they attain their preretirement satisfaction levels one or two years after retirement. Whether this is an effect of retirement itself or a psychological adaptation is still an open issue.

References

Berkel, B., and A. Börsch-Supan. 2004. Pension reform in Germany: The impact on retirement decisions. *Finanzarchiv* 3 (September): 393–421.

Börsch-Supan, A. 2000. A model under siege: A case study of the Germany Retirement Insurance System. *The Economic Journal* 110:24–45.

Börsch-Supan, A. S. Kohnz, and R. Schnabel. 2004. Budget effects of pension reform in Germany. In *Social Security programs and retirement around the world: Fiscal implications,* ed. J. Gruber and D. A. Wise, 135–80. Chicago: University of Chicago Press.

Börsch-Supan, A. and R. Schnabel. 1998. Social Security and declining labor force participation in Germany. *American Economic Review* 88:173–78.
———. 1999. Social Security and retirement in germany. In *Social Security and retirement around the world,* ed. J. Gruber and D. A. Wise, 135–81. Chicago: University of Chicago Press.
Börsch-Supan, A., R. Schnabel, S. Kohnz, and G. Mastrobuoni. 2004. Micro modelling of retirement choices in Germany. In *Social Security programs and retirement around the world: Micro-Estimation,* ed. J. Gruber and D. A. Wise, 285–343. Chicago: University of Chicago Press.
Börsch-Supan, A., and C. Wilke. 2003. The German Social Security System: How it was and how it will be. MEA-Discussion Paper 43-2003. MEA, Universität Mannheim, and MRRC-Discussion Paper, University of Michigan, Ann Arbor.
Bound, J. 1991. Self-reported versus objective measures of health in retirement models. *Journal of Human Resources* 26:106–38.
Charles, K. K. 2002. Is retirement depressing? Labor force inactivity and psychological well-being in later life. NBER Working Paper no. 9033. Cambridge, MA: National Bureau of Economic Research.
Clark, A. E., Diener, E., Georgellis, Y., and Lucas, R. E. 2003. Lags and leads in life satisfaction: A test of the baseline hypothesis. DIW Discussion Paper no. 371. Berlin: German Institute for Economic Research.
Greene W. 2001. Estimating econometric models with fixed effects. New York University Finance Department Working Paper no. 01-10.
Jürges, H. 2003. Age, cohort, and the slump in job satisfaction among West German workers. *Labour* 17:489–518.
Landua D. 1993. Veränderungen von Zufriedenheitsangaben in Panelbefragungen. *Kölner Zeitschrift für Soziologie und Sozialpsychologie* 45:553–71.
Lindeboom, M., Portrait, F., and van den Berg, G. J. 2002. An econometric analysis of the mental-health effects of major events in the life of elderly individuals. *Health Economics* 11:505–20.
Schräpler, J. 2001. Respondent behaviour in panel studies: A case study of the German Socio-Economic Panel. DIW Discussion Paper no. 244. Berlin: German Institute for Economic Research.
Stock, J. H., and Wise, D. A. 1990. The pension inducement to retire: An option value analysis. In *Issues in the economics of aging,* ed. D. A. Wise, 205–30. Chicago: The University of Chicago Press.
van Praag, B. M. S., and B. E. Baarsma. 2001. The shadow price of aircraft noise nuisance. Tinbergen Institute Discussion Paper 2001-010/3.
Winkelmann, L. and R. Winkelmann. 1998. Why are the unemployed so unhappy? *Economica* 65:1–15.

IV

Health and Economic Circumstances

6

How Do the Better Educated Do It? Socioeconomic Status and the Ability to Cope with Underlying Impairment

David M. Cutler, Mary Beth Landrum, and
Kate A. Stewart

The pronounced gradient in health among people in different socioeconomic groups is well known. People who are richer or better educated live longer and have a higher quality of life than people in lower socioeconomic status (SES) groups. The reason for this difference is not well understood, however. Health results from decisions made throughout the life course (McGinness and Foege 1993), perhaps even before birth (Barker 1994). To date, most attempts to explain the gradient have come up shorthanded (Adler et al. 1993), even those exploring health differences among youths (Case, Lubotsky, and Paxson 2002). In this chapter, we focus on one particular dimension of the socioeconomic gradient in health. We examine how elderly people in different socioeconomic groups cope with disability in performing basic personal care activities, including dressing, bathing, and getting around inside, and activities required to live independently, such as preparing meals, grocery shopping, and managing money.

Gradients in disability by socioeconomic status have been found in a large number of studies (see, for example, Fried and Guralnik 1997; Stuck et al. 1999; Guralnik, Fried, and Salive 1996, and the references therein) and recent studies have documented growing disparities in disability by socioeconomic status (Crimmins and Saito 2001; Schoeni et al. 2005). Two re-

David M. Cutler is the Otto Eckstein Professor of Applied Economics and dean of the social sciences at Harvard University, and a research associate of the National Bureau of Economic Research. Mary Beth Landrum is an associate professor of biostatistics in the department of health care policy at Harvard Medical School. Kate A. Stewart is a researcher at Mathematica Policy Research, Inc., and was a PhD candidate in health policy at Harvard Medical School when this research was completed.

We are grateful to Michael Hurd and members of the National Bureau of Economic Research Aging Group for comments on an earlier version. This work was funded by the National Institute of Aging (R01AG019805).

cent studies have attempted to understand the causal pathways between socioeconomic status and disability by examining transitions between health states, using longitudinal data. Zimmer and House (2003) decompose the association between education, income, and prevalent disability into two pieces: onset of new disability and progression among those disabled. They find that both income and education is associated with onset, but only income predicts subsequent progression, suggesting that income can serve both to prevent ill health and allow individuals to better manage illness. Similarly, Melzer et al. (2001) examined incidence, recovery, and mortality rates by educational attainment and found that education was strongly associated with incidence of disability but not related to recovery or risk of death among the disabled. In these studies, recovery or progression of disability could result from a number of factors, including better management of the diseases underlying the limitations and better ability to cope with limitations. In this chapter, we examine a single piece of this puzzle and consider whether differences in coping strategies allow the better off to resolve their disability more effectively than the less well off.

The motivation for our analysis is provided in figure 6.1. Panel A of the figure shows the age- and sex-adjusted income and education gradients in impairment in any of a number of measures of self-care tasks, such as bathing, dressing, and related activities (the data set and specific measures of disability are described later). We show impairment even accounting for the use of personal and technological aids. There is a very pronounced education relation in this measure of disability. Among those with less than any high school education, about 8 percent of the elderly are disabled. In the highest education group—those who are college grads—the rate is half as high. There is a moderate income gradient in disability as well, although the difference is primarily between the very poor—those earning below $10,000—and everyone else.

Panel B of this figure shows the income and education gradients in impairment in various measures of independent functioning, such as the ability to shop or do light housework. The story is very similar. Over 20 percent of the elderly with less than any high school are disabled, compared to below 15 percent among those with some college or more. There is also an income gradient in impairment along these dimensions. With one exception (people earning $40,000–$49,000 per year), disability declines monotonically with higher income.

Our analysis considers two primary issues. First, we ask how much of this gradient in health is a result of underlying differences in functioning versus the ability to cope with impairments. We show that while the bulk of the difference is a result of underlying functioning—the better off have much less difficulty with these measures even in the absence of help—coping is important as well. The better educated are less likely to have functional disabilities in the first place, and cope with them better when they occur.

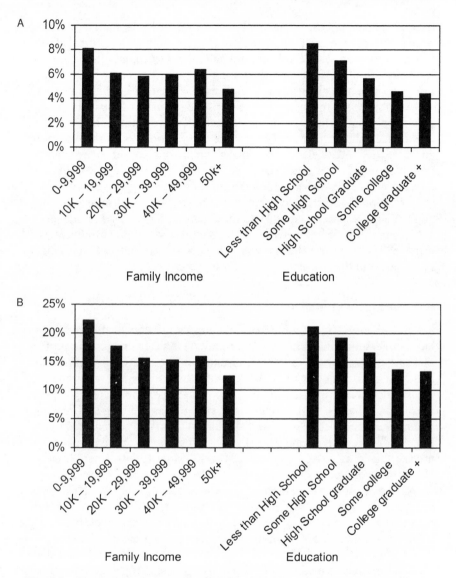

Fig. 6.1   Share of elderly reporting disability in ADLs or IADLS, even with use of help: *A*, **Any ADLs;** *B*, **Any IADLs**

Note: Estimates are adjusted for the age and sex mix of the population.

Second, we consider how the better educated elderly cope, and in particular whether the use of personal help and technological aids are important for successful coping. Better educated people use substantially more assistive technology than the less educated and are more likely to use paid help. Surprisingly, they are substantially less likely to use help from relatives, so that overall use of personal care is actually lower among the better educated than among the less educated, even given their functional status.

Knowing about use of aids or paid help does not explain the education gradient in coping, however. Controlling for type of coping strategies does not affect in a material way the pronounced education gradient in coping with disability. We speculate that perhaps the intensity of use varies across education groups, that there is an interaction between the technology that is available and the environment in which the person lives, or that the more educated are more likely to cope through behavioral and/or environmental modifications (coping strategies not examined in this paper). Because our data go only so far, we leave open the analysis of these specific hypotheses.

Our chapter is structured as follows. The first section discusses the disability measures we considered and the data used. The second section presents analyses of the link between socioeconomic status and disability. The third section examines alternative explanations for the education gradient in coping, and the last section presents our conclusions.

6.1   Measures of Disability

Disability is a complex concept, related to a person's health, his or her environment, and his or her role expectations. As such, there is no perfect measure of disability. While most research in the nonelderly defines disability in terms of ability to work, we follow the lead of most researchers in measuring disability in the elderly as the presence of impairments in activities of daily living (ADLs), self-care tasks such as dressing and bathing, and instrumental activities of daily living (IADLs)—tasks required to live independently, such as preparing meals, doing housework, and managing money. Our data source, Phase 1 of the National Health Interview Disability Supplement of 1994 and 1995 (NHIS-D)—includes information on six ADL measures: bathing, dressing, eating, transferring to and from bed, toileting, and getting around inside the home. Questions are also asked about six IADL measures: grocery shopping, managing money, preparing meals, heavy housework, light housework, and using the telephone.

For any particular measure of disability, there are three relevant concepts. The first is termed *intrinsic disability,* the share of people who report difficulty on an item in the absence of any help from other people or equipment. We measure intrinsic disability for ADL tasks using a set of three questions from the NHIS-D. First, respondents are asked about receiving help from another person[1] and about the use of special equipment to per-

---

1. Specific questions are: "Because of physical, mental, or emotional problems, do you get help from another person" and "Because of a physical, mental, or emotional problem do you need to be reminded to do or need to have someone close by to do them" for ADL tasks, and "Because of a physical, mental, or emotional problem do you get help or supervision from another person" for IADL tasks.

form the task. Respondents who do not report personal or equipment help to do the activity are asked if they have any difficulty performing the task. We consider respondents to have intrinsic ADL disability if they either receive help from another person, use equipment to perform a task, or deny either of these forms of help but report difficulty performing the task. The NHIS-D did not ask about the use of special equipment for IADL tasks. Thus we define respondents as having intrinsic IADL disability if they report receiving help with the task or report difficulty in the absence of help.

We define *residual disability* as the share of people who report difficulty on an item even with help from others or special equipment. In the NHIS-D, respondents who report using special equipment or receiving help to perform a task were also asked how much difficulty they have performing the task even with this help.[2] We consider a respondent to have residual disability if he or she reports at least some difficulty, even with the help or use of equipment, or if he or she reports that help or use of equipment is not received, but he or she but does have difficulty with the task.

The difference between intrinsic and residual difficulty is termed *coping*. Specifically, we define coping as that share of the population with intrinsic disability who do not have residual disability (i.e., the fraction of people for whom disability is completely resolved through the use of special equipment or help from another person).

There are many data sets that ask about either intrinsic disability (for example, the National Long Term Care Survey [NLTCS], the Medicare Current Beneficiary Survey [MCBS], and all years of the National Health Interview Survey [NHIS]). However, there are only a few data sets that ask about residual disability,[3] and to our knowledge only three data sets that asks about both intrinsic and residual disability—the NHIS-D, the 1993 AHEAD, and the First National Health and Nutrition Examination Survey (NHANES I) Epidemiologic Followup Study (NHEFS).[4] We chose

2. The response options for this question are no difficulty, some difficulty, a lot of difficulty, or completely unable.

3. For example, Verbrugge and Sevak (2002) also used residual disability measures in the NHIS-D to study the efficacy of various types of assistance; Verbrugge, Rennert, and Madans (1997) used measures of residual disability in the NHANES I, and Taylor and Hoenig (2004) and Agree (1999) studied residual disability using the Asset and Health Dynamics Among the Oldest Old (AHEAD). Several investigators have also examined coping with disability using other outcomes. For example, Agree and Freedman (2003) examined pain, fatigue, and time intensity associated with tasks, even when using help using the NHIS-D Phase 2 surveys, and Penning and Strain (1994) examined subjective feelings of well-being among those using assistance with daily tasks.

4. The 1993 AHEAD asks a similar set of questions about intrinsic and residual disability in ADLs as the NHIS-D. Specifically, respondents were first asked, "Does anyone ever help you . . . ," then for two of the ADLs (getting around inside and getting in and out of bed), respondents were asked, "Do you ever use equipment or devices when . . ." Respondents who report the use of either personal assistance or special equipment were then asked, "Even when someone helps you/using the equipment, do you have any difficulty . . ." Finally, respondents who deny personal or equipment help were asked, "Without any help or special equipment,

not to use the NHEFS because the data were collected in the 1980s and included only approximately 10,000 individuals. While the HRS/AHEAD data contains more detailed information on socioeconomic measures than the NHIS, we chose to use the NHIS-D in our analysis, for several reasons. First, the sample size is substantially larger for the 1994 to 1995 NHIS-D (almost 25,000 respondents age sixty-five and older, compared to approximately 8,000 respondents to the 1993 AHEAD). Second, the AHEAD data only contains information on residual disability in ADL measures, while the NHIS-D asked respondents about difficulty with help for ADL and IADL tasks. Finally, the AHEAD only asked respondents about the use of special equipment to aid in the performance of two of the ADL tasks.

The NHIS-D was conducted in 1994 and 1995 as a supplement to the regular National Health Interview Survey. The survey was administered in person at the same time as the NHIS Core and collected information on all members of the household age five and over. Several limitations of the NHIS-D should be noted. First, the NHIS is restricted to people living in the community. Disability rates are thus lower than those found in surveys that include institutionalized individuals (such as the NLTCS or the MCBS). Our analysis will not take into account SES differences in the likelihood of nursing home use. As residence in a nursing home suggests inability to cope with declining health and disability, our analysis may underestimate SES differentials in the ability to cope with disability.

Second, the NHIS-D contains imperfect measures of household income. Household income was measured in the 1994 and 1995 NHIS through two survey questions. First, respondents were asked if their family income was lower or higher than $20,000. Then respondents were asked to categorize their income into twenty-seven income groups. The detailed categories were not reported by approximately 20 percent of respondents in our sample.[5] For these respondents, the NCHS imputed family income using sequential hot-deck imputation within matrix cells.[6] Because of these mea-

---

do you have any difficulty . . ." In contrast, the NHEFS first asked about difficulty with twelve everyday tasks without assistance; "Please tell me if you have no difficulty, some difficulty, much difficulty, or are unable to do . . . at all when you are by yourself and without the use of aids." Those reporting much difficulty or being unable to do the task were then asked about assistance from another person or help from special equipment, and those using assistance were asked about the degree of difficulty when they used the assistance.

5. The weaknesses in this approach to assessing household income become apparent by contrasting it to the approach taken in the HRS. For example, while 45 percent of responding households to the 1993 AHEAD refused to report their exact household income, 75 percent of these respondents completed an unfolding cascade while an additional 11 percent completed some of the unfolding cascade, so that household income was completely missing for only 6 percent of the households.

6. The imputation was aided by detailed income and wealth data collected in the Family Resource Supplement. Specifically, respondents age sixty-five and over were cross-classified according to total monthly family income reported in the Family Resources Supplement and median household income in their sampling segment. Within these cells, respondents were then sorted according to marital status, educational attainment, gender, and race-ethnicity

surement issues, and because household income may not adequately reflect resources and assets in an elderly retired sample, we focus our primary attention on the relationship between coping and education, noting that our estimates of the relationship between household income, disability, and coping are inherently limited by the available data.

The NHIS-D also collects data on difficulty with several measures of physical functioning: lifting something as heavy as ten pounds, walking up ten steps without resting, walking a quarter of a mile, standing for about twenty minutes, bending down from a standing position to pick up an object from the floor, reaching up overhead or reaching out as if to shake someone's hand, using fingers to grasp or handle something, and holding a pen or pencil, and the use of specific assistive technologies (not in conjunction with ADL or IADL tasks) including canes, crutches, walkers, orthopedic shoes, manual and electric wheelchairs, scooters, and braces. Sociodemographic variables include information on respondents' age, race, gender, marital status, educational attainment, and household income, taken from the core survey. All analyses accounted for the complex survey design and for pooling data from both survey years using approximations based on Taylor-series linearizations.[7]

6.2   Descriptive Statistics

We start our empirical analysis with basic data on disability. Although the NHIS-D is administered to people of nearly all ages, we focus on the elderly population (ages sixty-five and older), since ADL and IADL disability rates are much higher in the elderly than in the nonelderly. This also allows us to compare our results with most of the existing literature, which has focused predominantly on the elderly population. In two years of administration, the NHIS-D collected data on 24,791 people age sixty-five and older.

Table 6.1 presents basic descriptive data on the population. Fifty-eight percent of the population is female and 89 percent is white. Fifty-seven percent of the population is married and a third is widowed. The education distribution is skewed toward less completed schooling. Twenty-two per-

---

for respondents who indicated their household income was less than $20,000, and according to educational attainment, hours worked per week, marital status, and number of adult workers in the family for those who reported their income to be over $20,000. Hot-deck imputation was then implemented within these sorted cells. For more details see "Methods used to impute annual family income in the National Health Interview Survey, 1990–1996" http://www.cdc.gov/nchs/products/elec_prods/subject/impute.htm. Last accessed December 22, 2005.

7. For details, see "Variance estimation for person data using Sudaan and the National Health Interview Survey (NHIS): Public use person data files, 1994–1995: Combining 1994 and 1995 data only" http://www.cdc.gov/nchs/data/nhis/94_95var.pdf. Last accessed December 22, 2005.

Table 6.1   Demographic characteristics of 65 and over population from NHIS-D, 1994 and 1995

	Percent of people ($N = 24,791$; weighted $N = 31,245,306$)
Male	41.7
Married	57.0
Div/sep	6.4
Widowed	32.5
Never married	4.0
Unknown marital status	0.1
Black/other	10.5
Age	
65–69	31.0
70–74	27.7
75–79	19.8
80–84	12.8
85 and over	8.6
Education	
Less than high school	21.8
Some high school	15.4
High school grad	34.7
Some college	13.7
College grad or higher	13.3
Unknown educational attainment	1.1
Annual Family Income	
0–9,999	18.3
10K–19,999	30.8
20K–29,999	21.3
30K–39,999	11.6
40K–49,999	6.5
50k+	11.5

cent of the sample did not start high school. Another fifteen percent started high school but did not finish. Modal income is between $10,000 and $20,000.

Table 6.2 shows data on disability and coping rates. Nearly 10 percent of the population reports some intrinsic ADL disability. This rate is comparable to other surveys that have asked about intrinsic disability among community dwelling elderly. For example, rates of ADL disability—defined as getting help or using special equipment with one or more ADL, among community-dwelling elderly age seventy were approximately 15 percent in the 1995 HRS and the 1994 NLTCS and slightly over 20 percent in the 1994 MCBS (Freedman et al. 2004). Over 6 percent of the respondents report residual disability (difficulty completing the task even with

Table 6.2   Intrinsic and residual disability in the population and ability to cope among the intrinsically disabled, by type of ADL and IADL (*N* = 24,791)

	Percentage reporting intrinsic disability	Percentage reporting residual disability	Percentage of respondents with intrinsic disability who cope effectively
Activities of daily living (any)	9.5	6.4	32.3
Bathing	7.7	4.7	39.1
Getting around inside	4.4	3.2	26.6
Dressing	4.4	2.9	33.5
Transferring	4.1	3.1	25.4
Toileting	3.7	2.3	36.9
Eating	1.4	0.9	37.8
Instrumental activities of daily living (any)	22.7	17.0	25.3
Heavy housework	21.6	15.7	27.0
Shopping	9.8	6.7	31.9
Light housework	7.3	5.4	26.1
Preparing meals	5.9	4.1	31.3
Managing money	4.8	3.0	36.9
Using the telephone	2.5	1.7	32.1

help or special equipment) on at least one ADL, meaning that approximately one-third of the elderly population effectively copes with an underlying health problem, so that all of their ADL limitations are resolved through the use of help or equipment.[8] Looking within categories, the most common ADL impairment is difficulty bathing (7.7 percent) and the least common is difficulty eating (1.4 percent). The other measures are relatively similar, at about 4 percent each. Coping rates vary less across the tasks, ranging from 25 percent for transferring to 39 percent for bathing.

A much larger share of the population—nearly one quarter—reports an intrinsic IADL disability. The ability to cope with IADL disability is smaller; only one-quarter of people report that help completely alleviates their difficulty in performing important tasks required for independent living. By a wide margin, the most common IADL disability is doing heavy housework (22 percent). Activities associated with lighter housework or

8. Verbrugge and Sevak (2002) found similar levels of coping across ADL and IADL tasks among NHIS-D respondents age fifty-five and older. These rates can also be compared to those reported by Agree (1999) in an analysis of the 1993 AHEAD. She found that 68 percent of respondents with ADL disability reported residual difficulty performing tasks. Verbrugge, Rennert, and Madans (1997), analyzing data from the NHANES I Epidemiologic Followup Study, found that assistance (either personal or equipment) resolved difficulty in about 25 percent of those with functional limitations and/or disability.

shopping are second in importance (7 to 10 percent). Coping rates are again not particularly different across the various categories, ranging from 26 percent for light housework to 37 percent for managing money.

Figure 6.1 presented the relation between socioeconomic status and residual disability. Figure 6.2 presents the complementary figure for intrinsic disability. As with residual disability, intrinsic disability is substantially different by income and education. The highest education group has

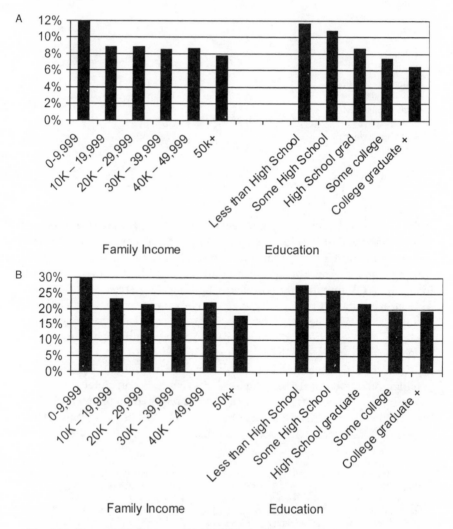

Fig. 6.2 Share of elderly reporting disability in ADLS or IADLS in the absence of receiving help: *A*, Any ADLs; *B*, Any IADLs

Note: Estimates are adjusted for the age and sex mix of the population.

an intrinsic disability rate for ADLs that is approximately half as large as the lowest education group. The variation across income groups is slightly smaller, but still large. There is large variation in IADL disability both by income and education.

The key issue for coping is the difference between intrinsic and residual disability. Figure 6.3 shows how coping varies by income and education. There is little variation in ability to cope with ADL impairments by income (fig. 6.3a). Only the highest income group has higher rates of coping than

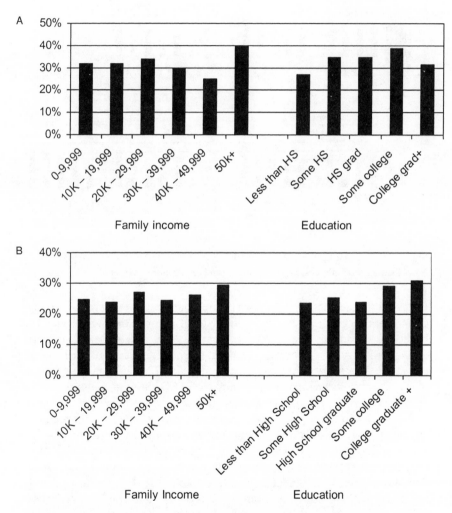

Fig. 6.3   Ability to cope for "any ADLs" and "any IADLs" by family income and education, adjusted for age and sex: *A*, Any ADLs; *B*, Any IADLs

Note: Estimates are adjusted for the age and sex mix of the population.

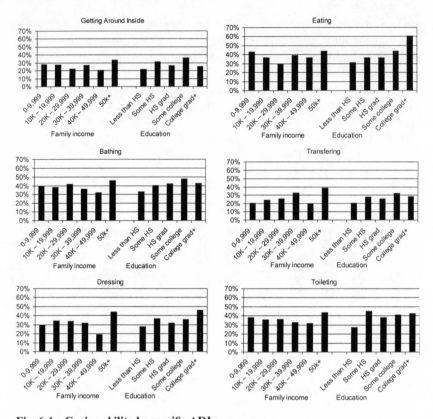

Fig. 6.4   Coping ability by specific ADLs
Note: Estimates are adjusted for the age and sex mix of the population.

the average, and the second-highest group has the lowest rates of coping. Coping ability generally increases with education, with the exception of the best educated group. Thirty-nine percent of those with some college cope with intrinsic ADL disability, compared to only 27 percent of the less well educated. The story is similar for coping with IADL impairments (fig. 6.3b). There is little variation in coping with IADL impairments across income groups, and a pronounced education gradient in coping.

Figures 6.4 and 6.5 show income and education gradients in coping, according to task. Education gradients in ADL coping are most pronounced for coping with difficulties in eating and dressing. This is interesting, given that these are areas where use of equipment is very minor, but use of personal help is much greater (shown in table 6.7). Education gradients in coping with IADL disabilities are largest for light and heavy housework—again, areas where personal help, especially paid help, can be very important. In contrast, there are few differences across income and educa-

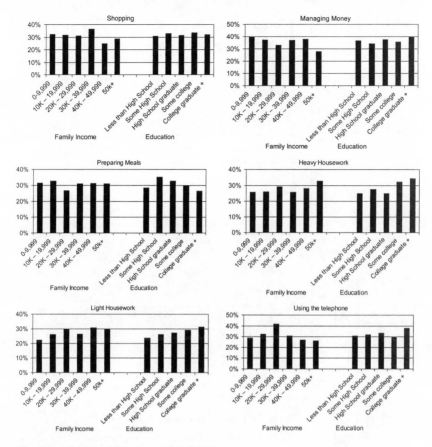

Fig. 6.5   Coping ability by specific IADLs

Note: Estimates are adjusted for the age and sex mix of the population.

tion groups in coping with difficulties managing money, grocery shopping, and using the telephone.

While figures 6.1 through 6.3 are age and sex adjusted, we also want to control for other demographic differences across groups. Table 6.3 reports basic regression results for intrinsic disability and table 6.4 shows results for residual disability. The first regression in each table is for any disability—either ADL or IADL impairment; the second and third regressions are for any ADL and IADL disability separately. In addition to five-year age and sex groups and their interaction and the income and education dummy variables, we include controls for marital status (married, widowed, or separated/divorced/single) interacted with gender and race (white or nonwhite).

Older and nonwhite respondents are more likely to report disability and

Table 6.3 Logistic regression models for intrinsic disability

Independent variable	Any disability		Any ADL disability		Any IADL disability	
	Coefficient (SE)	Adjusted percent	Coefficient (SE)	Adjusted percent	Coefficient (SE)	Adjusted percent
Income						
$0–$9,999		28.4		10.3		26.6
$10K–$19,000	-0.24 (0.05)*	24.2	-0.20 (0.06)*	8.7	-0.21 (0.05)*	22.9
$20K–$29,999	-0.29 (0.06)*	23.4	-0.11 (0.08)	9.4	-0.25 (0.06)*	22.3
$30K–$39,999	-0.32 (0.07)*	22.9	-0.10 (0.10)	9.4	-0.29 (0.08)*	21.7
$40K–$49,999	-0.18 (0.09)*	25.2	-0.05 (0.11)	9.9	-0.16 (0.09)	23.8
$50K +	-0.43 (0.08)*	21.1	-0.14 (0.11)	9.1	-0.41 (0.08)*	19.8
Education						
Less than high school		27.9		11.3		26.3
Some high school	-0.08 (0.05)	26.5	-0.07 (0.07)	10.7	-0.07 (0.05)	25.1
High school graduate	-0.24 (0.05)*	23.7	-0.30 (0.06)*	8.8	-0.24 (0.05)*	22.2
Some college	-0.40 (0.06)*	21.1	-0.45 (0.09)*	7.7	-0.39 (0.06)*	20.0
College grad or higher	-0.38 (0.07)*	21.4	-0.62 (0.09)*	6.6	-0.34 (0.07)*	20.7
Male	-0.33 (0.07)*		0.01 (0.12)		-0.38 (0.07)*	
Age 70–74	0.18 (0.06)*		0.43 (0.10)*		0.15 (0.06)*	
Age 75–79	0.55 (0.07)*		0.73 (0.10)*		0.51 (0.07)*	
Age 80–84	0.98 (0.07)*		1.42 (0.11)*		0.93 (0.07)*	
Age 85+	1.57 (0.08)*		1.94 (0.11)*		1.52 (0.08)*	

Age*sex			
70–74*male	0.05 (0.10)	0.28 (0.17)	0.06 (0.10)
75–79*male	-0.02 (0.11)	-0.14 (0.17)	-0.06 (0.11)
80–84*male	0.11 (0.10)	0.24 (0.17)	0.09 (0.10)
85plus*male	0.01 (0.12)	0.23 (0.17)	0.02 (0.12)
Widowed	0.32 (0.05)*	0.29 (0.07)*	0.33 (0.05)*
Divorced/separated/single	0.26 (0.18)*	0.34 (0.10)*	0.24 (0.08)*
Marital status*sex			
Widowed*male	0.02 (0.09)	-0.07 (0.13)	0.05 (0.09)
Divorced/separated/Single*male	0.02 (0.11)	-0.11 (0.16)	0.13 (0.11)
Black/other race	0.11 (0.06)	0.18 (0.08)*	0.12 (0.06)*
N	24,476	24,476	24,476

Notes: The definition of intrinsic ADL disability includes difficulty alone or without help or equipment; the definition for intrinsic IADL disability includes only difficulty alone or without help. Individuals missing values for educational attainment ($n = 295$) and/or marital status ($n = 25$) were dropped from regression analyses.

* $p < 0.05$.

Table 6.4   Logistic regression models for residual disability

	Any disability		Any ADL disability		Any IADL disability	
	Coefficient (SE)	Adjusted percent	Coefficient (SE)	Adjusted percent	Coefficient (SE)	Adjusted percent
Income						
$0–$9,999		21.5		7.1		19.8
$10K–$19,000	−0.19 (0.05)*	18.7	−0.20 (0.07)*	5.9	−0.17 (0.06)*	17.4
$20K–$29,999	−0.26 (0.06)*	17.8	−0.15 (0.09)	6.2	−0.25 (0.07)*	16.3
$30K–$39,999	−0.24 (0.08)*	18.0	−0.07 (0.12)	6.6	−0.23 (0.09)*	16.5
$40K–$49,999	−0.16 (0.09)	19.2	0.03 (0.13)	7.3	−0.15 (0.10)	17.6
$50K +	−0.42 (0.09)*	15.7	−0.27 (0.15)	5.5	−0.42 (0.09)*	14.2
Education						
Less than high school		22.1		8.3		20.0
Some high school	−0.11 (0.05)*	20.4	−0.18 (0.08)*	7.1	−0.09 (0.05)	18.7
High school graduate	−0.26 (0.05)*	18.2	−0.41 (0.07)*	5.8	−0.22 (0.05)*	16.9
Some college	−0.48 (0.06)*	15.4	−0.63 (0.11)*	4.7	−0.43 (0.06)*	14.3
College grad or higher	−0.49 (0.07)*	15.3	−0.67 (0.11)*	4.5	−0.42 (0.07)*	14.4
Male	−0.31 (0.08)*		0.04 (0.13)		−0.33 (0.05)*	
Age 70–74	0.12 (0.07)		0.45 (0.11)*		0.10 (0.07)	
Age 75–79	0.49 (0.07)*		0.72 (0.12)*		0.48 (0.07)*	
Age 80–84	0.89 (0.07)*		1.37 (0.12)*		0.83 (0.08)*	
Age 85+	1.40 (0.09)*		1.81 (0.13)*		1.33 (0.09)*	

Age*sex			
70–74*male	0.10 (0.11)	-0.42 (0.20)*	0.14 (0.11)
75–79*male	0.01 (0.11)	0.06 (0.19)	-0.06 (0.12)
80–84*male	0.11 (0.12)	-0.22 (0.18)	0.11 (0.12)
85plus*male	0.16 (0.13)	-0.26 (0.20)	0.15 (0.13)
Widowed	0.27 (0.06)*	0.12 (0.09)	0.29 (0.06)*
Divorced/separated/single	0.32 (0.07)*	0.30 (0.11)*	0.31 (0.08)*
Marital status*sex			
Widowed*male	0.01 (0.10)	-0.04 (0.16)	0.01 (0.10)
Divorced/separate/single*male	-0.04 (0.12)	-0.20 (0.19)	0.03 (0.12)
Black/other race	0.10 (0.07)	0.16 (0.09)	0.12 (0.07)
N	24,476	24,476	24,476

Notes: The definition of intrinsic ADL disability includes difficulty alone or without help or equipment; the definition for intrinsic IADL disability includes only difficulty alone or without help. Individuals missing values for educational attainment ($n = 295$) and/or marital status ($n = 25$) were dropped from regression analyses.

*$p < 0.05$.

women are more likely to report IADL disability. There is little indication that age effects varied by gender of the respondents. Single people, whether widowed or divorced/separated/never married, have higher rates of disability than do married people. Surprisingly, this effect is similar for men and women. Including these demographic variables has little impact on the education and income results. For example, the difference in residual ADL disability between the best educated and the least educated in figure 6.1 is 4.1 percentage points; the difference in table 6.4 is 3.8 percentage points. In the case of residual IADL disability, the unadjusted difference is 7.7 percentage points, and the adjusted difference is 5.6 percentage points. Our findings are thus not an artifact of demographic differences in the various groups.

Table 6.5 shows how coping differs by income and education, controlling for demographic factors and the severity of the underlying disability as measured by the number of reported limitations. Ability to cope is strongly negatively related to the number of limitations. In contrast to intrinsic or residual disability, there are few differences across demographic groups in coping with disability.[9] Similar to the age- and sex-adjusted results presented in figure 6.3, we find differential effects in coping by education but not by income. Coping with ADL disability is four to ten percentage points higher among all respondents with at least some high school compared to those who never started high school, with the highest rates of coping (38 percent) among those with some college education. Coping with IADL disability is about five percentage points higher among college graduates compared to those with a high school degree or less.

Because there may be differences in the relationship between coping with disability and socioeconomic status according to gender, we examined differences in coping separately by women and men. Figure 6.6 displays differences in coping by education and income in men and women (full regression results reported in tables 6A.1 and 6A.2 in the Appendix). In contrast to combined results in men and women, there are income differentials in coping among men, particularly at the highest levels of income. Coping rates are eleven percentage points higher among men with family incomes $50,000 and over compared to those with incomes under $10,000. Differences in coping by level of education are only evident among women, although the small number of males in our sample limits our power to detect these associations. Coping rates are four to eight percentage points higher in women with at least a high school diploma compared to women with less than high school education.

9. This is similar to results presented in Verbrugge and Sevak (2002), who find that need characteristics, such as severity of disability and poor health status, explain as much as 30 percent of the variance in resolving difficulty with ADL and IADL tasks while predisposing and enabling characteristics, such as age, race, marital status, and socioeconomic status, are much smaller factors in explaining ability to cope with disability.

Table 6.5   Logistic regression models for ability to cope

	Any disability		Any ADL disability		Any IADL disability	
	Coefficient (SE)	Adjusted percent	Coefficient (SE)	Adjusted percent	Coefficient (SE)	Adjusted percent
Income						
$0–$9,999		23.2		30.3		25.0
$10K–$19,000	-0.06 (0.10)	22.3	0.10 (0.14)	32.1	-0.05 (0.10)	24.0
$20K–$29,999	0.04 (0.11)	23.9	0.16 (0.16)	33.4	0.10 (0.11)	26.8
$30K–$39,999	-0.12 (0.15)	21.2	0.01 (0.19)	30.5	-0.06 (0.16)	23.9
$40K–$49,999	0.06 (0.18)	24.2	0.03 (0.26)	30.8	0.04 (0.16)	25.8
$50K +	0.16 (0.16)	26.0	0.43 (0.26)	38.7	0.17 (0.16)	28.2
Education						
Less than high school		20.9		27.3		24.4
Some high school	0.13 (0.10)	23.0	0.31 (0.14)*	33.1	0.06 (0.09)	25.5
High school graduate	0.11 (0.09)	22.6	0.44 (0.13)*	35.6	-0.06 (0.08)	23.5
Some college	0.35 (0.12)*	27.0	0.54 (0.21)*	37.5	0.20 (0.12)	28.2
College grad or higher	0.38 (0.12)*	27.6	0.19 (0.21)	30.8	0.26 (0.12)*	29.3
Male	0.01 (0.15)		-0.12 (0.27)		-0.11 (0.15)	
Age 70–74	0.22 (0.11)		-0.14 (0.20)		0.17 (0.12)	
Age 75–79	0.11 (0.13)		-0.07 (0.21)		0.04 (0.13)	
Age 80–84	0.14 (0.13)		0.03 (0.19)		0.18 (0.14)	
Age 85+	0.09 (0.14)		0.13 (0.19)		0.18 (0.14)	

(continued)

Table 6.5   (continued)

	Any disability		Any ADL disability		Any IADL disability	
	Coefficient (SE)	Adjusted percent	Coefficient (SE)	Adjusted percent	Coefficient (SE)	Adjusted percent
Age*sex						
70–74*male	-0.25 (0.19)		0.52 (0.32)		-0.29 (0.20)	
75–79*male	0.04 (0.21)		0.31 (0.33)		0.07 (0.21)	
80–84*male	0.05 (0.21)		-0.04 (0.33)		0.00 (0.22)	
85plus*male	-0.32 (0.22)		0.30 (0.35)		-0.24 (0.23)	
Widowed	0.07 (0.10)		0.34 (0.16)*		0.04 (0.10)	
Divorced/separated/single	-0.20 (0.14)		0.01 (0.21)		-0.19 (0.14)	
Marital status*sex						
Widowed*male	-0.01 (0.17)		-0.15 (0.26)		0.17 (0.17)	
Divorced/sep/single*male	0.13 (0.23)		0.19 (0.39)		0.31 (0.23)	
Black/other race	0.08 (0.11)		0.07 (0.17)		0.03 (0.11)	
Limitations						
IADL only	Ref		NA		NA	
1–2 ADLs	-0.31 (0.08)*		Ref		NA	
3 or more ADLs	-1.61 (0.16)*		-1.72 (0.14)*		NA	
3 or more IADLs	NA		NA		-0.86 (0.08)*	
N	5,868		2,266		5,557	

Notes: The definition of intrinsic ADL disability includes difficulty alone or without help or equipment; the definition for intrinsic IADL disability includes only difficulty alone or without help. These models include only respondents who reported intrinsic disability.
*p < 0.05.

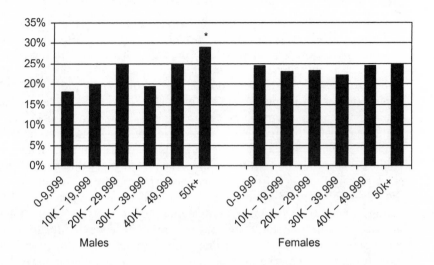

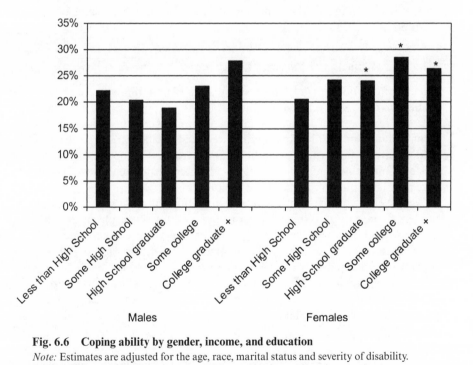

Fig. 6.6 Coping ability by gender, income, and education
Note: Estimates are adjusted for the age, race, marital status and severity of disability.
*Significantly different from lowest income or education category (*p*-value < 0.05)

We have also examined the impact of estimating models for disability, including income and education separately. Tables 6A.2 through 6A.7 in the appendix show the impact of income and education when the other variable is excluded from the model, for each of intrinsic disability (tables 6A.2 and 6A.3), residual disability (tables 6A.4 and 6A.5) and coping (tables 6A.6 and 6A.7) Comparing the Appendix tables to the equivalent regressions in tables 6.3 through 6.4 shows that for IADL disability, gradients in income and education are largely independent of each other. This may seem surprising but is relatively common in health studies, where income and education often pick up very different effects (Deaton and Paxson 2001). In the case of ADL disability, income by itself has an effect on disability that is almost entirely explained by education when both are included in the model. Income has very little effect on effective coping with disability, even in the absence of education in the model. Our results suggest that among the elderly, education is a more fundamental marker of socioeconomic status than is income (or at least income measured with error).[10] We present results with income and education included in the same equations throughout the rest of the chapter.

6.3   How Do the Better Educated Cope?

The central question raised by our results is how the better educated manage to cope with intrinsic disability. The first hypothesis we consider is that our results simply reflect difference in unmeasured health by educational attainment. While we examined residual disability in the subset of respondents with intrinsic disability and controlled for the number of reported limitations, it may be that more-educated respondents have less severe intrinsic disability that is more easily resolved.

We test this hypothesis by including an additional set of controls in our models, representing difficulty performing a set of seven physical tasks: lifting something as heavy as ten pounds (15 percent of the elderly report difficulty with this task), walking up ten steps without resting (19 percent), walking a quarter of a mile (25 percent), standing for about twenty minutes (18 percent), bending down from a standing position to pick up an object from the floor (17 percent), reaching up overhead or reaching out as if to shake someone's hand (8 percent), and using fingers to grasp or

10. This is in contrast to results presented by Agree (1999). Analyzing data from the 1993 AHEAD, she finds that residual disability among respondents with limitations in getting around inside the home has a nonlinear relationship with net worth, so that residual disability declines with net worth up to a certain point and then increases with increasing net worth. Education has a small and marginally significant relationship with residual disability.

Table 6.6   Logistic regression models for ability to cope, including functional limitations

	Any disability		ADL Only		IADL Only	
	Coefficient (SE)	Adjusted percent	Coefficient (SE)	Adjusted percent	Coefficient (SE)	Adjusted percent
Income						
$0–$9,999		23.8		30.8		25.4
$10K–$19,000	−0.09 (0.10)	22.2	0.05 (0.14)	31.7	−0.07 (0.10)	24.0
$20K–$29,999	−0.02 (0.11)	23.5	0.14 (0.16)	33.4	0.06 (0.11)	26.5
$30K–$39,999	−0.17 (0.16)	21.1	0.01 (0.19)	30.9	−0.08 (0.16)	23.9
$40K–$49,999	0.02 (0.17)	24.2	−0.03 (0.26)	30.3	0.03 (0.16)	25.9
$50K +	0.08 (0.17)	25.2	0.42 (0.27)	38.7	0.13 (0.16)	27.7
Education						
Less than high school		21.6		28.0		24.8
Some high school	0.10 (0.10)	23.2	0.27 (0.14)	33.0	0.04 (0.10)	25.6
High school graduate	0.05 (0.09)	22.4	0.39 (0.13)*	35.3	−0.08 (0.08)	23.4
Some college	0.27 (0.12)*	26.2	0.45 (0.20)*	36.4	0.16 (0.12)	27.8
College grad or higher	0.29 (0.13)*	26.6	0.14 (0.21)	30.5	0.20 (0.12)	28.6
N	5,868		2,266		5,557	

Notes: The definition of intrinsic ADL disability includes difficulty alone or without help or equipment; the definition for intrinsic IADL disability includes only difficulty alone or without help. These models include only respondents who reported intrinsic disability. Models all control for race, age*sex, sex*marital status, functional limitations, and the number of reported IADLs and ADLs. For any disability model, categorical variables for included 1–2 ADLs and 3 or more ADLs were included (IADL only was reference category). For the ADL and IADLs only models, dichotomous variables for 3 or more ADLs or 3 or more IADLs were included in the models, respectively.

*$p < 0.05$.

handle something (6 percent). The results from these models are presented in table 6.6.

Comparing estimated effects in tables 6.5 and 6.6, we find some evidence for this hypothesis, although it is not the whole explanation. For example, about a quarter of the difference between those with a college education in coping with IADL disability is explained by better underlying physical functioning, and the effect is no longer statistically significant. Better health explains less of the education differences in coping with ADL disability, but it is still some of it. Because we find that differences in physical functioning explain some of the observed gradient, we include controls for functional status in all future regressions.

Our second hypothesis concerns differences in the use of various coping strategies. The NHIS-D provides information on two broad coping strategies. The first strategy is getting help from other individuals. The survey asks respondents who report help from another person in completing an ADL or IADL task whether they received help from relatives or non relatives[11] and whether these helpers were paid.[12] We classify personal help into three groups: (1) help from a spouse, child, or parent, (2) other unpaid help, or (3) paid help.[13] The second strategy is to use assistive technologies. Respondents were asked about the use of special equipment to aid in ADL tasks.

Table 6.7 shows the use of various coping strategies used by those who report intrinsic disability in different domains. A vast majority of people (approximately 90 percent) with disability use at least one of the coping strategies. Overall, 64 percent of people with any ADL impairment use personal help—22 percent receiving help from a spouse, child, or parent, 21 percent using other unpaid help, and 25 percent using paid help—and 56 percent use assistive technology.

Coping strategies are very different across domains. Very few elderly use assistive technology to help with eating and dressing. For example, 81 percent of people with trouble eating use help from other people, and less than 10 percent use assistive technology. In contrast, approximately half of those with intrinsic disability in toileting or getting around inside use personal help, while over 60 percent use assistive technology.

Only questions about personal help are asked for people who report

---

11. The survey also distinguishes between household members and nonhousehold members.

12. Respondents are not asked about paid help if they report receiving help from a spouse, child, or parent only.

13. We initially considered unpaid help from relatives and nonrelatives separately. However, since only a small number of respondents report unpaid help from a nonrelative (4 percent and 6 percent of those with ADL and IADL disability, respectively), we combined the two categories.

Table 6.7   Use of equipment and personal help among respondents with intrinsic disability, by ADL and IADL category

	Equipment	Any personal help	Equipment and/or personal help
Activities of daily living (any) ($n = 2266$)	56.1	64.4	90.3
Bathing ($n = 1835$)	40.8	70.8	90.9
Getting around inside ($n = 1025$)	61.6	49.0	87.0
Dressing ($n = 1066$)	5.0	84.9	86.4
Transferring ($n = 995$)	28.3	60.9	74.6
Toileting ($n = 881$)	60.9	54.7	91.0
Eating ($n = 336$)	9.5	81.1	84.6
Instrumental activities of daily living (any)	N/A	88.4	88.4
Heavy housework ($n = 5,274$)	N/A	86.6	86.6
Shopping ($n = 2,399$)	N/A	91.3	91.3
Light housework ($n = 1,765$)	N/A	87.1	87.1
Preparing meals ($n = 1,432$)	N/A	86.9	86.9
Managing money ($n = 1,155$)	N/A	92.5	92.5
Using the telephone ($n = 596$)	N/A	82.8	82.8

IADL disability. Across domains, reported use of help is high, ranging from 83 percent for using the telephone to 93 percent for managing money.

Coping strategies also differ by SES group.[14] Tables 6.8 and 6.9 show regression results for the use of different coping strategies by income and education, and figures 6.7 and 6.8 display adjusted percentages of people using each type of help. The use of any personal help for ADL disability increases with income. Use of personal help is sixteen percentage points higher (76 percent versus 60 percent) in the group with income above $50,000 than the group with income below $10,000 (data not shown). Despite their higher incomes, the rich use paid help much less than the poor for both ADL and IADL disabilities. But they offset the reduced use of paid help with substantially more help from close relatives. This is consistent with the "strategic bequest" model of Bernheim, Shleifer, and Sum-

14. The prior literature on the effect of income and education on uses and types of assistance is mixed (see Agree, Freedman, and Sengupta 2004 and references there in). Most of this literature suggests that the predominant factor in determining use of assistance and types of assistance among those who use some assistance is need (i.e., severity and number of limitations and other measures of underlying health). For example, Verbrugge and Sevak (2002) found that need characteristics, such as degree of difficulty and number of limitations, explained 27 percent of the variation in use of assistance among those with ADL disability, while predisposing and enabling characteristics, such as age, race, marital status, education, and income explained only 6 percent of variation in use of assistance. Similarly, Mathieson, Kronenfeld, and Keith (2002) found that need characteristics explained 15 percent of variation in use of equipment among those with ADL and IADL limitations, while enabling characteristics explained only 2 percent of variance.

Table 6.8   Logistic regression models for use of equipment and help for "any ADL,"
                   conditioned on reported intrinsic ADL disability

	Model 1: Any equipment	Model 2: Any help from spouse, child, or or parent	Model 3: Any paid help	Model 4: Any other unpaid help	Model 5: Any type of personal help	Model 6: Any type of personal help and/or equipment
Income						
$0–$9,999						
$10K–$19,000	0.01	0.57	–0.30	0.17	0.13	0.15
	(0.12)	(0.17)*	(0.16)	(0.16)	(0.15)	(0.21)
$20K–$29,999	–0.19	0.85	–0.40	0.06	0.17	0.14
	(0.15)	(0.19)*	(0.17)*	(0.19)	(0.15)	(0.25)
$30K–$39,999	–0.04	0.90	–0.32	0.38	0.39	0.44
	(0.18)	(0.23)*	(0.20)	(0.20)	(0.21)	(0.35)
$40K–$49,999	0.03	1.28	–0.87	0.30	0.63	0.40
	(0.23)	(0.28)*	(0.28)*	(0.25)	(0.25)*	(0.40)
$50K +	–0.32	1.10	–0.55	0.56	0.85	0.14
	(0.21)	(0.26)*	(0.23)*	(0.23)*	(0.22)*	(0.30)
Education						
Less than high school						
Some high school	0.35	–0.36	–0.10	–0.49	–0.49	–0.09
	(0.13)*	(0.19)	(0.15)	(0.16)*	(0.16)*	(0.21)
High school graduate	0.49	–0.36	0.22	–0.45	–0.26	0.06
	(0.12)*	(0.15)*	(0.15)	(0.15)*	(0.14)	(0.21)
Some college	0.61	–0.74	0.34	–0.30	–0.49	0.22
	(0.17)*	(0.22)*	(0.20)	(0.20)	(0.19)*	(0.32)
College grad +	0.42	–0.99	0.40	–0.25	–0.65	–0.13
	(0.17)*	(0.25)*	(0.20)*	(0.23)	(0.21)*	(0.28)
Average use (%)	56.1	22.1	25.3	21.3	64.4	30.2
N	2,266	2,266	2,266	2,266	2,266	2,266

Notes: Models control for race, age*sex, sex*marital status, functional limitations, and whether respondents report difficulty with 3 or more ADLs.
*$p < 0.05$.

mers (1985); the possibility of an inheritance may spur children of better-off parents to provide more direct assistance (of course, other hypotheses are possible as well). Use of assistive technologies for help with ADL disability is relatively independent of income.

The pattern is the reverse for education. The better educated use more paid help than the less educated, but receive less help from close relatives. All told, the better educated use less personal care than the less educated (particularly for ADL tasks). For ADL tasks, the better educated offset their lower use of personal care with substantially higher rates of use of assistive technologies. On net, use of any form of help is high among all respondents and roughly equal by education and income.

The important question is how differential use of these technologies is

Table 6.9   **Logistic regression models for use of help for "any IADL," conditioned on reporting intrinsic IADL disability**

	Model 1: Any help from spouse, child, or parent	Model 2: Any paid help	Model 3: Any unpaid help	Model 4: Any help
Income				
$0–$9,999				
$10K–$19,000	0.25 (0.08)*	−0.19 (0.09)*	−0.13 (0.09)	−0.10 (0.14)
$20K–$29,999	0.20 (0.10)	−0.29 (0.11)*	−0.27 (0.11)*	−0.27 (0.15)
$30K–$39,999	0.55 (0.14)*	−0.41 (0.14)*	−0.32 (0.14)*	−0.11 (0.20)
$40K–$49,999	0.60 (0.16)*	−0.51 (0.18)*	−0.34 (0.18)	0.21 (0.28)
$50K +	0.59 (0.15)*	−0.52 (0.15)*	−0.40 (0.14)*	−0.19 (0.23)
Education				
Less than high school				
Some high school	−0.34 (0.10)*	0.36 (0.10)*	0.10 (0.10)	−0.11 (0.13)
High school graduate	−0.43 (0.08)*	0.63 (0.08)*	−0.07 (0.09)	−0.19 (0.11)
Some college	−0.83 (0.13)*	1.08 (0.11)*	−0.12 (0.12)	0.09 (0.18)
College grad +	−1.35 (0.16)*	1.30 (0.12)*	0.05 (0.13)	−0.05 (0.16)
Average use	25.49	29.90	27.31	88.44
N	5,557	5,557	5,557	5,557

Notes: Models all control for race, age*sex, sex*marital status, functional limitations, and whether respondent reports difficulty with 3 or more IADLs.
*$p < 0.05$.

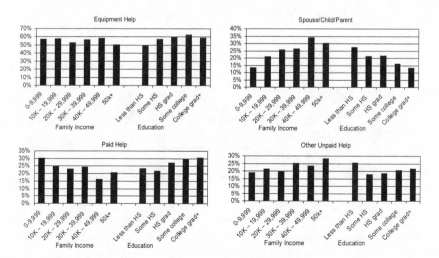

Fig. 6.7   **Use of help by income and education among respondents reporting intrinsic ADL disability**

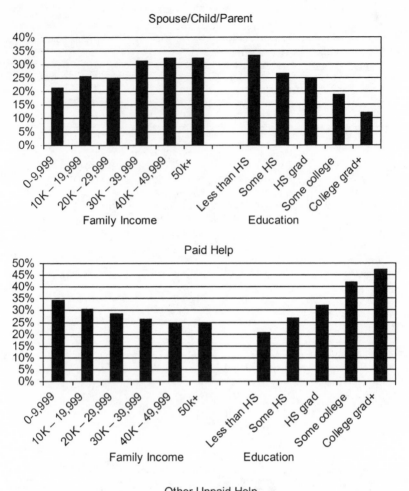

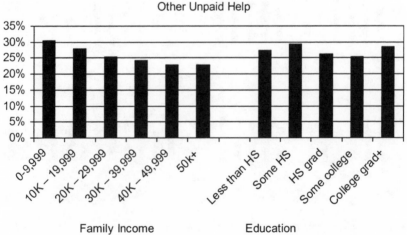

Fig. 6.8   Use of help by income and education among respondents reporting intrin-sic IADL disability

Table 6.10   **Logistic regression models for ADL coping, including covariates for use of equipment and help**

	Coefficient (SE)	Adjusted percent	Coefficient (SE)	Adjusted percent
Income				
$0–$9,999		34.3		34.9
$10K–$19,000	0.05 (0.15)	35.1	0.01 (0.16)	35.1
$20K–$29,999	0.18 (0.17)	37.5	0.13 (0.18)	37.2
$30K–$39,999	−0.10 (0.21)	32.4	−0.13 (0.21)	32.5
$40K–$49,999	−0.03 (0.27)	33.8	−0.06 (0.28)	33.8
$50K +	0.45 (0.28)	42.6	0.34 (0.29)	41.0
Education				
Less than high school	-	31.3	-	30.7
Some high school	0.28 (0.15)	36.3	0.32 (0.16)*	36.3
High school graduate	0.42 (0.14)*	38.9	0.48 (0.14)*	39.3
Some college	0.46 (0.21)*	39.7	0.51 (0.22)*	39.7
College grad or higher	0.18 (0.22)	34.5	0.27 (0.22)	35.4
Equipment and help				
AT only			0.10 (0.25)	
Spouse, child, parent help only			0.04 (0.29)	
Paid help only			−0.16 (0.31)	
Unpaid help only				
Multiple types of help			1.05 (0.29)*	
AT and any help			−0.16 (0.25)	
N	2,045		2,045	

Notes: These models include only respondents who reported intrinsic disability and use of either help and/or AT. Models all control for race, age*sex, sex*marital status, functional limitations, and whether respondents report difficulty with 3 or more ADLs.
*$p < 0.05$.

related to the ability to cope with impairment. We examine this issue by including measures of personal and assistive technology use in the equations for ability to cope with disability. Since respondents who use neither personal help nor equipment but report difficulty by definition have residual disability, we focus on the subset of respondents who use some kind of help (either personal or equipment). This omits only about 10 percent of the sample.[15]

The results of this analysis are shown in table 6.10 for ADL impairment and table 6.11 for IADL impairment. We report estimated effects without controlling for use of equipment and personal help in the first two columns in each table. These results differ from those reported in table 6.6 because of the restriction to the sample of respondents who use either personal help

15. There is unlikely to be any bias from this, as the analysis reported in the last columns of tables 6.8 and 6.9 already demonstrated that education had little effect on whether respondents used any help.

Table 6.11   **Logistic regression models for IADL coping, including covariates for use of equipment and help**

	Coefficient (SE)	Adjusted percent	Coefficient (SE)	Adjusted percent	Coefficient (SE)	Adjusted percent
Income						
$0–$9,999		28.2		27.5		27.5
$10K–$19,000	–0.06 (0.10)	27.0	0.02 (0.11)	27.9	0.03 (0.11)	28.0
$20K–$29,999	0.14 (0.12)	30.8	0.20 (0.12)	30.8	0.19 (0.12)	30.7
$30K–$39,999	–0.05 (0.16)	27.2	0.03 (0.17)	28.0	0.03 (0.17)	28.0
$40K–$49,999	–0.01 (0.17)	28.0	0.05 (0.18)	28.4	0.04 (0.18)	28.2
$50K +	0.17 (0.17)	31.5	0.27 (0.17)	32.1	0.26 (0.17)	32.0
Education						
Less than high school		27.8		29.1		29.0
Some high school	0.05 (0.10)	28.7	–0.00 (0.11)	29.0	–0.00 (0.11)	29.0
High school graduate	–0.04 (0.09)	27.0	–0.11 (0.09)	27.2	–0.11 (0.10)	27.2
Some college	0.14 (0.12)	30.6	0.02 (0.14)	29.3	0.02 (0.14)	29.4
College grad or higher	0.21 (0.13)	32.0	0.08 (0.13)	30.5	0.09 (0.13)	30.5
Help						
Spouse, child, parent help only			–0.27 (0.13)*		–0.28 (0.13)*	
Paid help only			–0.07 (0.13)		–0.07 (0.13)	
Unpaid help only						
Multiple types of help			1.59 (0.13)*		1.59 (0.13)*	
Mobility aids						
Cane or crutch					–0.10 (0.09)	
Walker					–0.11 (0.13)	
Manual wheelchair					0.03 (0.15)	
Electric wheelchair or scooter					0.70 (0.33)*	
Brace					–0.21 (0.16)	
N	4,905		4,905		4,905	

Notes: These models include only respondents who reported intrinsic disability and use of help. Models all control for race, age*sex, sex*marital status, functional limitations, and whether respondents report difficulty with 3 or more IADLs.

*$p < 0.05$.

or equipment. For these models we use mutually exclusive categories for the type of help received. For ADL disability these categories are equipment only (29 percent), help from a spouse, child, or parent only (14 percent), other unpaid help only (6 percent), paid help only (8 percent), multiple types of personal help (9 percent), and use of equipment and personal help (30 percent). For IADL disability the categories are help from a spouse, child, or parent only (29 percent), other unpaid help only (18 percent), paid help only (24 percent), and multiple types of personal help (30 percent). In each case, the omitted category in the regression models is other unpaid help only. Relative to this category, people who use multiple types of personal help are better able to cope with both ADL and IADL disability. Help from a close relative is also less effective than other unpaid help for coping with IADL disability, perhaps reflecting the fact that family members who have less formal knowledge and training with disabled people are less effective at helping to resolve disability.

Surprisingly, including measures of use of personal and assistive technologies does not affect the income or education coefficients in any material way. Comparing the two columns in table 6.10 shows that the coefficients on the higher-education groups are somewhat larger in the models with all of the help variables included, as in the models without the help variables. For example, the gap in coping with ADLs between those with some college and those with less than a high school degree is 8.4 percent without the measures of help and 9.0 percent with measures of help. Controlling for the types of help received for IADL disability (reported in table 6.11) explains more of the relationship between education and coping. However, these effects were small and not statistically significant, even in the absence of controls for types of help received.

The NHIS-D did not ask about the use of equipment to aid IADL tasks but did ask all respondents (regardless of whether they reported disability) about use of specific mobility aids, including a cane or crutch, a walker, a manual wheelchair, an electric wheelchair or scooter, or a brace. In the fifth and sixth columns of table 6.11, we present a model that also controls for the use of these specific mobility aids. While use of an electric wheelchair or scooter was a more effective coping strategy than other mobility aids (or the use of no mobility aids), use of specific technologies does not have any additional explanatory power once we control for differences in the types of personal help received.

Because both the use of coping strategies and their effectiveness may vary by gender, we also examined coping controlling for the use of help separately in men and women. Table 6.12 shows rates of use of various coping strategies by gender. Over 50 percent of men and women use equipment for ADL tasks. Men are more likely to get personal help with ADL tasks (69 percent versus 62 percent), particularly help from a spouse, child, or parent (31 percent versus 18 percent). However, women are more likely to obtain paid help than men (28 percent versus 21 percent), and there are few differences in use of other unpaid help for ADL tasks. For IADL tasks, differences across gender in help from family members and paid help are smaller. For example, 27 percent of men obtain help from a spouse, child, or parent for IADLs, compared to 25 percent for women. However, women are more likely to use other unpaid help for IADL tasks, compared to men (29 percent versus 24 percent).

We present analysis of coping ability by gender in tables 6A.8–6A.11 in the appendix. There is little evidence that the effectiveness of coping strategies varies by gender. In addition, patterns observed in combined samples generally hold in each gender. For example, in both men and women, ad-

Table 6.12   Use of equipment and personal help among respondents with intrinsic disability, by any ADL and any IADL category, separately for men and women*

	Men		Women	
	Any ADL	Any IADL	Any ADL	Any IADL
Any equipment	54.6		56.8	
Any personal help	69.3	87.5	62.0	88.9
Spouse/child/parent	31.0	27.4	17.7	24.6
Paid	20.5	28.1	27.7	30.7
Other unpaid	21.2	24.2	21.3	28.7
Either equipment or personal help	91.5		89.7	
N	751	1,729	1,515	3,828

*Categories are not mutually exclusive

justing for types of help increases differences by education in coping with ADL limitations.

Because both coping strategies and the size of the education gradient in coping vary according to specific activity, we also examined whether coping strategies explained task-specific education gradients. We examined four particular ADL and IADL restrictions: difficulty getting around inside and dressing (both ADL impairments), and difficulty shopping and doing light housework (IADL impairments). Two of these impairments seem particularly amenable to help from assistive technology, particularly mobility aids—getting around inside and shopping. The other two are activities where there are strong education gradients in coping ability, shown in figures 6.4 and 6.5.

Table 6.13 shows the impact of coping strategies on coping with these two ADL difficulties and table 6.14 shows comparable results for the IADL difficulties. In each case, the first two columns report results without the coping measures and the next two columns displays results controlling for the coping measures.[16] Once again, use of coping strategies does not explain the better coping of higher-education groups with specific ADL or IADL tasks. Surprisingly, type of coping strategy or use of specific mobility aids had little effect on ability to cope with specific task, and thus had little effect on the impact of education and income.

16. Questions about the type of help received were not asked in regard to specific tasks, so we cannot differentiate between respondents who use multiple types of help for each of their limitations from a respondent who uses paid help for some tasks and gets help from a spouse for other. Thus, for ADL disability we collapse our categories for type of help into equipment and personal help, equipment only, and personal help only. In addition, since respondents with IADL disability were not asked about equipment help, we control for specific mobility aids in models examining specific IADL tasks.

Table 6.13 Logistic regression models for coping for getting around inside and dressing, including covariates for use of equipment and help

	Getting around inside				Dressing			
	Coefficient (SE)	Adjusted percent	Coefficient (SE)	Adjusted percent	Coefficient (SE)	Adjusted percent	Coefficient (SE)	Adjusted percent
Income								
$0–$9,999		33.6		33.6		34.6		34.4
$10K–$19,000	−0.13 (0.22)	31.1	−0.13 (0.22)	31.2	0.32 (0.23)	41.2	0.32 (0.23)	41.0
$20K–$29,999	−0.44 (0.28)	25.6	−0.43 (0.28)	25.7	0.30 (0.27)	40.7	0.31 (0.27)	40.9
$30K–$39,999	−0.15 (0.31)	30.7	−0.15 (0.31)	30.7	−0.04 (0.30)	33.9	0.02 (0.30)	34.9
$40K–$49,999	−0.59 (0.43)	23.2	−0.61 (0.43)	22.9	−0.67 (0.45)	22.5	−0.66 (0.44)	22.7
$50K +	0.23 (0.33)	38.3	0.23 (0.33)	38.2	0.51 (0.30)	45.4	0.53 (0.31)	45.6
Education								
Less than high school		27.3		27.1		32.2		31.9
Some high school	0.37 (0.23)	34.2	0.40 (0.23)	34.5	0.51 (0.21)*	42.7	0.52 (0.21)*	42.5
High school graduate	0.18 (0.21)	30.6	0.19 (0.22)	30.6	0.24 (0.20)	37.0	0.28 (0.20)	37.5
Some college	0.49 (0.32)	36.5	0.52 (0.33)	36.9	0.45 (0.28)	41.3	0.46 (0.28)	41.2
College grad +	0.20 (0.34)	30.8	0.20 (0.34)	30.7	0.99 (0.28)*	53.4	1.03 (0.28)*	53.8
Equipment and help								
Equipment only			0.17 (0.27)				0.59 (0.75)	
Help only			0.34 (0.27)				0.94 (0.41)*	
N	890		890		924		924	

Notes: These models include only respondents who reported intrinsic disability and use of either help and/or AT. Models all control for race, age*sex, sex*marital status, functional limitations, and whether respondents report difficulty with 3 or more ADLs.

*p < 0.05.

Table 6.14   Logistic regression models for coping for shopping and light housework, including covariates for specific mobility aids

	Shopping				Light housework			
	Coefficient (SE)	Adjusted percent	Coefficient (SE)	Adjusted percent	Coefficient (SE)	Adjusted percent	Coefficient (SE)	Adjusted percent
Income								
$0–$9,999		33.6		33.6		25.9		25.7
$10K–$19,000	0.06 (0.13)	34.8	0.06 (0.13)	34.9	0.23 (0.17)	30.4	0.24 (0.17)	30.4
$20K–$29,999	0.13 (0.16)	36.4	0.12 (0.16)	36.2	0.41 (0.20)*	34.3	0.43 (0.20)*	34.4
$30K–$39,999	0.31 (0.19)	40.3	0.30 (0.19)	40.1	0.26 (0.24)	31.0	0.27 (0.24)	31.0
$40K–$49,999	-0.16 (0.22)	30.3	-0.19 (0.22)	29.9	0.44 (0.27)	34.8	0.46 (0.27)	35.1
$50K +	-0.07 (0.21)	32.1	-0.09 (0.21)	31.8	0.33 (0.25)	32.5	0.32 (0.25)	31.9
Education								
Less than high school		34.7		34.6		28.7		28.7
Some high school	0.06 (0.15)	35.9	0.05 (0.16)	35.7	0.10 (0.17)	30.6	0.09 (0.17)	30.5
High school graduate	-0.03 (0.13)	34.1	-0.02 (0.13)	34.2	0.10 (0.15)	30.7	0.10 (0.15)	30.7
Some college	0.01 (0.20)	34.8	0.02 (0.20)	34.9	0.12 (0.22)	31.1	0.14 (0.23)	31.5
College grad +	-0.04 (0.22)	33.7	-0.04 (0.22)	33.7	0.23 (0.23)	33.4	0.22 (0.24)	33.2
Mobility Aids								
Cane or crutch			-0.18 (0.10)				0.06 (0.11)	
Walker			0.04 (0.11)				-0.20 (0.14)	
Manual wheelchair			0.07 (0.14)				-0.02 (0.16)	
Electric wheelchair or scooter			0.49 (0.34)				0.56 (0.39)	
Brace			-0.26 (0.23)				-0.01 (0.25)	
N	2,187		2,187		1,534		1,534	

Notes: These models include only respondents who reported intrinsic disability and use of either help and/or AT. Models all control for race, age*sex, sex*marital status, functional limitations, and whether respondents reported difficulty with 3 or more IADLs.

*$p < 0.05$.

6.4   Conclusion

Analyses of socioeconomic gradients in health are notoriously difficult, and ours turns out to be complex as well. We show that the better educated are better able to cope with underlying disability than the less educated. These differences are large: the ability to cope with disease varies by as much as eight percentage points across education groups. We also show that the type of help differently educated groups receive is different. The better educated are more likely to use assistive technologies than the less educated and are more likely to receive paid help than help from close relatives. Despite our best attempts, however, we are unable to show that it is the use of these different forms of aids that explains differences in the ability to cope.

With the data that we have, we cannot examine this puzzle more completely. But there are several hypotheses that might be tested using other data. One hypothesis is that the more educated use care more intensively. For example, among users of paid help, the less educated might use two hours of paid care per week, while the better educated might use four hours. The additional two hours could substantially reduce impairment, but we cannot determine that with our data. Several other researchers have observed sociodemographic differences in the intensity of personal care. For example, Weiss et al. (2005) analyzed data from the 1993 AHEAD and found that Hispanics received more hours of informal care per week than African Americans and non-Hispanic whites. Kemper (1992), in a small study of highly disabled individuals, found that income was positively associated with both the likelihood of receiving paid help and the number of hours of help among users of paid help. Those who completed high school were also more likely to use paid help, but not more hours of help conditioning on using any paid help.

A related hypothesis is that the quality of the care received might be higher for the more educated compared to the less educated. The personal help received could be better trained and the equipment might be newer or less subject to failure.

A third hypothesis is that the more educated may be more willing or able to use behavior and environmental modifications to cope with their disability. For example, the more educated might be more likely to cope with difficulty in preparing meals by buying prepared foods, or they might be more able to make home modifications that allow them to function with their disability. Few surveys collect data on the use of behavior modifications and environmental adaptations. Norburn et al. (1995), analyzed data from the 1991 National Survey of Self-Care and Aging and estimated that 75 percent of the community elderly coped with their loss of functioning by changing their behavior, while one third made adaptations in their environment. Surprisingly, they found that these coping strategies were not associated with income or education. Similarly, Mathieson, Kronenfeld, and Keith (2002), analyzing the National Survey of Self-Care and Aging, found that household income and education were not related to the likelihood of making home modifications, although subjective measures of resources, such as reporting having enough income to buy little extras, did increase the likelihood of making home modifications.

A final hypothesis is that the environments that the more educated live in are more conducive to the use of technology or personal aids. If the better educated live in homes or shop in stores where there is more space, ramps, and elevators, use of a wheelchair may be able to fully resolve the underlying impairment. That might be less true in a crowded house or a store with narrow aisles and steps. Data on the specific physical features of the home or environment are limited. However, Gitlin et al. (2001) reported an average of thirteen environmental problems in a small study of approximately 300 elderly. Similarly, analyzing data from the 1995 American Housing Survey, Sandra Newman (2003) found that 23 percent of elderly individuals had unmet needs for housing modifications, and the number of reported unmet needs was negatively associated with household income.

In summary, we find that while the majority of socioeconomic differences in disability can be attributed to differences in underlying functioning—the better off have much less difficulty with these measures, even in the absence of help—coping is important as well. In addition, while we find differences in the way people receive help with functional limitations across educational and income groups, these differences do not explain the education gradient in coping. More work is needed to disentangle the complex interrelationships between underlying functional limitations, coping strategies, and the environment in which people live in order to further understand how the better educated are better able to cope with underlying disability.

Appendix

Table 6A.1   **Logistic regression models for ability to cope by sex**

	Any disability: Men		Any disability: Women	
	Coefficient (SE)	Adjusted percent	Coefficient (SE)	Adjusted percent
Income				
$0–$9,999		18.2		24.6
$10K–$19,000	0.11 (0.20)	19.9	–0.09 (0.11)	23.0
$20K–$29,999	0.41 (0.22)	24.9	–0.08 (0.13)	23.2
$30K–$39,999	0.08 (0.28)	19.4	–0.14 (0.17)	22.2
$40K–$49,999	0.40 (0.30)	24.7	–0.01 (0.20)	2445
$50K +	0.63 (0.28)*	29.0	0.00 (0.18)	24.7
Education				
Less than high school		22.2		20.5
Some high school	–0.11 (0.19)	20.4	0.22 (0.12)	24.2
High school graduate	–0.21 (0.18)	18.9	0.21 (0.10)*	24.1
Some college	0.05 (0.23)	23.0	0.46 (0.15)*	28.6
College grad or higher	0.31 (0.24)	27.8	0.34 (0.16)*	26.4
Age				
70–74	0.00 (0.16)		0.23 (0.12)*	
75–79	0.14 (0.18)		0.13 (0.13)	
80–84	0.14 (0.18)		0.18 (0.13)	
85 plus	–0.29 (0.19)		0.13 (0.14)	
Marital status				
Widowed	0.08 (0.15)		0.04 (0.10)	
Div/sep	0.02 (0.20)		–0.21 (0.15)	
Race				
Black/other race	0.04 (0.20)		0.11 (0.13)	
Severity of limitations				
1–2 ADLs	–0.12 (0.15)		–0.39 (0.10)*	
3 or more ADLs	–1.32 (0.24)*		–1.73 (0.18)*	
N	1865		4003	

Notes: The definition of intrinsic ADL disability includes difficulty alone or without help or equipment; the definition for intrinsic IADL disability includes only difficulty alone or without help. These models include only respondents who reported intrinsic disability. Reference groups for age, marital status, race, and severity of limitations are age 65–59, married respondents, white respondents, and respondents reporting only IADL disability, respectively.
*$p < 0.05$.

Table 6A.2 **Logistic regression models for intrinsic disability, income only**

Independent variable	Any disability		Any ADL		Any IADL	
	Coefficient (SE)	Adjusted percent	Coefficient (SE)	Adjusted percent	Coefficient (SE)	Adjusted percent
Income						
$0–$9,999		29.8		11.1		27.8
$10K–$19,000	−0.28 (0.05)*	24.6	−0.27 (0.06)*	8.9	−0.26 (0.05)*	23.2
$20K–$29,999	−0.38 (0.06)*	23.1	−0.23 (0.08)*	9.2	−0.34 (0.06)*	22.0
$30K–$39,999	−0.44 (0.07)*	22.0	−0.27 (0.10)*	8.8	−0.40 (0.07)*	21.0
$40K–$49,999	−0.31 (0.08)*	24.1	−0.24 (0.11)*	9.0	−0.28 (0.08)*	22.9
$50K +	−0.59 (0.07)*	19.8	−0.36 (0.11)*	8.2	−0.55 (0.07)*	18.7
N	24,476		24,476		24,476	

Notes: The definition of intrinsic ADL disability includes difficulty alone or without help or equipment; the definition for intrinsic IADL disability includes only difficulty alone or without help. Individuals missing values for educational attainment ($n = 295$) and/or marital status ($n = 25$) were dropped from regression analyses.

*$p < 0.05$.

Table 6A.3 **Logistic regression models for intrinsic disability, education only**

Independent variable	Any disability		Any ADL		Any IADL	
	Coefficient (SE)	Adjusted percent	Coefficient (SE)	Adjusted percent	Coefficient (SE)	Adjusted percent
Education						
Less than high school		28.8		11.4		27.0
Some high school	−0.10 (0.05)*	26.9	−0.08 (0.07)	10.7	−0.09 (0.05)	25.5
High school graduate	−0.29 (0.04)*	23.5	−0.31 (0.06)*	8.7	−0.29 (0.05)*	22.1
Some college	−0.48 (0.06)*	20.6	−0.47 (0.09)*	7.6	−0.46 (0.06)*	19.5
College grad or higher	−0.49 (0.06)*	20.5	−0.64 (0.09)*	6.6	−0.44 (0.07)*	19.8
N	24,476		24,476		24,476	

Notes: The definition of intrinsic ADL disability includes difficulty alone or without help or equipment; the definition for intrinsic IADL disability includes only difficulty alone or without help. Individuals missing values for educational attainment ($n = 295$) and/or marital status ($n = 25$) were dropped from regression analyses.

*$p < 0.05$.

Table 6A.4   **Logistic regression models for residual disability, income only**

Independent variable	Any disability		Any ADL		Any IADL	
	Coefficient (SE)	Adjusted percent	Coefficient (SE)	Adjusted percent	Coefficient (SE)	Adjusted percent
Income						
$0–$9,999		22.9		7.8		20.9
$10K–$19,000	–0.24 (0.05)*	19.1	–0.28 (0.07)*	6.1	–0.22 (0.05)*	17.7
$20K–$29,999	–0.36 (0.06)*	17.5	–0.29 (0.09)*	6.0	–0.34 (0.07)*	16.1
$30K–$39,999	–0.38 (0.08)*	17.2	–0.27 (0.11)*	6.1	–0.36 (0.08)*	15.8
$40K–$49,999	–0.32 (0.09)*	18.0	–0.19 (0.13)	6.6	–0.30 (0.10)*	16.6
$50K +	–0.60 (0.08)*	14.4	–0.52 (0.15)*	4.9	–0.58 (0.09)*	13.2
N	24,476		24,476		24,476	

Notes: The definition of intrinsic ADL disability includes difficulty alone or without help or equipment; the definition for intrinsic IADL disability includes only difficulty alone or without help. Individuals missing values for educational attainment ($n = 295$) and/or marital status ($n = 25$) were dropped from regression analyses.
*$p < 0.05$.

Table 6A.5   **Logistic regression models for residual disability, education only**

Independent variable	Any disability		Any ADL		Any IADL	
	Coefficient (SE)	Adjusted percent	Coefficient (SE)	Adjusted percent	Coefficient (SE)	Adjusted percent
Education						
Less than high school		22.8		8.4		20.6
Some high school	–0.13 (0.05)*	20.7	–0.19 (0.08)*	7.1	–0.11 (0.05)*	19.0
High school graduate	–0.30 (0.05)*	18.2	–0.43 (0.08)*	5.7	–0.27 (0.05)*	16.8
Some college	–0.54 (0.06)*	15.0	–0.66 (0.11)*	4.6	–0.50 (0.06)*	13.9
College grad or higher	–0.58 (0.07)*	14.6	–0.70 (0.10)*	4.5	–0.52 (0.07)*	13.7
N	24,476		24,476		24,476	

Notes: The definition of intrinsic ADL disability includes difficulty alone or without help or equipment; the definition for intrinsic IADL disability includes only difficulty alone or without help. Individuals missing values for educational attainment ($n = 295$) and/or marital status ($n = 25$) were dropped from regression analyses.
*$p < 0.05$.

Table 6A.6   **Logistic regression models for coping, income only**

Independent variable	Any disability		Any ADL		Any IADL	
	Coefficient (SE)	Adjusted percent	Coefficient (SE)	Adjusted percent	Coefficient (SE)	Adjusted percent
Income						
$0–$9,999		22.4		29.3		24.6
$10K–$19,000	−0.02 (0.09)	22.1	0.15 (0.14)	32.2	−0.04 (0.10)	23.9
$20K–$29,999	0.11 (0.11)	24.3	0.25 (0.16)	34.0	0.12 (0.11)	26.9
$30K–$39,999	−0.02 (0.15)	22.1	0.11 (0.19)	31.3	−0.00 (0.15)	24.6
$40K–$49,999	0.16 (0.17)	25.2	0.11 (0.27)	31.4	0.10 (0.16)	26.4
$50K +	0.28 (0.15)	27.4	0.52 (0.24)*	39.5	0.24 (0.15)	29.2
N	5,868		2,266		5,557	

Notes: The definition of intrinsic ADL disability includes difficulty alone or without help or equipment; the definition for intrinsic IADL disability includes only difficulty alone or without help. Individuals missing values for educational attainment ($n = 295$) and/or marital status ($n = 25$) were dropped from regression analyses.

*$p < 0.05$.

Table 6A.7   **Logistic regression models for coping, education only**

Independent variable	Any disability		Any ADL		Any IADL	
	Coefficient (SE)	Adjusted percent	Coefficient (SE)	Adjusted percent	Coefficient (SE)	Adjusted percent
Education						
Less than high school		20.7		26.9		24.2
Some high school	0.13 (0.10)	22.9	0.33 (0.14)*	32.9	0.06 (0.09)	25.4
High school graduate	0.11 (0.08)	22.6	0.47 (0.13)*	35.7	−0.04 (0.08)	23.5
Some college	0.36 (0.12)*	27.0	0.58 (0.20)*	37.9	0.21 (0.11)	28.3
College grad or higher	0.41 (0.11)*	28.1	0.27 (0.20)	31.7	0.29 (0.11)*	29.9
N	5,868		2,266		5,557	

Notes: The definition of intrinsic ADL disability includes difficulty alone or without help or equipment; the definition for intrinsic IADL disability includes only difficulty alone or without help. Individuals missing values for educational attainment ($n = 295$) and/or marital status ($n = 25$) were dropped from regression analyses.

*$p < 0.05$.

Table 6A.8   **Logistic regression models for ADL coping among males only, including covariates for use of equipment and help**

	ADL only: Men			
	Coefficient (SE)	Adjusted percent	Coefficient (SE)	Adjusted percent
Income				
$0–$9,999		33.4		33.4
$10K–$19,000	−0.13 (0.29)	31.2	−0.09 (0.30)	31.9
$20K–$29,999	0.14 (0.35)	35.9	0.14 (0.36)	35.8
$30K–$39,999	0.03 (0.44)	33.9	0.08 (0.44)	34.8
$40K–$49,999	0.70 (0.45)	46.3	0.61 (0.48)	44.1
$50K +	0.24 (0.45)	37.6	0.14 (0.44)	35.8
Education				
Less than high school		30.3		29.3
Some high school	0.40 (0.25)	37.3	0.40 (0.26)	36.0
High school graduate	0.24 (0.23)	34.4	0.39 (0.24)	35.7
Some college	0.55 (0.32)	40.1	0.66 (0.35)	40.6
College grad or higher	0.19 (0.39)	33.6	0.36 (0.38)	35.4
Equipment and help				
AT only			−0.00 (0.39)	
Spouse, child, parent help only			0.19 (0.41)	
Paid help only			−0.43 (0.54)	
Unpaid help only				
Multiple types of help			1.25 (0.48)*	
AT and any help			−0.33 (0.40)	
N	689		689	

Note: These models include only respondents who reported intrinsic disability and use of either help and/or AT. Models control for race, age · sex, sex · marital status, functional limitations, and whether respondents report difficulty with three or more ADLs.

*$p < 0.05$.

Table 6A.9   **Logistic regression models for ADL coping among females only, including covariates for use of equipment and help**

	ADL only: Women			
	Coefficient (SE)	Adjusted percent	Coefficient (SE)	Adjusted percent
Income				
$0–$9,999		34.9		35.4
$10K–$19,000	0.18 (0.18)	38.2	0.15 (0.19)	38.1
$20K–$29,999	0.20 (0.20)	38.6	0.15 (0.20)	38.1
$30K–$39,999	−0.13 (0.24)	32.5	−0.17 (0.24)	32.4
$40K–$49,999	−0.38 (0.35)	28.3	−0.34 (0.35)	29.4
$50K +	0.52 (0.35)	44.7	0.44 (0.36)	43.5
Education				
Less than high school		32.4		32.0
Some high school	0.22 (0.19)	36.5	0.27 (0.20)	36.9
High school graduate	0.48 (0.18)*	41.3	0.52 (0.18)*	41.4
Some college	0.39 (0.25)	39.6	0.44 (0.26)	39.9
College grad or higher	0.11 (0.30)	34.5	0.18 (0.31)	35.1
Equipment and help				
AT only			0.12 (0.30)	
Spouse, child, parent help only			−0.07 (0.35)	
Paid help only			−0.08 (0.35)	
Unpaid help only				
Multiple types of help			0.98 (0.36)*	
AT and any help			−0.07 (0.32)	
N	1,356		1,356	

Note: These models include only respondents who reported intrinsic disability and use of either help and/or AT. Models control for race, age · sex, sex · marital status, functional limitations, and whether respondents report difficulty with three or more ADLs.

*$p < 0.05$.

Table 6A.10   **Logistic regression models for IADL coping among males only, including covariates for use of equipment and help**

	IADL only: Men			
	Coefficient (SE)	Adjusted percent	Coefficient (SE)	Adjusted percent
Income				
$0–$9,999		20.4		19.5
$10K–$19,000	0.27 (0.20)	24.9	0.42 (0.22)	25.5
$20K–$29,999	0.62 (0.23)*	31.6	0.79 (0.25)*	31.6
$30K–$39,999	0.32 (0.30)	25.7	0.50 (0.34)	26.9
$40K–$49,999	0.30 (0.34)	25.4	0.45 (0.34)	25.9
$50K +	0.89 (0.27)*	37.1	1.13 (0.30)*	37.7
Education				
Less than high school		27.2		28.4
Some high school	−0.15 (0.21)	24.5	−0.24 (0.25)	24.7
High school graduate	−0.25 (0.19)	22.8	−0.37 (0.20)	22.7
Some college	0.11 (0.21)	29.2	0.08 (0.23)	29.8
College grad or higher	0.32 (0.25)	33.6	0.21 (0.25)	31.9
Help				
Spouse, child, parent help only			−0.45 (0.25)	
Paid help only			−0.29 (0.22)	
Unpaid help only				
Multiple types of help			1.50 (0.21)*	
N	1,510		1,510	

Note: These models include only respondents who reported intrinsic disability and use of either help and/or AT. Models control for race, age · sex, sex · marital status, functional limitations, and whether respondents report difficulty with three or more ADLs.

*p < 0.05.

Table 6A.11   Logistic regression models for IADL coping for females only, including covariates for use of equipment and help

	IADL only: Women			
	Coefficient (SE)	Adjusted percent	Coefficient (SE)	Adjusted percent
Income				
$0–$9,999		30.5		29.8
$10K–$19,000	−0.14 (0.12)	27.9	−0.06 (0.12)	28.8
$20K–$29,999	−0.01 (0.15)	30.2	0.02 (0.16)	30.1
$30K–$39,999	−0.13 (0.18)	28.0	−0.07 (0.19)	28.6
$40K–$49,999	−0.04 (0.19)	29.7	−0.00 (0.20)	29.8
$50K +	−0.07 (0.19)	29.2	−0.01 (0.20)	29.6
Education				
Less than high school		28.6		29.8
Some high school	0.10 (0.11)	30.4	0.05 (0.13)	30.7
High school graduate	0.00 (0.10)	28.6	−0.06 (0.11)	28.8
Some college	0.14 (0.15)	31.3	−0.05 (0.16)	28.9
College grad or higher	0.05 (0.16)	29.5	−0.10 (0.17)	28.1
Help				
Spouse, child, parent help only			−0.20 (0.15)	
Paid help only			−0.02 (0.15)	
Unpaid help only				
Multiple types of help			1.66 (0.14)*	
N	3,395			

Note: These models include only respondents who reported intrinsic disability and use of either help and/or AT. Models control for race, age · sex, sex · marital status, functional limitations, and whether respondents report difficulty with three or more ADLs.
*$p < 0.05$.

References

Adler, Nancy E., Thomas Boyce, Margaret Chesney, Susan Folkman, and Leonard Syme. 1993. Socioeconomic inequalities in health: No easy solution. *Journal of the American Medical Association* 269 (24): 3140–45.

Agree, Emily M. 1999. The influence of personal care and assistive devices on the measurement of disability. *Social Sciences and Medicine* 48:427–43.

Agree, Emily M., and Vicki A. Freedman. 2003. A comparison of assistive technology and personal care in alleviating disability and unmet need. *The Gerontologist* 43 (3): 335–44.

Agree, Emily M., Vicki A. Freedman, and Manisha Sengupta. 2004. Factors influencing the use of mobility technology in community-based long-term care. *Journal of Aging and Health* 16 (2): 267–307.

Barker, David J. P. 1994. *Mothers, babies, and disease in later life.* London: BMJ Publishing Group.

Bernheim, B., Douglas, Andrei Shleifer, and Lawrence Summers. 1985. The strategic bequest motive. *Journal of Political Economy* 93:1045–76.

Case, Anne, Darren Lubotsky, and Christina Paxson. 2002. Economic status and health in childhood: The origins of the gradient. *American Economic Review* 92 (5): 1308–34.

Crimmins, Eileen M., and Yasuhiko Saito. 2001. Trends in health life expectancy in the United States, 1970–1990: Gender, racial and educational differences. *Social Science and Medicine* 52:1629–41.

Deaton, Angus, and Christina Paxson. 2001. Mortality, education, income and inequality among American cohorts. In *Themes in the economics of aging,* ed. D. A. Wise, 129–65. Chicago: University of Chicago Press.

Freedman, Vicki A., Eileen Crimmins, Robert F. Schoeni, Brenda C. Spillman, Hakan Aykan, Ellen Kramarow, Kenneth Land, et al. 2004. Resolving inconsistencies in trends in old-age disability: Report from a technical working group. *Demography* 41 (3): 417–41.

Fried, Linda P., and Jack M. Guralnik. 1997. Disability and older adults: Evidence regarding significance, etiology and risk. *Journal of the American Geriatric Society* 45:92–100.

Gitlin, Laura N., William Mann, Machiko Tomit, and Sue M. Marcus. 2001. Factors associated with home environmental problems among community-living older persons. *Disability and Rehabilitation* 23 (17): 777–87.

Guralnik, Jack M., Linda P. Fried, and Marcel E. Salive. 1996. Disability as a public health outcome in the aging population. *Annual Reviews of Public Health* 17:22–46.

Kemper, Peter. 1992. The use of formal and informal home care by the disabled elderly. *Health Services Research* 27 (4): 421–51.

Mathieson, Kathleen M., Jennie Jacobs Kronenfeld, and Verna M. Keith. 2002. Maintaining functional independence in elderly adults: The roles of health status and financial resources in predicting home modifications and use of mobility equipment. *The Gerontologist* 42 (1): 24–31.

McGinness, J. Michael, and William H. Foege. 1993. Actual cause of death in the United States. *Journal of the American Medical Association* 270:2207–12.

Melzer, David, Grant Izmirlian, Suzanne G. Leveille, and Jack M. Guralnik. 2001. Educational differences in the prevalence of mobility disability in old age: The dynamics of incidence, mortality and recovery. *Journal of Gerontology: Social Sciences* 56B (5): S294–S301.

Newman, Sandra. 2003. The living conditions of elderly Americans. *The Gerontologist* 43 (1): 99–109.

Norburn, Jean E. Kincade, Shulamit L. Bernard, Thomas R. Konrad, Alison Woomert, Gordon H. DeFriese, William D. Kalsbeek, Gary G. Koch, and Marcia G. Ory. 1995. Self-care and assistance from others in coping with functional status limitations among a national sample of older adults. *Journal of Gerontology: Social Sciences* 50B (2): S101–S109.

Penning, Margaret J., and Laurel A. Strain. 1994. Gender differences in disability, assistance, and subjective well-being in later life. *Journal of Gerontology: Social Sciences* 49 (4): S202–S208.

Schoeni, Robert F., Linda G. Martin, Patricia M. Andreski, and Vicki A. Freedman. 2005. Persistent and growing socioeconomic disparities in disability among the elderly: 1982–2002. *American Journal of Public Health* 95 (11): 2065–70.

Stuck, Andreas E., Jutta M. Walthert, Thorsten Nikolaus, Christophe J. Bula, Chritoph Hohmann, and John C. Beck. 1999. Risk factors for functional status decline in community-living elderly people: A systematic literature review. *Social Science and Medicine.* 48:445–69.

Taylor, Donald H., and Helen Hoenig. 2004. The effect of equipment usage and residual task difficulty on use of personal assistance, days in bed, and nursing home placement. *Journal of the American Geriatric Society* 52:72–79.

Verbrugge, Lois M., Catherine Rennert, and Jennifer H. Madans. 1997. The great efficacy of personal and equipment assistance in reducing disability. *American Journal of Public Health* 87 (3): 384–92.

Verbrugge, Lois M., and Purvi Sevak. 2002. Use, type and efficacy of assistance for disability. *Journal of Gerontology: Social Sciences.* 57B (6): S366–S379.

Weiss, Carlos O., Hector M. Gonzalez, Mohammed U. Kabeto, and Kenneth M. Langa. 2005. Differences in amount of informal care received by non-Hispanic whites and Latinos in a nationally representative sample of older Americans. *Journal of the American Geriatrics Society* 53:146–151.

Zimmer, Zachary, and James S. House. 2003. Education, income, and functional limitation transitions among American adults: Contrasting onset and progression. *International Journal of Epidemiology* 32:1089–97.

Comment   Michael D. Hurd

Introduction

A strong positive correlation between health and socioeconomic status (SES) is well established in the literature. Health can be measured by survival, self-rated health, disease conditions, ADL limitations, or other measures, and SES can be measured by income, wealth, education, and occupation, among others. Yet, a main finding of Cutler, Landrum, and Stewart is that education has a strong relationship with impairment and with coping with impairment, whereas income does not. For example, in figure 6.2, with the exception of the lowest income band, which has about 18 percent of the sample, there is little variation in the prevalence of an ADL limitation across income categories. Higher education helps to cope with ADL limitations, mainly through the use of equipment, but income does not (table 6.6). While these results may be correct, the data set on which they are based, the 1994 and 1995 National Health Interview Surveys (NHIS), has a deficient income measure, which will obscure the true relationship between income and other variables, including impairment. Furthermore, in estimations in which both income and education explain an impairment or coping with an impairment, the deficiencies in the measurement of income will affect estimated effects of education because of the positive correlation between income and education.

My discussion will focus on measurement error in income and how it will contaminate the estimated effects of education. Before that discussion, however, I note the low levels of ADL limitations reported in the NHIS: according to table 6.2, the rate was just 9.5 percent among those age sixty-five or over. The authors state that this rate is similar to the rate as measured in

Michael D. Hurd is a senior economist and director of the RAND Center for the Study of Aging and a research associate of the National Bureau of Economic Research.

other data sets. They cite a rate of 15 percent in 1995 AHEAD, which would be over the age range of seventy-two or over. My calculation in 1998 HRS over the age range sixty-five or over is 22.5 percent (weighted). The authors also cite rates of 15 percent in the NLTCS and about 20 percent in the MCBS. These rates of 15 percent to 22 percent are substantially higher than the NHIS rate, and the difference warrants investigation.

Measurement of Income in the NHIS

Income in the NHIS is assessed in the following manner: a respondent for the household is asked whether anyone in the household has income from earnings, and if so, which of the household members has earnings. This question format is repeated in turn for each of self-employment income, Social Security, pensions, SSI, Social Security DI, welfare, interest from savings, dividends, child support, and any other sources. At this point, the respondent has not been asked about amounts—just whether anyone has income from those sources. Then, in a single question, the respondent is asked about total household income received by all household members during the past year. This is a very difficult question to answer, and generally will lead to underestimates of income and to under-reporting of income in the tails of the distribution.

If the respondent does not give a quantitative answer, he or she is asked a single bracketing question: $20,000, or more or less than $20,000? Depending on the bracket, the respondent is asked to choose the income interval from a range card. The range card for the lower bracket has twenty intervals, each $1,000 wide, from zero to $20,000. The range card for the upper bracket has intervals of width $1,000 up to $35,000 and intervals of width $5,000 up to $75,000. It is well known from cognitive research that subjects tend to give responses in the middle of a range card, so I would expect a clustering of responses between about $8,000 and $14,000, which is in the middle of the first range card, and a clustering of responses between about $29,000 and $35,000, which is in the middle of the second range card.

We can compare the distribution of income in the NHIS with the distribution of income in the HRS among those sixty-five or over.[1] The HRS has a widely copied assessment of income that has been replicated over many waves and has been validated against the CPS. Figure 6C.1 shows that the HRS distribution has more mass in the tails and considerably less in the range of $10,000–$30,000. This would be expected from measurement error and the tendency of the NHIS range cards to pull respondents toward the middle of the distribution.

A second possible explanation for the difference in income is that HRS and NHIS have surveyed different populations, even though they target the same population. Figure 6C.2 shows the distribution of education in

---

1. I use HRS 1998 for this comparison because prior to 1998, HRS (including AHEAD) did not cover the entire age range sixty-five or over.

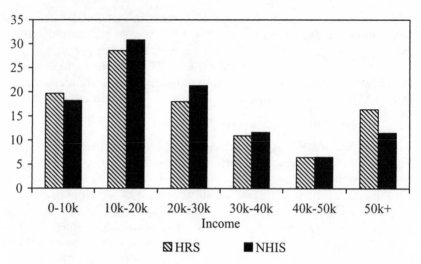

Fig. 6C.1   Income distribution (percentage)

HRS 1998 and in NHIS. The HRS sample has somewhat higher education levels than the NHIS. For example, in the HRS sample about five percentage points more attended some college or graduated from college than in the NHIS. While the differences are not large, the greater education in HRS could explain the higher fraction with income above $75,000, but it would not explain the greater fraction with income less than $10,000.

In AHEAD 1993, income was ascertained in the standard HRS manner by a series of questions about income from different categories such as dividends, earnings, and so forth. At the end of the income sequence the respondent for the household was also asked in one question for an annual total, much as in the NHIS. While some differences remain, we can get an idea of the observation error in income caused by the one-shot question by comparing the standard measure of income based on separate questions for each income category with the single-question measure.[2] As shown in table 6C.1, average income is similar: $24.5 thousand versus $21.3 thousand. Apparently the one-shot question undermeasures income by about 13 percent. However, the standard error is much smaller, $300 for the one-shot compared with $700 for the standard measure. This difference is a reflection of the tendency for the one-shot to pull reports toward the middle of the distribution.

Comparison of ADL Limitations between the HRS and NHIS

While the income comparisons accord with expectations, a more direct comparison is to compare the relationship between ADL limitations and

2. The standard measure and the one-shot measure were both gathered only in AHEAD 1993, which is the reason this analysis is based on AHEAD 1993.

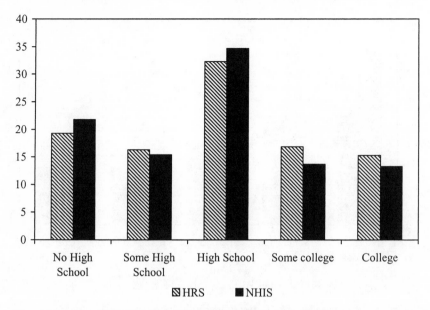

Fig. 6C.2   Distribution (percentage) of educational attainment

Table 6C.1   Income (thousands) in AHEAD 1993

	Mean	Standard error
Standard income assessment	24.5	0.7
One-shot income assessment	21.3	0.3

income in the HRS, where we believe we have an income measure that is relatively free of measurement error, with the relationship in NHIS, where we believe income has considerable measurement error, both systematic and random.[3] Even though the levels of ADL limitations in HRS and NHIS are very different, both measure some aspect of health and so should show variation with income and education in a manner that has been established in the literature. However, because the levels of ADL limitations are so different, I first show the relationship between ADL limitations and education. Figure 6C.3 shows the odds of having an ADL limitation by education category for the HRS and for the NHIS.[4] With the exception of the first education category, the odds levels and variation with education are

3. I will limit my discussion to ADL limitations because IADL limitations are more complex, reflecting individual choices about whether to perform an activity as well as intrinsic ability to perform it.
4. The odds ratios are adjusted for age and sex. The NHIS odds come from table 5A.3, renormalized on high school education (the largest education category). The HRS odds ratios are from my logistic regressions, based on HRS 1998.

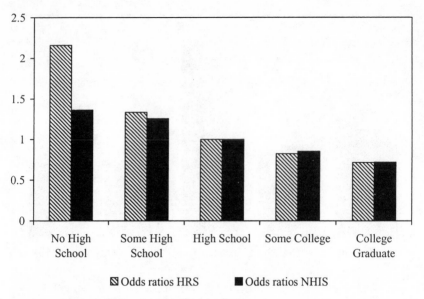

Fig. 6C.3   Relative odds of ADL limitation: Education

remarkably similar. Thus in the HRS the odds are about 38 percent higher among those with some high school (but not a high school degree) than among those with a high school degree; in the NHIS the odds are about 26 percent higher.

The patterns by income band are very different. Figure 6C.4 shows the adjusted odds ratios in the HRS and in the NHIS.[5] With the exception of the first income category, the odds ratios are essentially flat in the NHIS, whereas they show a sharp and (almost) consistent decline in the HRS. For example, among those with household income greater than $50,000 (about 16 percent of the sample in HRS) the odds are just 45 percent of the odds of those with household income of $20,000 to $30,000. This is the kind of relationship between income and health that is widely found by many researchers in many data sets.

When both income and education are included in the logistic specification and estimated over the HRS, the effects of education are attenuated as would be expected from the positive correlation between true income and education (fig. 6C.5).[6] Thus, the effect of "no high school" on relative risk is reduced from 2.12 in figure 6C.3 to 1.69 and the effect of "college grad"

5. The odds ratios are adjusted for age and sex. The odds ratios for the NHIS are based on table 5A.2, renormalized on income 10k–20k (the largest income category). The HRS odds ratios are from my logistic regressions, based on HRS 1998.

6. The odds ratios are adjusted for age and sex. The odds ratios for the NHIS are based on table 6.3, renormalized on income of 10k–20k, and high school education (the largest categories). The HRS odds ratios are from my logistic regressions, based on HRS 1998.

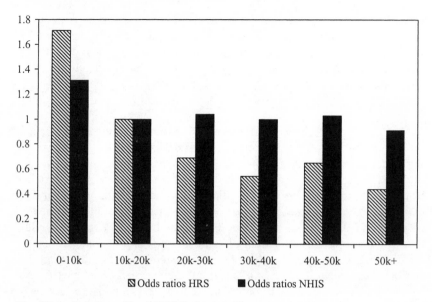

Fig. 6C.4   Relative odds of ADL limitation: Income

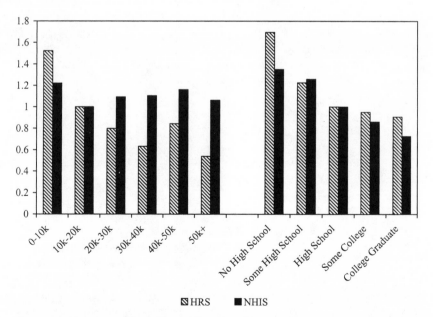

Fig. 6C.5   Relative odds of ADL limitation: Income and education

is reduced from 0.76 to 0.91. That is, the difference in relative risk between the lowest education band and the highest is reduced from 1.36 to 0.78 when income is included. In contrast, when income is included in the NHIS, relative risk with respect to education is virtually unchanged, as a comparison between figures 6C.3 and 6C.5 shows.

Conclusion

My discussion has been about the effects of the measurement of income on the estimation of the relationship between intrinsic ADL limitations and income and education. Measurement error on income will lead to underestimation of its effects, but because of the strong positive correlation between true income and education, the same measurement error will cause the effects of education to be overestimated. I found this to be the case in HRS data. Because of data limitations I did not perform similar analyses on coping and residual difficulties, but I expect that the results would be similar. I also noted the very low level of ADL limitations in the NHIS compared with other data sets. For these reasons I conclude that the results of this chapter need to be validated on a data set with a better measure of income and with a level of ADL limitations that is more consistent with data from other household surveys, such as the HRS, NLTCS, and MCBS.

Why Do Europeans Smoke More than Americans?

David M. Cutler and Edward L. Glaeser

7.1 Introduction

Americans have one of the lowest smoking rates in the developed world. As figure 7.1 shows, 19.1 percent of adult Americans smoke, as opposed to 34 percent of Germans or Japanese and 27 percent of the French or English. The American smoking rate is 10 percent less than the average among developed nations shown in the figure. This is the lowest rate in this sample apart from Sweden. This remarkable abstinence is all the more remarkable because there are many other areas where Americans are not notable for healthy behavior. For example, among the same sample of countries, America has easily the highest obesity rate (see figure 7.2) and our consumption of alcohol per adult is in the mean of the sample.[1] In this essay, we try to understand why smoking is so low in the United States.

America's abstinence from tobacco is not some long-standing aspect of U.S. culture; rather, it is very recent. As figure 7.3 illustrates, over the twentieth-century, cigarette smoking in the United States saw a remarkable rise from 267 cigarettes per capita in 1914 to over 4,300 cigarettes per capita in 1963 before plummeting to just over 2,000 per capita today.

David M. Cutler is the Otto Eckstein Professor of Applied Economics and dean for the social sciences at Harvard University, and a research associate of the National Bureau of Economic Research. Edward L. Glaeser is the Fred and Eleanor Glimp Professor of Economics at Harvard University, and a research associate of the National Bureau of Economic Research.

Both authors thank the National Institute of Aging. Mark Lurie and Elina Onitskansky provided superb research assistance.

1. This fact might suggest that American obesity and smoking are, in fact, negatively linked, where reductions in smoking led to higher obesity. There is little evidence to support this view. In general, across people there is no correlation between smoking and obesity (Cutler and Glaeser 2005), and across countries the correlation is also essentially zero.

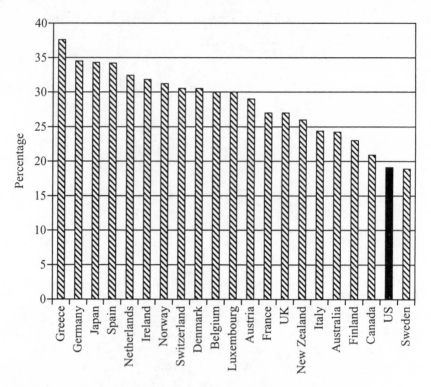

Fig. 7.1   Smoking rates in developed countries, 2000
Source: World Health Organization.

Through the 1960s, the United States had much higher per capita tobacco consumption than any Western European country. Figure 7.4 plots smoking rates per adult in 2000 on smoking rates in 1980 across countries. The line is the 45 degree line, so the distance between the point and line shows the extent that smoking declined between 1980 and 2000. America had the largest drop of any non-Scandinavian country in the sample.

We examine three potential explanations for the low level of smoking in the United States relative to other developed countries. First, we ask whether the effective price of cigarettes, which reflects both taxes and other regulations on tobacco, is higher in the United States. Second, we look at whether higher American income levels might explain the lower level of U.S. cigarette consumption, if better health is a luxury good. Third, we ask whether differences in beliefs about the consequences of smoking might be responsible for American exceptionalism.

It is clearly not the case that low cigarette smoking in the United States is the result of higher cigarette prices. Cigarettes are, on average, 37 percent cheaper in the United States than in the European Union. For ex-

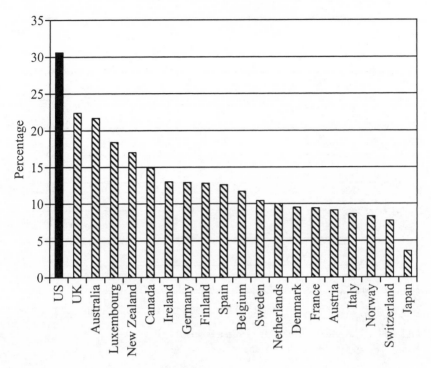

Fig. 7.2   Obesity rates in developed countries, 2000

Source: Organization for Economic Cooperation and Development (OECD) Health Statistics.

Note: Data are for about 2000 in all countries.

ample, the average price per pack in the United Kingdom is $6.25,[2] while the average price per pack in the United States is $3.60. The average tax per pack is 86 cents in the United States and 206 cents in France. Using standard estimates of the elasticity of cigarette consumption with respect to price, these facts suggest that, holding everything else constant, Americans would smoke 20 percent more than Europeans. Cross-national results on regulation are similar. If anything, tobacco consumption in the United States is less regulated than in most European countries, and controlling for regulation only makes American exceptionalism more extreme.

The relationship between income and cigarette consumption across countries is nonlinear. Cigarette consumption first rises with income and then declines. Our model in section 7.2 suggests that this can be interpreted as the confluence of two opposing effects: higher income levels make it eas-

2. These are legal prices. There may be some smuggling of cigarettes in the United Kingdom, which we do not account for.

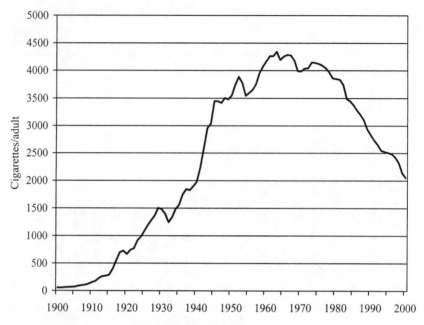

Fig. 7.3   Cigarette smoking in the United States
Source: Centers for Disease Control and Prevention.

ier to afford more cigarettes and also increase the costs of death and disease. Within-country estimates of income elasticities are much smaller than these cross-country estimates. As such, the ability of income differences to explain smoking differences between the United States and Europe depends primarily on one's beliefs about micro versus macro estimates of income elasticities. If one believes that there is a social multiplier so that macro estimates are indeed many times higher than micro estimates, and the estimated macro estimates are correct, then income differences can explain roughly one-quarter of the United States/Europe difference. If one believes that the micro estimates are correct and the macro estimates are spurious reflections of omitted variables, then income differences can, at best, explain one-tenth of the United States/Europe difference.

Finally, we turn to differences in beliefs about the health effects of smoking between the United States and Europe. Public opinion surveys suggest that Americans have some of the strongest beliefs that cigarettes are extremely harmful. Furthermore, there is an extremely strong negative correlation across individuals between beliefs about the harms of smoking and smoking, and a somewhat weaker correlation between the same variables across countries. Of course, cognitive dissonance (Akerlof and Dickens 1982) suggests that this relationship might exist because smokers like to

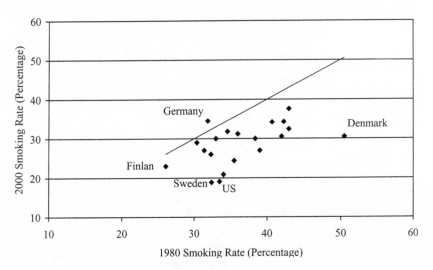

Fig. 7.4   Smoking rates in 1980 and 2000
Source: World Health Organization.

think that their habit isn't harmful. To address this possibility, we look only at beliefs among nonsmokers and again find a relationship between beliefs and smoking. Even among nonsmokers, the United States has some of the strongest antismoking beliefs.

A simple decomposition suggests that these belief differences can explain between one-quarter and one-half of the difference in smoking rates between the United States and Europe. We present some evidence suggesting that these differences in beliefs are themselves the result of concerted government action emphasizing the harms of smoking.

In the next section, we present a brief model that sets out the potential causes of lower cigarette consumption in the United States. In section 7.3 we review the evidence on price, tax, and regulation differences between the United States and Europe. Section 7.4 examines the relationship between income and cigarette consumption, showing that up to one-quarter of the difference between the United States and Europe can be explained by higher income in the United States. Finally, section 7.5 discusses the causes and consequences of differences in beliefs about the health consequences of smoking. The last section concludes.

7.2   Theoretical Determinants of Smoking

In this section, we present a simple model of cigarette consumption, beliefs, and income and use the model to theories we shall test. We assume a discrete time model where individuals receive income Y in each period. Individuals discount the future with discount factor β. To focus on the key issues, we assume there is no borrowing or lending between periods, and the only decision in each period is whether to smoke. Smoking is a one-zero choice that carries financial cost of P_c and yields utility of S, which differs across individuals.

In each period, the probability of surviving until the next period is believed to δ for nonsmokers and $\delta - \Delta$ for smokers. These beliefs can be changed, but we assume they are the same for everyone at a point in time. The utility flow if dead is normalized to zero. The flow of utility for non-smokers is $U(Y)$, and the flow of utility for smokers equals $U(Y - P_c) + S$. The stationary nature of this problem means (somewhat counterfactually) that individuals will always make the same decision about smoking each period. Total expected discounted utility for smokers equals $[U(Y - P_c) + S]/[1 - \beta(\delta - \Delta)]$ and for nonsmokers equals $[U(Y)]/(1 - \beta\delta)$. Smokers trade off the flow benefits of enjoying cigarettes against both the cash costs of smoking and the costs in terms of lost health. With these assumptions, Proposition 1 follows:

PROPOSITION 1. *There exists a value of $S > 0$, denoted S^*, at which individuals are indifferent between smoking and not smoking. Individuals with values of S greater than S^* strictly prefer smoking, and individuals with values of S less than S^* strictly prefer not smoking. The value of S^* is rising with P_c, β, δ, and Δ.*

The value of S^* suggests that the population will be split between those who smoke and those who don't smoke based on the heterogeneous preference for tobacco. If S is distributed with a cumulative distribution $F(S)$ and density $f(S)$, then the share of people who smoke will equal $1 - F(S^*)$, and an increase in S^* will cause smoking to fall by $-f(S^*)$.

The comparative statics of the model are straightforward. Because greater mortality risk is a primary cost of cigarette consumption, people who are more patient and value the future more will smoke less. Rising prices will generally cause fewer cigarettes to be consumed. Higher taxes on cigarettes will raise prices and should reduce consumption. Some regulations, such as bans on smoking indoors, may also act to raise the effective cost of consuming cigarettes, though regulations could matter through other channels as well.

The comparative statics on δ can be seen as reflecting the complementarities across health risks. When individuals have a low probability of survival (i.e., a low value of δ), then the health costs of smoking are discounted heavily, and smoking becomes more attractive. If one is likely to die from other reasons, one tends to worry less about the harms from smoking.[3] The comparative static on Δ can be interpreted as either relating to the actual

---

3. The heavy use of cigarettes among soldiers during wartime may be one particular example of this phenomenon.

impact of cigarette smoking on health or to the perceived impact of cigarette smoking on health. As individuals perceive that cigarettes are more harmful, they will smoke less.

The comparative static on income is somewhat more complex:

PROPOSITION 2. *The value of S^* is rising with Y if and only if $(1 - \beta\delta + \beta\Delta)/ (1 - \beta\delta) > [U'(Y - P_c)]/[U'(Y)]$. If $\lim_{Y \to 0} U'(Y) = \infty$, $\lim_{Y \to \infty} [U'(Y - P_c)]/ U'(Y) = 1$, and $- U''(Y)/U'(Y)$ is strictly increasing with Y, then there exists a value of Y below which $\partial S^*/\partial Y < 0$ and above which $\partial S^*/\partial Y > 0$.*

Income has two important effects on consumption, which work in opposite directions. Higher levels of income mean that the cash cost of cigarettes is less important; thus, there will be higher smoking as people get richer. Countervailing this, however, is that the value of life increases with income, and this will lead to less smoking. Under some cases—when the health effect becomes relatively more important as income rises—these two effects can lead to a nonmonotonic relationship between income and cigarette consumption. This will be the case if, for example, $U(.)$ is a power function.

To further investigate the comparative static on beliefs about the harms of smoking, we examine how beliefs about smoking interact with other characteristics of individuals. Our next proposition describes how changes in Δ affect different groups sorted along other margins.

PROPOSITION 3. *An increase in Δ will cause a greater decrease in smoking among (a) those with higher income, (b) those with a higher baseline probability of survival (δ), and (c) those who are more patient (a higher value of β).*

Proposition 3 tells us that if there is a change in beliefs about the mortality risks of smoking, then we should expect to see a greater reduction in smoking among people who are rich, patient, or likely to live long lives if they don't smoke. The intuition behind these results is that the value of living longer is greater for those who value the future highly, or who are likely to live, or who get more utility from living. Thus, information suggesting a way to live longer will be adopted more readily by those groups.

This effect is very different from the effect of an increase in prices. Because rich people care relatively more about survival and less about additional cash outlays than the poor, prices should have a smaller impact on the rich than on the poor. Price increases will have the same effect on people who differ only in discount rates or baseline levels of survival. We state this, and related results, formally in Proposition 4.

PROPOSITION 4. *An increase in the price of cigarettes, P_c, will cause a greater decrease in the share of the less rich that smoke. Cigarette price increases will have the same effect on people with different discount rates or different baseline levels of survival.*

Propositions 3 and 4 offer a general test of whether differences in smoking between the United States and Europe differ because of beliefs or prices. If beliefs differ, then we should expect the reduction in U.S. smoking to be concentrated among the wealthy, patient, and healthy. If prices differ, then we should expect differences in smoking to be concentrated among the poor, and we should expect no differences in groups on the basis of health or patience.

Finally, we extend the model to allow for social interactions in smoking. We assume that utility from smoking equals $S + g \times \text{Share}_{\text{smokers}}$, where S is an individual specific taste for smoking, and g is a constant that reflects the impact of having other smokers to interact with. Smoking interactions might occur because of social norms (smoking among nonsmokers becomes stigmatized) or because of habit persistence in tobacco consumption (being around smoke increases the desire to smoke). It is straightforward to show the following:

As in Propositions 3 and 4, we assume that there is always someone who smokes and someone who doesn't smoke and that $\overline{S} - \underline{S} > g$, where $\overline{S}$ and $\underline{S}$ are the upper and lower bounds of the taste for smoking. This implies the following:

PROPOSITION 5. *The share of the population in a country that smokes will be declining with P_C, β, δ, and Δ, and the negative impact of these variables on smoking will be larger with g. Assuming that the distribution of tastes for smoking is uniform within the population on the interval $[\underline{S}, \overline{S}]$ and that there is always someone who smokes, the impact of any other variable across groups will equal $(\overline{S} - \underline{S})/(S - \underline{S} - g) > 1$ times the impact of these variables within groups.*

As is usual, positive complementarities cause there to be a social multiplier so that exogenous characteristics that affect smoking become quantitatively more important (Becker and Murphy 2000; Glaeser, Sacerdote, and Scheinkman 2003). As a result, within-country estimates of coefficients may understate the importance that these coefficients can have on cross-country smoking patterns.

Our model suggests a relatively straightforward empirical implementation. We estimate equations for smoking at the individual and group level, relating the smoking decision to income, prices, and beliefs about the harms of tobacco. The regression is of the form:

(1) $\text{Share}_{\text{Smoker}} = \alpha + \beta_{\text{Price}}\text{Price} + \beta_{\text{Belief}}\text{Belief} + \beta_{\text{Income}}\text{Income}.$

This specification then implies that:

(2) $\text{Difference in Share}_{\text{Smoker}} = \beta_{\text{Price}}(\text{Price}_{\text{EU}} - \text{Price}_{\text{US}})$

$$+ \beta_{\text{Belief}}(\text{Belief}_{\text{EU}} - \text{Belief}_{\text{US}})$$

$$+ \beta_{\text{Income}}(\text{Income}_{\text{EU}} - \text{Income}_{\text{US}}).$$

Our objective is to provide estimates of the differences in cigarette prices, beliefs about cigarette risks, and income between the United States and the European Union, as well as to estimate the impact of these variables on the share of the population that smokes. With these estimates, we can decompose the difference in smoking patterns between the United States and Europe.

7.3 Data

Data on tobacco consumption are plentiful, but not always consistent. Almost all countries have some data on tobacco consumption, typically from national surveys. We use these data as much as possible. A compendium of such data is kept by the World Health Organization (WHO).[4]

For some of our analyses, we wish to examine subgroups of the population, for example, by income or education. While most surveys will have such data, tabulations of national data frequently do not contain such detail. In addition, we want to know about beliefs about the harms of smoking, which are measured far less frequently. For these analyses, we use the Eurobarometer survey in 1994, matched with the U.S. National Survey of Drug Use and Health of the same year. Unfortunately, Eurobarometer did not survey all countries. Thus, we are restricted to fourteen European countries in these analyses.

In addition, average smoking rates from the Eurobarometer data are somewhat different from average smoking in official national data. For the fourteen countries with both sources of data, the correlation coefficient is 0.50. The greatest difference is in Denmark, where official data from a survey conducted by PLS Consult and the Danish Council on Smoking and Health show substantially smoking rates that are 11 percentage points less than the Eurobarometer data. It is possible that differences in specific questions or samples explain these differences, though we cannot be sure without access to the raw data. Other large differences are in France, Finland, Italy, and the Netherlands. We use the reported national data as we can, to ensure the largest possible sample size, and use the Eurobarometer data for questions involving socioeconomic aspects of smoking or beliefs about the harms of smoking. Fortunately, the two estimates are relatively similar when we substitute one for the other.

As shown in the following, income has a large and nonlinear effect on smoking. When we examine bivariate relationships between smoking and other factors (prices, regulations, or beliefs), it is important to have a relatively homogeneous sample of countries by income. Within Europe, the major income outlier is Greece, with a per capita income that is 60 percent

4. See, especially, the World Health Organization's Health for All Database, http://www .euro.who.int/hfadb.

below the European average ($10,607 in Greece versus $25,858 in Europe in 2000) and 25 percent below the next lowest country (Spain, at $14,138). For this reason, we omit Greece from many of our regressions, though we present raw data for Greece in the tables and show the country in the figures.

7.4   Differences in Prices, Taxes, and Regulation between the United States and Europe

A long economic literature on smoking has focused on the impact of cigarette prices on smoking. This literature began by using time series data within the United States (Schoenberg 1933) and expanded to looking at cross-state variation created by differences in excise taxes (Maier 1955). More modern estimates have become increasingly sophisticated and relate cigarette smoking to either lagged or expected cigarette prices (Baltagi and Levin 1986; Becker, Grossman, and Murphy 1994). The most compelling estimates follow Lyon and Simon (1968) and use within-state variation, examining the response of consumption to a change in the state excise tax on cigarettes.[5]

Lyon and Simon (1968) estimate the price elasticity of smoking at −.51. Chaloupka (1991) estimates long-run price elasticities between −.27 and −.36 for the entire population. As Proposition 4 in the previous section suggests, Chaloupka finds higher price elasticities for poorer members of society. Becker, Grossman, and Murphy (1994) estimate short-run price elasticities ranging from −.36 to −.44 and long-run price elasticities ranging from −.73 to −.79. Gallet and List (2003) perform a meta-analysis of papers on cigarette demand and find a mean price elasticity of −.48. While there is a considerable range from −.27 to −.79, these estimates all suggest that differential cigarette prices can explain differences in cigarette consumption over time and space.

The first two columns of table 7.1 show prices and excise taxes across developed countries in 2000 (in U.S. dollars). The last column reports the price of cigarettes relative to the cost of one kilogram of bread—the normalization correcting for value added taxes on other commodities that might distort consumption decisions. These prices are the price of the cheapest national brand and do not account for any smuggling or nonmarket transactions. Stories of such transactions in some countries abound. For example, in 2002, the Italian police allegedly broke up a smuggling ring that smuggled three million Euros worth of cigarettes from Ro-

---

5. These results seem reasonably persuasive despite the possible endogeneity problem—high taxes might be put in place when states are experiencing an exogenous decline in cigarette smoking.

Table 7.1   **Cigarette prices in the United States and Europe**

Country	Price after tax of local brand (US$)	Tax (US$)	Price relative to bread
Austria	3.04	2.22	1.5
Belgium	2.93	2.20	1.5
Denmark	4.00	3.36	1.9
Finland	3.35	2.45	1.0
France	2.75	2.06	1.1
Germany	2.75	1.98	1.9
Greece	1.64	1.20	1.7
Ireland	4.47	3.35	1.9
Italy	1.93	1.41	0.9
Luxembourg	1.90	—	0.9
The Netherlands	2.56	1.84	1.7
Norway	6.48	5.05	2.7
Portugal	1.77	1.43	1.7
Spain	1.15	0.83	1.2
Sweden	3.64	2.51	1.5
Switzerland	2.80	1.46	1.2
United Kingdom	6.25	4.88	6.7
European average	3.22	2.39	1.9
United States	3.60	0.86	1.2

Sources: World Health Organization *The Tobacco Atlas,* 2002; Guindon, Tobin, and Yach (2002).

Notes: United Kingdom includes Northern Ireland. The European average is for all countries with complete data. Dash indicates data not available.

mania into Italy each month.[6] However, data on illegal sales are not generally available.

The table makes clear that price differences cannot explain why Americans smoke less than Europeans. Nominal cigarette prices are higher in the United States than abroad, but prices relative to other commodities are lower. At least part of this is because the tax on cigarettes is much lower in the United States than in much of Europe. Indeed, cigarette prices are generally higher in Europe than in the United States. Relative to other commodities, prices in the United States are 37 percent lower than in Europe. With an elasticity of –.5, this implies that smoking should be nearly 20 percent greater in the United States.

As figure 7.5 shows, there is little correlation across countries between the cost of cigarettes (measured relative to the cost of bread) and cigarette consumption across developed countries. Indeed, the United States has both relatively low prices and relatively low consumption. The regression line is slightly positive, although not statistically significant. While it is pos-

6. See http://www.crji.org/arhiva/e_020312.htm.

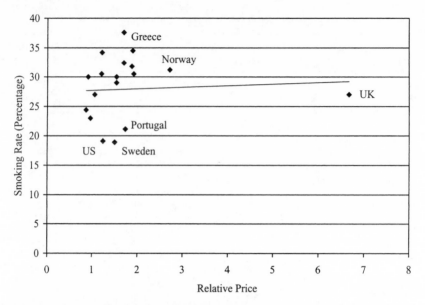

Fig. 7.5   Cigarette smoking and the relative price of tobacco
Source: World Health Organization.
Note: Regression excludes Greece.

sible that forces like greater smuggling of cigarettes in Europe than in the United States might mean that our price estimates overstate the differences across countries, the graph makes it clear that it is extremely unlikely that the United States actually has much higher cigarette prices than other countries.

Cash outlays are one component of cigarette costs; the time cost is another. Evans, Farrelly, and Montgomery (1999) have shown that workplace bans on smoking have a significant impact on cigarette consumption within the United States. The bans are effective, at least in part, because they raise the cost of smoking. We also calculated a regulation index within the United States based on the number of types of places where cigarette smoking is banned: government workplaces, private workplaces, and restaurants. We assign a 1 to each state where smoking is prohibited, a 0.5 to each state where smoking is restricted to specific areas, and a 0 if there is no regulation. As a simple summary measure, we sum the presence of a ban in the three settings. The data to construct the regulatory index come from the Center for Disease Control.

As figure 7.6 shows, there is a negative 38 percent correlation coefficient between this regulation index and the share of smokers in a state. A statistically significant negative relationship result persists even when we control for a wide range of other controls including tobacco prices and income. As

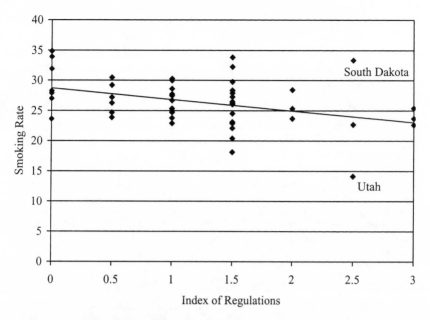

Fig. 7.6   Smoking and regulations in U.S. states
Source: Centers for Disease Control and Prevention.

such, it is at least possible that greater regulation of smoking in the United States might be a cause of the lower smoking rate in America.

To make cross-country comparisons, we look at the same government regulations across European countries. Data on cigarette restrictions come from the WHO Tobacco Control Database. While there are some discrepancies between these reports and what we know about regulation in the United States, we have decided to use the WHO estimates rather than to create our other alternative measures. These measures are generally corroborated by the World Bank data as well.[7]

Table 7.2 lists the principle forms of regulation on tobacco usage in public places in the United States and the European nations. In each case, we give the country a 1 if smoking is prohibited in that setting, a 0.5 if there are partial restrictions or voluntary agreements, and 0 if there is no regulation. It is apparent that the United States is not particularly regulatory. The United States does have some regulations on consumption in public places, but most European countries do as well. While it is possible that U.S. regulations are more seriously enforced than their European counterparts, and certainly the United States has private restrictions on smoking in workplaces that may be less prevalent in other countries, the United

---

7. See http://www1.worldbank.org/tobacco/brieflist_db.asp.

Table 7.2   **Cigarette regulation in the United States and Europe**

| Country | Total | Smoke-free workplace | | Restaurants |
		Government	Private	
Austria	2.0	1.0	1.0	0.0
Belgium	2.5	1.0	1.0	0.5
Denmark	1.0	0.5	0.5	0.0
Finland	2.5	1.0	1.0	0.5
France	2.5	1.0	1.0	0.5
Germany	1.5	0.5	0.5	0.5
Greece	2.5	1.0	1.0	0.5
Ireland	3.0	1.0	1.0	1.0
Italy	3.0	1.0	1.0	1.0
Luxembourg	0.0	0.0	0.0	0.0
The Netherlands	2.5	1.0	1.0	0.5
Norway	3.0	1.0	1.0	1.0
Portugal	2.5	1.0	1.0	0.5
Spain	1.0	0.5	0.5	0.0
Sweden	2.5	1.0	1.0	0.5
Switzerland	1.0	0.5	0.5	0.0
United Kingdom	0.5	0.0	0.0	0.5
European average	1.97	0.76	0.76	0.44
United States	1.05	0.49	0.25	.31

Sources: World Health Organization, Tobacco Control Database; CDC State database.
Notes: Data are for around 2000. United Kingdom includes Northern Ireland.

States doesn't stand out relative to the other countries in formal regulations. Indeed, the average of the index for the European Union is 1.97, compared to the value of 1.0 in the United States. Because the United States is less regulated than the European Union, it seems hard to believe that this variable explains less American smoking.

Figure 7.7 shows the relationship between our regulation index and smoking rates across countries. As the regression lines shows, there is no statistically significant relationship between the two. A literal interpretation of this regression suggests that regulations are irrelevant for smoking decisions. Of course, the evidence provided by Evans, Farrelly, and Montgomery (1999) and the U.S. states provides far more compelling results that regulation does matter. Rather, we interpret the cross-country results as suggesting that measurement of regulations and their enforcement at the country level are so noisy that it is impossible to say anything cleanly about the role of regulation in smoking. While our conclusions thus need to be interpreted with some care, the United States does not appear to tax or regulate tobacco consumption particularly highly, making these explanations unlikely to account for the lower smoking rate in the United States.

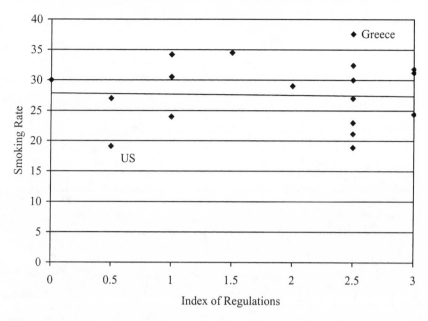

Fig. 7.7   Smoking and regulations across countries
Source: World Health Organization.
Note: Regression excludes Greece.

7.5   Income and United States Europe Differences

We now turn to the relation between income and smoking across countries. There is a rich body of evidence on the income elasticity of demand
for cigarettes. Unfortunately, estimates from this literature differ substantially from study to study (Gallet and List 2003). Given that our model suggests a possible nonmonotonic relationship between income and cigarette
consumption, the lack of a clear consensus on the income elasticity of
smoking is not so surprising.

Early estimates of the income elasticity of smoking were based on national time series or cross-state information. For example, Maier (1955)
reports generally positive income elasticities using cross-state data. Gallet
and List (2003) report twenty-four papers estimating income elasticities
for tobacco using state or provincial data; the median income elasticity
across these estimates is .3.

We have several ways to estimate the income elasticity of smoking. One
method is with international data. Income and smoking rates are available
for seventy-five countries. Figure 7.8 shows the relation between smoking
and the log of per capita income in those countries. The regression line al-

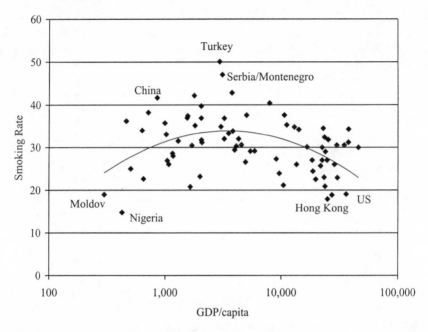

Fig. 7.8   Smoking and income, international data
Sources: World Health Organization and World Bank.

lows for a quadratic relationship, as suggested by the model. The quadratic fits reasonably well:

$$\text{Share Smoking} = -76.5 + 26.9 \ln(\text{GDP}) - 1.65 \ln(\text{GDP})^2; \ R^2 = .20,$$
$$\quad\quad\quad (30.5) \quad (7.36) \quad\quad\quad\quad (.43)$$

where $\ln(\text{GDP})$ is the logarithm of per capita gross domestic product (GDP) in 2000 in U.S. dollars, and standard errors are in parentheses beneath coefficient estimates. The maximum predicted value is reached at an income of \$3,200. The effect of a 1 log point increase in per capita GDP is –7.7 at the income of the United States. Even with its high income, however, the United States is a negative outlier; smoking is lower in the United States than one would expect by income alone. The residual for the United States is about –6 percent.

We can get a similar estimate of the income elasticity of spending using data from U.S. states. Figure 7.9 shows that the correlation between per capita income and smoking across states within the United States is negative. A 1 log point increase in income is associated with a 7.8 percent decrease in the smoking rate in a univariate regression. This is very similar to the international data.

Individual-based estimates of cigarette consumption show weaker esti-

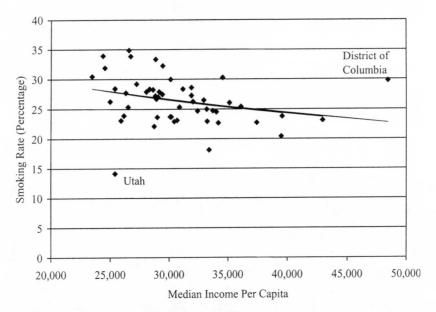

Fig. 7.9   Smoking and median income, states

Sources: Centers for Disease Control and Prevention and U.S. Census Bureau.

Note: The regression line is estimated using the logarithm of per capita income as the dependent variable.

mates. For example, Gallet and List (2003) report ten papers estimating the income elasticity of demand for tobacco using individual data, with the median elasticity estimate across those papers being .06, which is both small and positive.

In table 7.3, we show smoking rates across income quartile within the United States and Europe. We also show smoking rates by broad education category. Smoking declines with income (or education) in the United States. The difference is large; smoking rates for those in the top quintile are one-third lower than smoking rates for those in the bottom quintile. In Europe, the relationship between smoking and income is flat. As a result, the gap between the United States and Europe is smallest among poorer individuals and greatest among the rich.

Using the U.S. data, we estimate a nonlinear income elasticity, where a discrete variable that takes on a value of one for regular smokers is regressed on country dummies and the logarithm of income and the logarithm of income squared.[8] The probit regression yields the estimate:

---

8. Only monthly income is asked about in the Eurobarometer data. To get a more precise income elasticity, we use the annual data available in the United States.

Table 7.3   **Smoking rates in developed countries (%)**

Country	Smoking rate 2000	Smoking rate 1994	Rate by income quartile Top	2nd	3rd	Bottom	Rate by education >12 years	<12 years
Austria	29	—	—	—	—	—	—	—
Belgium	30	30	30	35	30	28	30	30
Denmark	31	42	34	48	44	38	42	46
France	27	37	37	36	37	37	41	34
Finland	23	30	—	—	—	—	—	—
Greece	38	36	41	41	40	22	44	31
Germany	35	32	36	33	30	27	34	32
Ireland	32	30	32	28	32	30	26	35
Italy	24	30	28	32	29	28	33	29
Luxembourg	30	29	25	21	36	36	29	29
The Netherlands	32	40	36	35	38	45	43	39
Norway	31	34	—	—	—	—	32	44
Portugal	21	25	32	24	28	11	37	22
Spain	34	34	30	38	38	24	42	31
Sweden	19	—	—	—	—	—	—	—
Switzerland	31	—	—	—	—	—	—	—
United Kingdom	27	31	20	32	32	33	22	36
European average	30	33	32	34	35	30	35	33
United States	19	23	21	24	29	31	22	25

Sources: Official smoking data for 2000 are from the World Health Organization's Health for All Database, and are generally compiled from national surveys. All other data are authors' tabulations. U.S. data are from the National Survey of Drug Use and Health. European data are from Eurobarometer.

Notes: European and U.S. data are for the population aged 15+ in 1994. Germany is West Germany. United Kingdom includes Northern Ireland. The European average is for countries that have complete data (e.g., excluding Norway). Dashes indicate data not available.

$$\text{Smoker} = .330 \ln(\text{Income}) - .024 \ln(\text{Income})^2 + \text{Country Dummies.}$$
$$\phantom{\text{Smoker} = }(.372) \phantom{\ln(\text{Income}) - } (.019)$$

There are 15,213 observations. The coefficients on income and income squared are not statistically significant. They are also somewhat smaller than the national data. An increase in incomes of $10,000 per person would reduce smoking rates by 2.1 percent.

It is not completely clear what income elasticity to use for the United States-Europe comparison. We consider first the elasticity in the international data. The mean income of the European countries that we have included is about $25,000 dollars in 2000. The U.S. income in the same year is about $36,000, for a difference of about 36 percent. Using the preceding equation, this translates into a predicted difference in smoking rates of 2.6 percent (roughly .36 × –7.7), or one-quarter of the total difference in smoking between the United States and Europe.

Our individual level estimates of the income elasticity of smoking are smaller than the macro estimates, so calculations using the micro estimates suggest that the income differences can explain even less of the cross-country differences.[9] Indeed, because the median income elasticity estimate shown by Gallet and List (2003) is positive, using that estimate would make the puzzle even larger.

7.6   Differences in Beliefs about the Health Consequences of Smoking

Finally, we turn to the impact of beliefs about smoking on smoking rates. We start our analysis with survey evidence on beliefs about the health consequences of smoking, leaving aside for the moment where those beliefs come from. In 1994, the Eurobarometer survey asked respondents whether they "tend to agree or disagree: smoking causes cancer and death." We code people who "tend to agree" as believing that smoking is harmful. To match this with U.S. data, we used the 1994 National Survey of Drug Use and Health, which asks "how much people risk harming themselves physically and in other ways when they smoke one or more packs of cigarettes per day: no risk, slight risk, moderate risk, or great risk?" For comparability with the Eurobarometer questions, we consider people who think that smoking has a moderate or great risk.[10]

These particular survey questions are obviously imperfect. Cancer is only one health consequence of smoking. In many cases, the relevant question is not whether smoking causes cancer but rather the increased probability of developing cancer that results from smoking behavior. Nonetheless, this is the best data that we have.

Table 7.4 shows the distribution of beliefs across countries about whether smoking causes cancer. The first column reports the share of the entire population believing that smoking causes cancer. The United States has one of the highest rates of believing that smoking is harmful; 91 percent of Americans report believing that smoking causes cancer. Given the high proportion of Americans that believe in UFOs and the literal truth of the Bible, this must represent one of the most remarkable instances of the penetration of scientific results in the country. Beliefs about the cancer-causing role of cigarettes in some European countries, like Finland, Greece, Norway, and Portugal, are almost identical to those in the United States, but in other places beliefs are far weaker. For example, in Germany, only 73 percent of respondents said that they believed that smoking causes cancer.

One possible interpretation of this data is that exogenous trends in

---

9. The nonlinear relationship means that inequality should also be considered when looking at the smoking differences across countries. We leave this for future work.

10. It is not entirely clear what level of risk corresponds to "tend to agree" in the Eurobarometer data. One might also include those who believe there is a slight risk of smoking. In this case, the beliefs about the harms of smoking would be higher still in the United States.

Table 7.4 Belief differences across countries

Country	Total	Nonsmokers	Smokers
	Percent believing smoking is harmful		
Belgium	78	85	63
Denmark	85	91	78
Finland	91	95	81
France	82	89	72
Germany	73	84	52
Greece	91	96	83
Ireland	85	91	73
Italy	77	85	57
Luxembourg	86	92	73
The Netherlands	81	87	72
Norway	90	94	83
Portugal	92	94	84
Spain	84	86	78
United Kingdom	87	92	75
European average	84	90	73
United States	91	94	83

Sources: Authors tabulations. European data are from Eurobarometer. U.S. data are from the General Social Survey.

Notes: European and U.S. data are for 1994. Germany is West Germany. United Kingdom includes Northern Ireland.

smoking affect beliefs about the harms of cigarettes, through a form of cognitive dissonance. Smokers may persist in believing that cigarettes don't cause cancer because their habits are more justifiable if they refuse to believe that there are health consequences of their actions. To address this, columns (2) and (3) show beliefs about the harms of smoking among nonsmokers and smokers, respectively. This concern does not appear to be evident. Both smokers (83 percent) and nonsmokers (94 percent) in the United States strongly believe that smoking is harmful to health. By contrast, 52 percent of German smokers and 84 percent of German nonsmokers shared that belief. Beliefs appear to be specific to the society, much more than to the individual who smokes or does not.

An added piece of evidence supporting the view that Europeans and Americans differ in their beliefs about smoking is the differential relationship between income and smoking in the United States and Europe. The preceding model emphasized the cross-effect between beliefs and income. If smoking is thought to be harmful, then we should particularly see high income people avoid smoking because they have a greater demand for healthy life. This is exactly what table 7.3 shows; in comparison to Europe, it is the richer groups of the U.S. population who smoke the least.

We use several methods to quantify the impact that these beliefs differences have on the smoking rate. We begin with time series evidence and then turn to cross-individual, cross-state, and cross-country evidence. Lung cancer did not become prevalent in the United States until cigarette use became relatively common. As seen in figure 7.3, this occurred in the first third of the twentieth century. Thus, scientific evidence about the link between smoking and cancer dates from that era. The first published article alleging a link between cigarette smoking and lung cancer appeared in the *American Journal of Cancer* in 1932 (McNally 1932). The article was relatively speculative, though; more concrete evidence linking cigarettes and cancer was published eighteen years later by Wynder and Graham (1950) in the *Journal of the American Medical Association.* This was followed by a 1954 Sloan-Kettering study that reported experiments where tar from cigarettes had caused cancerous tumors in mice (Sloan-Kettering Institute for Cancer Research 1954).

Popular knowledge about the harms of smoking almost certainly dates from *Readers' Digest,* which ran an article in 1952 titled "Cancer by the Carton." The news was picked up by other newspapers and media outlets, including even Edward R. Murrow's (a particularly famous smoker) *See It Now* television program. These early reports and the related publicity created the first cigarette cancer scare in the early 1950s. The 1950s saw nascent public beliefs form about the harms of smoking. In a January 1954 Gallup survey, 41 percent of people answered "yes" to the question "Do you think cigarette smoking is one of the causes of lung cancer, or not?"

Figure 7.3 shows the time path of cigarette smoking during this time period. From 1933 to 1952, cigarette smoking rose every year. Indeed, between 1920 and 1952, cigarette consumption fell only during the bleakest years of the great depression (confirming the positive income elasticity of cigarette consumption at lower income levels). Between 1952 and 1954, cigarette smoking took its first dramatic drop. From 1952 to 1953, smoking dropped by 3 percent, followed by an additional 6 percent the following year. While it is possible that this drop was due to something other than changing beliefs about the health risks of cigarettes, contemporary observers certainly thought that the decline in smoking was the result of the health scare. For example, the treasurer of the American Tobacco Company said in 1954 that "there is a tendency to ascribe the drop in cigarette consumption almost entirely to the so called 'cancer scare'" (*New York Times,* May 7, 1954, p 35).

The reaction in the marketplace proceeded along several dimensions. On the one hand, manufacturers and the public responded by making cigarettes somewhat safer. Use of filtered cigarettes rose from less than 2 percent in 1952 to more than 20 percent in 1955. Edward R. Murrow on the air linked the rise of filtered cigarettes to heightened fears about the dangers of cigarettes. On the other hand, the cigarette industry fought back through advertising. Using their vast advertising budgets and spending on their own rival research (which unsurprisingly found that cigarettes were harmless), cigarette companies were able to overcome the negative pub-licity associated with these early studies. Smoking rose again from 1954 through 1963.

Increasing evidence in the medical community showed the harms from smoking, and in 1964, the Surgeon General issued his famous warning about the health consequences of smoking. In 1966, the Federal Trade Commission required cigarettes to be sold with a label warning that "ciga-rettes may be hazardous to your health." Both the federal government and private groups like the American Cancer Society mounted campaigns meant to increase awareness of the health consequences of smoking. The fruits of this campaign are apparent in public opinion surveys. In 1960, 50 percent of Americans believed that cigarette smoking was one of the causes of lung cancer. By 1969, the share was 71 percent (Cutler and Kadiyala 2003). One sees this in the consumption data as well. In 1964 alone, cigarette smoking fell by 3 percent, and smoking was down by 8 per-cent by 1970.

Since the 1950s, beliefs about the harms of smoking have cemented. The Gallup Organization (Gallup 1981) documented a rising belief that smok-ing was dangerous. By the 1980s, Viscusi (1992) finds that people actually overestimated the health risks of smoking. As noted previously, over 90 percent of Americans now believe that smoking causes cancer.

A strong circumstantial case links the decline of smoking to the expan-sion of information about the harms of smoking. In addition to figure 7.3, data on the share of people who have ever smoked show a decline begin-ning in cohorts coming of smoking age after 1964. Other evidence about the link between perception and smoking comes from individual correla-tions between beliefs and actions. Smoking rates among those who believe that smoking a pack or more of cigarettes per day has a great risk are only 23 percent, compared to 52 percent among those who do not believe that link.[11] If beliefs causally affect smoking (and not the reverse, as with cog-nitive dissonance), it suggests a large impact of beliefs on actions.

One way to get around the reverse relationship between smoking and be-liefs is to consider subsets of the population where beliefs are not reflective of actions. Specifically, we consider how the smoking rate in a state or country is related to the beliefs of nonsmokers about the harms of smok-ing. Of course, if beliefs are formed through a social learning process, then the beliefs of nonsmokers in high-smoking states may reflect the influence of other variables that are related to smoking. But we do not have any ob-vious alternative to this strategy.

Figure 7.10 shows cross-state data on smoking rates and the share of

11. In a probit regression, where we also control for age, gender, race, education, and in-come, the effect of believing that smoking is a great risk drops to 27 percent.

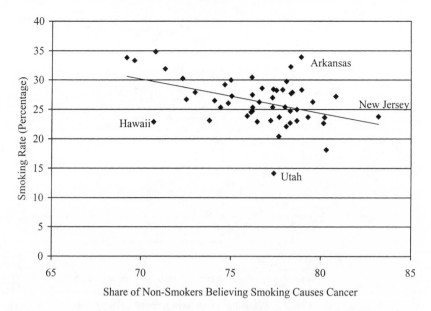

Fig. 7.10   Smoking and the beliefs of nonsmokers about the harms of smoking, states

Sources: Centers for Disease Control and Prevention and National Survey of Drug Use and Health.

nonsmokers who believe that smoking is a great risk.[12] There is a clear negative relation between the two. A 1 percent increase in the share of nonsmokers who think that cigarettes cause cancer is associated with a 0.6 percent decrease in the share of people who smoke cigarettes. This cross-state relationship is robust to controlling for income, price, a regulation index, education, and a dummy variable for states that produce tobacco. The coefficient on beliefs drops only to .5, including all of these controls.

We complement the analysis across U.S. states with cross-country evidence. Figure 7.11 shows the relationship across countries between the share of nonsmoking respondents who believe that cigarettes cause cancer and the share of smokers.[13] The regression line is negative and roughly the same magnitude as the state data; a 1 percent increase in the share of the population that thinks that cigarettes cause cancer is associated with a .47 percent decrease in the share of the population that smokes. Because of the small number of observations, the coefficient is not statistically significant.

12. Note that the mean differs from table 7.4 because we use only the share of people reporting that smoking is a great risk, rather than a great or moderate risk. We do this to highlight the certainty of beliefs.

13. We use Eurobarometer data for smoking rates because we are using the beliefs data from that survey.

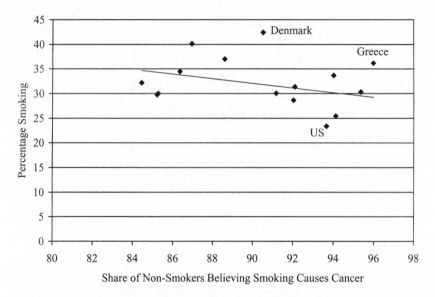

Fig. 7.11   Smoking rates and beliefs about smoking, cross-country data

Sources: Authors' tabulations of Eurobarometer survey data and National Survey of Drug Use and Health.

Note: Regression excludes Greece.

If one assumes that beliefs are formed independently of smoking rates, we can use these estimates and ask how much of the difference between U.S. and European cigarette consumption is associated with differences in beliefs. The difference in beliefs between the United States and Europe is about 7 percentage points overall and 4 percent among nonsmokers. Using the state-level estimate of the impact of beliefs on smoking or the international evidence, the more widespread belief about the harms of smoking explains between 2 and 4 percent lower smoking rates in the United States—the former taking only the difference in beliefs among nonsmokers and the latter taking the difference in beliefs overall. These translate into 20 and 40 percent of the total smoking difference across countries. On the whole, our evidence suggests that differences in beliefs are the most important factor explaining the differences in smoking between the United States and Europe.

7.7   Conclusion

There is a dramatic difference in smoking rates between the United States and Europe. This difference is largest for the most educated and richest members of the two regions, but applies throughout the distribution. This difference is not longstanding, and it exists despite the fact that along many other dimensions (witness obesity), Europeans are far healthier than Americans.

There is no evidence that this difference is the result of cigarette taxes or direct government regulation of cigarettes. Cigarettes are taxed more highly in Europe than in the United States. Some of the difference between the United States and Europe—perhaps a quarter—is the result of higher U.S. incomes. There appears to be something of a smoking Kuznets curve where cigarette consumption first rises and falls with income. Both the United States and Europe are on the downward slope of the Kuznets curve, where higher incomes are associated with less smoking.

The most important factor, however, appears to be differences in beliefs about the health consequences of smoking between the United States and Europe. Ninety-one percent of Americans think that cigarettes cause cancer; only 84 percent of Europeans share that view. Using different estimates of the relation between beliefs and cigarette consumption, we estimate that this difference can explain between one-quarter and one-half of the total smoking difference between the United States and Europe. Moreover, the history of cigarettes within the United States suggests that American beliefs about smoking seemed to come about only after substantial information about the harms of smoking were presented—first by private researchers, then by the Federal government. "Soft paternalism" is a major factor in lower rates of smoking.[14]

The possibility of a feedback from smoking to beliefs about smoking suggests that the impact of this information may be even larger than we have estimated. In areas where fewer people smoke, nonsmoker sentiment might be stronger, leading to a further reduction in cigarette use.

As a final thought, it is worth wondering why the United States, with its lower propensity toward regulation and paternalism generally, had more effective interventions in the changing of beliefs about smoking. The smoking history of the United States suggests that entrepreneurial actions on the part of antismoking interest groups were quite important. Initially, the American Medical Association and later organizations specifically focused on cancer and heart disease and effectively used the market for ideas both directly to influence beliefs and indirectly, by influencing the government. By contrast, European pressure groups were much weaker and less effective at influencing public opinion and policy. According to this view, while greater U.S. entrepreneurship and economic openness led to more smoking during an earlier era (and still leads to more obesity today), it also led to faster changes in beliefs about smoking and ultimately less cigarette consumption.

---

14. We distinguish information campaigns from "hard paternalism," including regulating smoking and raising taxes.

Appendix

Proofs of Propositions

Proof of Proposition 1. At $S = S^* = [\beta\Delta U(Y)]/(1 - \beta\delta) + U(Y) - U(Y - P_C)$, the utility from smoking and not smoking are equal. Because the utility from smoking is monotonically and continuously increasing in S, and the utility from not smoking is independent of S, for values of $S > S^*$, smoking strictly dominates not smoking and for values of $S < S^*$, not smoking strictly dominates smoking.

Differentiation then yields $\partial S^*/\partial P_C = U'(Y - P_C) > 0$, $\partial S^*/\partial\beta = \Delta U(Y)/(1 - \beta\delta)^2 > 0$, $\partial S^*/\partial\Delta = \beta U(Y)/(1 - \beta\delta) > 0$, and $\partial S^*/\partial\delta = \beta^2\Delta U(Y)/(1 - \beta\delta)^2 > 0$.

Proof of Proposition 2. Differentiation yields: $\partial S^*/\partial Y = [(1 - \beta\delta + \beta\Delta) U'(Y)]/(1 - \beta\delta) - U'(Y - P_C)$, which is positive if and only if $1 + \beta\Delta/(1 - \beta\delta) > U'(Y - P_C)/[U'(Y)]$. Further differentiation then yields $d/dY [U'(Y - P_C)/U'(Y)] = [U''(Y - P_C)U'(Y) - U'(Y - P_C)U''(Y)]/[U'(Y)^2]$, which is strictly negative if $-U''(Y - P_C)/[U'(Y - P_C)] > -U''(Y)/[U'(Y)]$. This is always true if $-U''(Y)/[U'(Y)]$ is strictly decreasing in Y. The assumption $\lim_{Y \to 0} U'(Y) = \infty$ guarantees that for some value of Y sufficiently close to P_C, $U'(Y - P_C)/[U'(Y)] > (1 - \beta\delta + \beta\Delta)/(1 - \beta\delta)$, and the assumption $\lim_{Y \to 0} U'(Y - P_C)/[U'(Y)] = 1$ guarantees that for some sufficiently high value of Y, $(1 - \beta\delta + \beta\Delta)/(1 - \beta\delta) > U'(Y - P_C)/[U'(Y)]$. Thus, there must exist a value of Y at which $(1 - \beta\delta + \beta\Delta)/(1 - \beta\delta) = U'(Y - P_C)/[U'(Y)]$. Monotonicity then implies that for levels of Y greater than that, $\partial S^*/\partial Y > 0$, and for levels of Y less than that, $\partial S^*/\partial Y < 0$.

Proof of Proposition 3. Within any two groups, the impact of an increase in Δ on the share of the group that smokes will equal $-f(S^*)\partial S^*/\partial\Delta = -f(S^*)\beta U(Y)/(1 - \beta\delta)$. If S is uniformly distributed, then this becomes $\beta U(Y)/(1 - \beta\delta)$ times a negative constant. Differentiation shows that this quantity is clearly greater for groups with more income, higher values of β, and higher values of δ.

Proof of Proposition 4. Within any two groups, the impact of an increase in P_C on the share of the group that smokes will equal $-f(S^*)\partial S^*/\partial P_C = -f(S^*) U'(Y - P_C)$. If S is uniformly distributed, then this becomes $U'(Y - P_C)$ times a negative constant. This is declining in Y and independent of β and δ.

Proof of Proposition 5. Now $S^* = \beta\Delta U(Y)/(1 - \beta\delta) + U(Y) - U(Y - P_C) - g \times \text{Share}_{\text{smokers}}$. Across population subgroups, the derivative of the share smoking will equal $[-1/(\bar{S} - \underline{S})](\partial S^*/\partial x)$ holding $\text{Share}_{\text{smokers}}$ constant, which yields derivatives of $-U'(Y - P_C)/(\bar{S} - \underline{S})$, $-1/(\bar{S} - \underline{S})[\Delta U(Y)/$

$(1 - \beta\delta)^2]$, $-1/(\overline{S} - \underline{S})[\beta\Delta U(Y)/(1 - \beta\delta)^2]$ and $-1/(\overline{S} - \underline{S})[\beta U(Y)/(1 - \beta\delta)]$ for P_C, β, δ, and Δ, respectively. Across countries, Share$_{\text{smokers}}$ = $(\overline{S} - S^*)/(\overline{S} - \underline{S})$, so the equation can be solved to yield: $S^* = (\overline{S} - \underline{S})/(\overline{S} - \underline{S} - g)[\beta\Delta U(Y)/(1 - \beta\delta) + U(Y) - U(Y - P_C) - g \times g\overline{S}/(\overline{S} - \underline{S})]$. The derivative of the share of cigarette smokers with respect to any variable equals $[-1/(\overline{S} - \underline{S})](\partial S^*/\partial x)$, which equals $-U'(Y - P_C)/(\overline{S} - \underline{S} - g)$, $-1/(\overline{S} - \underline{S} - g)[\Delta U(Y)/(1 - \beta\delta)^2]$, $-1/(\overline{S} - \underline{S} - g)[\beta\Delta U(Y)/(1 - \beta\delta)^2]$, and $-1/(\overline{S} - \underline{S} - g)[\beta U(Y)/(1 - \beta\delta)]$ for P_C, β, δ, and Δ, respectively. All of these are decreasing in g, so as g gets larger, the impact of all of these variables on aggregative smoking consumption will increase. Furthermore; the ratio of the relationship between these variables across subgroups within country to the relationship between these variables and smoking across countries will equal $(\overline{S} - \underline{S})/(\overline{S} - \underline{S} - g) > 1$.

References

Akerlof, George, and William Dickins. 1982. The economic consequences of cognitive dissonance. *American Economic Review* 72 (3): 307–19.

Baltagi, Badi H., and Dan Levin. 1986. Estimating dynamic demand for cigarettes using panel data: The effects of bootlegging, taxation and advertising reconsidered. *Review of Economics and Statistics* 68 (1): 148–55.

Becker, Gary S., Michael Grossman, and Kevin M. Murphy. 1994. An empirical analysis of cigarette addiction. *American Economic Review* 84 (3): 396–418.

Becker, Gary S., and Kevin M. Murphy. 2000. *Social economics.* Cambridge, MA: Harvard University Press.

Chaloupka, Frank J. 1991. Rational addictive behavior and cigarette smoking. *Journal of Political Economy* 99 (4): 722–42.

Cutler, David M., and Edward L. Glaeser. 2005. What explains differences in smoking, drinking, and other health-related behaviors? *American Economic Review* 95 (2): 238–42.

Cutler, David M., and Srikanth Kadiyala. 2003. The return to biomedical research: Treatment and behavioral effects. In *Measuring the gains from medical research: An economic approach,* ed. Kevin Murphy and Robert Topel, 110–62. Chicago: University of Chicago Press.

Evans, William N., Matthew C. Farrelly, and Edward Montgomery. 1999. Do workplace smoking bans reduce smoking? *American Economic Review* 89 (4): 728–47.

Gallet, Craig A., and John A. List. 2003. Cigarette demand: A meta-analysis of elasticities. *Health Economics* 12 (1): 821–35.

Gallup, George. 1981. Smoking rates decline as more perceive health hazard. Gallup Organization. Mimeograph.

Glaeser, Edward L., Bruce Sacerdote, and Jose Scheinkman. 2003. The social multiplier. *Journal of the European Economics Association* 1 (2): 345–53.

Guindon, G. Emmanuel, Steven M. Tobin, and Derek Yach. 2002. Trends and affordability of cigarette prices: Ample room for tax increases and related health gains. *Tobacco Control* 11 (1): 35–43.

Lyon, Herbert L., and Julian L. Simon. 1968. Price elasticity of the demand for cigarettes in the United States. *American Journal of Agricultural Economics* 50 (4): 888–95.

Maier, Frank A. 1955. Consumer demand for cigarettes estimated from state data. *Journal of Farm Economics* 37 (4): 690–704.

McNally, William D. 1932. The tar in cigarette smoke and its possible effects. *American Journal of Cancer* 16:1502–14.

Schoenberg, Erika H. 1933. The demand curve for cigarettes. *Journal of Business* 6:15–33.

Sloan-Kettering Institute for Cancer Research. 1954. *Progress report VIII.* New York: Sloan-Kettering Institute for Cancer Research.

Viscusi, W. Kip. *Smoking: Making the risky decision.* New York: Oxford University Press.

Wynder, Ernst L., and Evarts Graham. 1950. Tobacco smoking as a possible etiologic factor in bronchiogenic carcinoma: A study of 684 proven cases. *Journal of the American Medical Association* 143:329–36.

Trends in Prescription Drug Use by the Disabled Elderly

Jay Bhattacharya, Alan M. Garber, and
Thomas MaCurdy

8.1   Introduction

With the implementation of the Medicare Modernization Act in 2006, the federal government became responsible for the financing of prescription drugs for all Medicare recipients. Though there have been several attempts to forecast how much financial risk will be borne by the government in future years as a consequence of the introduction of Medicare Part D, no forecast has separately analyzed the effect of disability on Part D spending. This is unfortunate because the disabled elderly are among the groups that might be most affected by pharmaceutical innovations and changes in the way prescription drugs are financed. They use health services heavily, visit physicians more frequently, enter the hospital more often, and use long-term care more heavily than the nondisabled. It is likely that the same is true of their consumption of prescription drugs, although usage of medications has not been studied nearly as extensively as the use of products

Jay Bhattacharya is an assistant professor at the Center for Primary Care and Outcomes Research, Stanford University School of Medicine, and a faculty research fellow of the National Bureau of Economic Research. Alan M. Garber is the founding director of both the Center for Health Policy (CHP) and the Center for Primary Care and Outcomes Research (PCOR) at Stanford University, where he is the Henry J. Kaiser Jr. Professor; a professor of medicine; and professor, by courtesy, of economics and of health research and policy, and a research associate of the National Bureau of Economic Research. Thomas MaCurdy holds a joint appointment as a senior fellow at the Hoover Institution and a professor of economics at Stanford University, and is a research associate of the National Bureau of Economic Research.

This research is supported by Grants P30 AG 17253 and P01 AG05842 from the National Institute on Aging, and by the Department of Veterans Affairs. We are grateful for the assistance of Tikhon Bernstam and Grecia Marrufo.

and services that Medicare traditionally covered. Similarly, there has been little work examining the patterns of pharmaceutical use by individuals under sixty-five who qualify for Medicare through the Disability Insurance.

In this paper, we use the Medicare Current Beneficiary Survey (MCBS) to analyze trends in the utilization of pharmaceuticals by disabled and nondisabled beneficiaries in the community (noninstitutionalized) between 1992 and 2001. We examine both the over-sixty-five population and the population under sixty-five that qualifies for Medicare by virtue of their disability. We compare the rates of growth of prescription drug use in these two groups, along with changes in the share of medical expenditures attributable to prescription drugs. We examine both overall prescription drug uses and use by class. We then discuss the implications of changing disability rates for drug benefits and for overall health care expenditures.

8.2   Background

Providing medical care for the disabled is expensive, and pharmaceutical products account for a nontrivial fraction of that expense. In recent years, disability prevalence among elderly and near-elderly populations has been changing dramatically, but in opposite directions. In this section, we review these changes, and argue that the implementation of the Medicare drug benefit greatly increases the importance of this debate.

There is broad literature documenting trends in disability in the elderly population. In the past two decades, much support can be found for the hypothesis that active life span is increasing faster than total life span—see Fries (1980). Contributors to this literature have relied upon different surveys and different definitions of disability, but have consistently found declines, sometimes sharp and accelerating declines, in disability among the elderly. Recent work, however, suggests that such declines may not continue into the future. Lakdawalla, Bhattacharya, and Goldman (2004) find evidence of increasing functional limitation rates in the 1990s in younger populations. Why these trends are happening, and whether these trends will continue into the future has important implications for the financing of Medicare.

Manton, Corder, and Stallard (1997) use the 1982, 1984, 1989, and 1994 National Long Term Care Surveys (NLTCS) to investigate trends in the prevalence of disability in the elderly population. They find that the age-adjusted prevalence of disability in 1994 decreased by 3.6 percent from 1982 (from 24.9 percent to 21.3 percent). Manton and Gu (2001) update the results of Manton, Corder, and Stallard (1997) using the latest wave of the NLTCS and confirm a continuing decline in disability among the elderly, especially among the oldest age groups. Other authors find similar declines in disability in the 1980s and 1990s using different data sets— Freedman and Martin (1998) find declines between 1984 and 1993 in the

Surveys of Income and Program Participation (SIPP); Crimmins, Saito, and Reynolds (1997) find declines in the 1984 to 1990 Longitudinal Study of Aging (LSOA) and the 1982 to 1993 National Health Interview Survey (NHIS). Crimmins, Saito, and Ingegneri (1989) confirm that disability-free life expectancy increased in the 1980s.

Pardes et al. (1999) and Manton (2003) attribute these improvements in elderly disability prevalence to developments in medical technology that enable seniors to delay both disability and death. Manton (2003) suggests that because the future of medical technology is bright, further improvements can be expected, and these improvements will decrease the demand for costly care, such as nursing homes, by future elderly cohorts. Manton and Gu (2001) project that if declines in elderly disability continue at current rates, Medicare financial insolvency will be delayed significantly, perhaps indefinitely.

Lakdawalla, Bhattacharya, and Goldman (2004) argue that these conclusions ignore an important fact. Because disability is typically a long-lasting health state, an individual who is disabled when near elderly is likely to be disabled when elderly. Thus, studying disability trends in younger populations is important for forecasting future trends in disability, which none of the preceding studies do. Lakdawalla, Bhattacharya, and Goldman (2004), using data from the 1984 to 2000 U.S. National Health Interview Surveys (NHIS) to track changes in disability for this population, find that, while disability rates fell slightly for the near elderly population between 1984 and 1990, they rose dramatically for those under fifty-five years old between 1990 and 2000. They attribute a substantial portion of these trends to rising obesity rates. Further decline in the prevalence of disability among incoming Medicare cohorts, they argue, is by no means a certain prospect.

Bhattacharya et al. (2003) and Lakdawalla et al. (2003a,b) forecast the implications of cohort-specific disability trends for future Medicare and nursing home expenditures, respectively. They find that for the next decade, the documented declines in elderly disability should lead to declines in real per capita Medicare expenditures, holding all else equal. However, as the younger, more disabled, cohorts age into Medicare, these trends will reverse themselves. This will lead to increasing per capita Medicare expenditures in the decades that follow.

This debate about future disability trends and their implications for Medicare took place before the passage of Medicare Modernization Act. None of the forecasts account for the effects of the new drug benefit. In addition, with the exception of Moxey et al. (2003), very little work has been done examining how spending by disabled individuals on prescription drugs differs from spending by nondisabled individuals. Moxey et al. (2003), using 1996 data from the MCBS, find that Medicare beneficiaries with "three or more comorbidities and/or difficulty with any [activity of daily living limitations]" spend between $2,000 and $3,000 per year on pre-scription drugs. Beneficiaries with "zero comorbidities, no difficulty with [activity of daily living limitations]," by contrast, spend less than $700 per year on prescription drugs.[1] These numbers suggest that the passage of the Medicare drug benefit will magnify the effect of changing disability trends on future Medicare financing.

8.3   MCBS Pharmaceutical Data

The MCBS is a longitudinal survey covering a nationally representative sample of around 12,500 Medicare beneficiaries per year. Those under sixty-five who qualify for Medicare by virtue of their disability are over-sampled to permit separate analyses of this population, with a sample size of about 2,000 per year. (Hereafter, we refer to this population as the Dis-ability Insurance, or DI disabled, because such Medicare recipients must first qualify for Social Security's DI program.) While the MCBS samples Medicare beneficiaries in nursing homes, we focus in this paper on the non-institutionalized population because the pharmaceutical data for the two populations are not directly comparable.[2]

The MCBS has been conducted annually since 1992, and we use the 1992 to 2001 data here. The MCBS uses a rolling panel design, with individual respondents being followed for four years and then replaced. All of our analyses are weighted to be representative of the underlying population of Medicare beneficiaries in each year.

The MCBS collects detail on health status and health care use and costs. Information on drug usage and expenditures in MCBS resides in two files, one for beneficiaries living in the community, and a second for beneficiar-ies living in institutions, which we do not use in this paper. The first of these files, the community file (RIC_PME) is a prescription level file. It includes records for all prescriptions consumed by each beneficiary in 2001 while living in the community, based upon self-reports. In preparation for the in-terview, respondents are asked to keep a detailed log of their prescriptions, including refills. Over-the-counter medications are excluded.

This file also contains transaction price information for those prescrip-tions. Transaction prices are sometimes taken as the price reported (30 per-cent of the records in 2001) to have been paid by a sample respondent. In the remaining cases, transaction prices are computed by starting with the average wholesale prices (AWP) for the pharmaceutical product, and dis-

---

1. There are some important limitations to the work by Moxey et al. (2003). In particular, they do not separately examine younger disabled individuals who qualify for Medicare through the Social Security Disability Insurance program. Furthermore, they do not look at how the prescription drug expenditures have changed over time.

2. We also exclude end-stage renal disease Medicare patients from our analysis as well for similar reasons.

counting this amount based upon the source paying for the prescription (for example, Medicaid, Health Maintenance Organization [HMO], Veterans Affairs [VA], Retail, and so on).

Average wholesale prices in the RIC_PME (hereafter PME) file are imputed from to the Medicaid Information System (MIS) using information on drug name, form, strength and amount, after these fields are verified and modified to be consistent with drugs descriptions in the First Data-Bank, which is a comprehensive categorization of pharmaceutical products on the market. The MCBS matches each prescription record to its corresponding AWP from the PME file by as many of the four fields—drug name, form, strength, and unit—as possible. When a PME record does not match all four fields with a drug available in MIS, an AWP is simulated from the distribution of scripts in the MIS with as many fields as matched.

8.4 Methods

Our main aim in this paper is to characterize trends in pharmaceutical consumption for disabled and nondisabled Medicare populations for the years $t = 1992 \ldots 2001$. The primary outcome variable that we are concerned with is pharmaceutical expenditures for different subpopulations of the Medicare population based upon disability status (say, j), $P(t|j)$, as a fraction of total nonpharmaceutical expenditures, $M(t|j)$, plus pharmaceutical expenditures:

(1) $$f(t|j) = \frac{P(t|j)}{P(t|j) + M(t|j)}$$

As a measure of trends, $f(t|j)$ has the advantage of being invariant to inflation. Hence, we need not make difficult decisions about which deflator—the Consumer Price Index, the Medical Care Price Index, or some other index—to use in comparing expenditures in different years.

In the remainder of the section, we describe our approach to various methodological necessities, including defining disability, classifying pharmaceutical products into therapeutic classes, and the underreporting of prescription drug use by MCBS respondents.

8.4.1 Defining Disability

Because disability is a primary predictor of Medicare expenditures, we examine trends for people with and without disabilities. Precision in the definition of disability is crucial, and it is particularly important to use a definition that is objective—not subject to manipulation—in order to avoid moral hazard. In this section, we describe our approach to identifying disabled populations in the MCBS.

For the Medicare population, there are (at least) two conceptually distinct definitions of disability, one that applies to the under-sixty-five population, another to the over-sixty-five population. The first definition is an administrative definition. In order for someone under sixty-five to qualify for Medicare, that individual must first receive Social Security Disability Insurance (SSDI) payments, and then meet the twenty-four-month qualifying period, during which the individual does not work due to the disabling condition. This definition implies that there may be people who are younger than age sixty-five and disabled, in the common use of the term, yet do not meet the administrative requirements to qualify for Medicare. However, because we are primarily interested here in Medicare expenditures, we do not attempt to examine such people.

The second definition focuses instead on the inability to perform a set of standardized activities (functional limitations) and is assessed in a survey setting like the MCBS by respondent self-reports. Respondents are asked a series of questions regarding their difficulties in doing six different concrete activities of daily living (ADL): bathing or showering, dressing, eating, getting in and out of beds and chairs, walking, and using the toilet. We divide MCBS respondents over sixty-five into three groups based upon the number of these ADLs respondents have difficulty performing. The first nondisabled group reports no difficulties; the second has problems in either one or two of these tasks exactly; the third has difficulties with three or more tasks. This is a perfectly standard partitioning of the elderly by their extent of functional limitations—see Manton and Gu (2001). Many studies have shown that expected health care expenditures (not including pharmaceutical expenditures) in the elderly population are least for the nondisabled, intermediate for those with one to two ADL limitations, and highest for those with three to four limitations.[3] An individual who qualifies initially for Medicare through the SSDI program, and then turns sixty-five, is considered disabled for our purposes only if that individual exhibits functional limitations.

8.4.2   Tracking Changes in Health and in the Types of Drugs Used by Medicare Recipients

Pharmaceutical expenditures for a group of people, such as the disabled, can change for many reasons. Two primary reasons are changes in the set of available prescription medications and changes in the composition or health of the group. To examine these explanations more closely, we examine what sorts of drugs entail the greatest expenditures for each group.

In table 8A.1 we reproduce a mutually exclusive and exhaustive list of therapeutic classes to which each drug in the MCBS PME file is assigned. This therapeutic classification system contains thirty-five separate classes. The large number of categories makes it impractical to present trends in pharmaceutical expenditure for each category. Consequently, we collapse

---

3. See, for example, Bhattacharya et al. (2003).

this classification system into a simpler system, still mutually exclusive and exhaustive, but consisting of only five classes: psychotherapeutic agents, analgesic agents, cardiovascular agents, antiarthritic agents, and all other drugs. The first four classes include several of the most commonly pre- scribed medications for Medicare patients—see Waldron and Poisal (1999). The fifth, catch-all category, includes drugs that are unclassified in the broader MCBS thirty-five-class system. These unclassified drugs make up a declining proportion of the "all other drugs" category over time—un- classified drug products made up over 15 percent of drug spending in 1996 and 1997, before falling off to around 8 percent in 2000.[4]

Let $P_1(t|j) \ldots P_5(t|j)$ represent pharmaceutical expenditures by group j on drugs in the five classes we examine, where $P(t|j) = \Sigma_{k=1}^{5} P_k(t|j)$. In our results, we report trends in $f_1(t|j) \ldots f_5(t|j)$, which are defined analogously to equation (1):

$$(2) \qquad f_k(t|j) = \frac{P_k(t|j)}{P(t|j) + M(t|j)} \text{ for } k = 1 \ldots 5$$

Chronic disease is certainly an important reason for high expenditures on prescription drugs. There is no reason to suppose that the health of dis- abled and nondisabled populations in Medicare has remained static over the past decade. The MCBS asks respondents as series of detailed ques- tions ("Has your doctor ever told you that you have . . . ?") about their health status. To track how changes in the Medicare population have in- duced changes in use of drugs, for each group j, we identify the individ- uals in the top 10 percent of the $P(t|j)$ distribution. For these top drug spenders, we plot trends in the prevalence of several of the most common chronic diseases, including hypertension, arthritis, mental illness, diabetes, osteoporosis, and Alzheimer's disease.

8.4.3 MCBS Underreporting of Pharmaceutical Use

To prepare the RIC_PME file, which contains information on prescrip- tion drugs for the MCBS, the Center for Medicare and Medicaid Services (CMS) relies mainly on self-reports by survey respondents. Although re- spondents are asked in advance to keep track of their use of prescribed medications, respondents can forget to report some of the medications that they take. To prevent this problem, respondents are asked to collect all pre- scription drug containers and insurance receipts during the year before the interview and to present these materials to the interviewer. The self-reports are then confirmed against this objective evidence of pharmaceutical product use. Though there is still a potential for underreporting—for ex-

---

4. Among the unclassified drugs include various emollients and creams that are popular among people who use Medicare home health services. The decline in this category presum- ably reflects the declining use of home health services after the 1997 Balanced Budget Act, which cut Medicare payments for such services.

ample, respondents may have failed to save containers or receipts—establishing a corroboration between the self-reports and the objective evidence lends credence to the MCBS estimates.

To address these sorts of problems, the CMS Information and Methods Group suggests adjusting MCBS pharmaceutical expenditure data upward by 17 percent—Poisal (2003). Poisal arrives at this figure by conducting a pharmacy follow-back audit for a subset of the 1999 MCBS respondents. We apply this correction factor for underreporting to our estimates.

There is an additional source of underreporting error in the MCBS pharmaceutical data. In addition to the RIC_PME file, which contains detailed the information described in the preceding on each prescription, the MCBS reports total expenditures on prescription drugs, as well as other medical care expenditures, in a person-level summary file. We use the RIC_PME file to construct our estimates of the numerator in our $f(t|j)$ measures—$P(t|j)$—while we use the person-level summary file to construct our estimates of the denominators—$M(t|j) + P(t|j)$.

While the MCBS documentation suggests that the total pharmaceutical expenditure numbers from these two files should match, we find in practice that this is not always the case. In nearly every year, between 5 to 6 percent of the people in the person-level summary file who have positive drug expenditures do not appear in the PME file, though they should. This will tend to understate the numerator in our $f(t|j)$ measures.[5] Conversely, between 1 to 2 percent of the people in the PME file who have prescription expenditures in a given year do not appear to have any in the in the summary file, though they should. This will tend to understate the denominators in our $f(t|j)$ measures. While these two effects tend to offset each other, our calculations suggest that the net effect is an underestimate of the true value of $f(t|j)$, assuming that anyone reporting pharmaceutical expenditures in the RIC_PME file should be reporting them in the person-level summary file, and vice-versa. Our estimates of pharmaceutical expenditure trends should thus be seen as underestimates.

8.5   Results

In this section, our goal is to characterize how the role that the different types and extent of disability play in determining expenditures on prescription drugs in the Medicare population.

---

5. In 1996, this figure is anomalously high—36 percent of the people in the person-level summary file who have positive drug expenditures do not appear in the PME file. We were unable to determine why this is the case. The pharmaceutical expenditure numbers developed using the 1996 MCBS should thus be seen as severe underestimates.

8.5.1   Changes in the Size and Composition of the Medicare Population

We start by examining growth in the population of disabled and nondisabled Medicare recipients—Population $(t|j)$. Table 8.1 shows these numbers for 1992 to 2000, based upon the MCBS population sample weights. The two biggest net sources of growth in the Medicare population over the decade were the Medicare DI population, which added over 1.7 million people, and the nondisabled elderly population, which added over 2.4 million people. By contrast, the number of elderly disabled fell slightly over the period. There were nearly 600,000 fewer elderly with one to two ADL limitations in 2000 than there were in 1992, and about 130,000 fewer with three or more ADL limitations. These numbers confirm trends reported elsewhere in the literature of burgeoning younger disabled populations—Autor and Duggan (2001) and Lakdawalla, Bhattacharya, and Goldman (2004)—and declining disability among elderly populations—Manton and Gu (2001).

Table 8.2 explores the Medicare DI population in more detail. It shows the DI population by primary cause of DI eligibility, as reported in the MCBS. Mental illness is the modal identified cause of DI recipiency (15 percent of all DI recipients). With an average age of forty-four, these patients are also among the youngest recipients. Patients with mental retardation (7.6 percent of DI recipients) are even younger (40.8 years old). Disability resulting from chronic diseases and severe acute events such as strokes (5.3 percent of DI recipients) and cardiovascular disease (10.3 per-

Table 8.1   **Trends in noninstitutionalized Medicare population**

| | | Elderly | | |
Year	Disability Insurance	Difficulty with 0 ADLs	Difficulty with 1–2 ADLs	Difficulty with ≥3 ADLs
1992	3,285,364	21,647,427	6,281,249	2,932,333
1993	3,536,864	22,479,300	5,914,561	2,848,153
1994	3,776,145	22,849,250	5,781,001	2,876,014
1995	4,002,487	23,269,384	5,612,604	2,844,031
1996	4,107,449	24,162,911	5,440,830	2,649,575
1997	4,386,421	24,069,791	5,583,173	2,652,202
1998	4,641,815	24,314,895	5,597,334	2,534,695
1999	4,827,507	23,851,277	5,976,560	2,755,146
2000	4,994,876	24,113,225	5,706,425	2,802,296
Change 1992–2000	1,709,512	2,465,798	−574,824	−130,037
Percent change 1992–2000	52	11.3	−9.2	−4.4

Source: 1992–2000 Medicare Current Beneficiary Survey.
Note: ADLs = activities of daily living.

Table 8.2   Primary cause for Social Security Disability Insurance eligibility

		Within cause	
Cause	Percent	Mean age	Male (%)
Back/spine/disc	11.3	52.3	66.0
Poor eyesight	3.9	49.8	49.9
Poor hearing	1.0	45.2	53.4
Kidney disease	0.6	48.0	56.6
Stroke/seizure disorder	5.3	50.0	61.3
Car/bicycle/train accident	2.6	48.3	68.8
Multiple sclerosis	1.8	49.4	29.4
Muscular dystrophy	0.4	47.8	54.7
Cerebral palsy	0.6	45.9	45.3
Broken bones/hip	1.3	53.5	77.9
Cardiovascular conditions	10.3	55.0	65.1
Cancer	2.5	51.7	49.7
Diabetes	1.7	55.2	63.0
Arthritis	7.1	53.3	51.9
Mental Retardation	7.6	40.8	59.2
Alzheimer's disease	0.1	55.8	83.5
Mental illness	14.9	44.1	59.3
Osteoporosis	0.3	52.9	32.6
Parkinson's disease	0.1	47.5	59.2
Emphysema/asthma	1.9	54.8	87.4
Partial paralysis	3.0	55.1	55.3
Loss of limb	0.3	47.6	75.4
Other cause	20.5	50.4	81.3

Source: 1992–1998 Medicare Current Beneficiary Survey.

cent of DI recipients) are nearly as common as mental illness and retardation as causes of DI recipiency. However, these patients tend to be older (fifty-five years old in the case of cardiovascular conditions and fifty years old in the case of stroke). Similarly, patients with arthritis (7.1 percent of DI recipients) and with back, spine, or disc injuries (11.3 percent of DI recipients) are, on average, older than fifty years. Given these patterns in the Medicare DI population, we should expect that use of psychiatric, pain, and antiarthritic medications are the among the most popular drugs used by this group.

8.5.2   Trends in Pharmaceutical Expenditures

Figure 8.1 shows trends in per capita nominal pharmaceutical expenditures for disabled and nondisabled Medicare populations. That is, it shows trends in $\pi(t|j) = [P(t|j)]/[\text{Population}(t|j)]$ for $j = $ DI disabled, elderly with zero ADL limitations, elderly with one to two ADL limitations, and elderly with three or more ADL limitations. There is a striking growth in per capita pharmaceutical expenditures for all of these groups between

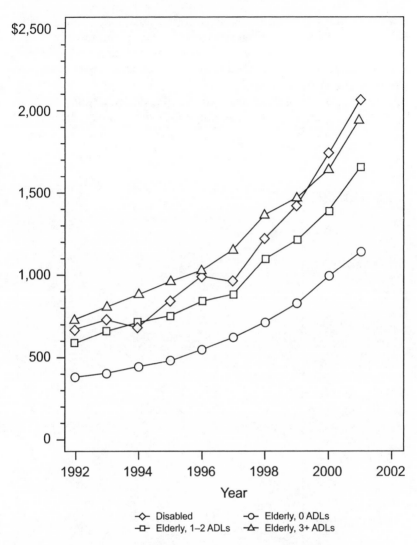

Fig. 8.1   Per capita pharmaceutical expenditures by disability category
Source: 1992–2001 Medicare Current Beneficiary Survey.

1992 and 2001. For example, elderly nondisabled populations spent about $400 per capita in 1992, and more than $1,100 per capita in 2001. This group consists of some of the least intensive spenders of prescription drugs. For the elderly with one to two ADL limitations, pharmaceutical expenditures per capita grew from about $600 in 1992 to almost $1,700 in 2001. In 1992, the elderly with three or more ADL limitations spent the most on pharmaceutical products—nearly $750 per person. As was the case for the other groups, this figure grew substantially to about $1,950 in 2001. The DI disabled per capita pharmaceutical expenditures grew similarly, but more. In 1992, per capita expenditures were under $700 and rose to over $2,000 in 2001. The DI disabled now spend the most of all these groups on prescription drugs.

Figure 8.2 shows total nominal expenditures on prescription drugs for the groups. As a group, elderly nondisabled spend the most in total on prescription drugs. This is not surprising because this is the largest group of Medicare beneficiaries (see table 8.1). Define $\Delta P_j \equiv P(2001|j) - P(1992|j)$,

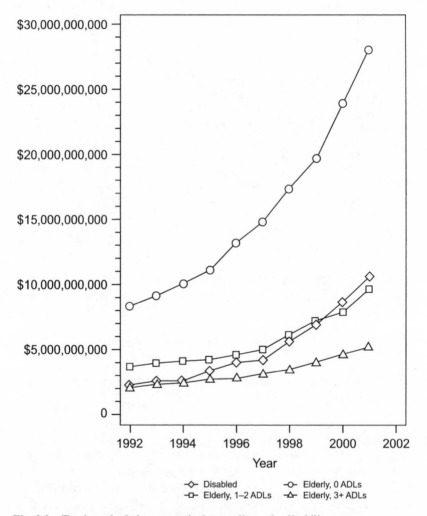

Fig. 8.2   Total nominal pharmaceutical expenditures by disability category
Source: 1992–2001 Medicare Current Beneficiary Summary.

$\Delta \text{Pop}_j \equiv \text{Population } (2001 \mid j) - \text{Population } (1992 \mid j)$, and $\Delta \pi_j \equiv \pi(2001 \mid j) - \pi(1992 \mid j)$. Then:

$$(3) \qquad \Delta P_j = \pi(1992 \mid j)\Delta \text{Pop}_j + \text{Population } (1992 \mid j)\Delta \pi_j.$$

Because Population (1992 | nondisabled) is the largest among the groups, and $\Delta \text{Pop}_{\text{nondisabled}}$ is also largest, a \$1 growth in per capita expenditures for the nondisabled translates to the largest growth in total expenditures. Although the elderly with three or more ADL limitations spend more per capita than the elderly with one to two ADL limitations, the greater size of the latter group means it spends more in total. For both groups, even though population size declined between 1992 and 2001, total expenditures on prescription drugs as a group rose. Total pharmaceutical expenditures by the DI disabled grew sharply because that group saw both a large increase in population and per capita expenditure.

Because figures 8.1 and 8.2 present pharmaceutical expenditures in nominal dollars, some of the growth in expenditures shown there is due to inflation. Figure 8.3, which presents trends in $f(t \mid j)$, does not have this problem because both numerator and denominator are measured in nominal dollars. The results from figure 8.3 are striking. For all four groups, pharmaceutical expenditures as a percent of total medical expenditures were largely flat until 1997, after which $f(t \mid j)$ increased sharply.[6] The largest increases in pharmaceutical expenditures were for the DI Medicare population. For this group, prescription drugs rose between 1992 and 2001 from about 12.5 percent of total medical expenditures to just under 25 percent. The elderly also saw a steep growth in these numbers over this period, though not quite as steep. The nondisabled elderly went from 11 percent to about 19 percent; the elderly with one to two ADL limitations went from about 9.5 percent to 15 percent; and the elderly with three or more ADL limitations went from under 7 percent to 11 percent. These last two elderly groups depend more heavily upon inpatient and outpatient medical care than do the nondisabled elderly and the DI Medicare populations, and this is reflected in their lower positions on the graph. The main point, though, is that all groups are relying much more heavily on prescription drugs for their care than they were just a few years ago.

8.5.3   Trends in the Composition of Prescribed Drugs

Figure 8.4 shows the growth in expenditures on prescription drugs in different therapeutic classes. There are five panels, corresponding to each class in our simplified therapeutic class scheme.

Panel A of figure 8.4 shows trends in expenditures on psychotherapeutic

---

6. The biggest changes to Medicare in 1997 came with the passage of the 1997 Balanced Budget Amendment (BBA). Analyzing the effects of the BBA on pharmaceutical expenditures by the Medicare population is beyond the scope of this paper, but is a topic worthy of study.

Fig. 8.3   Pharmaceutical expenditure as a fraction of total expenditure (including drugs)

Source: 1992–2001 Medicare Current Beneficiary Summary.

agents as a fraction of total medical care expenditures. The DI population is the big story in this panel—its expenditures on these drugs expanded from 2 percent of total expenditures to 4 percent. Given the prominence of mental illness as a primary cause of DI eligibility, the high level of expenditures on psychotherapeutic drugs by this group should not come as a surprise, though the increase over the decade is still striking. Meanwhile,

Fig. 8.4 Expenditures on prescription drugs in different therapeutic classes: *A,* Expenditures on psychotherapeutic agents as a fraction of total expenditure (including drugs); *B,* Expenditures on analgesic agents as a fraction of total expenditure (including drugs); *C,* Expenditures on cardiovascular agents as a fraction of total expenditure (including drugs); *D,* Expenditures on antiarthritic agents as a fraction of total expenditure (including drugs); *E,* Expenditures on all other therapeutic agents as a fraction of total expenditure (including drugs)

Source: 1992–2001 Medicare Current Beneficiary Survey.

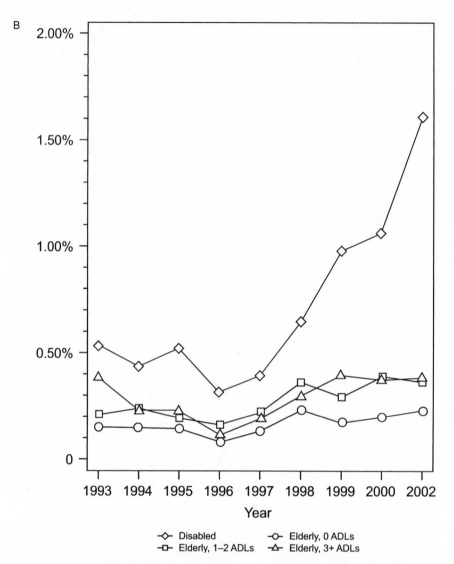

Fig. 8.4 **(cont.) Expenditures on prescription drugs in different therapeutic classes:** *A,* **Expenditures on psychotherapeutic agents as a fraction of total expenditure (including drugs);** *B,* **Expenditures on analgesic agents as a fraction of total expenditure (including drugs);** *C,* **Expenditures on cardiovascular agents as a fraction of total expenditure (including drugs);** *D,* **Expenditures on antiarthritic agents as a fraction of total expenditure (including drugs);** *E,* **Expenditures on all other therapeutic agents as a fraction of total expenditure (including drugs)**

Source: 1992–2001 Medicare Current Beneficiary Survey.

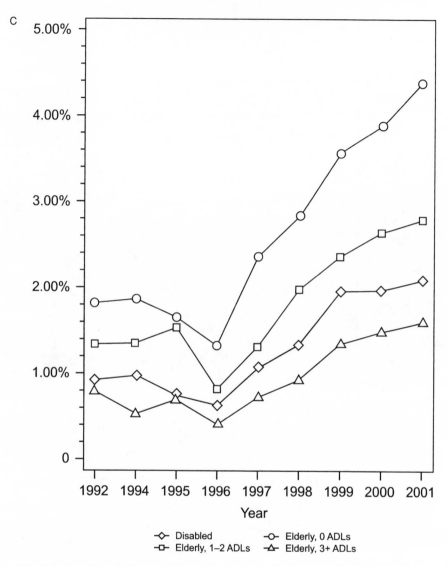

Fig. 8.4   (cont.)

elderly expenditures on these drugs, regardless of the number of ADL limitations, stayed low (about 0.5 percent of total expenditures) and flat over
the period.

Panel B of figure 8.4 tells a similar story for analgesic agents. These rose
from about 0.5 percent of total expenditures to over 1.5 percent between
1992 and 2001 for the DI population, but stayed flat for the elderly population at roughly 0.1 percent to 0.4 percent of total expenditures.

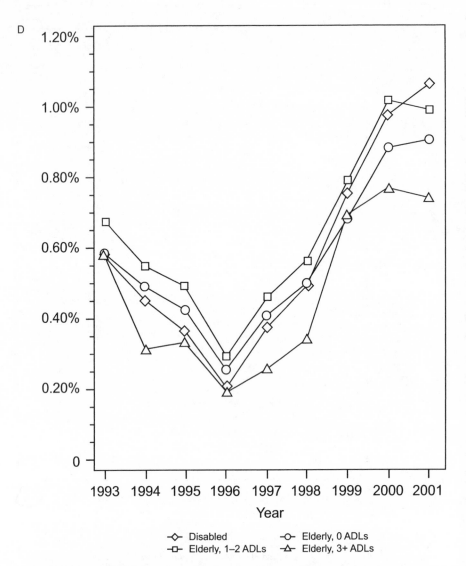

D

Fig. 8.4 (cont.) Expenditures on prescription drugs in different therapeutic classes:
A, Expenditures on psychotherapeutic agents as a fraction of total expenditure (including drugs); *B,* Expenditures on analgesic agents as a fraction of total expenditure (including drugs); *C,* Expenditures on cardiovascular agents as a fraction of total expenditure (including drugs); *D,* Expenditures on antiarthritic agents as a fraction of total expenditure (including drugs); *E,* Expenditures on all other therapeutic agents as a fraction of total expenditure (including drugs)

Source: 1992–2001 Medicare Current Beneficiary Survey.

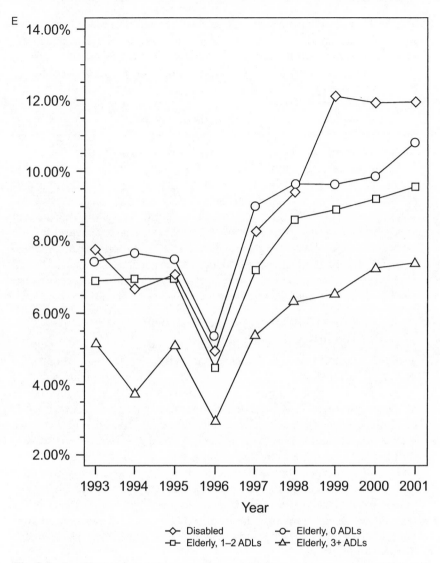

Fig. 8.4   (cont.)

Panel C of figure 8.4 shows that expenditures on cardiovascular drugs have risen for all groups, DI disabled and elderly alike, unlike analgesics and psychotherapeutic drugs. The sharpest growth has been among non-disabled elderly, where expenditures on these drugs grew from 1.9 percent of total expenditures to 5.4 percent between 1992 and 2001. This proportion grew for other groups as well, but not quite as sharply.

Similarly, panel D of figure 8.4 shows expenditure growth between 1992 and 2001 for antiarthritic drugs. This time, the change in use of these drugs seems similar for the four groups. For both cardiovascular and antiarthritic drugs, much of the increase in $f(t|j)$ took place after 1996—before then, expenditures on cardiovascular and antiarthritic drugs were flat or declining. One hypothesis is that the rise in expenditures after 1996 reflects the release into the market of some new and expensive cardiovascular and antiarthritic drugs, including (the now infamous) COX-2 inhibitors, angiotensin receptor blockers, and disease modifying antirheumatic drugs, though exploring this hypothesis further is beyond our scope.[7]

Finally, panel E of figure 8.4 shows changes in $f(t|j)$ for all other drugs between 1992 and 2001. These drugs make up roughly half of the pharmaceutical expenditures (that is psychotherapeutic, analgesic, cardiovascular, and antiarthritic drugs together make up about half of pharmaceutical expenditures), though this fraction varies from year to year and for the different groups. All of the groups show a similar patter in their expenditures on this catch-all category of drugs. After declines between 1992 and 1996, there are sharp increases in expenditures for all other drugs between 1997 and 2001, though the increases are sharpest for the DI disabled.

8.5.4   Changes in the Disease Prevalence among the Top 10 percent of Drug Spenders

Figure 8.5 plots trends in the self-reported health status of the highest 10 percent of drug spenders in the four groups. Table 8.3 summarizes these graphs by reporting changes between 1992 and 2001 in the prevalence of these conditions among these high drug spenders. Panels A through F of figure 8.5 track changes in the prevalence of hypertension, arthritis, mental illness, diabetes, osteoporosis, and Alzheimer's Disease, respectively, for these high drug spending four groups. We select these conditions to examine either because they are costly to treat, or because there have been new pharmaceutical therapies developed to treat them in the 1990s. The panels are arranged in declining order of average disease prevalence in the population. Because we are examining only the noninstitutionalized population, the prevalence of some of these diseases (especially Alzheimer's disease) appears low.

The most important finding of figure 8.5 and table 8.3 is that the most intensive users of prescription drugs in the noninstitutionalized Medicare population have become significantly less healthy between 1992 and 2001. The prevalence of all of these conditions have risen, sometimes sharply, for the disabled and nondisabled alike. These prevalence increases were not evenly divided across groups, though.

---

7. In part, the anomalously low expenditures on pharmaceuticals in 1996 can be explained by mismeasurement, for reasons described in note 5.

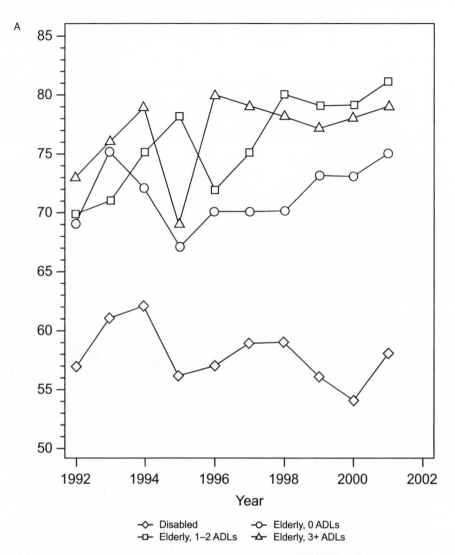

A

—◇— Disabled   —○— Elderly, 0 ADLs
—□— Elderly, 1–2 ADLs   —△— Elderly, 3+ ADLs

Fig. 8.5   Self-reported health status among top 10 percent of drug spenders: *A,*
Prevalence of hypertension among top 10 percent of drug spenders; *B,* **Prevalence of**
arthritis among top 10 percent of drug spenders; *C,* **Prevalence of mental illness**
among top 10 percent of drug spenders; *D,* **Prevalence of diabetes among top 10 per-**
cent of drug spenders; *E,* **Prevalence of osteoporosis among top 10 percent of drug**
spenders; *F,* **Prevalence of Alzheimer's disease among top 10 percent of drug**
spenders

Source: 1992–2001 Medicare Current Beneficiary Survey.

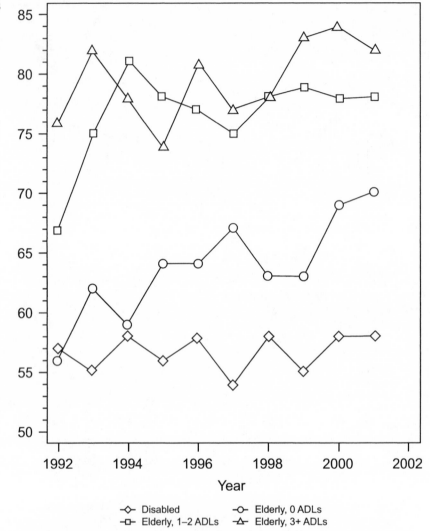

Fig. 8.5   (cont.) **Self-reported health status among top 10 percent of drug spenders:** *A,* **Prevalence of hypertension among top 10 percent of drug spenders;** *B,* **Prevalence of arthritis among top 10 percent of drug spenders;** *C,* **Prevalence of mental illness among top 10 percent of drug spenders;** *D,* **Prevalence of diabetes among top 10 percent of drug spenders;** *E,* **Prevalence of osteoporosis among top 10 percent of drug spenders;** *F,* **Prevalence of Alzheimer's disease among top 10 percent of drug spenders**

Source: 1992–2001 Medicare Current Beneficiary Survey.

C

Fig. 8.5 (cont.)

Among the high-spending DI population, there has been a remarkably large and steady increase in the prevalence of mental illness—an increase of forty-two cases per 100 population in just ten years time. This increase reflects both changes in the composition of the Medicare DI population over this time period as well as the introduction and dissemination of effective medications to treat certain psychiatric conditions, like depression and bipolar disorder. The only other change of any size for this population

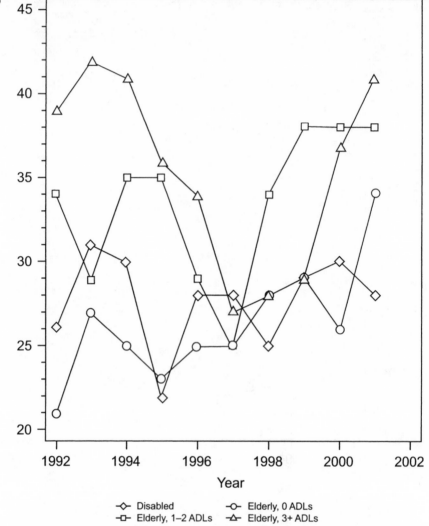

Fig. 8.5 (cont.) Self-reported health status among top 10 percent of drug spenders:
A, Prevalence of hypertension among top 10 percent of drug spenders; *B,* Prevalence
of arthritis among top 10 percent of drug spenders; *C,* Prevalence of mental illness
among top 10 percent of drug spenders; *D,* Prevalence of diabetes among top 10 percent of drug spenders; *E,* Prevalence of osteoporosis among top 10 percent of drug
spenders; *F,* Prevalence of Alzheimer's disease among top 10 percent of drug
spenders

Source: 1992–2001 Medicare Current Beneficiary Survey.

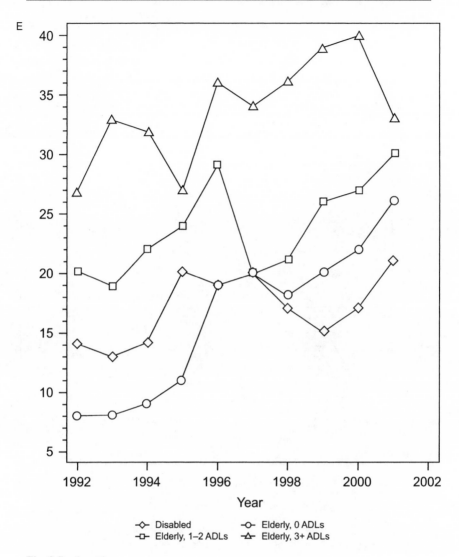

Fig. 8.5   (cont.)

is in the prevalence of osteoporosis, which rose by seven cases per 100 people.

Among the high-spending nondisabled elderly population, the prevalence of several diseases has substantially increased over this period. Osteoporosis prevalence grew by eighteen cases per 100, arthritis prevalence grew by fourteen cases per 100, diabetes prevalence grew by thirteen cases per 100, and mental disorders grew by twelve cases per 100. These diseases

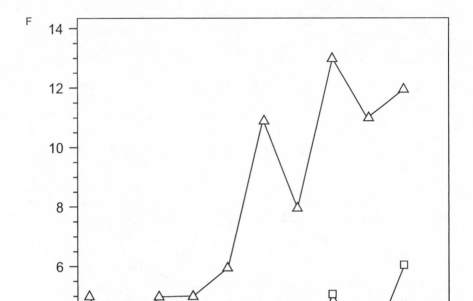

F

◇ Disabled   ○ Elderly, 0 ADLs
□ Elderly, 1–2 ADLs   △ Elderly, 3+ ADLs

Fig. 8.5   (cont.) Self-reported health status among top 10 percent of drug spenders:
A, **Prevalence of hypertension among top 10 percent of drug spenders;** *B,* **Prevalence**
of arthritis among top 10 percent of drug spenders; *C,* **Prevalence of mental illness**
among top 10 percent of drug spenders; *D,* **Prevalence of diabetes among top 10 per-**
cent of drug spenders; *E,* **Prevalence of osteoporosis among top 10 percent of drug**
spenders; *F,* **Prevalence of Alzheimer's disease among top 10 percent of drug**
spenders
Source: 1992–2001 Medicare Current Beneficiary Survey.

Table 8.3   **Change in disease prevalence among top 10 percent of drug spenders
(1992–2001; cases in group per 100 noninstitutionalized population)**

	Disability Insurance	Elderly		
		0 ADLs	1–2 ADLs	3 + ADLs
Hypertension	+1	+6	+11	+6
Arthritis	+1	+14	+11	+6
Mental disorders	+42	+12	+25	+31
Diabetes	+2	+13	+4	+2
Osteoporosis	+7	+18	+10	+6
Alzheimer's disease	+1	+1	+4	+7

Note: ADLs = activities of daily living.

suggest that prescription medications have become more important in the early (that is, before the development of any functional limitation) treatment of chronic diseases.

High-spending elderly with ADL limitations have also had substantial increases in the prevalence of chronic conditions, including osteoporosis, arthritis, and hypertension. Unlike the nondisabled elderly, these groups have not had a large increase in diabetes prevalence. While the nondisabled elderly had a large increase in the prevalence of mental disorders, the increase among these elderly disabled groups has been larger still—twenty-five cases per 100 for those with one to two ADLs, and thirty-one cases per 100 for those with three or more ADLs. Again, this increase reflects both real changes in the health of these groups and the development of new medications. The increase in Alzheimer's disease prevalence among these groups has not been as large as the increases in some other conditions.[8]

8.6   Conclusions

Though there are many nuances in our results, our most important findings can be summarized simply:

- For the disabled and nondisabled, elderly and nonelderly, expenditures on prescription drugs as a fraction of total medical expenditures grew sharply between 1992 and 2001. Much of the growth took place between 1996 and 2001.

8. One important determinant of the community prevalence of Alzheimer's disease is the probability of entering a nursing home conditional on having the disease. In recent years, this probability has been falling—see Lakdawalla et al. (2003a,b). The changes in Alzheimer's disease prevalence in the noninstitutionalized population is thus an overestimate in the change in disease prevalence in the overall population.

- The growth in pharmaceutical expenditures was especially great for DI Medicare recipients, who were the fastest growing segment of the Medicare population in the 1990s.
- The DI Medicare population had large increases in expenditures on all drug categories we examined (psychotherapeutic, analgesic, antiarthritic, cardiovascular, and all other drugs), with especially large increases for psychotherapeutic drugs. The top 10 percent of people in this group in terms of pharmaceutical expenditures had an astoundingly large increase in the prevalence of mental illness, with smaller increases in other chronic diseases.
- The elderly Medicare population had increases between 1992 and 2001 in expenditures for cardiovascular, antiarthritic, and all other drugs. Among the top 10 percent of elderly drug spenders, with and without functional limitations, there were moderate increases in the prevalence of several chronic diseases, including hypertension, arthritis, diabetes, and osteoporosis. Among the top 10 percent of elderly drug spenders with functional limitations, the prevalence of mental illness also increased sharply.

These findings have important implications for future Medicare financing and policy. We briefly explore two related implications here, though there are certainly others. The first implication relates to the costs of the new Medicare drug benefit. Our results come from the 1990s, long before the implementation of Medicare Part D. During that period, many Medicare recipients had little or no insurance coverage for their prescription drugs, and hence faced significant out-of-pocket payments for them. To the extent that the new drug benefit reduces the out-of-pocket price paid by Medicare enrollees, it will further increase demand for prescription drugs. Hence, all else equal, the increasing trend in prescription drug expenditures we present here underestimate the financial exposure faced by Medicare under the prescription drug plan. Reductions in cost sharing for drugs should accelerate these trends by increasing moral hazard. Estimating carefully the effect of Part D cost-sharing on the demand for pharmaceutical is thus a vital topic for further research.[9]

Finally, these findings reinforce the importance of forecasting disability rates accurately. If disability prevalence among the elderly continues to decline sharply, then the addition of Part D to Medicare might be financially manageable. If, on the other hand, the increasingly disabled near elderly age into Medicare in a disabled state, and the set of DI Medicare enrollees continue to grow, Medicare faces a substantial additional financial risk from the introduction of Part D. Any attempt to forecast future pharma-

---

9. A complete forecast would also incorporate the effect of increased use of pharmaceuticals on the demand for other types of medical care, as well as on mortality and morbidity rates.

ceutical expenditure growth without including the disabled population will result in an underestimate of future growth of pharmaceutical expenditures.

Appendix

Table 8A.1 First DataBank pharmaceutical therapeutic class

Analgesics	Electrolyte, caloric, and fluid replacement
Anestetics	Ear, eyes, nose, and throat (EENT)
Antiobesity drugs	preparations
Antiarthritics	Gastrointestinal preparations
Antiasthmatics	Hormones
Antihistamines	Hypoglycemics
Anti-infectives	Miscellaneous medical supplies, devices,
Anti-infectives, miscellaneous	and other
Antineoplastics	Muscle relaxants
Antiparkinson drugs	Psychotherapeutic drugs
Autonomic drugs	Sedative and hypnotics
Blood	Skin preparations
Cardiac drugs	Thyroid preps
Cardiovascular	Biologicals
Central nervous system (CNS) drugs	Prenatal vitamins
Contraceptives	Vitamins, all others
Cough and cold preparations	Psychotherapeutic drugs
Diagnostic	Unclassified drug products
Diuretics	

References

Autor, D., and M. Duggan. 2001. The rise in disability recipiency and the decline in unemployment. NBER Working Paper no. 8336. Cambridge, MA: National Bureau of Economic Research.

Bhattacharya, J., D. Cutler, D. P. Goldman, M. D. Hurd, G. F. Joyce, D. N. Lakdawalla, C. W. A. Panis, and B. Shang. 2003. Disability forecasts and future medicare costs. In *Frontiers in health policy research.* Vol. 6, ed. Alan Garber and David Cutler. Cambridge, MA: MIT Press.

Crimmins, E. M., Y. Saito, and D. Ingegneri. 1989. Changes in life expectancy and disability-free life expectancy in the United States. *Population and Development Review* 15 (2): 235–67.

Crimmins, E. M., Y. Saito, and S. L. Reynolds. 1997. Further evidence on recent trends in the prevalence and incidence of disability among older americans from two sources: The LSOA and the NHIS. *Journal of Gerontology: Social Sciences* 52B (2): S59–S71.

Freedman, V. A., and L. G. Martin. 1998. Understanding trends in functional limitations among older americans. *American Journal of Public Health* 88:1457–62.

Fries, J. F. 1980. Aging, natural death, and the compression of morbidity. *New England Journal of Medicine* 303:130–35.

Lakdawalla, D., J. Bhattacharya, and D. Goldman. 2004. Are the young becoming more disabled? *Health Affairs* 23 (1): 168–76.

Lakdawalla, D., D. Goldman, J. Bhattacharya, M. Hurd, G. Joyce, and C. Panis. 2003a. Forecasting the Nursing Home Population. *Medical Care* 41 (1): 8–20.

———. 2003b. A response to the points by Manton and Williamson on "Forecasting the nursing home population." *Medical Care* 41 (1): 28–31.

Manton, K. G. 2003. Response to "Forecasting the nursing home population" by Lakdawalla et al. *Medical Care* 41 (1): 21–24.

Manton, K. G., L. Corder, and E. Stallard. 1997. Chronic disability trends in elderly United States populations: 1982–1994. *Proceedings of the National Academy of Science* 94:2593–98.

Manton, K. G., and X. L. Gu. 2001. Changes in the prevalence of chronic disability in the United States black and nonblack population above age 65 from 1982 to 1999. *Proceedings of the National Academy of Science* 98 (11): 6354–59.

Moxey, E. D., J. P. O'Connor, K. D. Novielli, S. Teutsch, and D. B. Nash. 2003. Prescription drug use in the elderly: A descriptive analysis. *Health Care Financing Review* 24 (4): 127–41.

Pardes, H., K. G. Manton, E. S. Lander, H. D. Tolley, A. D. Ullian, and H. Palmer. 1999. Effects of medical research on health care and the economy. *Science* 283 (5398): 36–37.

Poisal, J. A. 2003. Reporting of drug expenditures in the MCBS. *Health Care Financing Review* 25 (2): 23–36.

Waldron, C. J., and J. A. Poisal. 1999. Five most commonly used types of pharmaceuticals. *Health Care Financing Review* 20 (3): 119–23.

Comment   Jonathan Skinner

There are few analyses of pharmaceutical drug utilization in the general elderly population, and most of those are cross-sectional (e.g., Safran et al. [2005], although see Centers for Medicare and Medicaid Services [CMS] n.d.). Thus, Bhattacharya, Garber, and MaCurdy should get special credit for tackling an extremely difficult problem, which is tracking prescription drug use among the elderly and disabled population between 1992 and 2001. The Medicare Current Beneficiary Survey (MCBS) can be extremely tricky to use as a longitudinal data set, and the fact that their estimates look reasonable and tell a compelling story is all the more remarkable. For this alone, the authors deserve applause. Understanding pharmaceutical cost growth is a particularly important topic, given the future potential of even

Jonathan Skinner is the John Sloan Dickey Third Century Professor in Economics at Dartmouth College, and a research associate of the National Bureau of Economic Research.

more rapid growth in prescription drug expenditures as the Medicare Part D plan takes effect.

In these comments, I make two general points. First, the paper raises a number of fascinating issues surrounding the substitution effects between prescription drug use and more conventional (Part A and B) health care expenditures. Is it possible to get traction on this important question using these MCBS data—for example, are regions where pharmaceutical expenditures are rising the most rapidly also the ones experiencing the most modest growth in conventional health expenditures? Or are regions where pharmaceutical utilization is rising most rapidly (for example, in the use of cholesterol-lowering statin drugs) also the ones where specific illnesses are falling the most rapidly (e.g., cardiac disease)? These are all questions that could be addressed using these data, and I look forward to seeing more.

And second, the paper is motivated by the ongoing debate regarding the future progression of disability. In the view of Manton and his colleagues, we can look forward to a steady downward trend in disability among the elderly population (Manton, Corder, and Stallard 1997). By contrast, Bhattacharya and his colleagues suggest that rising patterns of obesity and mental illness currently in the middle-aged population could lead to increasing disability rates in the future, with presumably adverse consequences for the Medicare budget (Lakdawalla et al. 2003). Fortuitously, the data presented here by the researchers shed light on this debate because they have carefully estimated levels and growth for both disability rates and expenditures on pharmaceuticals conditional on disability. In the following, I consider whether we need to know the resolution of this debate before we can reasonably predict or forecast future pharmaceutical (and overall) health care costs.

Bhattacharya, Garber, and MaCurdy consider four populations enrolled in the Medicare program: those under age sixty-five on Social Security Disability Insurance, elderly people without any deficits in their Activities of Daily Living (ADL = zero), moderately disabled (one to two ADLs), and more severely disabled elderly people (three or more ADLs). Figure 8.1 in their paper shows remarkable similarities in the growth rates from 1992 to 2001 of pharmaceutical expenditures within each of the four groups. By my crude approximations, annual nominal expenditure growth for each group appears to lie within a remarkably narrow band of 11 to 12 percent.[1]

We also know from the authors' table 8.1, both levels and changes in these categories during the period 1992 to 2000. (Assume the 2000 disability measures are matched to the 2001 expenditures.) My figure 8C.1 uses their data

---

1. After adjusting by the gross domestic product (GDP) deflator, real expenditure growth is 1.7 percentage points below nominal expenditure growth.

Figure 8C.1 Actual and counterfactual changes in disability measures for the over-sixty-five population, 1992–2000

Source: Bhattacharya, Garber, and MaCurdy (chapter 8 in this volume, authors' assumptions).

to show the breakdown of the population served by the Medicare program, including the under-sixty-five population covered under Disability Insurance. In 1992, 10 percent of the total covered Medicare population was disabled and under age sixty-five, 18 percent were over sixty-five and experienced one or two ADLs, and 9 percent were elderly and experienced three or more. The remainder, 63 percent were over sixty-five but without any disability. By 2000, the percent disabled had climbed to 13 percent, but the fraction of elderly people with ADLs had fallen (figure 8C.1). How much of an impact did the slight decline in disability have on per capita pharmaceutical expenditures? The short answer is: barely detectable.

This point can be made more forcefully by taking an extreme counterfactual case. Assume a magic drug that cuts disability rates in the U.S. population by more than 50 percent. In this happy counterfactual world, disability rates have plummeted to just 5 percent (under sixty-five), 5 percent (three or more ADLs) and 10 percent (one to two ADLs) in 2000 (see figure 8C.1). In contrast to the true rate of 65 percent of the enrolled Medicare population with no ADLs, this counterfactual case assumes that 80 percent of the population has no disabilities.

Had this occurred, what would have happened to growth rates in pharmaceutical expenditures? Still not much. Rather than annual growth rates of 11.5 percent, there would have been growth rates of 10.4 percent. Both growth rates are likely to be unsustainable, although at a rate of 11.5 percent, the day of reckoning will arrive somewhat earlier, a point made more generally for Medicare expenditure projections in Lee and Skinner (1999). This result contrasts with the work by Bhattacharya et al. (2004), who suggest that Medicare expenditures will actually decline in the short term because of improvements in disability. However, their result is easily understood given that they assume future disability-constant growth rates in Medicare expenditures to be equal to the inflation rate. In their projection, real Medicare expenditures (adjusted for inflation) will clearly decline as the population becomes healthier, at least for the next several decades.

But as long as overall medical expenditures grow substantially more rapidly than inflation—as has been the case for the last half-century—the importance of changes in disability for spending projections will remain second-order. This is not to say that disability rates aren't of first-order importance to the health and well-being of the American population. Indeed, were disability rates to attain the desirable levels posited in the counterfactual, an 11.5 percent growth rate in pharmaceutical expenditures would be well worth it.

References

Bhattacharya, Jay, David Culter, Dana Goldman, Michael Hurd, Geoffrey Joyce, Darius Lakdawalla, Contantijn Panis, and Baoping Shang. 2004. Disability forecasts and future medicare costs. In *Frontiers in health policy research.* Vol. 7, ed. Alan Garber and David Cutler, 75–94. Cambridge, MA: MIT Press.

Centers for Medicare and Medicaid Services (CMS). n.d. *Health and health care of the Medicare population 2000,* Ch. 2. http://www.cms.hhs.gov/apps/mcbs/MCBS src/2000/00cb2.pdf.

Lakdawalla, Darius, Dana Goldman, Jay Bhattacharya, Michael Hurd, Geoffrey Joyce, and Constantijn Panis. 2003. Forecasting the nursing home population. *Medical Care* 41(1): 8–20.

Lee, Ronald, and Jonathan Skinner. 1999. Will aging baby boomers bust the federal budget? *Journal of Economic Perspectives* 13 (1): 117–40.

Manton, Kenneth G., Larry Corder, and Eric Stallard. 1997. Chronic disability trends in elderly United States populations: 1982–1994. *Proceedings of the National Academy of Science* 94:2593–98.

Safran, Dana G., Patricia Newman, Cathy Schoen, Michelle S. Kitchman, Ira B. Wilson, Barbara Cooper, Angela Li, Hong Chang, and William H. Rogers. 2005. Prescription drug coverage and seniors: Findings from a 2003 national survey. *Health Affairs* Web Exclusive (April 19).

9

Health and Well-Being in Udaipur and South Africa

Anne Case and Angus Deaton

Health and wealth are two of the most important components of well-being. Rankings of well-being based on income or on health alone will differ from more comprehensive rankings, depending on the way that income and health are related. Strong causal links run in both directions between income and health, as well as through third factors, so that we cannot hope to understand one without understanding both. The availability of purchasing power parity (PPP) exchange rates allows relatively sound comparisons of income across countries, while some dimensions of population health—particularly life expectancy, mortality rates of infants and children, and anthropometric measures—are also straightforward to compare across countries. Consequently, much of the research on international health and income has focused on the cross-country relationships between population health and national income. Starting from Preston (1975, 1980), these relationships have been used to investigate the causes of mortality decline, particularly the relative roles of income and of medical knowledge. And data on adult height have been used to investigate the causes of the historical decline in mortality (see, in particular, Fogel 1997, 2004; Floud, Wachter, and Gregory 1990; and Steckel 1995).

Anne Case is the Alexander Stewart 1886 Professor of Economics and Public Affairs at Princeton University, and a research associate of the National Bureau of Economic Research. Angus Deaton is the Dwight D. Eisenhower Professor of International Affairs at Princeton University, and a research associate of the National Bureau of Economic Research.

This paper develops and extends the preliminary work briefly reported in "Health and Wealth among the Poor: India and South Africa Compared," *American Economic Review Papers and Proceedings* (Case and Deaton 2005). We gratefully acknowledge funding from the National Institute on Aging R01 AG20275-01, P01 AG05842-14, and from the John D. and Catherine T. MacArthur Foundation through its Research Network on Poverty and Inequality in a Broader Perspective. We thank Amitabh Chandra for helpful comments.

The Commission for Macroeconomics and Health (World Health Organization 2001) used the same data to argue that it is health care, acting through health status, that is an important engine of economic growth. Another strand of research, particularly associated with Amartya Sen, for example, Sen (1999), and embodied, for example, in the United Nations Development Programme's (UNDP) Human Development Index, argues that cross-country comparisons of well-being must look at health (and education) together with national income. And Becker, Philipson, and Soares (2005) have recently argued that if national income is extended to include the value of years lived, "extended" national incomes, unlike national incomes, are converging across countries so that international inequality is decreasing, at least on a between-country-level basis and according to their specific measure.

International comparisons of the link between health and income using data on individuals are more difficult than those using populations, if only because many nonfatal measures of health are not obviously comparable from place to place. Another difficulty is that, until relatively recently, surveys that collect information on income rarely collect comprehensive information on health, while most standardized health surveys, the Demographic and Health Surveys (DHS) being the most notable examples, contain at best rudimentary and unsatisfactory information on economic status. Even so, and following Filmer and Pritchett (2001), the information on ownership of durable goods in the DHS surveys has been widely used to construct principal component indexes, often referred to as "wealth" or "income," that have been used to document the link between various measures of health and "wealth" across many countries using the DHS surveys. But because the indexes are computed independently for each country, because the list of goods included differs from country to country, and because the relationship between the index and actual wealth or actual income cannot be documented in the absence of wealth or income data, these results, useful although they are, tell us very little about the relationship between income and health either within or between countries.

In this paper, we present largely descriptive results from three field sites in India and South Africa. We report direct comparisons of a number of objective and subjective measures of economic and health status in the sites, one in the district of Udaipur in rural Rajasthan; one in the shack township of Khayelitsha near Cape Town; and one in the demographic surveillance site of Agincourt, Limpopo Province, a rural area that was once part of a Bantustan in apartheid South Africa. We are ultimately interested in improving our ability to make comparisons of well-being across such places, using both economic and health measures. We are also concerned with the relationship between income and health and, in particular, with the fundamentalist "wealthier is healthier" hypothesis that health automatically follows economic development, within and across countries. Although the term comes from the title of a paper by Pritchett and Summers (1996), who indeed argued that it was income, not health care, that determined population health, the idea that income, through better nutrition, clothing, and housing, was the primary determinant of health in the history of now rich countries was argued by McKeown (1979), and, more recently and in more detail and with more nuance, by Fogel (1997, 2004). While these historical views have been convincingly challenged, most notably by Szreter (1988), Guha (1994), Preston (1996), and Easterlin (2004), the argument that economic growth is automatically good for health remains widely accepted, particularly among those arguing for the benefits of globalization; see, for example, Dollar (2001) and World Bank (2002). If the "wealthier is healthier" hypothesis is *not* true, economic growth needs to be supplemented by appropriate public and private action to directly improve population health, independently of whether better health promotes better economic levels of living.

The paper is laid out as follows. Section 9.1 provides a brief background on levels and trends in population health and income in India and South Africa within the broad context of levels and trends in international health. Section 9.2 describes our three field sites and documents various dimensions of their health and economic status. Section 9.3 analyzes the correlates of health and well-being in our sites. Our results show that the economically better-off South Africans are healthier in some respects, but not in others. They are taller and heavier, but their self-assessed health is no better; they suffer from depression and anxiety to about the same degree; they have a remarkably similar pattern of prevalence of various health conditions; and both adults and children in South Africa, particularly in the urban site, are more likely to go without food for lack of money. Even if some of the self-reported deprivations, such as hunger, are assessed relative to different local expectations, the effects on anxiety and mental health appear to be absolute and absolutely comparable. Because health, like well-being, is multidimensional, and because the components of health do not correlate perfectly with one another, nor with income-based measures, income on its own is likely to be misleading as a short-cut measures of international health. Even within places, such as the three examined here, the links between health and wealth are far from universally strong.

9.1   Population Health in India and South Africa

Figure 9.1 reports the familiar Preston curve for 2000, with life expectancy at birth plotted against gross domestic product (GDP) per capita measured in (current) purchasing power parity (PPP) dollars. The United States is the richest country shown (Luxembourg is excluded, and would appear far to the right), but has lower life expectancy than most of the other rich countries. India, with per capita income of $2,045 in 2000, is a

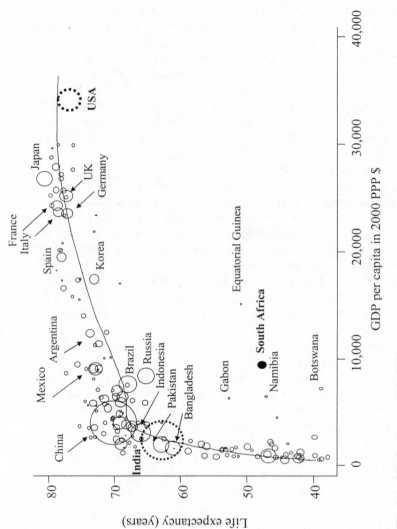

Fig. 9.1   The Preston curve in 2000
Sources: World Bank and Penn World Table.

little below the "hinge" of the Preston curve, the point at which there is a sharp fall in the slope of the regression function and that is often identified as the point where countries cross the epidemiological transition, from infectious to chronic disease, and from childhood to old age mortality. South Africa, like several other countries in sub-Saharan Africa, lies far below the Preston curve. Together with falling life expectancy in the countries of the former Soviet Union, South Africa and its neighbors have caused the "dent" in the Preston curve just above the "hinge," a feature that was not present in earlier curves.

Figure 9.2 shows the evolution of the Preston curves by decade from 1960. India has made steady if unspectacular progress in both health and income. It is instructive to compare India with China, where progress has (sometimes) been much more rapid, leading to an almost forty-year increase in life expectancy over the forty-year period. But much of the Chinese improvement comes from the fact that the starting point is during the famine associated with the Great Leap Forward of 1958 to 1961 in which it is estimated that 29 million people died (Macdonald 2003). After 1970 (or by starting at an earlier date), China did indeed make progress in increasing life expectancy, although the most rapid progress was *prior* to the acceleration of economic growth after 1980; indeed, China provides one of the strongest counterexamples to the "wealthier is healthier" hypothesis; see, in particular, Drèze and Sen (2002, chapter 4). India's progress has been much steadier than China's although, like China, its health improved most rapidly during periods of relatively slow economic growth.

As can be seen from figure 9.2, South Africa's history of health and income is almost as spectacular as China's. In the 1960s and 1970s, before HIV and AIDS, South Africa was well below the curve because of apartheid. Indeed, if the country had been split into two, one rich and white, one poor and black, both would have been close to the curve, although in very different positions. Put differently, the distribution of income between whites and blacks (with the mean income of whites around seven times that of blacks), makes average income a poor indicator of health, even if individual incomes were closely related to individual health. In 2000, South Africa's income per capita was $7,409, more than three times that of India in the same year. But if we adjust the South African figure for the distribution of income between whites and blacks in South Africa, using the (rough) 7:1 rule, Africans in South Africa are only about 50 percent better off than Indians in terms of GDP per capita.

Figure 9.2 shows that, until 1990, South Africa was making gradual progress toward the curve, improving population health albeit with little growth in real income. Between 1990 and 2000, life expectancy collapsed. In 1990, life expectancy in South Africa was three years greater than in India while, by 2000, it was fourteen years less, and the reversal would be even

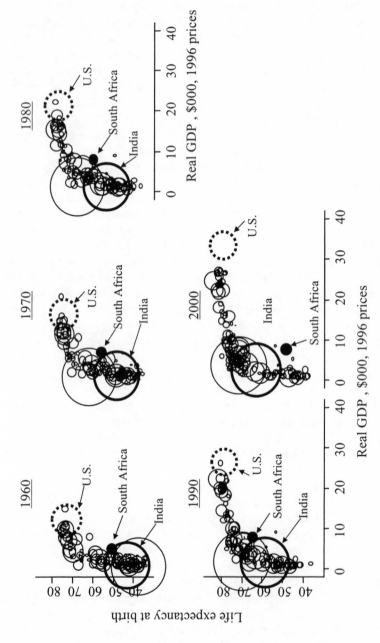

Fig. 9.2 Preston curves 1960 to 2000 (India, South Africa, and United States highlighted)

more dramatic if we were to exclude South African whites, for whom there has been no decrease in life expectancy.

Figure 9.3 shows the changes in life expectancy together with average growth rates. The left panel uses World Bank data for 1960 and 2000, while the right panel uses data from the United Nations (UN) population division and refers to 1955 to 1960 and to 1995 to 2000. One important difference is that the UN data, by averaging over years, exclude the effects of the 1960 famine in China. This change is responsible for a considerable flattening of the population weighted regression slope in the right-hand panel. Another difference that is important for our purposes is the treatment of South Africa. Because the UN data begin two and a half years earlier, the starting life expectancy is lowered and the ending life expectancy raised, so that the decline over the forty-year period is much reduced. Both figures show a substantial and statistically significant correlation between changes in life expectancy and changes in income, although there are many countries that are far away from the regression lines. The consistent progress in India is clear in both graphs; together with China, India's economic growth and its progress in health have been responsible for enormous reductions in income and health poverty for a substantial fraction of the population of the world. The catastrophe in sub-Saharan Africa is also well illustrated in the graphs. For many countries of the region, both per capita real income and life expectancy are lower now than they were in the late 1950s; the extreme point at the bottom left of the right-hand panel is the Democratic Republic of the Congo. Yet the HIV and AIDS mortality in South Africa (for example) has little to do with the decline in income during the late apartheid years, nor with the very slow economic growth since 1994. And in the two poster countries for the "wealthier is healthier" story, India and China, decade-by-decade averages show, if anything, a negative correlation between economic growth and improvements in health. Almost all coherent theories of mortality decline would predict that, over a period of forty years, there would be correlation between income and health; health services, public health, and education are all positively associated with both health and income. But, decade by decade, there is nothing to guarantee that, left to itself and unaided by public policy, economic growth will improve population health.

9.2   Agincourt, Khayelitsha, and Udaipur

We are here concerned with samples from three poor populations in India and South Africa. The first is a stratified sample of 1,000 households (more than 5,700 persons) in 100 villages in the Udaipur district in India, interviewed between August 2002 and August 2003, and described by Banerjee, Deaton, and Duflo (2004a,b). The second survey is of a random sample of 300 households (1,243 persons) collected between March and

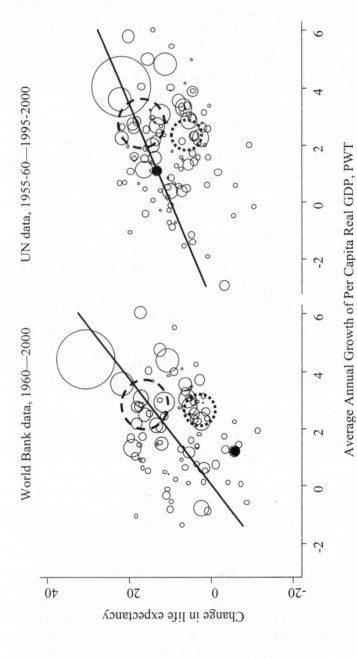

Fig. 9.3   Changes in life expectancy versus GDP growth
Sources: World Bank and UN data.

July 2003 in Khayelitsha, a township of approximately 500,000 people near Cape Town. The township is composed of both houses that receive services (water and electricity) and unserviced shacks. Almost all households in Khayelitsha have a family connection to the Eastern Cape (Transkei, Ciskei, and one of the poorest areas of the country), from where their families recently migrated.

The third survey, also from South Africa, is from the Demographic Surveillance Site in Agincourt in Limpopo Province, about 500 km northeast of Johannesburg, near the border with Mozambique, where one of us (Case) was part of a team that drew a stratified random sample of 475 households (with nearly 3,000 members). All resident adult members of these households were interviewed in the period from January to August, 2004. (The questionnaires for both Agincourt and Khayelitsha are available at http://www.princeton.edu/~rpds/sa_questionnaires.html.)

The Agincourt field site is far from urban areas and has very little infrastructure. Until 1994, it was part of a "homeland" or Bantustan that was designated by the Apartheid government as a "resettlement area" where people from the townships were "supposed" to live. It is semiarid savannah, with low and unpredictable rainfall and, although people live by cultivation, the area is better suited for wild game, as in the neighboring Krueger National Park. According to INDEPTH Network (2002, chapter 16):

> The main ethnic group is Shangaan, although Mozambicans, originally refugees, constitute more than a quarter (29 percent) of the total population. Both groups are Shangaan-speaking, and the Mozambicans are culturally affiliated with the South African host population. . . . Unemployment is estimated at 40–50 percent. Formal-sector employment involves migrant men who work in the mines, in the manufacturing and service industries of larger towns, and on nearby game and commercial farms and timber plantations. (198)

Survey instruments for all three sites were designed to collect information on economic and health status and, while each was adapted to its own environment, the questionnaires were developed in parallel and contain many identical questions. In Khayelitsha and Agincourt, a "knowledgeable household member" was first interviewed and asked questions about all persons in the household. All adults identified as household members were then interviewed separately and asked questions about their physical and mental health, their education, income, earnings and expenditures. In Udaipur, one household member answered an abbreviated consumption questionnaire that had been used previously by the Indian National Sample Survey. Each member was asked a battery of questions on health and mental health.

9.2.1   Economic and Educational Status

A first look at our Indian and South African households is provided in table 9.1, where it is apparent that our South African population is economically better-off, with the rural sample about half as well-off as the urban sample, and the rural Indians less than half as well-off as the rural South Africans. Monthly total expenditure per head is estimated to be 220 PPP (2003) dollars per head on average in Khayelitsha, 127.5 PPP dollars per head in Agincourt, but only 42.8 PPP dollars per head in rural Udaipur. These estimates are likely noisy, but they are not wildly out of line with other survey evidence in India (52.7 $PPP mean expenditures from the 2002 to 2003 round of the National Sample Survey in rural Rajasthan) and South Africa (289 $PPP mean monthly income per household member [106 $PPP median] among Western Cape African households, and 185 $PPP mean monthly income per member [50 $PPP median] among Limpopo households in the 2001 South African Census). The median PPP value of food expenditure per head, which is probably more accurate, is three times as high in Khayelitsha (58 $PPP) and twice as high in Agincourt (38 $PPP) as in Udaipur (18 $PPP).

Ownership of household durable goods, which is the indicator used for analyses based on the DHS (and many other health surveys) is higher in South Africa than in Udaipur. For a group of eight goods in both surveys, the median number owned is one among the Indian households, and three and two in the two South African sites. In both South African sites, four times as many households have electricity than in Udaipur. Telephones and cell phones (39 percent in Khayelitsha, 52 percent in Agincourt) and televisions (50 percent and 42 percent) are common in South Africa, but are rare in rural Udaipur (1 percent and 4 percent). These three sites also illustrate the danger of the mechanical use of indexes of durable goods ownership as short-cut measures of economic status. Electric appliances cannot be used where there is no electrification, nor cellphones where there is no reception (as in most of rural India today) so that, at the least, there is a danger of double counting. Bicycles are much more useful in some places than others and are essentially useless in a shack township whose access to the city is along a busy freeway. Although it is true that, within any given site, ownership or lack of it is likely to be a useful indicator of economic status, variations in ownership across sites will also be a function of geography, prices, and public provision of complementary infrastructure.

Using simplified versions of the United States Department of Agriculture's (USDA) questions for measuring food insecurity, household respondents were asked whether there had been a time in the last year when, because of lack of money, an adult missed a meal, or had not eaten for a whole day, or whether a child had missed a meal. In spite of (or conceivably because of) their apparently better nutrition, Africans reported that adults

Table 9.1   **Household-level characteristics: Udaipur, Agincourt, and Khayelitsha**

	Udaipur		Agincourt		Khayelitsha	
	Mean	Median	Mean	Median	Mean	Median
Household size	5.63	5	5.49	5	4.15	4
No. of children (0–13)	2.39	2	2.02	2	1.16	1
Expenditure per member ($PPP per month)	42.8	34.1	127.5	86.4	220.0	183.9
Food expenditure per member ($PPP per month)	20.9	17.5	53.0	38.2	71.3	57.5
Structure is electrified (%)	21.1		83.3		84.3	
Assets						
Percent of households owning:						
Telephone or cell phone	1.4		52.1		39.0	
Stove—electric or gas	15.0		38.5		44.0	
Stove—wood, coal, or paraffin	99.1		31.0		81.3	
Television	3.7		42.5		50.3	
Radio or stereo	17.1		66.3		71.3	
Sewing machine	5.1		8.7		6.7	
Car	0.5		12.7		8.0	
Bicycle	16.3		8.9		2.0	
No. of assets owned	1.58	1	2.6	2	3.02	3
Hunger						
Percent of households reporting:						
An adult skipped a meal	28.3		39.7		59.0	
An adult went all day without eating	11.0		18.8		27.0	
A child skipped a meal	10.5		24.5		37.9	
Financial status[a]						
Percent of households reporting:						
Wealthiest category	0.7	—	0	—	0	—
Second highest	1.7	62.8	4.8	255.0	1.0	596.9
Third highest	10.6	47.2	39.6	112.3	38.0	229.3
Fourth highest	32.2	38.7	31.9	75.1	44.0	161.3
Poorest category	54.8	31.2	23.7	46.3	17.0	121.7
No. of observations	1,022	1,022	469	469	300	300

Notes: The report of children missing meals is conditional on the presence of a child less than age fourteen in the household. Statistics for Udaipur and Agincourt are calculated using sampling weights. Purchasing power parity (PPP) conversions are made using the 2000 consumption PPPs from the Penn World Tables updated to the dates of the surveys using Indian, South African, and U.S. Consumer Price Indexes. Dashes indicate there are no households in this category.

[a]Median values are median expenditure per person ($PPP).

missed meals twice as frequently, went whole days without food more than twice as frequently, and children went without food nearly four times as frequently as did the Indian children; see table 9.1. While it is possible that these results have something to do with the difference between an urban, more-monetized, versus an agricultural, less-monetized environment, anecdotal clinical evidence from Khayelitsha maintains that child malnourishment is common and is often associated with maternal obesity; see also Doak et al. (2005) who provide international evidence on the prevalence of households containing both malnourished and obese individuals.

Household respondents were also asked to rate their own economic status using a question of the form "how would this household classify its financial situation these days," using a ten-rung ladder in India, and a 5 point scale in Khayelitsha and Agincourt. Table 9.1 shows that these responses are well correlated with measured expenditure per capita and that the Indian households (correctly) characterized themselves as very poor relative to the Africans. Between the South African sites, those living in Agincourt perceive themselves as poorer on average than those in Khayelitsha. Even so, the Indian and African respondents are clearly not using the same (PPP) scale; in the "poor" category, just above the poorest ranking, median PPP expenditures per head in Khayelitsha are twice as large as those in Agincourt and are four times higher than those in Udaipur. Note that this apparent adaptation takes place even across the two South African sites for which the survey instruments are identical and where there is no question of the appropriateness of PPP conversions (though price levels may well differ). Respondents in Khayelitsha consistently report themselves as poorer than respondents in Agincourt at the same levels of household total consumption per capita.

Information on education and on health status of adults in our surveys is presented in table 9.2, where when possible we also present statistics for U.S. blacks and U.S. whites for comparison with a much higher income environment. Until recently, women in rural Rajasthan did not go to school, and more than 90 percent of the women in the Udaipur sample are illiterate. Although almost half of all men can read and write, average completed education is less than three years. The populations of Khayelitsha and Agincourt are better educated, although only by comparison; more than a fifth of men and more than a third of women in Agincourt report themselves to be illiterate and, while the proportions are much lower in Khayelitsha, years of education are not very different, eight and nine for men and women in Khayelitsha and eight and seven in Agincourt.

Table 9.2 and figure 9.4 also show the distribution of self-reported health status on a standard 5 point scale in which larger numbers indicate worse health. These distributions are remarkably similar across the three developing country sites but, just as with self-reported financial status, this surely reflects adaptation or lower health expectations in India and can

Table 9.2   Individual characteristics: Udaipur (U), Agincourt (A), Khayelitsha (K), U.S. black (USB), and U.S. white (USW)

	Men					Women				
	U	A	K	USB	USW	U	A	K	USB	USW
Education										
Illiterate (%)	57.2	21.4	6.8			92.1	35.2	5.5		
Years completed	2.9	7.6	8.1	12.8	13.7	0.6	6.5	8.7	12.9	13.8
Anthropometrics										
Mean height (SD) in centimeters	164 (7.6)	172 (7.6)	167 (12.7)	177 (4.6)	177 (4.7)	152 (7.9)	160 (6.6)	157 (7.9)	163 (3.0)	163 (2.9)
BMI less than or equal to 18.5 (%)	62.7	9.9	7.2	2.4	0.9	56.8	6.3	1.5	1.3	3.1
25 less than or equal to BMI < 30	0.6	14.8	19.1	34.2	41.5	1.6	28.5	27.2	28.0	26.9
30 less than or equal to BMI < 40	0.1	5.1	5.1			0.3	16.6	36.4		
40 less than or equal to BMI	0.2	0.8	1.7			0.2	1.6	11.5		
BMI > 30	0.3	5.9	6.8	27.5	28.4	0.5	18.2	47.9	48.8	31.3
Self-reported health										
1. Excellent	12.4	15.9	18.5	30.1	35.0	8.7	10.8	10.4	24.1	32.0
2. Very good	31.9	32.4	24.2	28.1	33.8	26.5	25.8	21.0	28.5	34.4
3. Good	33.2	32.6	32.1	27.5	22.2	32.0	35.9	33.9	29.8	24.0
4. Fair	15.6	15.9	18.2	10.3	6.5	25.4	23.9	25.1	13.7	7.3
5. Poor	6.9	3.2	7.0	4.0	2.5	7.4	3.6	9.6	4.0	2.3
Mean	2.73	2.58	2.71	2.20	2.08	2.96	2.84	3.03	2.45	2.13

(continued)

Table 9.2 (continued)

	Men					Women				
	U	A	K	USB	USW	U	A	K	USB	USW
	Blood pressure									
Normal	55.0	54.1	48.6			61.0	57.0	45.3		
High-normal	25.1	26.4	24.7			23.0	21.2	24.4		
Stage 1	14.0	14.4	17.6			10.3	12.8	17.9		
Stage 2	3.8	3.5	6.1			4.2	4.6	8.3		
Stage 3 or higher	2.0	1.5	3.0			1.5	4.4	4.1		
Stage 1 or higher	19.8	19.4	26.7	35.8	28.1	16.0	21.8	30.3	42.0	32.8

Notes: Maximum observations used in calculations for Udaipur are 1,057 men and 1,242 women, for Agincourt are 529 men and 770 women, and for Khayelitsha are 309 men and 398 women. Means for Udaipur, Agincourt, and the United States were calculated using sampling weights. Blood pressure measures for Agincourt are based on the average of a second and third reading taken. Blood pressure is categorized as high-normal if the systolic reading is greater than 130 or the diastolic reading is greater than 80; stage 1 hypertensive if systolic is greater than 140 or diastolic is greater than 90; stage 2 hypertensive if systolic is greater than 160 or diastolic is greater than 100; stage 3 or higher if systolic is greater than 180 or diastolic is greater than 110.

Data for the United States are for non-Hispanic white and black adults aged twenty to seventy-four. Data on heights, body mass index (BMI), and blood pressure for the United States are based on published tables from NHANES 1999–2002. U.S. hypertension results are reported for all individuals stage 1 hypertensive or higher, which include all persons currently taking antihypertensive medication. Data on educational attainment and self-reported health status are from the National Health Interview Survey 2001. Standard deviations (SD) for heights in the United States were approximated using a design effect of 2.50. Blank cell indicate data unavailable.

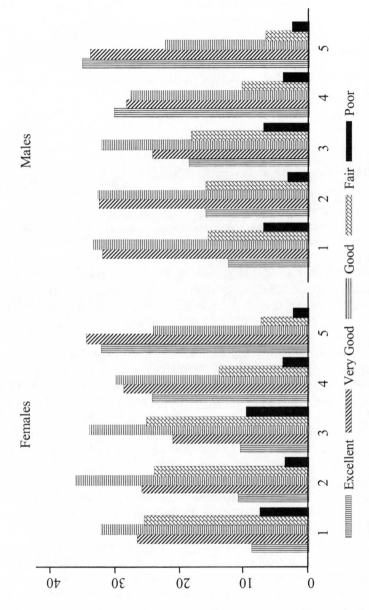

Fig. 9.4 Self-reported health status in five populations: 1. Udaipur, 2. Agincourt, 3. Khayelitsha, 4. U.S. blacks, 5. U.S. whites

hardly be taken as an exception to the "wealthier is healthier" rule. But while self-reported health status is adapted to people's circumstances, that adaptation is far from complete. While there is not much improvement in self-reported health status across the three developing country sites—except for men in the "excellent" category—both blacks and whites in the United States report that they are much healthier: 32 percent of white women and 24 percent of black women in the United States report themselves to be in excellent health, which stands in sharp contrast to reports from South Africa and India, in which only 10 percent of women report excellent health. Figure 9.4 also shows that women report worse health status than men, something that appears to be a worldwide phenomenon.

9.2.2   Measures of Health Status: Height, Weight, Body Mass Index, and Hypertension

Measures of height and weight are useful because they are directly comparable across countries and are (relatively) objective, given that they are not self-reported but measured by the survey teams in all three sites. Adult height, which does not change much until old age, or until differential selection by mortality or migration affects the population, provides a useful indicator of long-term nutritional status, which in turn is influenced both by the availability of food and by the disease environment, particularly during middle infancy. Indeed, much of the variation in adult height is set by age four, in that deficiencies in growth up to that age cannot be made up later (Dahlmann and Peterson 1977), so that contemporary cross sections of adult height are informative about the epidemiological and nutritional environment many years in the past. Similarly, the burden of chronic disease among contemporary middle-aged adults is likely to be higher among those whose early growth was compromised by a negative health and nutritional environment up to age four of which their current height is an indicator. Among adults in currently rich countries, height tends to rise most rapidly with year of birth among the older members of the population, many of whom experienced an adverse epidemiological environment in childhood, and then flatten out among the younger adults, born in a more benign environment. In Europe, Schmidt, Jørgensen, and Michaelsen (1995) have shown that the flattening out of heights among military conscripts tends to occur about two decades after the end of the decline in postneonatal mortality, itself an indication of improvements in nutrition and infections, driven both by higher living standards and public health measures such as the provision of safe drinking water.

Table 9.2 shows that both South African groups are taller than the Indians, and all are considerably shorter than contemporary Americans measured in the National Health and Nutrition Examination Survey (NHANES III, 1988–1994). The poorer South African group, in Agincourt, is taller (5 cm for men, and 3 cm for women) than the better-off group in Khayelitsha. The rural Indians are shorter still, 3 cm (men) and

5cm (women) shorter than the Khayelitsha group. It is possible that there is some genetic component to height across South African ethnic groups, but it is generally believed that the genetic contribution to intergroup comparisons of height is small relative to the contribution from the nutritional and disease environment (Floud, Wachter, and Gregory 1990, figures 5.4, 5.5, 6.1). In this context, note the very large variation in heights in all three sites compared with the United States. The standard deviation of heights in India and South Africa is roughly twice that in the United States and is exceptionally large for men in Khayelitsha. A healthier environment not only improves *average* health, but it also sharply reduces disparities because it is the poorer individuals who bear the greatest burden of infectious disease and poor nutrition. Both average height and the standard deviation of height are indicators of the health environment.

Figure 9.5 shows graphs of height against age for ages zero to fifty in the top panel and for children only in the bottom panel. (Gaps exist between ages thirteen and eighteen for the South African surveys; young adults of these ages were not measured.) In order to avoid possible bias from differing proportions of men and women and different ages, we first calculated averages of women's and men's heights separately and then took the (simple) average of these two at each age. While adult heights are higher in the two South African sites than in Udaipur, child heights in Khayelitsha and Udaipur at each age are indistinguishable. (Results are very similar when children's heights are plotted separately by sex.) Although children in Agincourt are slightly taller at each age from four to ten, there is no height deficit in middle infancy in Udaipur compared with Khayelitsha, suggesting that (unless the adolescent growth spurt accounts for a different proportion of adult heights in the two sites) the height discrepancy among the adults will not exist in the next generation, and that the health environment in Udaipur has caught up with that in South Africa. Of course, we must treat these results with caution if only because, in localized sites like these, health selective migration is potentially important in a way that is not true for the population as a whole. Furthermore, as shown in figure 9.6, the Indian children are lighter than the South Africans. Weight for age is usually taken to be an indicator of short-run nutritional status, but in the context of international comparisons, it is unclear why height and weight for age should give such different pictures.

Figure 9.7 shows heights against age for adults only. The U.S. data at the top of the graph, taken from NHANES III, show the slow down in the growth of height for those born after about 1950, after which it is plausible that improvements in infant health had exhausted their potential for increases in adult height. The Udaipur data also show some slowdown (or even halt) in the rate of height increase for those born after around 1960. There is possibly also some flattening in the curves for Khayelitsha and Agincourt, although in both cases the samples are too small to permit definitive conclusions. (Note that, in spite of appearances, the data in the top panel of figure

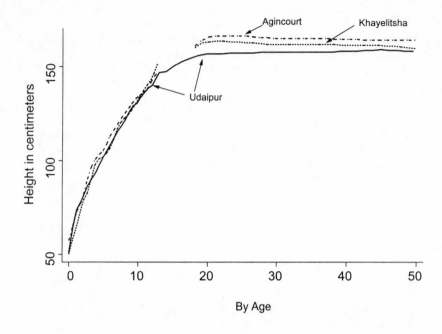

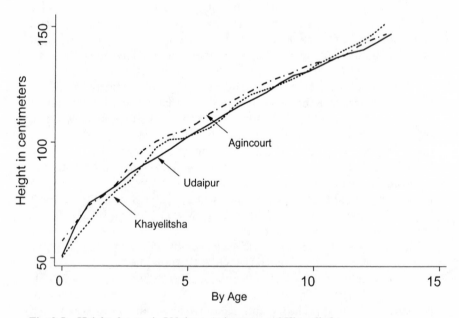

Fig. 9.5   Heights by age in Udaipur, Agincourt, and Khayelitsha

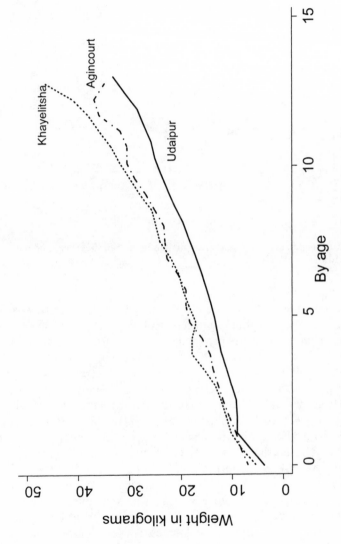

Fig. 9.6 Children's weights by age: Udaipur, Agincourt, and Khayelitsha

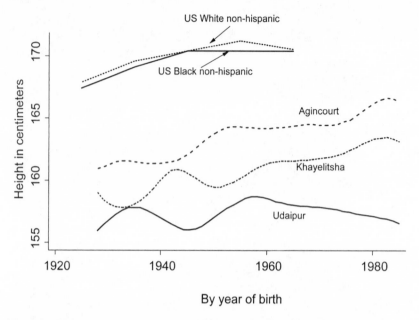

By year of birth

Fig. 9.7   **Heights of adults by year of birth in India, South Africa, and the United States**

9.5 are the same as those in figure 9.7; they look different because of the larger scale and the plotting against date of birth rather than age.)

If the height differences across the sites are large, they are dwarfed by differences in weight. Table 9.2 shows the distribution of body mass index (BMI) across the sites and again presents statistics from the United States for comparison. Sixty-three percent of men and 57 percent of women in rural Udaipur have a BMI of less than 18.5, which is the international cutoff for *underweight* (World Health Organization [WHO] Expert Consultation 2004). Few of the South Africans are underweight, but 75 percent of the women in Khayelitsha are stage 2 (BMI between 25 and 30) or stage 3 (BMI over 30) *obese.* In Agincourt, obesity among women is less startling, but still highly prevalent, with 47 percent of women stage 2 or 3. Men are much leaner than women, and somewhat leaner in Agincourt than in Khayelitsha. The fraction of women with a BMI over 30 in Khayelitsha is close to that for black women in the United States. These results are consistent with results found for a much larger, nationally representative sample of Africans measured in the 1998 South African Demographic and Health Survey (see Puoane et al. 2002). They are also consistent with the existence of substantial obesity among women, particularly urban women, in other middle-income developing countries, although none appears to approach the prevalence in South Africa (Martorell et al. 2000, table 1).

The pronounced differences in BMI, both between countries and between men and women in South Africa, can also be seen in figure 9.8, which presents the distributions of BMI by country and sex. (Agincourt is omitted for clarity, but lies between Udaipur and Khayelitsha.) In both countries, women's BMIs show greater variance than do men's, but the difference in South Africa is especially noteworthy.

Hypertension, in part associated with obesity, is also more prevalent among the South Africans and is somewhat more prevalent among women than men in Khayelitsha and Agincourt, although perhaps less than might be expected given the gender differences in obesity. The prevalence of hypertension in urban Khayelitsha is similar to what we find in the United States among whites, though it remains much lower than prevalence among U.S. blacks (data from NHANES 1999–2002.) South African townships are already suffering from the posttransitional health problems of diabetes and stroke, which have yet to make an appearance in rural Rajasthan.

In our three sites, many respondents will not have seen a physician or health care professional for the physical problems they face, and so asking the types of questions one finds in, say, the National Health Interview Survey on whether "a doctor or nurse or health care professional has ever told you that you have [particular chronic conditions]" is not illuminating. Instead, we ask participants about the physical symptoms they have encountered in the last thirty days. Figure 9.9 and table 9.3 show the prevalence of

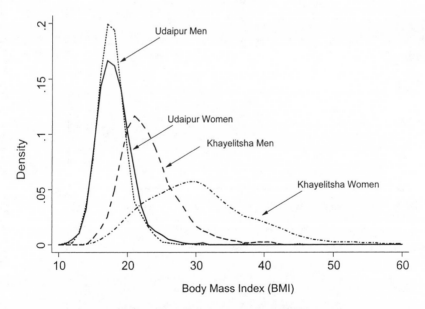

Fig. 9.8   Body mass indexes by sex: Udaipur and Khayelitsha

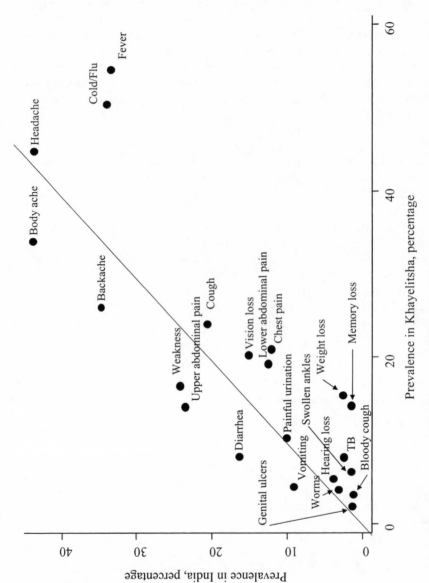

Fig. 9.9 Prevalence of conditions in Udaipur and Khayelitsha

Table 9.3   **Physical symptoms: Udaipur (U), Agincourt (A), Khayelitsha (K), and United States (% of adults reporting)**

	Men				Women			
Symptoms	U	A	K	US	U	A	K	US
Cold/flu	36.8	42.5	47.2	12.2	31.8	38.2	52.9	13.3
Fever	30.7	6.2	51.6		35.9	7.5	57.0	
Persistent cough		12.9	23.2			11.4	24.6	
Dry cough	25.5				16.6			
Productive cough	8.8				13.1			
Cough with blood	1.5	1.1	3.6		1.1	0.9	3.5	
Chest pain	11.9	12.0	19.4		12.4	17.7	22.1	
Body ache	32.3	15.8	28.1		53.7	28.8	38.5	
Head ache	37.0	41.8	33.9	11.0	49.6	54.2	53.7	23.1
Back ache	27.8	12.9	20.0	28.6	40.7	21.1	30.9	34.2
Vomiting	7.0	2.1	4.2	4.0	10.8	3.6	4.5	5.6
Diarrhea	15.5	10.9	7.1		17.5	10.3	8.8	
Weakness	22.1	13.5	16.8		26.2	19.3	16.4	
Worms in stool	2.9	2.2	3.9		3.3	0.7	4.0	
Pain in upper abdomen	18.9	10.1	11.3		27.5	10.5	16.1	
Pain in lower abdomen	10.1	6.0	6.5		14.7	15.7	29.0	
Genital ulcers	0.5		0.6		2.2		3.0	
Painful urination	11.6	8.0	6.5		8.8	7.3	13.1	
Swollen ankles	1.0	4.3	3.9		2.2	5.4	8.1	
Severe weight loss	1.7	7.5	14.6		3.4	9.5	16.1	
Memory loss	1.2	9.4	12.0		2.0	11.3	15.9	
Vision	14.7	11.2	19.1	7.4	15.6	18.1	21.2	10.5
Hearing	3.3	3.3	4.5	3.7	4.4	5.2	6.0	2.5
Tuberculosis	3.9	4.6	10.0		1.4	2.0	6.3	

Notes: Reports refer to symptoms the respondent has experienced in the past thirty days, with the following exceptions. Reports for tuberculosis (TB) refer to whether a doctor, nurse, or a staff member at a clinic or hospital has ever told the respondent that he or she has TB. For Khayelitsha and Agincourt, vision and hearing impairment is for current vision and hearing, with glasses or a hearing aid. The Udaipur survey asked whether the respondent had experienced "weight loss" in the past thirty days; the South African surveys asked about "severe weight loss." The U.S. statistics are calculated from National Health Interview Surveys (NHIS) 2002 and 2003. For the United States, vomiting includes vomiting and diarrhea. The numbers of responses for the Indian survey range from 1,050 to 1,055 for men, and from 1,238 to 1,242 for women. Numbers of responses for the Khayelitsha survey range from 308 to 310 for men, and from 395 to 398 for women, and for the Agincourt survey are 529 for men and 769 for women. The number of responses for the NHIS range from 26,872 to 26,913 for men, and from 34,885 to 34,942 for women. Means for Udaipur, Agincourt, and the United States are weighted using sampling weights. Blank cells indicate data unavailable.

twenty-two health conditions that were asked in all three surveys. Participants in India report more body ache, backache, vomiting and diarrhea, and more pain in the upper abdomen. The South Africans report more chest pain, swollen ankles, and weight loss. More notable is the similarity between the three different sites. Figure 9.9 presents prevalence rates for Udaipur and Khayelitsha; the correlation across the reported health conditions in the figure is 0.84. Americans are only half as likely to report vision problems as are South Africans or Indians, but almost as likely to report hearing problems. Perhaps vision impairment is more easily remedied than is hearing.

We also included in all three sites questions on depression and anxiety, results for which are reported in table 9.4. Substantial percentages of men and women in all three poor sites reported that over the last year they had had a period of a month or longer during which they worried most of the time and, of those, between 38 and 55 percent said that this worrying had significantly interfered with their normal activities. Similarly, indicators of depression (feeling sad, crying a lot, not feeling like eating) were prevalent in the three sites, with no evidence of better mental health among the better-educated and better-off South Africans. Women consistently report worse mental health than do men, something that is also true in the United States among both blacks and whites. But perhaps the most notable feature of the table is the much better mental health of the Americans relative to both the South Africans and Indians, even when the questions "I felt sad" or "everything was an effort" are identical. American whites are certainly economically better-off than any of the other groups, yet we find no evidence that American blacks have worse mental health than American whites nor, in our developing country data, that those who live in urban Khayelitsha have better mental health than those who live in rural Rajasthan, in spite of a fourfold difference in levels of consumption.

9.3   The Correlates of Health

We examine the relationship between household resources, BMI, and hypertension in table 9.5. The upper panel presents regression results in which BMI is regressed on the number of assets owned by the household, with controls for age and sex. In all three sites, we find a significant positive relationship between BMI and assets owned. Controlling for age and sex, each additional asset is associated with an increase in BMI on the order of 0.3 to 0.5 points. This may be either because lack of resources constrains a household's ability to purchase food or because adults living in wealthier households are not required to do as much strenuous work. To gain a better sense of the mechanisms at play, we add to the BMI regressions a control for whether households report that "in most months" an adult went all day without eating because there wasn't enough money for food. In all three sites, adult BMI is negatively correlated with this indicator, conditional on the number of assets, age, and sex, although only significantly so in our urban Khayelitsha site. Adding this control to our regressions reduces the coefficient on assets owned, but only slightly.

That higher BMIs are associated with a greater risk of hypertension can be seen in the bottom panel of table 9.5 and in figure 9.10. Table 9.5 reports changes in the probability of being stage 1 hypertensive or higher, given a

Table 9.4   Depression and anxiety: Udaipur (U), Agincourt (A), Khayelitsha (K), U.S. whites (USW), and U.S. blacks (USB)

	Men					Women				
	U	A	K	USW	USB	U	A	K	USW	USB
Percent of adults who report that *some or most of the time* they:										
Depression										
Cried a lot	7.4	2.9	11.3			30.2	14.2	27.9		
Felt sad	31.9	29.9	37.2	8.1	11.5	49.0	40.4	38.9	12.6	17.1
Did not feel like eating	25.3	22.4	31.4			39.4	31.0	35.4		
Did not feel like working	28.7					46.7				
Could not get going		18.9	31.7				29.4	37.9		
Everything was an effort		24.0	39.5	10.7	13.4		32.0	47.7	13.9	18.3
Sleep was restless	21.2	33.6	44.3			36.1	45.4	47.2		
Restless or fidgety				14.8	14.1				18.1	18.7
Nervous				12.6	11.2				18.4	16.2
Hopeless				4.9	5.4				7.1	8.4
Worthless				4.3	4.7				6.0	6.6
Conditional on answering some or most of the time: this interfered with life or activities "a lot"				11.4	11.9				12.6	13.0
Anxiety										
Percent of adults reporting:										
A period of 1 month or longer worried most of the time	30.8	33.8	22.0			24.3	40.9	30.9		
Conditional on worrying: this interfered with normal activity "a lot"	46.0	52.0	52.3			37.6	55.2	46.2		

Notes: Among those who report a period of one month or longer of worry, reported is the fraction who said this interfered with their ability to carry out normal activities "a lot." Means for Udaipur, Agincourt, and the United States are weighted using sampling weights. Blank cells indicate data unavailable.

Table 9.5   Hypertension, body mass index, and economic status

	Udaipur			Agincourt			Khayelitsha		
Dependent variable: Body mass index									
An adult went all day without eating in most months	—	-.662	-.375	—	-2.645	-1.463	—	-2.287	-1.792
		(.370)	(.759)		(1.075)	(1.089)		(.855)	(.869)
No. of assets	.393	—	.387	.301	—	.285	.378	—	.328
	(.083)		(.084)	(.054)		(.056)	(.116)		(.118)
Age	.014	.013	.014	.066	.062	.066	.122	.123	.124
	(.008)	(.008)	(.008)	(.008)	(.009)	(.008)	(.019)	(.019)	(.019)
Female	.480	.511	.482	2.567	2.533	2.571	7.149	7.155	7.155
	(.234)	(.235)	(.234)	(.302)	(.305)	(.302)	(.480)	(.482)	(.479)
No. of observations	2,118	2,125	2,118	1,257	1,257	1,257	683	683	683
Dependent variable: High blood pressure									
Body mass index		.004			.010			.009	
		(.001)			(.002)			(.003)	
No. of assets		.004			.005			-.018	
		(.006)			(.004)			(.009)	
Age		.004			.008			.015	
		(.001)			(.001)			(.001)	
Female		-.039			-.037			-.027	
		(.017)			(.023)			(.042)	
No. of observations		2,082			1,244			668	

Notes: Body mass index coefficients were estimated from OLS regressions, and blood pressure coefficients from probit regressions. In the lower panel, we report changes in the probability of stage 1 hypertension or higher, given a change in each right-side variable. Standard errors are reported in parentheses. Regressions for Udaipur and Agincourt are weighted using sampling weights. Dashes indicate variable was not included in regression.

change in each of the right-side variables, estimated using probit regressions. Holding constant age, sex, and asset ownership, an increase in BMI of 1 point is associated with a 1 percentage point increase in the probability of hypertension in our South African sites, and a .40 percentage point increase in Udaipur. This difference across sites suggests that there might be a nonlinear response, with BMI having little effect on the risk of hypertension at low levels, but a larger effect among the obese. However, figure 9.10 shows that the main difference between Udaipur and South Africa is attributed to a shift effect, whereby the Indians are at higher risk for hypertension, independently of their levels of BMI, and presumably due to some other unmeasured risk factor.

We have also looked at the effects of BMI and weight on self-reported health status. The results are strongest for the effect of weight, where the relationship differs in an interesting way across the sites. In Udaipur, where *underweight* is the main problem, greater body weight is *positively* associated with self-assessed health; conditional on age and sex, an additional

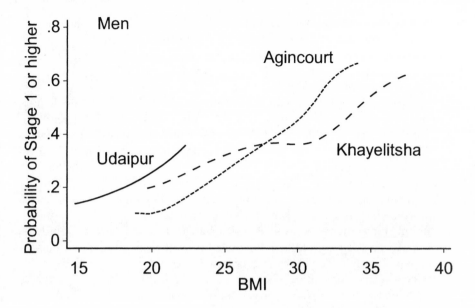

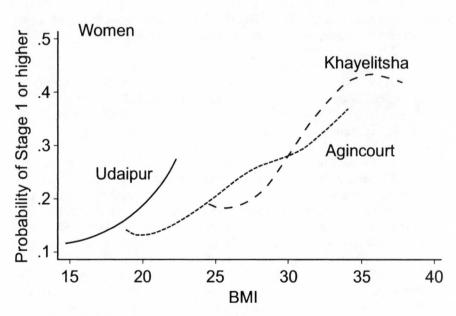

Fig. 9.10   Body mass index and hypertension

kilo improves self-assessed health by 0.015 on a 5 point scale. The same effect is seen, albeit attenuated (0.005) in Agincourt, but is effectively zero in Khayelitsha. By contrast, in the United States, both blacks and whites report themselves in *worse* health (–0.01) when they weigh more, an effect that is stronger among women.

One way to calibrate the effects of health conditions is to examine their impact on self-reported health status. In all three sites, virtually all health conditions have a significant deleterious effect on self-reported health status, whether we control for household expenditures, assets, or education. When run separately for men and women, there are a few cases in which the symptom has no significant effect, but these are relatively rare conditions, like memory loss for women (but not men) and genital ulcers for men (but not women) in India, and genital ulcers, worms, cough with blood, and vomiting for women in Khayelitsha. When all health conditions are jointly regressed on self-reported health status, the coefficients are around one-third smaller than when they are regressed one at a time, as is to be expected given comorbidities. The effects of each condition on self-reported health are typically somewhat larger in India than in South Africa and are only weakly correlated across the sites; for example, weight loss and a cough with blood have much larger effects on health status in Udaipur, while the reverse is true for hearing problems and for diarrhea, which is much more prevalent among the Indians. (See Case and Deaton [2004] for further details on these results.)

We can also examine whether anxiety, depression, and self-assessed health status have similar correlates across our sites. The first two columns of table 9.6 present results for anxiety, which we model as an indicator variable equal to 1 if the respondent answered that he or she had experienced a period of a month or longer, in the preceding twelve months, when most of the time he or she felt worried, tense, or anxious. The second set of columns examines the determinants of a depression index, which is the number of depression-related questions to which the respondent answered that he or she had felt that way some or most of the time in the past week. The last two columns examine self-reported health status on a 5 point scale for the South African surveys and a 10 point scale for the Indian survey. All indicators are such that higher values refer to worse outcomes so that the signs are expected to be the same across all columns.

For each outcome, we examine the impact of a number of variables that we believe a priori could affect anxiety, depression, and health status. These include the number of reported limitations in activities of daily living (ADL), which is the sum of the number of ADLs for which the respondent expressed having any sort of difficulty. In addition, we include three types of economic controls: indicators that an adult or child missed a meal because there wasn't adequate money for food, the number of assets the

Table 9.6   **Anxiety, depression, and self-reported health status**

	Anxiety		Depression		Health status	
		Khayelitsha				
No. of limitations in ADLs	.005	.006	.452	.451	.206	.204
	(.017)	(.017)	(.107)	(.107)	(.047)	(.047)
Indicator: Adults skipped meals	.122	.123	−.059	−.064	.089	.083
	(.037)	(.037)	(.226)	(.227)	(.093)	(.093)
Indicator: Children skipped meals	.052	.050	.091	.094	−.063	−.059
	(.043)	(.042)	(.249)	(.249)	(.103)	(.103)
No. of assets owned	−.012	−.014	−.121	−.117	.001	.007
	(.008)	(.008)	(.048)	(.048)	(.020)	(.020)
Years of completed education	—	.011	—	−.021	—	−.031
		(.007)		(.039)		(.016)
Age	.005	.007	.038	.036	.029	.025
	(.001)	(.001)	(.008)	(.010)	(.004)	(.004)
Indicator: Female	.078	.072	.517	.531	.293	.315
	(.033)	(.033)	(.196)	(.198)	(.081)	(.082)
No. of observations	706	706	701	701	696	696
		Agincourt				
No. of limitations in ADLs	.017	.017	.332	.332	.281	.282
	(.013)	(.013)	(.061)	(.061)	(.032)	(.032)
Indicator: Adults skipped meals	.118	.114	.532	.488	.275	.259
	(.037)	(.037)	(.170)	(.170)	(.079)	(.080)
Indicator: Children skipped meals	−.032	−.028	.330	.331	−.082	−.087
	(.039)	(.039)	(.184)	(.184)	(.086)	(.086)
No. of assets owned	−.011	−.011	−.084	−.066	−.008	.001
	(.005)	(.006)	(.025)	(.026)	(.012)	(.012)
Years of completed education	—	.000	—	−.046	—	−.023
		(.004)		(.018)		(.009)
Age	.002	.002	.019	.011	.018	.014
	(.001)	(.001)	(.004)	(.005)	(.002)	(.002)
Indicator: Female	.066	.068	.543	.536	.188	.183
	(.028)	(.028)	(.133)	(.133)	(.062)	(.062)
No. of observations	1,207	1,206	1,210	1,209	1,211	1,210

(continued)

household owns, and the years of education the respondent has completed. In each regression, we also control for the respondent's age and sex.

Results are similar for our two very different South African sites. Limitations in ADLs have a large and significant effect on depression in both Khayelitsha and Agincourt, with an additional limitation associated with a 0.3 to 0.5 point increase in the depression index on average. In addition, ADL limitations are significantly associated with self-assessed health status, with additional limitations increasing (worsening) self-assessed health in both sites by 0.2 to 0.3 points. When adults in the household skip meals, this increases the probability of reporting a period of anxiety by 12 per-

Table 9.6   Anxiety, depression, and self-reported health status

	Anxiety		Depression		Health status	
		Udaipur				
No. of limitations in ADLs	.020	.020	.369	.368	.196	.198
	(.007)	(.007)	(.029)	(.029)	(.021)	(.021)
Indicator: Adults skipped meals	.043	.046	.383	.380	.091	.081
	(.025)	(.026)	(.095)	(.095)	(.062)	(.062)
Indicator: Children skipped meals	.170	.169	−.222	−.222	.149	.151
	(.044)	(.043)	(.150)	(.150)	(.100)	(.100)
No. of assets owned	.002	−.001	−.030	−.028	−.077	−.070
	(.007)	(.007)	(.030)	(.028)	(.017)	(.018)
Years of completed education	—	.006	—	−.003	—	−.014
		(.004)		(.014)		(.008)
Age	.001	.002	.004	.003	.008	.007
	(.001)	(.001)	(.003)	(.003)	(.002)	(.002)
Indicator: Female	−.101	−.086	.383	.377	−.045	−.081
	(.022)	(.024)	(.085)	(.092)	(.057)	(.062)
No. of observations	2193	2190	2196	2193	1805	1802

Notes: Anxiety refers to an indicator variable that the respondent reported a period of one month or longer in the past twelve months in which he or she "felt worried, tense, or anxious." Estimates for anxiety are from probit regressions. We report the change in the probability of reporting anxiety, given a change in each right-side variable. Depression is the simple sum of the number of times the respondent answered that "some or most of the time" he or she had the depression symptoms. For Agincourt and Khayelitsha, these refer to the following eight depressive symptoms: feeling sad, miserable, depressed, that everything was an effort, sleep was restless, respondent did not feel like eating, could not get going, and the respondent cried a lot. For Udaipur, these refer to the following five depressive symptoms: feeling sad, did not feel like working, sleep was restless, did not feel like eating, and the respondent cried a lot. Dashes indicate variable not included in the regression.

centage points in both South African settings. In contrast, children missing meals is not a significant determinant of anxiety in either Khayelitsha or Agincourt, but is significantly associated with depression in Agincourt. Assets appear to be protective against anxiety and depression in both sites, but have no significant association with self-assessed health. Of the socioeconomic variables included in our analyses, it is education that is significantly associated with better health in both Agincourt and Khayelitsha.

Taken together, these suggest different aspects of socioeconomic status (SES) protect in different ways: education appears to protect health status, but has little effect on anxiety or depression, while assets protect against depression, but not against poor health is these sites.

In both South African sites, older adults are significantly more likely to report anxiety, depression, and poor health, although changes in all three measures with age are more pronounced in Khayelitsha than in Agincourt. Women report more anxiety in both sites, and their depression indexes are 0.5 points higher on average.

Some of the results for Udaipur mirror those seen in our South African sites. Limitations to ADLs increase depression and worsen self-assessed health identically to what was seen for South Africa. Adults missing meals leads to depression in Udaipur, similar to Agincourt. However, many results for Udaipur are quite different from those observed for South Africa. Women in Udaipur report significantly *less* anxiety than do men, and their self-assessed health is no worse than men's. Anxiety and depression do not increase systematically with age in our Indian site. Education is associated with better health, but not significantly so.

9.4   Conclusions

This paper has presented a descriptive account of health and economic status in three sites in rural India and in rural and urban South Africa. The broader populations of the two countries are in very different positions in the international hierarchy of life expectancy and income. While India's population health is about where it would be predicted to be given its level of GDP per capita, South Africa, like the United States, has poor health relative to its income and, because of HIV and AIDS, has a current life expectancy that is lower than India's. But even before the onset of the epidemic, South Africa's life expectancy was lower than would be expected from its income, largely because of the degree of inequality between its population groups. If we use mortality as a measure of economic success (Sen 1998), both South Africa and the United States are less successful than would be warranted by their resources, even without taking into account the distribution of income within them. Over the last forty years, India's population health has improved along with its levels of real income; though, decade by decade, the rate of progress in health has not been closely correlated with progress in economic growth. South Africa's population health improved through much of the same period, in spite of little or no economic growth, either under apartheid, or in the decade since. But with HIV and AIDS, it has shared in the collapse of life expectancy that is widespread through sub-Saharan Africa.

The lack of any simple and reliable relationship between health and wealth also characterizes our three field sites, one in rural Rajasthan, and two in South Africa, one in a shack township and one a rural area that, until 1994, was a Bantustan area. Income levels across the three sites are roughly in the ratio of 4:2:1, with urban South Africa richest and rural Rajasthan poorest, while ownership of durable goods, often used as a shortcut measure or check of living standards, are in the ratio of 3:2:1. These differences in economic status are reflected in respondents' own reports of financial status, although not to the same degree as the monetary measures; people know that they are poor, but appear to adapt their expectations to local conditions, at least to some extent. The South Africans are certainly taller and heavier than the Indians—although their children are no taller at the same age—but their self-assessed physical and mental health is no better, and they report that they more often have to miss meals for lack of money. And in spite of differences in incomes across the three sites, they report a very similar list of symptoms. Where the "wealthier is healthier" hypothesis seems to work is in comparisons between the three poor sites and much richer Americans. White Americans self-report better health than do black Americans, but both report substantially better physical and mental health than do South Africans and Indians in our three sites.

In spite of their much lower incomes, urban women in South Africa have fully caught up with black American women in terms of the prevalence of obesity and are catching up in terms of hypertension. These women have the misfortune to be experiencing many of the diseases of affluence without experiencing affluence itself.

References

Banerjee, Abhijit, Angus Deaton, and Esther Duflo. 2004a. Health care delivery in rural Rajasthan. *Economic and Political Weekly,* February 28, 2004, 944–49.
———. 2004b. Wealth, health, and health services in rural Rajasthan. *American Economic Review* 94 (2): 326–30.
Becker, Gary S., Tomas J. Philipson, and Rodrigo R. Soares. 2005. The quantity and quality of life and the evolution of world inequality. *American Economic Review* 95 (1): 277–91
Case, Anne, and Angus Deaton. 2004. Health and wealth among the poor: India and South Africa compared. Princeton University, Research Program in Development Studies. http://www.princeton.edu/~rpds/downloads/case_deaton_healthwealth.pdf.
———. 2005. Health and wealth among the poor: India and South Africa compared. *American Economic Review* 95 (2): 229–33.
Dahlmann, Nicolaus, and Kurt Petersen. 1977. Influences of environmental conditions during infancy on final body stature. *Pediatric Research* 11 (5): 695–700.
Doak, C. M., L. S. Adair, M. Bentley, C. Monteiro, and B. M. Popkin. 2005. The dual burden household and the nutrition transition paradox. *International Journal of Obesity* 29:129–36.
Dollar, David. 2001. Is globalization good for your health? *Bulletin of the World Health Organization* 79 (9): 827–33.
Drèze, Jean, and Amartya K. Sen. 2002. *India: Development and participation.* Delhi: Oxford University Press.
Easterlin, Richard A. 2004. How beneficent is the market? A look at the modern history of mortality. In *The reluctant economist,* 101–38. Cambridge, UK: Cambridge University Press.
Filmer, Deon, and Lant H. Pritchett. 2001. "Estimating wealth effects without expenditure data—or tears: An application to educational enrollments in states of India. *Demography* 38 (1): 115–32.
Floud, Roderick, Kenneth Wachter, and Annabel Gregory. 1990. *Height, health,*

and history: Nutritional status in the United Kingdom, 1750–1980. Cambridge, UK: Cambridge University Press.

Fogel, Robert W. 1997. New findings on secular trends in nutrition and mortality: Some implications for population theory. In *Handbook of population and family economics,* ed. Mark Rosenzweig and Oded Stark, 433–81. Amsterdam: Elsevier.

———. 2004. *The escape from hunger and premature death, 1700–2100.* Cambridge, UK: Cambridge University Press.

Guha, Sumit. 1994. The importance of social intervention in England's mortality decline: The evidence reviewed. *Social History of Medicine* 7 (1): 89–113.

INDEPTH Network. 2002. *Population and health in developing countries.* Ottawa, Canada: International Development Research Center.

MacDonald, Alphonse L. 2003. Famine in China. In *Encyclopedia of population,* ed. P. Demeny and G. McNicoll, 388–90. New York: Macmillan Reference.

Martorell, Reynaldo, Laura Kettel Khan, Morgen L. Hughes, and Laurence M. Grummer-Strawn. 2000. Obesity in women from developing countries. *European Journal of Clinical Nutrition* 54:247–52.

McKeown, Thomas. 1979. *The role of medicine: Dream, mirage, or nemesis?* Princeton, NJ: Princeton University Press.

Preston, Samuel H. 1975. The changing relation between mortality and level of economic development. *Population Studies* 29:231–48.

———. 1980. Causes and consequences of mortality declines in less developed countries during the twentieth century. In *Population and economic change in developing countries,* ed. Richard A. Easterlin, 289–360. Chicago: University of Chicago Press.

———. 1996. *American longevity: Past, present, and future.* Maxwell School Center for Policy Research Policy Brief no. 7/1996. Syracuse, NY: Maxwell School Center for Policy Research.

Pritchett, Lant, and Lawrence H. Summers. 1996. Wealthier is healthier. *Journal of Human Resources* 31 (4): 841–68.

Puoane, Thandi, Krisela Steyn, Debbie Bradshaw, Ria Laubscher, Jean Fourie, Vicki Lambert, and Nolwazi Mbananga. 2002. Obesity in South Africa: The South African Demographic and Health Survey. *Obesity Research* 10 (10): 1038–48.

Schmidt, I. M., M. H. Jørgensen, and K. F. Michaelsen. 1995. Heights of conscripts in Europe: Is postneonatal mortality a predictor? *Annals of Human Biology* 22 (1): 57–67.

Sen, Amartya K. 1998. Mortality as an indicator of economic success and failure. *Economic Journal* 108 (446): 1–25.

———. 1999. *Development as freedom.* New York: Knopf.

Steckel, Richard H. 1995. Stature and the standard of living. *Journal of Economic Literature* 33 (4): 1903–40.

Szreter, Simon. 1988. The importance of social intervention in Britain's mortality decline C. 1850–1914: A reinterpretation of the role of public health. *Social History of Medicine* 1 (1): 1–37.

World Bank. 2002. *Globalization, growth, and poverty: Building an inclusive world economy.* Washington, DC: World Bank.

World Health Organization. 2001. *Macroeconomics and health: Investing in health for economic development.* Geneva: World Health Organization.

World Health Organization Expert Consultation. 2004. Appropriate body-mass index for Asian populations and its implications for policy and intervention strategies. *Lancet* 363 (9403): 157–63.

Comment   Amitabh Chandra

In 1996, Lant Prichett and Lawrence Summers produced a highly influential paper that was boldly titled "Wealthier is Healthier." Their work along with the important contributions of their predecessors, notably Thomas McKeown and Robert Fogel, has advocated the sanguine view that increases in national income will improve population health. There is no disputing the striking cross-sectional association between income and conventionally used measures of health such as infant mortality and life expectancy (see figure 1 of Pritchett and Summers 1996). Indeed, since the pioneering work of Preston (1975), who first illustrated the striking relationship between life expectancy and income, social scientists have been primed to believe that countries will move along these curves as their incomes increase; so seductive is the power of graphical regularities. The key question for any scientist interested in population health is the degree to which this association is causal. If Preston curves shift upward or rightward over time, then the cross-sectional relationship is completely specious.

Motivated by this ambitious agenda and armed with a cornucopia of data, largely collected by their own tenacious efforts, Anne Case and Angus Deaton have written a magnificent paper, which provides a nuanced interpretation for the aforementioned observation that wealthier is healthier. Few questions in economics or, for that matter, in all of social science can claim to be as fundamental to human well-being as this one. First, they consider their macroeconomic evidence: for most countries, the historical record points to a fragile relationship between decennial change in gross domestic product (GDP) growth per capita and improvements in life expectancy. In India and China, which together account for over two-thirds of the human experience since 1950, the preceding relationship is essentially zero (and often negative) for ten-year changes that occurred in the late twentieth century. We can bicker about whether these regressions should be weighted or whether they should report jackknifed coefficients, but we should not miss the substantive point: it is astonishing to note that even for countries that lie on the "steep" part of the Preston curve, those who have not yet transcended the epidemiological transition, the relationship between per capita incomes and improvements in health is tenuous.

Amitabh Chandra is an assistant professor of public policy at the John F. Kennedy School of Government, Harvard University, a faculty research fellow at the National Bureau of Economic Research, and an NBER Aging fellow.

This research is funded by NIA P01 AG19783-02. I thank, without implicating, Lisa Berkman, Sandy Jencks, Ichiro Kawachi, and participants in the Robert Wood Johnson Health and Society Program for helpful conversations that have greatly improved my understanding of population health.

Economic growth appears to move the entire Preston curve to the right, raising incomes, but with no effect on measured population health. This result has important implications for the literature on the health effects of globalization. I do not know the magnitude of the relationship between globalization and its effects on economic growth (as proxied by changes in per capita income), but let us assume that this channel is large and robust. In the context of the Case-Deaton results, the role of per capita income is estimated to be too minor to actually improve population health in the short run. Critics of globalization may cheer at the impotence of the wealthier is healthier mechanism, but their glee is premature; Case and Deaton are the harbingers of unpleasant news for both champions and critics of globalization. If we hypothesize that globalization is detrimental for population health, either by increasing inequality and relative deprivation or by reducing per capita incomes, then the evidence for that proposition is also extremely weak.

Even over forty years' changes, the relationship between average per capita income growth and health is weaker than one may have expected (figure 9.3). This is a result with enormous policy relevance: virtually every theory of development would predict that nations with higher average growth rates over thirty to forty years would be able to realize improvements in health. This relationship may operate through improved investments in nutrition, public health, or women's education. The conspicuous lack of a relationship in both decennial and longer-term changes challenges the empirical basis for providing aid initiatives that are biased toward targeting economic growth. Rather than assume that economic growth causes governments to push policy levers that affect health, might it be wiser to offer incentives to push these levers directly? What levers are these? What is the historical record on such policies, and what are the determinants of successful policies that improved population health? Addressing this question is beyond the scope of this paper, but should provide an active research agenda for development economists.

"Wealthier is Healthier" and Its Discontents

Much of the belief (among economists) that "wealthier is healthier" has its intellectual antecedents in work of Prichett and Summers (1996; henceforth, PS) who studied the relationship between increases in real income, infant mortality, and life expectancy. For many reasons, the popularity of this argument is overstated: (1) PS found an inverse relationship between the first two variables, but not between the first and third. This is surprising: given that life expectancy at birth is largely determined by infant and child mortality (not in the post HIV era, but that is not of relevance for the time period studied by PS), the lack of a relationship causes a skeptical reader to ponder the robustness of their principal result. Clearly, more research into this puzzle is warranted. (2) It is not clear that outcomes such as infant mortality are the sufficient statistics for population health. The incidence of chronic conditions in the adult population such as diabetes, kidney disease, tuberculosis, and asthma will not affect life expectancy tabulations for several decades. (3) Higher growth rates may mask the fact that economic gains from higher growth rates may accrue to a small fraction of the population; if 5 percent of people get 95 percent of the increase in income, then it would be difficult to see a relationship between per capita and health (or the result is being driven for those whom incomes increases). In other words, if the increase in income is unbalanced across the population, population health may increase less than the health of those who benefit from income gains.

To some degree, the popularity of this theory is also a consequence of economists' intellectual predilection that higher incomes *must* improve health: either through access to better healthcare, or through the provision of better public health, population health *must* progress. The first channel may or may not be protective of health. While it is probably not damaging, higher incomes for richer countries may translate into marginal investments in health care. Better dental care, use of antihistamines, and more frequent office visits are utility enhancing but have not been shown to affect long-term measures of health. More intensive use of technologically advanced medicine has been shown to be inversely associated with "quality care" in the United States (Baicker and Chandra 2004). As Jack Wennberg and his colleagues at Dartmouth have argued for decades, "more is not better" (Fisher et al. 2003a,b).

Conscious of these concerns, Case, Deaton, and their collaborators collect data from three poor populations in India and South Africa. They obtain on assets, anthropometrics, self-reported health, depression, anxiety, blood pressure, and a rich set of health conditions. This is an extraordinarily challenging enterprise and one that established a new standard for empirical work in economics: it is no longer sufficient for us to claim "no data" as an excuse for less rigorous empirical work. The results from this new micro data set are striking. Despite having income levels in the ratio of 4:2:1 between South African communities and Udaipur, and ownership of durable goods in the ratio of 3:2:1, the correlation across the prevalence of twenty-two symptoms is 0.84 (figure 9.9). I was struck by three facts: South Africans are more likely to report missing meals, there is anecdotal evidence of child malnourishment, and the prevalence of obesity among South African women is striking. In addition to casting doubt at the wealthier is a healthier hypothesis, they also portend worsening outcomes in years to come. While it has been suggested that the association between obesity and mortality is decreasing over time as medical science improves its understanding of obesity (Flegal et al. 2005), this view appears to be idiosyncratic to the second and third waves of the National Health and Nutrition Examination Survey (NHANES) relative to the first. Attempts to replicate this result in other data sets have failed (Calle et al. 2005). It is probably best to interpret the presence of obesity (as measured by a body mass index [BMI] greater than 30) as doubling the risk of death (all cause) relative to those with BMI of 23.5 to 24.9 (Calle et al. 1999). With this interpretation, being wealthier is certainly not healthier: a point that is further reiterated when we note the significantly higher obesity rates among African American women who are undoubtedly richer than their South African counterparts.

Let us explore three potential explanations why the maxim "wealthier is healthier" may not be as accurate as previously thought. With these explanations, I am not arguing that "wealthier is unhealthier." Rather, I am interested in pushing the observation that (1) income is neither necessary nor sufficient for improved population health, and (2) even though increasing income may be protective of population health, there may be aspects of this increase that *may* undo some the protective gains in certain populations.

Public Health

Efficacious public health polices may be the drivers of large gains in population health, but may be the consequence of good governance, foreign aid, and knowledge transmission, none of which require higher income as a prerequisite. In the framework of Preston curves, such policies move the Preston curve upward; population health improves without any change in incomes. To understand public health's role more concretely, we would want to understand the history of efficacious public health programs that targeted smallpox and cholera in 1960s and early 1970s in India. Were these campaigns the consequence of political willpower, the presence of an extensive public health service, or generous funding from the World Health Organization (WHO)? Similarly, in March 2006, the media was abuzz with reports that global measles deaths had fallen 48 percent over a five-year period. This improvement was attributed to a massive WHO-coordinated immunization program in regions of sub-Saharan Africa, where measles and its attendant maladies—pneumonia and diarrhea—are responsible for hundreds of thousands of deaths. The majority of these deaths have been preventable since 1960, when an economical and highly potent vaccine for measles was invented. This decline in child mortality is clearly not associated with improvements in sub-Saharan incomes, and one would like to know the details of how and why this particular initiative was so successful forty years after the discovery of the innovation that made it feasible. Finally, the iodization of salt is championed as being one of the great success stories of public health, but we do not have a single high-quality evaluation of this intervention. What was its effect in reducing the incidence of goiter (and consequently, retardation and perhaps educational attainment)? One key testable prediction from the hypothesis that public health interventions improved health is that the variance of outcomes should fall with the successful implementation of these programs. In the spirit of these questions, David Cutler and Grant Miller (2005) study the historical record in America between 1900 and 1936, and argue that the provision of clean water can explain half the decline in total mortality, three fourths of the decline in infant mortality, and two-thirds of the decline in child mortality. Their calculations suggest that every dollar invested in this program yielded 23 dollars in social benefit; even the upper bounds of the "wealthier is healthier" hypothesis do not generate returns of this magnitude. More work on the precise mechanisms by which population health improves would help both governments and aid agencies.

The Nutrition Paradox

I would like to draw attention to the "nutrition-paradox" that we have begun to see in developing countries. Caballero (2005) provides an extremely lucid introduction to this phenomena, which refers to the finding that many households in poorer countries have an underweight *and* overweight family member, and my discussion draws from his article. Doak et al. (2005) demonstrate that 60 percent of families with an underweight member also have someone who is overweight. This trend is not ubiquitous across all countries, but tends to be seen in middle-income countries (i.e. those with annual per capita incomes of approximately $3000). Monterio et al. (2004a) demonstrate that being poor is protective of female obesity in low-income countries, but is a risk-factor in middle income countries. We do not understand the mechanisms underlying this phenomenon. Any coherent explanation must be able to reconcile (1) the inverse U-shaped relationship between the prevalence of obesity and per capita incomes (note that most of the historical record points to obesity being a disorder that accompanies prosperity), (2) its concentration in women, and (3) the puzzle that other members of the same household are malnourished. Factors such as a decrease in agricultural labor, or increased access to calorically rich foods, would explain the growth of obesity in adults. Why this should be concentrated among women is a question to which I have no answer, unless the factors noted previously apply disproportionately to women. The large prevalence of female obesity noted by Case and Deaton in Khayelitsha is not unique to that part of the world. Monteiro, Conde, and Popkin (2004) study the experience of Brazil and demonstrate that economic growth has reduced the prevalence of underweight women but has replaced it with obesity (in 1997, 9.5 percent of the poorest women were underweight, while 13 percent were overweight; in 1989, those numbers were 9.7 percent and 8 percent, respectively, while in 1975, the corresponding percentages were 17 percent and 4.7 percent).

Explaining the joint prevalence of obese and underweight members of the same family is difficult. If the underweight members of the family are children, and the obese are adults, then we may be able to appeal to an explanation that is grounded in the quality of calories ingested. Caballero (2005, 1515) sums this up succinctly:

> Although many of these low-cost commercial foods are energy-dense, they may be nutrient-poor. And nutrient density is particularly important for growing children. For example, on a per-calorie basis, a five-year-old boy needs five times as much iron in his diet as a man. Cheap, energy-dense, nutrient-poor foods may adversely affect the growth of the child but may provide sufficient calories for the adult to gain excess weight.

I agree with his assessment, but we should note that the explanation is speculative and has not been proven. Much more work needs to be done to determine how diets interact with gender and age to produce overweight mothers and underweight children.

In contrast to piecewise theorizing, where one uses multiple theories to reconcile different parts of the data, it may be useful to evaluate the empirical content of the "fetal origins" hypothesis in explaining some of the facts on obesity. This tantalizing hypothesis come in many flavors, but one version that may be particular relevant for interpreting the results in Case and Deaton's paper is noted by Caballero (2005): might early exposure to an environment with pervasive malnourishment activate genes that are responsible for the body accumulating body fat? This response would be maximizing in an evolutionary context, but devastating for an individual who is exposed to an environment where energy-dense foods are cheaply available. From the work of Daviglus et al. (2004), we know that obesity in young adulthood is associated with a significant increase in the Medicare expenditures on treating cardiovascular disease and diabetes. Despite the potential importance of this theory, most tests of the fetal-origins hypothesis continue to be muddled because of their uncontrolled nature, but the study by Ravelli, Stein, and Susser (1976) does stand out. In this report, 300,000 men who were exposed to the Dutch famine of 1944 had their health assessed at the age of nineteen (as part of military conscription). For those exposed to the famine in the first half of the pregnancy, significantly higher obesity rates were noted. More recent evidence comes from a recent study by David Barker (the principal advocate of the fetal-origins hypothesis). Barker et al. (2005) examine the trajectory of height, weight, and BMI in a sample of Finns who were admitted to a hospital with heart disease. These individuals were more likely to have BMIs that were below average through the age of about two. After this age, a massive increase in BMI was seen (operating through increases in weight, not height). This accelerated gain in BMI is related to the presence of insulin resistance later in life.

While our understanding of the physiology underlying the fetal-origins hypothesis continues to improve, persuasive tests of this hypothesis in human populations continue to be evasive but clamor for the attention of empirical economists. For those interested in embracing this challenging enterprise, Harding (2001) provides accessible summaries for the principal role of in utero (fetal) and neonatal nutrition in influencing the adult disease. McMillen, Adam, and Muhlhausler (2005) and McMillen et al. (2006) discuss the considerable evidence from rat and sheep populations that shed light on this hypothesis.

Relative Deprivation

An alternative explanation for why healthier may not be healthier may lie in the role of the relative depravation hypothesis. Here the idea is that a person's health and well-being is affected by his or her relative depravation—the degree to which the health of person i deteriorates as the income of person j increases. The causal mechanism that leads to adverse outcomes is the greater (alleged) incidence of depression, stress, and the willingness of engage in risky behaviors. Evaluating this hypothesis is a difficult task, for one needs high quality data on health outcomes, a concrete definition of who constitutes an agent's reference group (is it people in one's neighborhood, coworkers at a firm, or individuals with similar demographics?), and knowledge of what margin of a reference group's prosperity (earnings, income, wealth) affects an agent's well-being. Few data sets provide measures that allow this question to be competently executed, but that does not mean that it does not have merit. Historically, support for explanations grounded in relative deprivation has been the purview of epidemiologists (although the concept is noted in Dusenberry 1949), and I would hazard the guess that economists have a natural antipathy to it, for it wreaks havoc with the applicability the Pareto principle that guides much of our thinking on welfare calculations. In fairness to economists, it is not the case that the epidemiological literature is particularly convincing; much of the empirical work would not meet economists standards for identification (see Deaton and Lubotsky [2003] for an example of economists challenging the premise that income inequality per se is associated with higher mortality).

Despite these concerns, the fact that Swedes with a PhD have substantially lower mortality than those with a master's degree is unlikely to be explained by conventional explanations such as greater incomes, better health care, or better maternal nutrition (Erikson 2001). A recent paper by Banks et al. (2006) notes that white Americans are in substantially worse health than the English, even after accounting for differences in health insurance. While some interpret this result as providing support for the importance of preventative health (a belief that flies in the face of the scant evidence on the returns to preventative medicine in a developed-country context), it is also possible that even higher incomes and health care expenditures in America improve health, but greater levels of relative deprivation undo some of these gains. Once again, this is pure speculation on my part. More careful work would evaluate this explanation rigorously. More recent work by economists has begun to do precisely this. Eibner and Evans (2005) provide a summary of much of the literature and push our understanding of the empirical evidence in support of this hypothesis. They use individual death records to establish a compelling association between specific measures of relative deprivation and all-cause death, self-reported health, BMI, and prevalence of engaging in risky behaviors. Interestingly, one's location in the income distribution, that is, "rank," seems not to matter. Luttmer (2005) notes that agents are less happy when the earnings of their neighbors increase; relative consumption may enter the utility function in addition to the absolute level of consumption. If the relative deprivation hypothesis is true, then it has massive implications for the wealthier is healthier hypothesis; a country that is able to realize a 10 percent income shock for every citizen, while preserving one's rank in the distribution, would still see the health of those at the bottom worsen (a person who earned $40k now earns $44k, whereas someone who earned $100k now earns $110k; the initial difference of $60k is now $66k) as relative deprivation increases.

The research program underlying this paper poses questions of absolute importance. Obtaining the correct answer has the power to improve the lives of billions, but it is equally humbling to ponder the lethality of the incorrect answer. Much is known, but much more still needs to be known. We are grateful to Case and Deaton for showing us how to know it.

References

Baicker, K., and A. Chandra. 2004. Medicare spending, the physician workforce, and beneficiaries' quality of care. *Health Affairs* Web Exclusive (April 7).

Banks, J., M. Marmot, Z. Oldfield, and J. P. Smith. 2006. Disease and disadvantage in the United States and in England. *Journal of the American Medical Association* 295:2037–45.

Barker, D. J. P., C. Osmond, T. J. Forsen, E. Kajantie, and J. G. Eriksson. 2005. Trajectories of growth among children who have coronary events as adults. *New England Journal of Medicine* 353:1802–09.

Caballero, B. 2005. A nutrition paradox—Underweight and obesity in developing countries. *New England Journal of Medicine* 352:1514–16.

Calle, E. E., L. R. Teras, and M. J. Thun. 2005. Obesity and mortality. *New England Journal of Medicine* 353:2197–99.

Calle, E. E., M. J. Thun, J. M. Petrelli, C. Rodriguez, and C. W. Heath. 1999. Body-mass index and mortality in a prospective cohort of U.S. adults. *New England Journal of Medicine* 341:1097–1105.

Cutler, D., and G. Miller. 2005. The role of public health improvements in health advances: The twentieth-century United States. *Demography* 42 (1): 1–22.

Daviglus, M. L., K. Liu, L. L. Yan, A. Pirzada, L. Manheim, W. Manning, D. Garside, et al. 2004. Relation of body mass index in young adulthood and middle age to Medicare expenditures in older age. *Journal of the American Medical Association* 292:2743–49.

Deaton, A., and D. Lubotsky. 2003. Mortality, inequality and race in American cities and states. *Social Science & Medicine* 56:1139–1153.

Doak, C. M., L. S. Adair, M. Bentley, C. Monteiro, and B. M. Popkin. 2005. The dual burden household and the nutrition transition paradox. *International Journal of Obesity* 29:129–36.

Dusenberry, J. S. 1949. *Income, saving and the theory of consumer behavior.* Cambridge MA: Harvard University Press.

Eibner, C., and W. N. Evans. 2005. Relative deprivation, poor health habits, and mortality. *Journal of Human Resources* 40:591–620.

Erikson, R. 2001. Why do graduates live longer? In *Cradle to grave: Life-course change in modern Sweden,* ed. J. O. Jonsson and C. Mills, 211–27. Durham, England: Sociology Press.

Fisher, E. S., D. E. Wennberg, T. A. Stukel, D. J. Gottlieb, F. L. Lucas, and É. L. Pinder. 2003a. The implications of regional variations in Medicare spending. Part 1: The content, quality, and accessibility of care. *Annals of Internal Medicine* 138:273–87.

———. 2003b. The implications of regional variations in Medicare spending. Part 2: Health outcomes and satisfaction with care. *Annals of Internal Medicine* 138:288–98.

Flegal, K. M., B. I. Graubard, D. F. Williamson, and M. H. Gail. 2005. Excess deaths associated with underweight, overweight, and obesity. *Journal of the American Medical Association* 293:1861–67.

Harding, J. E. 2001. The nutritional basis of the fetal origins of adult disease. *International Journal of Epidemiology* 30:15–23.

Luttmer, E. F. P. 2005. Neighbors as negatives: Relative earnings and well-being. *Quarterly Journal of Economics* 120:963–1002.

McMillen, I. C., C. L. Adam, and B. S. Muhlhausler. 2005. Early origins of obesity: Programming the appetite regulatory system. *Journal of Physiology* 565:9–17.

McMillen, I. C., L. J. Edwards, J. Duffield, and B. S. Muhlhausler. 2006. Regulation of leptin synthesis and secretion before birth: Implications for the early programming of adult obesity. *Reproduction* 131:415–27.

Monteiro, C. A., W. L. Conde, B. Lu, and B. M. Popkin. 2004. Obesity and inequities in health in the developing world. *International Journal of Obesity* 28:1181–86.

Monteiro, C. A., W. L. Conde, and B. M. Popkin. 2004. The burden of disease from undernutrition and overnutrition in countries undergoing rapid nutrition transition: A view from Brazil. *American Journal of Public Health* 94:433–34.

Preston, S. H. 1975. The changing relation between mortality and level of economic development. *Population Studies* 29:231–48.

Pritchett, L., and L. H. Summers. 1996. Wealthier is healthier. *Journal of Human Resources* 31 (4): 841–68.

Ravelli, G. P., Z. A. Stein, and M. W. Susser. 1976. Obesity in young men after famine exposure in utero and early infancy. *New England Journal of Medicine* 295:349–53.

10

The SES Health Gradient on Both Sides of the Atlantic

James Banks, Michael Marmot, Zoe Oldfield, and
James P. Smith

10.1 Introduction

In a recent paper, we documented large differences in health status between the Americans and the English (Banks et al. 2006). In this paper, we extend that work by examining the relative health status of mature men in both countries. There are several advantages to limiting the focus to men. First, there are well-documented and significant health differences by gender in most countries, with men experiencing worse health outcomes for

James Banks is professor of economics at University College London and the Institute for Fiscal Studies, Michael Marmot is professor of epidemiology and public health at University College London, Zoe Oldfield is a senior research economist at the Institute for Fiscal Studies, and James P. Smith is a senior economist at RAND.

The authors are grateful for the very helpful suggestions made by participants at the NBER conference on the economics of aging and, in particular, to our discussant Dan McFadden. Angus Deaton provided detailed written comments on the first draft that were very constructive. Helpful comments were also received from Meena Kumari, of University College London, especially regarding the biological markers. The expert programming assistance of Iva Maclennan is gratefully acknowledged. The English Longitudinal Study of Ageing has been supported by grants from the National Institute on Aging, US, NIH (2RO1AG7644-01A1, 2RO1AG017644) and several British Government departments, specifically the Department for Education and Skills; the Department for Environment, Food and Rural Affairs; the Department of Health; the Department of Trade and Industry; the Department for Work and Pensions; HM Treasury; the Inland Revenue; the Office of the Deputy Prime Minister; and the Office for National Statistics. Funding for the Health and Retirement Study was provided by grant NIA U01AG009740. Michael Marmot is supported by a Medical Research Council (MRC) Research Professorship. James Banks and Zoe Oldfield's research was supported by the National Institute on Aging through grant number (P01 AG008291-13) and the Economic and Social Research Council (ESRC) through the project "Late Life Work and Retirement" (RES-000-23-0588), with co-funding from the ESRC Centre for the Microeconomic Analysis of Public Policy (grant number M544285003). James P. Smith's research was supported by the National Institute on Aging, US, NIH (P01 AG008291-13).

certain diseases and women more likely to have other illnesses. The causes of disease may also vary by gender with work-related health problems a more common cause among men and health consequences of childbirth more relevant for women. Documenting international differences by gender is important because it may shed light on the underlying reasons why these cross-country differences emerge.

An important case in point relates to the possibility of health affecting income and wealth, a pathway that is undoubtedly more relevant for men than for women in both the United States and England, at least for current cohorts approaching retirement. Of those currently ten or so years before retirement, men will have had much higher levels of labor force activity than women. A new serious health event that takes place during that time may well trigger labor force exits before the planned retirement age. If income replacement is not complete, these labor force withdrawals will also be associated with lower household incomes and wealth.

The strength of this pathway has already been established in recent research on the United States (Smith 1999, 2004), but little is known about its importance in other countries, including England. One advantage of selecting these two countries is that England has set up institutional arrangements whose goal is to isolate individuals from the economic consequences of poor health not only in terms of any medical expenditures they may have to pay. While by no means complete, a similar argument applies to earnings and job losses, where social insurance in the United Kingdom is also arguably more generous. The more generous income maintenance system in the United Kingdom should mitigate any effects that adverse health changes may have on income and wealth there compared to the United States.

In this paper, we will investigate the size of health differences that exist among men in England and the United States and how those differences vary by socioeconomic status (SES) in both countries. Three SES measures will be emphasized—education, household income, and household wealth—and the health outcomes investigated will span multiple dimensions as well.

International comparisons have played a central part of the recent debate involving the SES-health gradient. For example, Wilkinson (1996) cited cross-country differences in levels of income equality and mortality as among the most compelling evidence that unequal societies have negative impacts on individual health outcomes. In spite of the analytical advantages of making such international comparisons, until recently good microdata measuring both SES and health in comparable ways have not been available for both countries. Fortunately, that problem has been remedied with the fielding of two surveys—the Health and Retirement Survey (HRS) and the English Longitudinal Study of Aging (ELSA). In order to facilitate the type of research represented in this paper, both the health and SES measures in ELSA and HRS were purposely constructed to be as directly comparable as possible.

Because income and wealth inequality are greater in the United States than the United Kingdom, Wilkinson's (1996) argument would imply poorer health outcomes among those at the bottom in the United States and a steeper social health gradient in the United States compared to the United Kingdom. If differences in social hierarchies are greater in the United States than in United Kingdom, whether driven by income inequality, social stratification in the workforce, or other forms of ranking where degree of difference matters, the theories of Wilkinson (1996) and Marmot (1999) tend to imply steeper SES gradients in the United States. Similarly, if one sees the United States as a more competitive winner-take-all system with lower levels of social support in the community and state, theories that emphasize negative impacts of psychosocial stress on those at the bottom also point to steeper U.S. health gradients compared to those in England.

This paper is divided into nine sections. The next describes the two primary data sources that will be used in this analysis. Section 10.3 highlights the most salient aspects of the male SES health gradients in self-reported diseases in both countries, emphasizing both their similarities as well as their differences. Section 10.4 documents the very different portrait of across-country differences in health that is obtained when self-reported general health status is used instead as the primary health status measure. Section 10.5 documents that these differences in male health in the two countries are not due to standard behavioral risk factors, such as smoking, drinking, and obesity. Section 10.6 explores the degree to which differential measurement of self-reports of health status between the two countries accounts for the differences that emerge in the SES health gradient. The issue of the relevance of absolute and relative income scales to make international comparisons is addressed in section 10.7. Section 10.8 explores whether there are important health affects on male labor force activity and household income in England, and section 10.9 examines health gradients by financial wealth in the two countries.

10.2   Data

This research will initially rely on four important surveys from the two countries, each designed to contain comparable measures of both SES and health outcomes.

10.2.1   Health and Retirement Survey (HRS)

For the United States, our research will be based on a combined set of cohort surveys of the over-age fifty populations in the United States—the original HRS, the Assets and Health Dynamics of the Oldest Old

(AHEAD), the Children of the Depression Age (CODA), and the War-Babies Cohort.[1] The objective of these surveys is to monitor economic transitions in work, income, and wealth, as well as changes in many dimensions of health status among those over fifty years old.

In these surveys, questions were included on demographics, income and wealth, family structure, and employment. Questions were asked in each wave about self-reports of general health status, the prevalence and incidence of many chronic conditions, functional status and disability, and medical expenditures. Other related health variables include depression scales, health insurance, smoking, physical exercise, weight and height (so that body mass index [BMI] can be calculated). No clinical measures of health are currently available in the HRS.

To be comparable with the ELSA survey, which was fielded in the same year, we use the 2002 wave of these combined surveys, which we will refer to as HRS02. Thus, HRS02 is representative of all birth cohorts born in 1947 or earlier who will be fifty-four and over in that year. To insure that any differences between the countries that emerge are not due to special issues that exist in the African American or Hispanic communities in the United States, the American data presented here exclude those two populations.

10.2.2   National Health and Nutrition Examination Survey (NHANES)

Because clinical measures will form part of the evidence presented here and these are not available in the HRS, we turned instead to the most recent National Health and Nutrition Examination Survey (NHANES), which were fielded between 1999 and 2002. The NHANES contains data obtained through personal interviews and physical and lab exams (blood, urine, and swabs) for people two months and older. Information is available on the self-reported prevalence of a wide variety of illnesses and individual characteristics including age, gender, race, marital status, household income (in brackets), and education. In addition, physical exams and laboratory measurements were performed on respondents so that clinical prevalence of disease can be calculated. While the NHANES is a nationally probability sample of the noninstitutionalized civilian population, African Americans and Latinos were severely oversampled.

The NHANES 1999 to 2002 contains 21,004 interviews with medical exams on 19,759 respondents. To maintain comparability with our previous data from the HRS, African Americans and Latinos are excluded from the analyses that follow. In addition, we mostly limit our samples to two age

1. The HRS is a national sample of about 7,600 households (12,654 individuals) with at least one person in the birth cohorts of 1931 through 1941 (about fifty-one to sixty-one years old at the wave 1 interview in 1992). The AHEAD includes 6,052 households (8,222 individuals) with at least one person born in 1923 or earlier (seventy or over in 1993). In 1998, the HRS was augmented with baseline interviews from the cohorts of 1924 to 1930 (the CODA cohort—2,320 individuals) and 1942 to 1947 (the War Babies—2,529 individuals).

groups—fifty-five to sixty-four for comparability with the HRS and those aged forty to seventy. Sample sizes for the age group fifty-five to sixty-four are too small except for the most basic description. All data based on the NHANES are weighted.

10.2.3   English Longitudinal Survey of Aging (ELSA)

In ELSA, around 12,000 respondents from three separate years of the Health Survey for England (HSE) survey were recruited to provide a representative sample of the English population aged fifty and over on February 29, 2002. A major advantage of HSE sampling is that baseline data on respondents' health (details of morbidity, lifestyle, diets, and blood samples) had already been collected. The health data was supplemented by collection of baseline social and economic data in the first wave of ELSA. Future rounds of ELSA, to be fielded every two years, will track changes in health and economic position.

Like the HRS02, ELSA is quite strong in measurement of various dimensions of SES. Detailed education data, employment, income, wage, and asset modules have been fielded, and the quality of the baseline data appears to be quite high (Marmot et al. 2003). In particular, those who keep their finances separate are separately asked about their incomes and assets, whereas for those with jointly held income, assets, and debts, a financial respondent provides information on behalf of the couple. This section of the questionnaire is modeled closely on the HRS, adopting many of its innovations such as the use of unfolding brackets to minimize nonresponse.

The ELSA data is especially rich in the health domain. Its health module collects data on self-reported general health, specific diagnoses of disease (hypertension, heart disease, diabetes, stroke, chronic lung diseases, asthma, arthritis and osteoporosis, cancer, and emotional and mental illness including depression, memory and cognitive assessment, disability and functioning status (e.g., activities of daily living [ADLs] and instrumental activities of daily living [IADLs]), difficulty with pain, health behaviors (smoking, alcohol consumption, and physical activity), and symptoms of heart disease (dizziness and chest pain [the Rose Angina Questionnaire]). While certainly not identical, many of these modules closely parallel those available in the HRS.

Health measurement in ELSA is arguably superior to that available in the American counterpart. Advantages include the prior physical measurement (blood samples, waist, height, hip, blood pressure) and respondent health measurement available in the HSE from which the ELSA sample was drawn. Moreover, wave 2, which was carried out in 2004 and 2005, comprised a further face-to-face interview with nurse visits that repeated the HSE measurement of biological markers, collected additional biological samples (fasting bloods, cortesol), and included a further battery of physical functioning tests (grip strength, balance test, chair stand, lung function test). Further nurses' visits are planned for every second wave, and the walking speed test is intended to be repeated as part of the core ELSA interview every two years.

The biological measures are of interest for several reasons. They include markers such as fibrinogen (which controls blood clotting and is a risk factor for cardiovascular disease [CVD]), HbA1c (a test for diabetes), C-reactive protein (CRPC—measuring the concentration of a protein in serum that indicates acute inflammation and possible arthritis), and cholesterol. Such measures can be used not only to validate respondents' self-reports and to gauge overall health, but they can also inform us about preclinical levels of disease of which the respondents may not have been aware and, therefore, to which they have not yet able to react behaviorally. The preclinical gradient in disease is a largely unexplored area of research in large population-based samples.

10.2.4   2003 Health Survey for England (HSE)

For the purposes of this paper, clinical measures for England were obtained from the 2003 HSE, which is part of an annual survey monitoring health.[2] The 2003 HSE is a survey of 18,553 respondents of all ages, including children. For the purposes of this analysis, we draw similar age subsamples to those described in the preceding for those aged between forty and seventy. The survey protocols included an interview visit followed by a nurse visit where saliva and blood samples were drawn. Hence, all analyses are weighted using weights designed to control for sample design and aggregated nonresponse into the nurse-visit section of the HSE interview. The blood samples collected at this nurse visit were analyzed for total and high-density lipoprotein (HDL) cholesterol, fibrinogen, C-reactive protein, and glycated hemoglobin. Respondents were also asked to self-report on any diseases they may have. The 2003 HSE placed special emphasis on CVD and the behavioral risk factors associated with CVD such as drinking, smoking, and eating habits. The survey also covered health status risk factors such as blood pressure, cholesterol, and diabetes.[3]

10.3   Establishing the Facts—The Nature of the Gradient in the United Kingdom and United States

In this section, we present some basic descriptive statistics that contrast the shape of the SES health gradient in these two countries. The health gra-

---

2. Although we also have biomedical information for those ELSA respondents who were originally sampled in the 1998 HSE, the use of the more recent year of data provides us with a wider array of biomedical measures and a larger sample. In addition, the comparison to the recent years of the NHANES is more contemporaneous.

3. For more details, see Health Survey for England (2003).

dient is first defined across two of the more widely used dimensions of SES—years of schooling and family income. These two dimensions of SES may capture quite different reasons for the origin and existence of the gradient. In the United States, education is separated into three groups: zero to twelve, thirteen to fifteen, and sixteen or more years of schooling. We experimented with different education classifications in the United Kingdom in order to engender comparability although the resulting classification inevitably involves some inherent stance about the nature of education in each of the two countries. In the end, we use the following three-way division: qualified to a level lower than "O-level" or equivalent (typically zero to eleven years of schooling), qualified to a higher level but lower than "A-level" or equivalent (typically twelve to thirteen years of schooling), and a higher qualification (typically more than thirteen years of schooling).

Constructing income groups is more straightforward. In both countries, family income is adjusted for household size using the Organization for Economic Cooperation and Development (OECD) equivalence scale, and divided into three age-specific income terciles. To insure that the observed patterns are not confounded by variation in either SES or health by age, our comparisons are restricted to those who are fifty-five to sixty-four years old.

Even more so than SES, there are a multitude of possible measures of health status. Among others, these would include the existence and severity of an assortment of physical and emotional diseases; the ability to function effectively in workplace, home, and other important every day settings; and self-assessments of more general health status.

Table 10.1 lists the fraction of men aged fifty-five to sixty-four reporting specific diseases where the data are stratified by income terciles and by years of schooling. A separate panel exists for the following seven diseases—diabetes, hypertension, all heart disease, heart attacks, strokes, cancer, diseases of the lung, and cancer. We next present short summaries of the major patterns that emerge for each disease.

10.3.1   Diabetes

Our comparisons begin with diabetes. Diabetes is a disease in which the body does not produce or properly use insulin, a hormone required to convert sugar into energy. Both genetics and environmental factors such as obesity and lack of exercise appear to increase risks of being a diabetic. Type 1 diabetes results from a failure of the body to produce insulin, while the far more common type 2 diabetes results from an inability of the body to properly use insulin.

For men, overall prevalence rates of diabetes are twice as high in the United States (14.4 percent) compared to those in England (7.1 percent). There is a steep negative gradient across income terciles as we move from

Table 10.1			Health outcomes in England and the United States, by income tercile and years of schooling (men aged 55–64)					

	Years of schooling							
	England				United States			
Income tercile	Low	Medium	High	Total	Low	Medium	High	Total
Diabetes								
1	9.0	5.4	8.5	8.1	23.2	15.8	15.2	20.4
2	9.2	7.1	6.7	7.9	14.1	15.2	15.7	14.8
3	5.4	3.9	6.4	5.5	8.1	6.8	11.0	9.5
Total	8.3	5.5	6.8	7.1	16.6	12.6	12.7	14.4
Hypertension								
1	42.8	30.7	29.2	37.5	54.5	50.5	40.9	51.6
2	35.1	36.1	34.9	35.3	51.3	48.6	42.4	48.5
3	33.0	27.2	31.9	30.9	41.9	40.9	41.6	41.5
Total	37.9	31.3	32.2	34.4	50.8	46.6	41.7	46.8
All heart disease								
1	21.4	15.6	11.5	18.2	26.7	25.8	17.8	25.2
2	12.5	8.9	10.4	11.0	14.8	19.1	15.3	16.0
3	9.5	10.3	8.7	9.3	12.8	13.8	14.8	14.1
Total	15.6	11.2	9.7	12.6	19.2	19.3	15.3	17.9
Heart attack								
1	11.6	10.2	7.9	10.6	16.4	10.7	10.4	14.3
2	5.2	4.7	3.2	4.6	5.1	7.8	8.5	6.6
3	2.3	5.5	4.7	4.3	5.6	2.3	4.9	4.6
Total	7.3	6.4	4.9	6.3	9.7	6.8	6.5	8.0
Stroke								
1	5.3	3.3	2.0	4.2	7.0	4.7	3.7	6.0
2	2.1	3.0	3.0	2.6	5.3	4.8	5.0	5.1
3	2.6	3.6	1.3	2.2	3.8	0.9	0.8	1.5
Total	3.5	3.2	1.9	3.0	5.7	3.5	2.2	4.0
Lung disease								
1	10.4	6.5	4.9	8.5	12.6	8.7	5.2	10.6
2	8.3	4.9	4.0	6.2	8.5	9.4	2.9	7.4
3	5.0	3.4	2.1	3.2	5.2	4.5	2.3	3.4
Total	8.4	4.7	3.1	5.8	9.5	7.6	2.8	6.8
Cancer								
1	4.7	2.9	6.9	4.7	7.2	5.5	9.7	7.2
2	5.1	5.5	1.2	4.2	6.0	8.8	4.8	6.4
3	1.3	0.6	3.4	2.1	5.9	10.1	8.4	8.2
Total	4.1	3.0	3.5	3.6	6.5	8.3	7.7	7.3

Sources: English data is from first wave of ELSA. U.S. data is from the 2002 wave of the HRS.

the lowest to the highest income groups in each society. This income gradient is much sharper in the United States so that the disparity in diabetes prevalence between the countries expands as we move down the income scale. For example, in this age group, rates of male diabetes are 12 percentage points (around 150 percent) higher in the United States in the lowest income tercile compared to only 4 percentage points (around 80 percent) higher in the highest income tercile. One in every five American men among those in the lowest income class in this age range is a diabetic.

The two countries are more distinct across education groups where the gradient is quite steep and negative in the United States but less pronounced in England. The net result is that when we compare the "bottom of the bottom"—those simultaneously in the lowest education group and the lowest income quintile—to those respondents at the "top of the top"—those simultaneously in the highest group in both measures of SES—the disparities between both countries are maximized. For example, within the joint lowest education-lowest income tercile grouping, 23 percent of American men report having diabetes compared to 9 percent of English men. In contrast, within the top of the top, the comparable data indicate a difference of about 5 percentage points between men in the two countries (11 percent compared to 6 percent).

This contrast between the dual education-income SES extremes in both countries will receive some emphasis in our ongoing summary of the comparative nature of the health gradient. And at least for diabetes, the data appear to show that in a within-country comparative sense, Americans who rank in the lowest SES echelons are in worse health than their British counterparts at the bottom of the British SES hierarchy. But this is not simply an issue of the social health gradient. American men in the highest income-education class have higher diabetes prevalence (11 percent) then English men in the lowest education-income class (9 percent). Those at the bottom of the SES hierarchy are at greater risk of being diabetic in America and England, but there is a substantially higher risk, independent of SES, in the United States compared to England.

10.3.2   Hypertension

Respondents in both ELSA and HRS were asked if a doctor has ever told them they had high blood pressure. Hypertension (high blood pressure), a major risk factor for CVD, is a relatively common condition, especially for men, with a prevalence that grows rapidly with age. Before the introduction of new effective drugs, the recommended treatment consisted of some combination of exercise and diet, particularly to reduce excessive weight and salt.

In many ways, the cross-national patterns for prevalence of high blood pressure (HBP) mirrors those just documented for diabetes. Overall male prevalence is considerably higher in the United States—a difference of about 12 percentage points (46.8 percent in the United States compared to 34.4 percent in the United Kingdom). Negative gradients exist across education and income in both countries, with indications of a slightly steeper education and income gradient in the United States. The net result is that differences between the two countries are once again largest at the bottom of the bottom of the SES hierarchy compared to the top of the top.

10.3.3 Heart Disease

Coronary heart disease (CHD) is one of the leading causes of human mortality, especially among men. Disease disparities by SES in CHD have attracted increased research attention in recent years in part because the SES disparities are so large. In addition, recent research has suggested that psychosocial factors, including many that are economic in origin, may offer important clues about some of the underlying causes of these differentials (Steptoe and Marmot 2004).

Table 10.1 shows that CHD is far more common among American men compared to English men in this age range. Overall prevalence is about 6 percentage points higher in the United States. As has been documented in many studies (see Steptoe and Marmot 2004), there are very pronounced gradients in heart disease across both education and income groups. These gradients characterize both countries leaving substantially higher risks for the underclass in both countries.

10.3.4 Heart Attacks

Our attention now shifts to a far more serious form of CVD—having had a heart attack in the past. Overall prevalence among men remains somewhat higher in the United States (8.0 percent) than in England (6.3 percent). Negative SES health gradients are still the order of the day in both countries, but the gradient across income is decidedly steeper than it is across years of schooling. Because both absolutely and relatively the income gradient is steeper in the United States, intercountry differences in prevalence are maximized when the comparison centers on the bottom of the bottom. The American male rate of heart attacks exceeds British rates by 4.8 percentage points at the bottom of the bottom, compared to only 0.6 of a percentage point at the top of the top.

10.3.5 Stroke

Stroke occurs with the sudden death of some brain cells due to a lack of oxygen impairing the blood flow to the brain by blockage or rupture of an artery to the brain. We find very similar patterns for strokes as reported in the preceding for heart attacks. Male prevalence rates are slightly higher in the United States than in England (4 percent versus 3 percent). Sharp negative gradients persist across both education and income in both England and the United States so that those at the bottom of the bottom face the larger prevalence risk in both countries. In England, the risk of having had suffered a stroke is four times larger at the bottom of the bottom compared to those at the top of the top. The comparable relative risk differential in the United States is almost nine to one. Consequently, the biggest disparities between the two countries clearly lie within the bottom of bottom (7.0 percent compared to 5.3 percent), while at the top of the top, prevalence is actually somewhat lower among American men (0.8 percent compared to 1.3 percent).

10.3.6   Diseases of the Lung

Lung disease, an impairment or disorder that impairs the function of the lungs, is one of the leading causes of death in both England and the United States. There are several forms of lung disease, but a common separation involves obstructive and restrictive lung disease. Obstructive lung diseases, such as emphysema, bronchitis, or asthma, cause a narrowing or blockage of the airways resulting in decreased exhaled airflow. Restrictive lung disease involves a decreased ability of the lung to expand and to transfer oxygen to the blood. Lung disease is a useful addition for international comparisons because the root causes are believed to be quite different than the other diseases that we have examined. Smoking and a variety of indoor and outdoor pollutants are believed to be the major reasons for lung diseases.

In spite of these quite different root causes, table 10.1 demonstrates that diseases of the lung also exhibit similar cross-country differentials and within-country patterns although the scale of the overall differences between the two countries is reduced—the higher prevalence rates in America are 6.8 percent compared to 5.8 percent in England. Sharp income and education gradients exist in both countries, with a much steeper income gradient in the United States. The contrast at the extremes of SES mimic the findings for the other diseases that we have examined—much larger across-country disparities to the disadvantage of American men among those at the very bottom SES tier compared to those at the very top.

10.3.7   Cancer

Cancer prevalence among men is much higher in the United States, with a surprisingly large difference between the two countries (7.3 percent compared to 3.6 percent). In sharp contrast to all other diseases that we examined, the SES gradient in cancer prevalence is almost nonexistent across either education or income. There are two factors that make reliance on cancer prevalence alone to characterize health status across groups or countries more problematic. Given how serious the illness is, the SES gradient with cancer may be affected by both differential diagnosis and differential mortality. In either country, those in lower SES groups may be unaware that they have cancer or be at greater risk of dying quickly from their cancers, thereby camouflaging the true nature of the incidence and prevalence across different SES groups. Because screening rates for cancer are in general thought to be higher in the United States than in England, this may also play a role in the higher rates of cancer in the United States, as may greater incident mortality from cancer in England (Melia and Johns [2004] or Sirovich, Schwartz, and Woloshin [2003]).

These issues certainly require more investigation. However, the magnitude of these cross-country differences in cancer prevalence appears to us too large to be fully explained by these factors alone. Differences in cancer prevalence between England and the United States also exist in the high education and income groups where differential detection and incident mortality should play a weaker role. For example, the differences in cancer prevalence are quite large for those at the top of the top, those individuals in both countries who are simultaneously in the highest education group and highest income tercile. In that group, prevalence among American men is 7.7 percent compared to 3.5 percent among English men. These higher rates of American cancer prevalence are similar to those at the bottom of the bottom.

Whatever the causes for the higher cancer prevalence in the United States, the absence of any social gradient in the disease in either country suggests that these reasons may be quite different than those producing higher rates of American illness in the other diseases we have examined.

10.4   International Comparisons Using General Health Status

In the previous section, we have compared disease prevalence rates of men between the ages of fifty-five to sixty-four in two countries—England and the United States. Our comparisons included many different types of diseases that together would account for most of human mortality. Two clear messages flow from these comparisons—Americans men are much less healthy than English men of the same age, and there exists a very dramatic social gradient in health across most of these diseases using either education or income as the marker of one's SES group. These conclusions confirm findings obtained in our recent study that considered all adults as opposed to men and women separately (Banks et al. 2006).

Before moving on to try to discuss potential explanations for these results, it is necessary to highlight an apparently stark contradiction to our findings. A frequently used measure of health status—especially for international comparisons—is to use individuals' self-evaluation of their overall health. A standard metric relies on a 5 point scale—excellent, very good, good, fair, and poor, a scale that was included in both the HRS and ELSA. To simplify without losing its main attributes, we converted that scale into two dichotomous outcomes—good health (answers of "excellent" or "very good") and bad health (answers of "fair" and "poor"), with those answering simply "good" falling into neither category.

Table 10.2   **Reports of general health status in England and the United States, by income tercile and years of schooling (men aged 55–64)**

| | Years of schooling | | | | | | | |
| | England | | | | United States | | | |
Income tercile	Low	Medium	High	Total	Low	Medium	High	Total
	Good health							
1	26.2	36.6	54.3	33.9	32.1	48.6	59.6	39.8
2	42.1	49.8	48.2	45.8	44.8	52.9	58.6	50.1
3	49.6	58.4	60.1	57.0	57.0	68.8	71.6	67.7
Total	37.0	49.6	55.9	46.3	42.0	56.9	66.8	53.6
	Bad health							
1	51.2	26.9	21.2	40.1	39.9	24.2	15.8	32.9
2	31.8	22.1	17.8	25.5	16.5	13.6	10.4	14.4
3	22.1	8.3	11.3	13.2	11.6	8.4	7.9	8.9
Total	37.9	18.1	14.9	25.4	25.0	14.9	9.5	17.6

Sources: English data is from first wave of ELSA. U.S. data is from the 2002 wave of the HRS.

Table 10.2 lists the fractions of American men and English men who are in good health and in bad health according to this definition. In spite of the fact that disease prevalence rates are higher in America than in England, and sometimes considerably so, for every disease included in table 10.1, using self-reported health scales, American men rate themselves as healthier than their English counterparts. Nor are the differences between the two countries trivial—the proportion of English men reporting bad health is 8 percentage points higher than it is in the United States. Controlling for education or income does not eliminate the contradiction—in every education-income cell in table 10.2, a higher fraction of American men report good health than do their English counterparts.

The puzzle using general health status scales extends to its description of the gradient as well. While reports of good health in both countries increase with education and income, the relative magnitude of the gradient actually appears steeper in England, the reverse of the ordering of the two countries when we examined specific diseases in table 10.1. To illustrate, 51 percent of English men between the ages of fifty-five to sixty-four who are at the bottom of the bottom claim that their health is "bad" compared to 13 percent of English men at the top of the top. The comparable numbers among American men are 40 percent and 10 percent, respectively, so that the across-country disparities are once again maximized at the bottom of the bottom, but in this case, it is to the disadvantage of English men within the lowest SES tiers.

The apparent contradiction between these two standard measures of health status—self-reported disease prevalence and self-reported health status—for international comparisons raises questions of which of the two provides the more reliable index and why the contradiction exists in the first place. One possibility is that the self-reports of disease are incorrect in their ranking of the two countries by disease. However, we will provide evidence in section 10.6 using biological measures of disease that the disease prevalence self-reports are, in fact, not incorrect—one obtains the same image of Americans being sicker than the English using biological measures of disease.

A possible reconciliation of the two disparate portraits of relative health in the two countries is that we have only examined physical health in table 10.1. Self-reported general health status may be more sensitive to emotional and psychological aspects of health. To investigate this, table 10.3 lists the fraction of men between ages fifty-five to sixty-four who say that they have emotional problems. But even along the emotional dimension of health, American men appear to be worse off than English men are, and these differences are just as large as those documented for physical health in table 10.1. The sharp negative social gradients in health also appear in the emotional domain for both education and income in both countries.

Another possible reconciliation may lie in differential rates of comorbidity in the two countries. Even though prevalence rates for individual diseases may be lower in England than in the United States, those individ-

Table 10.3   **Health status in England and the United States, by income tercile and years of schooling (men aged 55–64)**

| Income tercile | Years of schooling ||||||||
| | England |||| United States ||||
	Low	Medium	High	Total	Low	Medium	High	Total
*Emotional problems*								
1	10.4	10.4	5.1	9.4	18.2	19.4	22.4	19.1
2	3.8	6.0	7.1	5.3	8.3	12.1	5.7	8.6
3	5.8	4.0	6.1	5.4	6.6	8.5	11.4	9.7
Total	7.0	6.4	6.2	6.6	12.0	12.9	11.3	12.0
*Comorbidity (percentage with two or more conditions, given you have at least one)*								
1	41.7	36.2	32.4	39.2	56.2	45.6	40.7	52.0
2	34.8	24.1	31.5	30.9	45.3	43.4	41.4	44.0
3	15.6	32.5	29.9	26.4	25.9	34.2	37.1	33.9
Total	34.4	30.1	30.8	32.4	46.9	41.6	38.7	43.2
*Percentage with one or more mobility limitations*								
1	58.3	45.9	38.4	51.7	67.0	56.2	40.7	60.8
2	45.0	42.2	34.1	41.4	51.0	51.2	33.3	46.8
3	36.3	21.1	25.2	26.9	41.5	51.2	33.6	38.8
Total	48.7	35.2	30.0	39.2	55.6	52.6	34.4	47.8

Sources: English data is from first wave of ELSA. U.S. data is from the 2002 wave of the HRS.

uals who are sick with one disease in England may simultaneously be ill with other diseases, leading them to self-report their health status as bad. However, the second panel of table 10.3, which shows rates of prevalence of two or more diseases from the set analyzed in table 10.1 among those with at least one illness, demonstrates that comorbidity rates are also higher in America than in England.

The next factor we examine in table 10.3 is whether differences in functional limitations can explain the tendency of English men to self-report themselves in poorer health. Although other domains of functional limitations and disability can and should be analyzed, the one we measure here is self-reported mobility limitations. Table 10.3 lists the fraction of male respondents in each country who report at least one limitation from the following set: walking a block; sitting for about two hours; getting up from a chair after sitting for long periods; climbing a flight of stairs without resting; stooping, kneeling, or crouching; reaching or extending arms about shoulder level; pushing or pulling large objects such as a living room chair; lifting or carrying weights over ten pounds; and picking up a dime from a table. Once again, even using a relatively broad level of disability, we find that Americans experience more difficulty than the English do.

With all these possible reasons eliminated, the reason that self-reported general health status may provide an incorrect portrayal of the overall health status in the two countries must lie elsewhere. One possibility is simply that there are omitted factors along the lines of those we have considered previously that affect subjective general health. Alternatively, there may well be problems with using subjective scales for international comparisons. A growing number of studies have documented that residents of different countries, even when their health is identical, use different thresholds when self-rating their own health (King et al. 2004; Kapteyn, Smith, and van Soest (2004)). In particular, this research demonstrates that Americans are relatively optimistic when evaluating their health status given the objective circumstances. For the same objective health circumstances, Americans are more likely to rate their health as good than residents of other countries are. Moreover, the use of different thresholds can confound the evaluation of health across SES groups even within the same country if the threshold standards vary by SES as well.[4] As a result of these problems, we conclude that using self-reported health scales will not be useful in making comparisons about the nature of the SES health gradient in the two countries.

Two further comments are in order. First, if international comparisons of subjective general health measures yield results that depend on differ-

---

4. The SES health gradients characterize the health gradient in this measure as well. Reports of good health rise with both education and income, and reports of bad health decline fall in both countries.

ential reporting behavior across countries, then the analysis of such measures within national populations may also be thought to be somewhat dependent on the same type of reporting differences, to the extent to which they arise across socioeconomic groups. Such an issue is not investigated here but left as an important topic for future research. Second, our preceding discussion should not be taken to diminish the interest in subjective general health measures. In a similar way in which one can argue an individual's subjective economic expectations are important to measure and study, regardless of whether they reflect the true underlying nature of economic processes, when thinking about attitudes to health and, in particular, willingness to undertake particular health behaviors such as improved diet, increased exercise, or reduced smoking and drinking, an individual's subjective perception of their own health state, and the particular benchmarks they use to rate it, may well be important.

10.5   Risk Factors and Their Role in the Gradient

It is standard practice in epidemiological studies to relate the prevalence or incidence of disease to a relatively small set of risk factors that make having the disease more likely. For diabetes and heart disease, these risk factors typically include smoking and drinking behavior and obesity, concepts that can be comparably defined in ELSA and HRS. Using the same format as in the preceding with cross stratifications by education and income terciles, table 10.4 lists among men aged fifty-five to sixty-four in both England and the United States average rates of smoking, obesity, being overweight, and heavy drinking (defined as drinking on more than four days per week in the HRS and twice a day or more/daily or almost daily in ELSA).

On average, male smoking behavior is remarkably similar in both countries with about one in five people in this age group currently smoking. Strong negative gradients across income and education exist in both countries, but these gradients appear somewhat steeper in England compared to the United States. Thus, differential male smoking behavior by itself cannot explain the higher concentration of disease (particularly those related to smoking) at the lower rungs of the joint SES classification in America. In fact, it actually deepens the mystery by making the adjusted differentials that much higher in America compared to England.

Obesity (defined as BMI greater than 30) is a risk factor for a number of diseases including heart disease and diabetes. In both countries, male rates of obesity decline with income and with education both unconditionally and after conditioning on the alternative SES measure. Especially along the income dimension of SES, differences between the two countries are largest in the lowest income tercile. Among those in the lowest income tercile, male obesity rates are 13 percentage points higher in the United

Table 10.4   **Male risk factors in England and the United States, by income and years of schooling (aged 55–64)**

	Years of schooling							
	England				United States			
	Low	Medium	High	Total	Low	Medium	High	Total
Percentage smoking								
Income quintile								
1	33.5	29.5	20.7	30.1	29.7	24.2	16.2	26.5
2	29.2	20.5	11.8	22.3	22.7	28.8	17.9	23.1
3	25.9	16.0	10.0	15.7	20.1	14.7	9.6	13.0
Total	30.3	21.1	12.5	22.2	25.0	22.9	12.5	20.3
Percentage obese								
Income tercile								
1	24.8	17.1	16.1	21.4	36.0	37.4	25.4	34.7
2	22.7	22.9	13.3	20.4	34.2	39.9	25.8	33.6
3	29.4	19.4	17.7	21.1	27.1	35.0	25.6	27.7
Total	25.1	20.1	16.3	21.0	33.6	37.6	25.6	31.8
Percentage overweight								
Income tercile								
1	42.5	47.4	46.0	44.3	41.0	47.6	54.7	44.5
2	46.0	47.6	54.9	48.7	45.9	47.1	40.8	44.9
3	43.0	50.7	51.6	49.2	49.3	50.0	50.8	50.3
Total	43.9	48.7	51.5	47.5	44.6	48.2	48.7	46.8
Percentage heavy drinking								
Income tercile								
1	25.3	35.3	39.2	30.2	18.8	17.5	19.6	18.7
2	30.0	30.7	46.1	34.3	21.5	25.8	33.1	25.3
3	31.5	51.2	49.6	45.5	27.1	30.3	33.8	31.6
Total	28.3	39.6	46.8	37.1	21.5	24.9	31.8	25.7

Sources: English data is from first wave of ELSA. U.S. data is from the 2002 wave of the HRS.

Notes: Obesity is defined as BMI >30; overweight is defined as BMI between 25 and 30; heavy drinking is defined as drinking on more than four days per week in the HRS, and twice a day or more/daily or almost daily in the ELSA.

States, while they are only 6 percentage points larger in the highest income tercile.

Finally, there are higher rates of heavy drinking among men in England than in the United States. Because heavy drinking is more common among those at the top of the education and income strata, it is also an unlikely explanation for the concentration of disease among those at the bottom in either country, although more moderate drinking in high SES groups could contribute to lower heart disease risk.

This short summary suggests that, collectively, these behavioral risk factors cannot explain either one of our two main conclusions—the lower health status among American men compared to English men and the strong negative health gradient across both education and income groups in both countries.

To more precisely evaluate this, we estimated a set of ordinary least squares regressions on the prevalence of all of diseases—diabetes, hypertension, heart attacks, stroke, arthritis, lung disease, and cancer. These models included the three education groups and three income quintiles used in the SES stratification in table 10.1, and measures of the following risk factors (obesity, overweight, smoking, and excess drinking). By and large, the set of risk factors included in the analysis perform in the expected direction. For example, being obese and overweight is associated with higher rates of diabetes, hypertension, heart attacks, stroke, arthritis, and lung disease, and being a current smoker is strongly associated with lung disease and stroke. While not presented here, the inclusion of this standard set of risk factors and SES measures such as income and education at best can explain only 20 to 30 percent of the overall difference in male health status between these two countries. They also fail to explain much of the social gradient in health (see Banks et al. 2006). The major explanations, therefore, must lie elsewhere.

10.6   Differences in Reporting Health Outcomes across the Atlantic

Whether one uses prevalence of specific illness or general health status as the health outcome measure, our description of comparative health conditions in England and America thus far relies completely on respondent self-reports. We have already showed that self-reported conditions and self-reported general health give qualitatively different pictures of health differences between America and England, potentially rendering the use of self-reported general health scales for international comparisons problematic.

Even if we confine ourselves to disease prevalence, self-reports are known to have several potential problems. Diseases may be unreported due to limited contact with the medical system, and, even when previously diagnosed, individuals may confuse having the disease under control with its being cured. If those within lower SES groups are less likely to report a health problem that they actually have, these reporting problems may have a SES gradient of their own. For our purposes, however, the key issue is whether differential reporting of health problems, especially by SES, differs between England and America. Protocols and thresholds for specific disease diagnosis may not be the same in the two countries so that a similarly ill patient may be diagnosed with the disease in one country but not the other.

One way of addressing how important this issue is to examine biological markers of disease in both countries. There are two related questions we will ask using biological markers: (1) are the disease patterns by SES using clinical indicators of disease similar to those obtained with respondent self-reports in both countries; and (2) are any of the most important cross-country differences that we have identified using self-reports due to differential reporting of illness between the two countries? In a recent paper (Banks et al. 2006), we demonstrated that biological markers confirmed the conclusion of higher rates of disease in the United States compared to England. In this section, we examine a set of biological markers to assess the extent to which that conclusion remains true for men.

10.6.1 Diabetes

All participants aged twelve and over in the NHANES and the HSE were evaluated for diabetes with a glycosylated hemoglobin A1c (HbA1c) test. This test records average blood glucose over a period of two or three months (the number of glucose molecules attached to hemoglobin, a substance in red blood cells). While there is no strict diagnosis threshold value, we will initially follow the American convention by using values greater than or equal to 6.5 percent as indicating clinical diabetes. Although not usually a screener for diabetes, HbA1c is highly correlated with fasting plasma glucose levels.

Table 10.5 illustrates the correspondence between male respondents' self-reports on whether a doctor had told them they had diabetes and those based on the HbA1c values among those fifty-five to sixty-four years old in the NHANES and in the HSE. In both countries, diabetes prevalence based on the two measures is actually very similar (in the United States 10.9 percent for self-reports and 10.5 percent for clinical, while the corresponding measures in England are 6.8 percent and 6.3 percent, respectively). Similarly, in both countries, the vast majority of men are similarly labeled on both self- and clinical reports (United States = 95.2 percent; England = 95.9 percent). By far, the most important pattern in table 10.5

Table 10.5   **Relationship between self- and biological reports for diabetes (men aged 55–64; 6.5% cutoff on HbA1c)**

	United States			England		
	Self-report%		Row	Self-report%		Row
Biological report	No	Yes	total%	No	Yes	total%
No	87.0	2.1	89.1	91.4	1.8	93.2
Yes	2.5	8.4	10.9	2.3	4.5	6.8
Column total	89.5	10.5		93.7	6.3	

Sources: U.S. data from the NHANES 1999–2002—uses 6.5 percent cutoff on HbA1c. English data from the HSE 2003—uses 6.5 percent cutoff on HbA1c.

confirms that whether one uses self- or clinical reports, diabetes prevalence among men is much higher in the United States than it is in England.

The convention in the health field (at least in the United States) is to call those above the clinical threshold who do not self-report diabetes the "undiagnosed population." In this age group in the United States, there are 2.5 percent such men, implying an overall diabetes prevalence of 12.6 percent, or equivalently that 20 percent of male diabetes in this population is undiagnosed. In England, the group above the clinical threshold who do not self-report as diabetics constitutes 2.3 percent of men in this age group, a rate of undiagnosis of 28 percent, which would raise overall prevalence there to 8.6 percent. Accepting these sorts of calculations at face value would not alter our basic finding that male diabetes is a far more serious problem in America compared to England.

However, there are also men who claim that that they are diabetics but who fall below the clinical threshold. The convention in the health field apparently is not to allow false positives, arguing that medication or insulin is likely to have placed them below the threshold. Not allowing any offset is surely too extreme because we know in panel surveys like the HRS some respondents negate their prior self-reports of diabetes in subsequent rounds. Because this is not our central concern, we will not also allow any offsets.[5] It is worth noting that this subset of the male population is somewhat higher in the United States than in England (2.5 percent compared to 2.3 percent). This could reflect better management and adherence to medical regimens in the United States.

Rates of undiagnosed diabetes in the United States is 20 percent and in England 28 percent. Using the NHANES II, which covered the period between 1976 and 1980, self-reported diabetes prevalence for all whites between ages fifty-five to sixty-four was 6.0 percent, while the undiagnosed rate was 5.9 percent. Similarly, data from NHANES III (1998 to 1994) show that about one-third of people with diabetes are unaware they have diabetes because their diabetes has not been diagnosed (Harris et al. 1998). Based on the current waves of the NHANES, undiagnosed diabetes is apparently much less of an issue today in the United States than in the past. This means that the widely cited growth in reported diabetes prevalence may be overstated. It also raises the possibility that some part of higher contemporaneous prevalence in the United States compared to England could have resulted from lower rates of undiagnosed disease in America if England did not share in this rapid secular decline in undiagnosed disease. This possibility, however, is soundly rejected by our data.

---

5. For example, 40 percent of those twenty-five to seventy years old in the NHANES who self-reported that they had diabetes but were clinical below the threshold were not taking either insulin or medication. Similarly, 60 percent of those who self-reported that they had HBP but who were clinically below the threshold were not taking medication, reducing salt, exercising more, reducing alcohol, or controlling their weight to reduce their hypertension.

Table 10.6   **Comparison of self- and biological reports for diabetes by socioeconomic
status (men aged 40–70)**

	United States			England		
	Self-reports	Biological reports	Percentage undiagnosed	Self-reports	Biological eports	Percentage undiagnosed
Education						
Low	13.5	16.7	30.9	5.5	6.8	35.4
Middle	8.9	9.8	25.4	3.6	4.1	34.4
High	7.4	6.8	18.8	4.2	4.1	20.2
Income						
Low	12.7	14.7	28.2	7.5	6.8	25.1
Middle	7.7	6.7	18.8	2.8	2.9	34.3
High	5.2	5.1	15.6	3.2	4.5	31.3
All	8.6	8.9	23.3	4.4	4.8	29.3

Sources: U.S. data from the NHANES 1999–2002—uses 6.5 percent cutoff on HbA1c. English data from the HSE 2003—uses 6.5 percent cutoff on HbA1c.

In addition to overall rates of undiagnosed disease, our primary interest centers on how clinical and self-reports differ by SES. Table 10.6 facilitates this comparison by listing for both countries male prevalence rates by self- and clinical reports by education and income groups and, in the final column, the percent who are undiagnosed diabetics. Due to sample size consideration in the NHANES, the age group in this comparison is expanded to those male white non-Hispanics between ages forty to seventy. A similar age restriction is imposed on the English sample.

This table supports three conclusions. First, there is a strong SES gradient to male diabetes prevalence in both countries whether self-reports or clinical measures are used. Second, the gradient is even stronger for education using the clinical criteria. Third, and as a direct corollary, rates of undiagnosed diabetes are higher among those at the bottom of the education hierarchy. For example, in the United States, among those in the lowest education category, the percent of men with undiagnosed diabetes is 31 percent. The comparable numbers for those men in the highest education and income group is a 19 percent rate of undiagnosed diabetes. In each education cell, rates of undiagnosed diabetes are higher in England than in the United States.

While the 6.5 percent threshold used in table 10.5 represents the conventional American diagnostic threshold, some have argued that the standard threshold in England is 7 percent. Higher clinical thresholds are a possible explanation for the lower rates of both clinical and self-reported diabetes there. To check on this possibility, table 10.7 replicates table 10.5 except that a clinical threshold of 7 percent is used instead of 6.5 percent. While diabetes prevalence rates are necessarily lower, the two tables are vir-

Table 10.7   Relationship between self- and biological reports for diabetes (men aged 55–64; 7% cutoff on HbA1c)

	United States			England		
	Self-report%		Row	Self-report%		Row
Biological report	No	Yes	total%	No	Yes	total%
No	87.8	5.1	92.9	92.9	2.5	95.3
Yes	1.5	5.6	7.1	0.8	3.9	4.7
Column total	89.2	10.8		93.7	6.3	

Sources: U.S. data from the NHANES 1999–2002—uses 7 percent cutoff on HbA1c. English data from the HSE 2003—uses 7 percent cutoff on HbA1c.

Table 10.8   Relationship between self- and biological reports for high blood pressure (men aged 55–64)

	United States			England		
	Self-report%		Row	Self-report%		Row
Biological report	No	Yes	total%	No	Yes	total%
No	52.4	4.7	57.1	41.9	15.8	57.8
Yes	9.8	33.1	42.9	18.8	23.5	42.2
Column total	62.2	37.8		60.7	39.3	

Sources: U.S. data from the NHANES 1999–2002. English data from the HSE 2003.

tually identical in their message on across-country differences, indicating that there simply is not sufficient density around these thresholds to alter our conclusions by much.

10.6.2   High Blood Pressure

In the NHANES and HSE as well as the HRS and ELSA, self-reports of hypertension are based on a question of whether a physician has informed you that you have high blood pressure or hypertension. For the clinical definition, we follow the recommendations in the Sixth Report of the Joint National Committee on the Prevention, Detection, Evaluation and Treatment of High Blood Pressure (1997)—systolic blood pressure equal to or greater than 140 mm Hg and/or diastolic blood pressure equal to or greater than 90 mm Hg and/or taking medication.

Using the NHANES and HSE, tables 10.8 and 10.9 provide a comparison between self- and clinical reports for HBP using the same format employed in the preceding for diabetes. Once again, among male respondents between the ages of fifty-five to sixty-four years old, in the vast majority of cases (84 percent), the average diagnosis rate is the same using either the self- or biological criteria. The rate of undiagnosed hypertension in this age group is 21 percent. Similar to diabetes, there has also been a steady secu-

Table 10.9   **Comparison of self- and biological reports for hypertension by socioeconomic status (men aged 40–70)**

	United States			England		
	Self-reports	Biological reports	Percentage undiagnosed	Self-reports	Biological reports	Percentage undiagnosed
Education						
Low	37.8	38.7	17.1	36.6	41.1	36.4
Middle	31.0	35.6	24.9	33.1	36.3	36.3
High	26.9	31.2	26.3	28.7	32.8	37.3
Income						
Low	34.0	37.8	22.2	42.7	40.0	27.6
Middle	25.0	29.7	28.9	28.8	34.9	40.0
High	28.7	32.0	23.5	27.9	32.0	38.4
All	29.3	33.2	24.6	32.0	36.0	36.7

Sources: U.S. data from the NHANES 1999–2002. English data from the HSE 2003.

lar decline in "undiagnosed hypertension in the United States." According to the Center for Disease Control and Prevention (CDC) Web site on Healthy People 2010, "Comparing the 1976–80 National Health and Nutrition Examination Survey (NHANES II) and the 1988–1991 survey (NHANES III, phase 1) reveals an increase from 51% to 73% in the proportion of persons who were aware that they had high blood pressure."

However, 5 percent of respondents say that they have HBP although their clinical readings claim otherwise. This group represents some unknown amalgam of the presence of false positives or individuals who may be controlling their HBP through means other than medication. Both clinical and self-reports of hypertension indicate a very strong SES gradient across either income or education.[6] However, in contrast to diabetes, the percent of individuals who are undiagnosed with HBP does not appear to rise with either dimension of SES, and, if anything, it may increase slightly.

The three remaining clinical measures that we examine are C-reactive protein, fibrinogen, and cholesterol. In these cases, there is no matching respondent self-reports, so the primary issue becomes whether the nature of the gradient and the differences across countries are similar to those obtained for self-reports on diseases for which these clinical measurements are well-established risk factors. This will include, in particular, cardiovascular disease and, to a lesser extent, arthritis. Table 10.10 lists data for men aged 40–70 for all these biological markers where the stratifying SES variable is education. A similar format is used in table 10.11 using family income terciles as the SES marker.

---

6. Note that there is a difference in the ranking of the two countries in hypertension prevalence in using the HSE and ELSA as the source. The reasons for this discrepancy are not apparent.

Table 10.10 Comparison of male self- and biological reports (aged 40–70), by years of schooling

	England				United States			
	Low	Medium	High	All	Low	Medium	High	All
Diabetes								
% prevalence (self-reports)	5.5	3.6	4.2	4.4	13.5	8.9	7.4	8.6
% prevalence (biological reports)[a]	6.8	4.1	4.1	4.8	16.7	9.8	6.8	8.9
Hypertension								
% prevalence (self-reports)	36.6	33.1	28.7	32.0	37.8	31.0	26.9	29.3
% prevalence (biological reports)[b]	41.1	36.3	32.8	36.0	38.7	35.6	31.2	33.2
C-reactive protein								
% high risk[c]	36.2	28.3	22.7	27.7	47.1	35.2	28.4	32.5
% moderate risk[d]	40.2	42.5	38.1	39.9	34.5	39.7	37.6	37.7
% low risk[e]	23.6	29.2	39.2	32.3	18.4	25.1	34.1	29.9
Mean (mg/dL)	0.41	0.34	0.29	0.33	0.51	0.38	0.31	0.36
Median (mg/dL)	0.20	0.17	0.13	0.16	0.28	0.20	0.15	0.18

Fibrinogen								
% high risk[f]	11.9	8.8	7.3	8.8	31.8	24.5	17.6	21.2
Mean (mg/dL)	309	302	287	296	377	355	342	350
Median (mg/dL)	300	290	280	290	367	347	333	342
HDL cholesterol								
% high[g]	22.3	25.9	30.8	27.2	12.5	9.4	14.3	12.9
% normal[h]	61.7	58.8	60.1	60.1	49.8	52.3	55.4	53.9
% low[i]	16.0	15.3	9.2	12.8	37.7	38.3	30.3	33.2
Mean (mg/dL)	52.1	52.9	54.9	53.6	45.3	43.5	46.9	45.9
Median (mg/dL)	50.3	50.3	54.2	50.3	42	42	45	44

Sources: U.S. data from the NHANES 1999–2002. English data from the HSE 2003.

Notes: See table 10.1 for definitions of income and education groups.

[a]HbA1c greater than 6.5 percent.

[b]Blood pressure equal to or greater than 140 mm Hg and/or diastolic blood pressure equal to or greater than 90 mm Hg and/or taking medication.

[c].3 mg/dL or higher.

[d]Between .1 mg/dL and .3 mg/dL.

[e].1 mg/dL or lower.

[f]400 mg/dL or higher.

[g]60 mg/dL or higher.

[h]Between 40 mg/dL and 60 mg/dL.

[i]40 mg/dL or lower.

Table 10.11   Comparisons of male self- and biological reports (aged 40–70), by income tercile (%)

	England				United States			
	Low	Medium	High	All	Low	Medium	High	All
Diabetes								
% prevalence (self-reports)	7.5	2.8	3.2	4.4	12.7	7.7	5.2	8.6
% prevalence (biological report)[a]	6.8	2.9	4.5	4.8	14.7	6.7	5.1	8.9
Hypertension								
% prevalence (self-reports)	42.7	28.8	27.9	32.0	34.0	25.0	28.7	29.3
% prevalence (biological report)[b]	40.0	34.9	32.0	36.0	37.8	29.7	32.0	33.2
C-reactive protein								
% high risk[c]	34.8	23.8	23.1	27.7	39.0	31.8	26.6	32.5
% moderate risk[d]	40.5	39.9	39.3	39.9	37.6	40.1	35.6	37.7
% low risk[e]	24.7	36.3	37.6	32.3	23.4	28.1	37.8	29.9
Mean (mg/dL)	0.43	0.27	0.30	0.33	0.42	0.35	0.30	0.36
Median (mg/dL)	0.19	0.14	0.14	0.16	0.23	0.18	0.13	0.18

Fibrinogen								
% high risk[f]	10.8	8.3	7.7	8.8	29.1	19.2	15.3	21.2
Mean (mg/dL)	311	294	288	297	365	348	335	350
Median (mg/dL)	300	290	280	290	358	340	326	342
HDL cholesterol								
% high[g]	24.4	26.2	33.3	27.2	13.4	10.3	14.8	12.9
% normal[h]	61.6	60.9	55.5	60.1	51.0	56.3	54.5	53.9
% low[i]	14.0	12.9	11.2	12.8	35.6	33.4	30.7	33.2
Mean (mg/dL)	52.9	53.2	55.2	53.6	45.9	45.2	46.6	45.9
Median (mg/dL)	50.3	50.3	54.2	50.3	43	44	45	44

Sources: U.S. data from the NHANES 1999–2002. English data from the HSE 2003.

Note: See notes to table 10.4.

[a]HbA1c greater than 6.5 percent.

[b]Blood pressure equal to or greater than 140 mm Hg and/or diastolic blood pressure equal to or greater than 90 mm Hg and/or taking medication.

[c].3 mg/dL or higher.

[d]Between .1 mg/dL and .3 mg/dL.

[e].1 mg/dL or lower.

[f]400 mg/dL or higher.

[g]60 mg/dL or higher.

[h]Between 40 mg/dL and 60 mg/dL.

[i]40 mg/dL or lower.

10.6.3   C-Reactive Protein

C-reactive protein (CRP) is an acute phase reactant released in response to acute injury, infection, or other inflammatory stimuli. Plaques in diseased arteries quite often contain inflammatory cells, and the release of acute phase reactants in response to this type of inflammation have been proposed as a marker for arteriosclerosis. Several studies have shown a positive association between C-reactive protein and coronary artery disease and that it serves as a good marker for future cardiovascular events (Mendall et al. 1996).

C-reactive protein measures the concentration of a protein in serum that indicates acute inflammation and possible arthritis. Tests for C-reactive protein were conducted on respondents in the NHANES and the HSE. Once again, we will be following convention by categorizing measurement into three groups "3 mg/L" or higher indicates high risk, between "1" and "3" is moderate risk, and less than "1" is low risk.

There are several quite striking patterns. First, male levels of C-reactive protein are higher in the United States than in England. To illustrate, among those forty to seventy years old, 33 percent of American men have levels placing them within the high-risk group compared to only 28 percent of English men of the same age. Second, health gradients are clearly alive and well in both countries for both education and income using C-reactive protein. In the United States, for example, 47 percent of those in the lowest education group are at high risk compared to 28 percent of those in the highest schooling class. In England, the comparable numbers are 36 percent and 23 percent, respectively. Across both the income and education dimensions, there appears to be a somewhat steeper gradient in the United States compared to England.

10.6.4   Fibrinogen

Fibrinogen is a protein produced by the liver that circulates in the blood and helps stop bleeding by assisting blood clots to form. High fibrinogen has been identified as an important risk factor for CVD. Fibrinogen and C-reactive protein levels appear to rise in response to stress stimuli and to take longer to return to normal levels among those in lower SES groups (Steptoe and Marmot 2004). The normal range is 200 to 400 mg/dl (mg/dl = milligrams per deciliter) and above 400 is considered a high risk for heart disease.

Tables 10.10 and 10.11 also document U.S. and English gradients in high risk for men aged forty to seventy.[7] Once again, these can only be described as dramatically higher levels in the United States. The percent at high risk in the United States is more than twice as large as it is in England, consis-

7. In the NHANES, fibrinogen tests are performed on those forty and over.

tent with the much higher levels of heart disease in America obtained from self-reports. Twenty-one percent of American men have measured fibrinogen levels that place them at high risk—the comparable rates in England are only 9 percent.

Among all of our clinical measures, fibrinogen exhibits perhaps the sharpest SES gradients, a statement that would be equally true whether we used education or income to stratify the data. These social health gradients are much steeper in the United States than they are in the England. For example, compare American men in the lowest education group with those in the highest education group—32 percent of those in the bottom are at high risk compared to only 18 percent of those at the top. The comparable numbers in England are 12 percent and 7 percent, respectively.

10.6.5   Cholesterol

Heart disease is caused by narrowing of the coronary arteries feeding the heart (arteriosclerosis). When the coronary arteries become narrowed by cholesterol and fat deposits and cannot supply enough blood to the heart, the result is CHD. When there is too much cholesterol in the bloodstream, some of the excess is deposited in the coronary arteries, where it contributes to the narrowing and blockages that can cause heart disease. The bad cholesterol, low-density lipoproteins (LDL-C), carries most of the cholesterol in the blood and is the main source of damaging buildup and blockage in the arteries. The NHANES and the HSE also contain measures of HDL-C the "good cholesterol" because high levels of HDL reduce risk for coronary heart disease by preventing plaques). We divide HDL-C levels into three groups—more than or equal to 60 mg/dL, which we describe as "high," 40 to 60mg/dl labeled "normal," and below 40 "low." Levels in our high range have been established as reducing the risk of heart disease.

Tables 10.10 and 10.11 present a parallel presentation for HDL-C. Once again, there are large differences in this biological marker favoring the English over the Americans. Remembering that high HDL-C is good for cardiovascular health, slightly less than one-third of Americans in our age range of fifty-five to sixty-four have levels in this range. The comparable number in the HSE sample is 45 percent. Almost three times as many Americans have low HDL readings compared to the English.

For income and especially for education, there are very sharp gradients in HDL-C levels in America compared to England. For example, among Americans between the ages of forty to seventy who have less than a twelfth grade education, 12.5 percent have high levels of HDL-C with an average reading of 45.3. In contrast, among Americans who have more than twelve years of schooling, 14.3 percent have high HDL-C, with a mean amount of 46.9. A similar if slightly muted gradient across income groups is also evident. When we combine and compare the education and income groups, those simultaneously in the highest education and income groups have more than twice the prevalence of HDL-C as those in the bottom end of both (35 percent compared to 16 percent). The social gradient in HDL levels is much more muted across either education or income in England.

10.7   The Use of Absolute or Relative Income Scales

Using terciles of income in both countries, income gradients appear to be steeper in the United States compared to England. Although we have largely followed convention for such international comparisons, we have been silent on the appropriate metric to adopt on the income scale. By using measures such as terciles, we have at least implicitly endorsed a relative income metric without really justifying it. The principal alternative is to compare social health gradients using absolute income levels in both countries. Although one can derive one from another with knowledge of the distribution of income, these comparative gradients will generally not be the same as one moves between an absolute and relative income metric.

For example, suppose that the two health-absolute income gradients are parallel and negatively sloped in the two countries, but that income dispersion is higher in the United States than in England (as it is). Then health income gradients across percentiles, terciles, deciles, or quintiles or any type of relative income metric will necessarily steepen in the United States compared to England when relative income metrics are used. Higher income dispersion in the United States compared to England necessarily implies that, compared to slopes measured on an absolute income scale, there will be a greater increase in slope of the U.S. health gradient (compared to the English one) when placed on the relative income scale.

Given this, the comparative nature of health gradients on alternative income scales cannot not tell us whether it is absolute or relative income that matters for health outcomes. Other tests are more appropriate to distinguish between them. For example, if all that matters for health is relative income, then preserving dispersion, income growth should not matter for health. Similarly, if all that matters is absolute income, increasing dispersion at the top of the income distribution should not affect health outcomes of those at the bottom of the income hierarchy. These are the correct tests for deciding whether absolute or relative income matters and not a comparison of which of these two health gradients are steeper in the United States compared to England.

In an international context, moving from relative income health gradients to absolute income gradients is more complicated then is generally recognized. There are several issues that have to be resolved. First, one must decide how to convert incomes measured in the currencies of one country into another. Purchasing power parity (PPP) is generally the preferred method because it is less subject to the vagaries of sharp financial fluctuations that can affect exchange rates. Purchasing power parity estimates are available and debated vigorously, but the conceptual and implementation problems here go beyond those thorny issues. In fact, it is these problems that make the use of relative scales so popular as all that matters are within-country rankings into groups.

We can illustrate the difficulties with the steps necessary to convert incomes to the same absolute scale using the ELSA and HRS. For openers, incomes are measured on a before-tax basis in the HRS but after tax in the ELSA, so it was necessary first to convert the ELSA incomes to before-tax, and there is undoubtedly some imprecision in our conversion. But the issues go beyond taxes.

To illustrate, table 10.12 gives a comparison of income levels and distributions in England and the United States as recorded in the ELSA and HRS for a sample of those fifty-five to sixty-four years old. To give an alternative benchmark in each country, data are also provided from the American Current Population Survey (CPS) and from the English Family Resources Survey (FRS). In this age group, using ELSA and HRS to measure reality, mean family incomes are 78 percent higher in the United States compared to England. These income differences expand noticeably across the income distribution—for example, 68 percent at the median and 95 percent at the 95th percentile. Two contributing factors to this magnitude are that two low-income groups—African Americans and Latinos—have been excluded from the American sample, and income differences between the two countries reach their peak at in this age group. An overvalued American currency could also overstate the real differences, but even with those caveats in mind, the across-country income difference seems large.

A significant part of this difference flows from the fact that family incomes in the HRS are much higher than those reported in the CPS for the same demographic subset of the population. For example, the HRS mean family income is 17 percent higher than the CPS, and the difference between these two U.S. surveys expands as we move up the income distribu-

Table 10.12   **Family income comparisons across the household surveys (Aged 55–64)**

Percentile	HRS	CPS	ELSA ($)	FRS ($)
Mean	80,928	68,918	45,560	47,432
25th	30,000	27,756	18,271	21,926
50th	56,192	52,000	33,256	37,106
75th	97,000	88,112	54,505	59,903
90th	167,400	136,500	85,109	89,286
95th	228,188	180,400	117,126	115,096

Notes: Sample—families with a head between the ages of fifty-five to sixty-four years old. All data are weighted.

tion. The difference between these two surveys is 8 percent at the median and 26 percent at the 95th percentile. Thus, if the CPS were compared to ELSA, the mean income difference between the two countries would be only 51 percent instead of 78 percent. Incomes in ELSA are about 4 percent lower than those obtained from the FRS so that a CPS-FRS yields a cross-country income differential of 45 percent.

The question then is whether one should believe the HRS or CPS, which requires first an understanding of why their reports of family income could be so different. Table 10.13 separates out that component of mean family incomes in the two surveys that flow from income from capital, and within that subcomponent the amount that is self-employment income and the amount that is the return on financial assets.

Income from capital essentially accounts for all the differences in mean income between the CPS and HRS. Within total capital income, three-quarters of the difference between the two surveys appears in a single item—self-employment income, which, on average, are almost $9,000 higher in the HRS compared to the CPS. This most likely stems from a difference in the questions asked. In the CPS, respondents are asked a net income question of the form, "How much did (name/you) earn from (his/her/your) own business after expenses?" In contrast, the question asked in the HRS is a gross income question of the form "about how much did your self-employment income amount to the last calendar year, including any profits left in the business, and before taxes and other deductions?" The form of the HRS question is unfortunate. Expenses are not income, and this creates an unnecessary inconsistency between HRS income measurement and the other prominent American surveys that attempt to measure income.

Income from financial assets (largely dividends and interest) accounted for the rest of the difference between the HRS and CPS. The issues involved in measuring these components of income were addressed in Hurd, Juster, and Smith (2003). A major innovation in the HRS was a change in the way this type of income was measured. In its original waves, the HRS measured capital income in a way very similar to that in the CPS. When these household survey measures were compared to those in National Accounts, it was

Table 10.13   Comparing CPS and HRS measures of family income

	CPS	HRS	Difference
Total family income	68,918	80,928	12,010
Total capital income	8,663	20,733	12,070
Self-employment income	4,400	13,268	8,868
Other income	4,263	7,465	3,202

Notes: Sample—families with a head between the ages of fifty-five to sixty-four years old. All data are weighted.

found that reporting in the household surveys was about half of the total from the National Accounts. The measurement innovation adopted by the HRS was to integrate questions about capital income with questions about the existence and amount of wealth held in the assets that produced that income. This integration produced in the HRS an across-wave increase of 63 percent in the amount of income derived from financial assets, real estate investments, and farm and business equity. As a result, capital income flows as measured in the HRS were now much closer to those in the National Accounts.

It is likely then that some of the differences between the CPS and HRS reflect better measurement in the HRS, and some reflect a poor question choice in the HRS for the self-employment component. Because our main interest rests in the American-English comparison, we would also conclude that incomes as measured in the HRS are to some degree artificially high relative to those in the ELSA. It is difficult to establish precisely the magnitudes involved, but HRS incomes could be as much as 10 percent too high at the mean with an even larger discrepancy at the top tiers of the income distribution.

These measurement issues can have important implications for how we interpret the income gradient in health across countries. Not only are income levels in the United States higher on average in the HRS, but also American income as measured by the HRS is more dispersed than the CPS indicates. The implications for the social health gradient are twofold. At a given income level, health will be worse in the HRS compared to the CPS, and the health gradient will become less steep in the HRS compared to the CPS.

To illustrate the problems involved in comparing health gradients across countries, Figures 10.1 and 10.2 plot for both countries the fraction of men in excellent or very good health (figure 10.1) and fair or poor health (figure 10.2) using income deciles in both England and the United States. From these graphs, we would conclude both that American men are healthier than English men (which is we know is false and due only to the use of self-reported general health) and that income health gradients are steeper in the United States compared to the England.

Figures 10.3 and 10.4 plot the same data but with each decile point indexed to an absolute income per week metric in both countries. Where one places these graphs for each country depends, of course, on the rate of conversion used between dollars and pounds (as well as on an assumption that this conversion rule does not vary by income position and certainly does not vary differentially by income position in the two countries). For these graphs, we used the 2002 exchange rate, which ex post may well represent an overvalued dollar. On each curve, data are marked by dark boxes (United States) and lighter circles (England).

The shape of the social gradient in health story now is quite different.

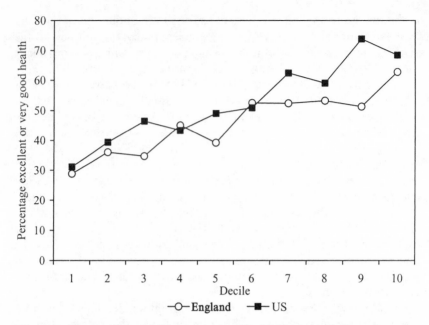

Fig. 10.1 Percentage in excellent or very good health by income deciles

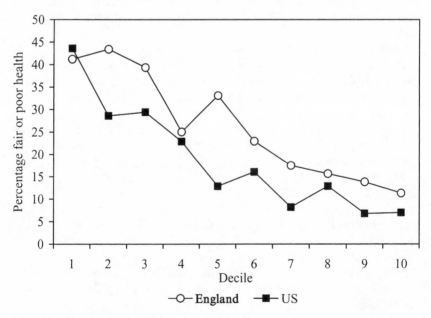

Fig. 10.2 Percentage in fair or poor health by income deciles

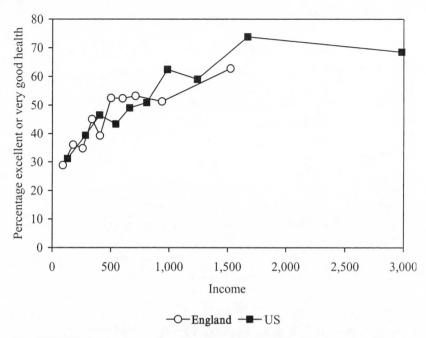

Fig. 10.3   Percentage in excellent or very good health by income

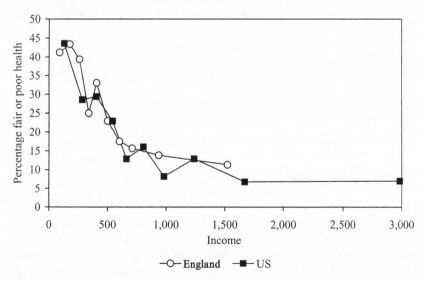

Fig. 10.4   Percentage in fair or poor health by income

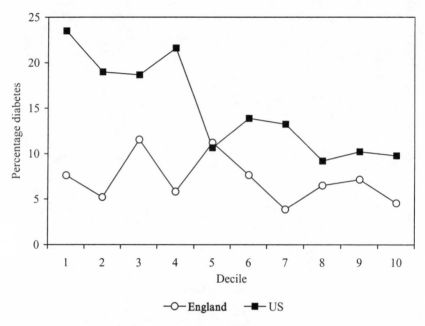

Fig. 10.5   Percentage with diabetes by income deciles

Across most of the income distribution, the curves lie essentially on top of each other so that at each income, male general health status (GHS) is the same in both countries, and the gradients are equally negatively sloped. The principal difference between the two countries in figures 10.3 and 10.4 is that the U.S. curve extends out much farther to the right given the much higher concentration of income at the top in the United States. Because those Americans within the extended part of the U.S. curve are relatively healthy, translating the data in figure 10.3 into figure 10.1 produces a U.S. curve that is above and steeper than the English health gradient.

Of course, we have argued that general health status is a treacherous health measure for international comparisons, so we will rely now instead on some comparisons based on disease prevalence.

Figures 10.5 to 10.10 compare the relative and absolute income gradients for three diseases—diabetes, heart diseases, and diseases of the lung—for which there appeared to be significant prevalence differences between the countries. Figures 10.5 and 10.6, which plot the prevalence of diabetes in the two countries, show that whether relative or income scales are used, male diabetes prevalence is higher in the United States compared to England. Across both absolute and relative income metrics, the differences between the two countries appear highest in the lower tiers of the income hierarchy, but they never fully disappear even among the highest income groups.

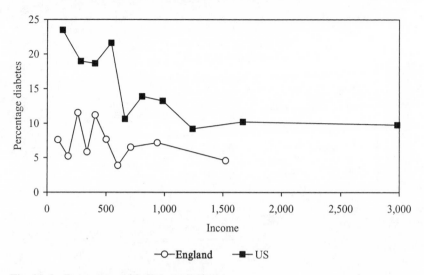

Fig. 10.6   Percentage with diabetes by income

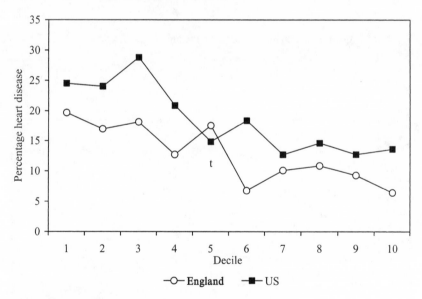

Fig. 10.7   Percentage with heart disease by income deciles

Figures 10.7 and 10.8 have a parallel set of plots for heart disease. Once again using either the relative or absolute income metric, at each income level, heart disease is more common among American men compared to their English counterparts. Using either metric, there is a sharp negative gradient in heart disease as one moves from the bottom to the top of the income hierarchy in both countries—and these figures also indicate that this

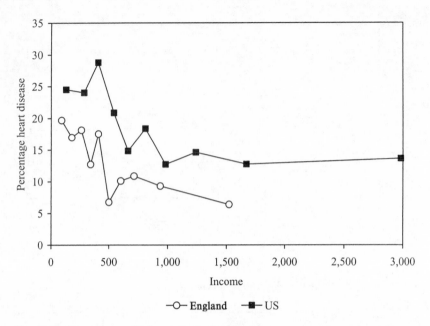

Fig. 10.8   Percentage with heart disease by income

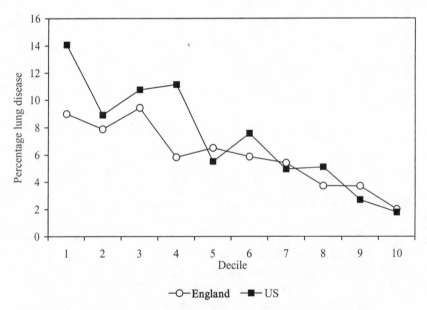

Fig. 10.9   Percentage with lung disease by income deciles

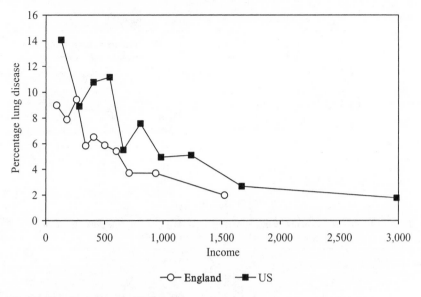

Fig. 10.10   Percentage with lung disease by income

income gradient goes well beyond the terciles we presented in early sections, extending to the 10th and 90th percentiles of the income distribution. These steep income health gradients also characterize diseases of the lung, which are plotted in figures 10.9 and 10.10—diseases of the lung are almost seven times more likely among American men in the lowest income decile compared to those in the highest income decile. While not quite as steep, the income gradients are also steeply downward sloped across the income distribution in England.

10.8   The Role of Feedbacks from Health to Income

In the overall project of which this paper represents an early progress report, we plan to investigate several important factors that may account for the different shape of the social health gradient in these two countries. Among other things, these factors will include the nature and organization of work in England and the United States, the manner in which social and power structures are organized and the hierarchies that result from them, and the relative importance of feedback effects from health to SES in the two countries. In this paper, we present an initial examination of the possible differential feedbacks from health to income in England and the United States.

Studies based on the HRS have shown that, especially in the preretirement age groups considered, here there are significant feedbacks from health shocks to labor force exits and to lower household incomes (Smith

Table 10.14   Poor health and work by income quartile: England

	Fraction in poor health (income quartile within age)				Fraction not working (income quartile within age)			
Age	1	2	3	4	1	2	3	4
50–53	0.313	0.164	0.127	0.060	0.336	0.075	0.037	0.030
54–57	0.360	0.258	0.098	0.117	0.409	0.209	0.079	0.067
58–61	0.331	0.270	0.162	0.099	0.697	0.426	0.211	0.184
62–65	0.354	0.380	0.233	0.140	0.838	0.729	0.434	0.442
66–69	0.339	0.382	0.274	0.130	0.952	0.878	0.879	0.642

Source: ELSA 2002.

Table 10.15   Proportion in poor health by work status: England (low education group—bottom income quartile)

	Work status	
Age	Working	Not working
50–53	0.238	0.800
54–57	0.077	0.850
58–61	0.000	0.571
62–65	0.143	0.463
66–69	0.000	0.354

1999, 2004). The new availability of ELSA allows us to take an initial look at whether similar feedbacks exist in England. Given the greater governmental support system in England compared to the United States, we anticipate that labor force exits due to health shocks might even be larger in England than in the United States, but that the income losses associated with these exits might be smaller.

Tables 10.14 and 10.15 (for England) and 10.16 and 10.17 (for the United States) provide an initial look at this issue by breaking down the income patterns we saw earlier into finer age groups across which labor market participation will differ. The left-hand panels show the fraction of those in poor or fair health at each age-specific income quartile. Especially for those in their early fifties, a large fraction of those in the bottom income quartile self-report themselves in poor health in both countries. For example, among those who are aged fifty-four to fifty-seven, one-third of those in the bottom income quartile self-report their health as poor or fair in England—the corresponding fraction in the United States is 42 percent.

In both countries, these fractions in poor health decline significantly as one moves up the income quartiles. In this age group, the fraction in poor or fair health is only one in every four in the second to the bottom income quartile and is about 12 percent in the highest income quartile. An even

Table 10.16   **Poor health and work by income quartile: United States**

Age	Fraction in poor health (income quartile within age)				Fraction not working (income quartile within age)			
	1	2	3	4	1	2	3	4
50–53	0.357	0.152	0.102	0.056	0.293	0.084	0.058	0.041
54–57	0.419	0.184	0.115	0.069	0.391	0.150	0.108	0.071
58–61	0.430	0.213	0.146	0.075	0.544	0.313	0.224	0.143
62–65	0.438	0.239	0.166	0.098	0.746	0.622	0.521	0.346
66–69	0.418	0.275	0.200	0.107	0.838	0.772	0.734	0.738

Source: HRS.

Table 10.17   **Proportion in poor health by work status: United States (low education group—bottom income quartile)**

Age	Work status	
	Working	Not working
50–53	0.265	0.687
54–57	0.273	0.704
58–61	0.291	0.705
62–65	0.314	0.566
66–69	0.290	0.496

Source: HRS.

more sharply declining fraction in poor health exists in the United States where the percent in poor health in the highest income quartile is about 7 percent among men of this age group.

These patterns by themselves are simply another way of expressing the social health gradient along the income divide and tell us nothing about the underlying mechanisms at work. The right-hand panels in these tables provide a step in that direction. These panels document for the same income quartiles the fraction in each quartile who are not working. A large fraction of those in the bottom income quartile again in both countries are not working even for those aged fifty-four to fifty-seven. In England, 41 percent of those in the bottom income quartile are not working compared to 7 percent who are not working in the highest income quartile. In this age group at least, the numbers who are not working are almost identical in the United States.

We have established then that in both England and the United States that nonwork and poor health are important attributes of those at the lower end of the income distribution and that work and good health characterize those at the top of the income distribution. But is there a reason to believe that nonwork and poor health are related?

Tables 10.15 and 10.17 complete the thought by showing that a very large fraction of those who are not working in the lowest income quartile in both countries self-report themselves in poor health. In England, 85 percent of those aged 54–57 in poor health are not working—in the United States, the corresponding fraction is 70 percent. Poor health is more closely related to nonwork in England than in the United States, lending some support to our first conjecture in the preceding that at least in these age groups, poor health is more likely to lead to labor force exit in England than in the United States.

These patterns in both countries are suggestive that there may well be important feedbacks from health to labor force exits to low incomes. While the strength of these pathways from health to income during the preretirement years has been established in the United States (Smith 1999, 2004), very little is currently known about them in England. The ELSA data now provides the opportunity for such a test. Even though our analysis does not use wave 2 data, ELSA is derived from a sample of individuals who had previously participated in the HSE, and there exists sufficient information about their labor force activity and incomes to estimate the impact of a new health event on both labor force activity and income.

Our tests for England of the pathway from health shocks to labor force exits, and any reductions in income that may accompany these exits are provided in tables 10.18 and 10.19. In table 10.18, we estimate the probability of a labor force exit for ELSA respondents between the time they participated in the 1998 HSE and the ELSA baseline interview. The 1998 HSE specialized in heart disease so that we can monitor the impacts of new illnesses of this type between these waves. In addition to controls for education, age, gender, marital status, and whether a person hit the state pension ages between 1998 and 2002, we also control for baseline health in the form

Table 10.18   **Probits for probability of stopping work**

Stopwork	dF/dx	z
Middle education	−.406	(2.83)
High education	−.286	(1.77)
Male	−.041	(2.07)
Age in 1998	.009	(3.26)
Middle education • age in 1998	.009	(2.67)
High education • age in 1998	.005	(1.56)
Married/cohabitation in 1998	.044	(2.04)
Hits state pension age between 1998 and 2002	.189	(5.51)
SRH = good	−.130	(2.76)
SRH = very good	−.230	(4.46)
SRH = excellent	−.202	(4.06)
Onset of diabetes/high blood pressure/angina	.041	(1.42)
Onset of heart attack/stroke	.221	(3.01)

Sources: The HSE (1998) and ELSA (2002).

Table 10.19   **Percentage change in family income**

	dF/dx	z	dF/dx	dF/dx
Middle education	.126	(0.78)	.121	(0.75)
High education	−.061	(0.39)	−.032	(0.21)
Male	.014	(0.91)	.029	(1.82)
Age in 1998	−.002	(0.94)	−.005	(1.98)
Middle education • age in 1998	−.002	(0.87)	−.002	(0.84)
High education • age in 1998	.001	(0.44)	.001	(0.23)
Married/cohabitation in 1998	.014	(0.78)	.017	(0.95)
SRH = good	.070	(1.39)	.057	(1.13)
SRH = very good	.110	(2.27)	.092	(1.90)
SRH = excellent	.088	(1.79)	.069	(1.41)
Hits state pension age between 1998 and 2002			.159	(5.08)
Hits state pension age • stops work			−.169	(5.31)
Onset of diabetes/high blood pressure/angina	−.007	(0.33)	−.004	(0.16)
Onset of heart attack/stroke	−.187	(3.30)	−.169	(3.00)
Cons	−.393	(3.32)	−.248	(1.85)

Sources: The HSE (1998) and ELSA (2002).

of self-reported health status. Two measures of new health events or health shocks are used, both involving the onset of an illness between the 1998 HSE and the baseline ELSA waves. The first represents the onset of a serious health shock—heart attacks and strokes—while the second includes less serious health onsets (diabetes, HBP, and angina).

Two equations are estimated. The first is a probit for the probability of a labor force exit between these two waves (table 10.18). The results obtained for the variables other than the new health events are as expected. The probability of a labor force exit declines with education, is lower for men than women, and increases in age. The probability of an exit is also higher is an individual becomes age eligible for a state pension between the two waves.

There are two types of health variables in this model. The first measures self-reported general health status at baseline, and labor force exits decrease as baseline health improves. Because the outcome conditions on working at baseline, this may suggest that new health events (not captured by our two measures) are more likely for the less healthy at baseline. Finally, there are two measures of new health events that are included in our model. For these variables, our estimates mimic findings from the HRS (see Smith 2004). In particular, serious health onsets (the onset of a heart attack or stroke) are strong predictors of labor market exits, while the onsets of more minor conditions have a much more reduced impact on work.

The second model is the percent family income change between the two waves (table 10.19). Our estimates indicate that a serious health onset reduces family income by 19 percent, while, not surprisingly given the small labor market effects, the impact of minor onsets is quite small. The second model listed in table 10.19 adds a control that indicates that the respondent reaches the state pension age between the waves. Reaching the state pension is associated with a reduction in family incomes of 17 percent if the individual stops working, indicating that there is not full income replacement associated with retirement. This implied replacement rate is quite similar to those computed in Banks, Blundell, and Smith (2003).

The estimates in the second model also indicate that family income reductions due to severe health shocks also result in family income declines of about 17 percent, very similar to those incurred for those who stop work due to reaching the state pension age. This suggests that overall income replacement rates are roughly similar no matter what the reason for labor market exit.

These results represent at best an initial stab at these important issues. They do suggest that feedbacks from health to labor force activity and to income are an important part of the SES health income gradient in England as well as the United States. Further analysis using the second wave of ELSA will be better able to provide more definitive tests of the differences as well as similarities that exist across countries.

10.9   Wealth as an Alternative Marker for the Social Gradient in Health

The simultaneous availability of alternative measures of financial resources beyond the traditional use of household income has sparked interest both in how these new measures impact on health and how they may also be affected by health. The most important of these new measures involves the financial wealth held by individuals and families. Even among families with the same amount of income, there is a substantial variation in the amount of financial wealth they possess. There are also large differences in financial wealth holdings between England and the United States (Banks, Blundell, and Smith 2003). Among those between ages forty and sixty, for example, Banks, Blundell, and Smith report that mean financial assets are more than twice as large in American households compared to English households although some of these differences are offset by higher housing wealth in Britain. These differences become much bigger at the top of the financial wealth distributions. At the 90th percentile, American households held $172,000 in financial assets compared to only $62,000 among English households. Financial wealth is far more unequally distributed than is family income, and this is much truer in America than in England.

The independent effects of wealth on health status over and above any impact income may have is a largely unexplored topic of research although accumulated wealth—in particular, the indication it gives of permanent income levels and the security it provides over and above current income—

could well link differently with health outcomes. In recent papers, Smith (1999, 2004) reported that neither financial assets nor family income predicted the new onset of disease among American middle-aged adults. On the other hand, Smith estimated relatively large effects of new health events on the wealth holdings of mature American households. Whether these results applied to England is very much an open question, the resolution of which must await analysis on multiple waves of the ELSA panel.

We rely here only on cross-sectional comparisons of social health gradients in the 2002 HRS and ELSA data using net financial wealth as the alternative SES marker. Table 10.20 lists prevalence rates of the same diseases listed in table 10.1, but now these prevalences are arrayed by quintiles of financial wealth instead of income.

Negative health gradients also exist in both countries across financial wealth quintiles, and once again the differences between the two countries in the overall levels of disease is enough to dominate the comparisons across wealth groups. For example, even though Americans in the highest quintile of net financial wealth have far more assets than English men do in any of their wealth quintiles, rates of diabetes are higher in the United States—American men in the highest wealth quintile have a minimum of $146,900 in net financial assets, while English men in the lowest wealth quintile have less than $800. But rates of diabetes in these two groups are about the same. Financial resources alone are clearly not sufficient to prevent diabetes.

Relatively speaking, however, the steepness of the gradients in health across the net financial wealth distribution is not so strikingly different across countries than in the income case. Indeed, if anything, the gradients

Table 10.20   **Health outcomes by net financial wealth (men aged 54–64)**

Net financial wealth quintile/range ($ thousands)	Diabetes	Hypertension	Heart attack	Stroke	Heart disease	Lung disease	Cancer
England							
1: <0.8	9.8	37.6	11.5	6.0	18.2	10.6	5.5
2: 0.8–14.4	7.7	36.8	6.9	3.0	16.4	6.3	2.7
3: 14.4–46.4	7.0	35.9	4.8	1.5	10.7	4.9	2.7
4: 46.4–112.7	5.6	32.9	5.0	2.8	9.4	5.1	2.5
5: >112.7	5.6	29.4	3.7	1.5	8.5	2.3	4.6
United States							
1: <0.5	21.0	54.2	15.4	5.3	25.9	13.1	4.5
2: 0.5–10.5	16.5	46.0	10.0	6.5	17.9	6.4	6.0
3: 10.5–42.3	10.6	46.5	5.6	3.2	14.5	5.9	9.7
4: 42.3–146.9	14.5	47.6	5.0	2.5	16.3	6.3	6.8
5: >146.9	10.2	40.5	4.8	2.7	15.8	3.0	9.2

Sources: English data is from first wave of the ELSA. U.S. data is from the 2002 wave of the HRS.

in terms of relative risks are a little steeper in the United Kingdom than in the United States when we rank individuals by net financial wealth.

We do not pursue the same detailed comparisons of relative and "absolute" gradients by wealth that we did for income in figures 5.1 to 5.5. Nevertheless, some idea of the effects of such an adjustment can be obtained from looking at the cut points for the wealth quintiles in each country, presented in table 10.20. The increased wealth inequality in the United States is immediately apparent, with the 20th percentile of the distribution being 62.5 percent of the corresponding value in England ($500 instead of $800) and the 80th percentile being 130 percent of the English value ($146,900 as opposed to $112,700). Forgetting the difference in the levels for a minute and concentrating on relative risks, because the health gradients by wealth quintile are equally steep in each country, the adjustment to a gradient measured across absolute levels of wealth will tend to make the gradient in the United States flatter than that observed in England over a common wealth range.

Clearly, this is a potentially interesting avenue for future research. One question is simply the degree of transatlantic variation in the extent to which individuals are ranked differently in the income and wealth distributions, which will presumably depend on the different institutional arrangements for income maintenance in the two countries and how each might depend on the level of financial wealth the household may have. A second question is the extent to which income and wealth correlate differently with risk factors and health behaviors in the two countries, and particularly those that may have occurred in early life. The final issue is then to relate any such differences to differences in health outcomes or factors (such as stress, status, or control, for example) that are linked with such health outcomes.

10.10   Conclusions

In this paper, we have presented data on some of the most salient issues regarding the social health gradient in health and the manner in which this health gradient differs for men in England and the United States. There are a several key findings. First, looking across a wide variety of diseases, average health status among mature men is much worse in America compared to England, confirming non-gender specific findings we reported in Banks et al. 2006. Second, there exists a steep negative health gradient for men in both countries where men at the bottom of the economic hierarchy are in much worse health than those at the top. This social health gradient exists whether education, income, or financial wealth is used as the marker of one's SES status. While the negative social gradient in male health characterizes men in both countries, it appears to be steeper in the United States. These central conclusions are maintained even after controlling for a standard set of behavioral risk factors such as smoking, drinking, and obesity and are equally true using either biological measures of disease or individual self-reports.

In contrast to these disease based measures of health, health of American men appears to be superior to the health of English men when self-reported general health status is used as the measure of health status. This apparent contradiction does not result from differences in comorbidity, emotional health, or ability to function, all of which still point to mature American men being less healthy than their English counterparts. The contradiction most likely stems instead from different thresholds used by Americans and English when evaluating their health status on subjective scales. For the same objective health status, Americans are much more likely to say that their health is good than are the English.

Finally, we present preliminary data that indicates that feedbacks from new health events to household income are also one of the reasons that underlie the strength of the income gradient with health in England. Previous research has demonstrated its importance as one of the underlying causes in the United States, and these results suggest that that conclusion should most likely be extended to England as well.

References

Adams, P., M. Hurd, D. McFadden, A. Merrill, and T. Ribeiro. 2003. Healthy, wealthy, and wise? Tests for direct causal paths between health and socioeconomic status. *Journal of Econometrics* 112:3–56.

Banks, J., R. Blundell, and J. P. Smith. 2003. Understanding differences in household financial wealth between the United States and Great Britain. *Journal of Human Resources* 38 (2): 241–79.

Banks, J., M. Marmot, Z. Oldfield, and J. P. Smith. 2006. Disease and disadvantage in the United States and in England. *Journal of the American Medical Association* 295:2037–45.

Goodman, N., I-F. Lin, M. Weinstein, and Y.-H. Lin. 2003. Evaluating the quality of self-reports of hypertension and diabetes. *Journal of Clinical Epidemiology* 56:148–54.

Harris, M. I., K. M. Flegal, C. C. Cowie, M. S. Eberhardt, D. E. Goldstein, R. R. Little, H. M. Wiedmeyer, and D. D. Byrd-Holt. 1998. Prevalence of diabetes, impaired fasting glucose, and impaired glucose tolerance in U.S. adults: The Third National Health and Nutrition Examination Survey, 1988–1994. *Diabetes Care* 21:518–24.

Health Survey for England (HSE). 2003. *Health Survey for England 2003.* Vol. 3, *Methodology and documentation.* London: The Stationery Office.

Hurd, M., F. T. Juster, and J. P. Smith. 2003. Enhancing the quality of data on income: Recent innovations from the HRS. *Journal of Human Resources* 38 (3): 758–72.

Kapteyn, A., J. P. Smith, and A. van Soest. 2004. Self-reported work disability in the United States and The Netherlands. Federal Reserve Bank of San Francisco. Working Papers in Applied Economic Theory no. 2002-22.

King, G., C. J. L. Murray, J. A. Salomon, and A. Tandon. 2004. Enhancing the validity and cross-cultural comparability of measurement in survey research. *American Political Science Review* 98 (1): 191–204.

Marmot, M. 1999. A multi-level approaches to understanding social determinants. In *Social epidemiology,* ed. L. Berkman and I. Kawachi, 349–67. Oxford: Oxford University Press.

Marmot, M., J. Banks, R. Blundell, C. Lessof, and J. Nazroo. 2003. Health, wealth, and lifestyles of the older population in England—The 2002 English Longitudinal Study of Ageing. London: Institute of Fiscal Studies.

Melia, J., S. Moss, and L. Johns 2004. Rates of prostate-specific antigen testing in general practice in England and Wales in asymptomatic and symptomatic patients: A cross-sectional study. *British Journal of Urology International* 94:51–56.

Mendall, M. A., P. Patel, L. Ballam, D. Strachan, and T. C. Northfield. 1996. C-reactive protein and its relation to cardiovascular risk factor. *BMJ,* 312:1061–65.

National Institutes of Health: National Heart, Lung, and Blood Institute. 1997. Sixth Report of the Joint National Committee on the Prevention, Detection, Evaluation and Treatment of High Blood Pressure. NIH Publication no. 98-04080. Washington, DC: NIH.

Salomon, J., A. Tandon, and C. Murray. 2004. Comparability of self rated health: Cross sectional multi-country survey using anchoring vignettes. *British Medical Journal* 328 (7434): 258–60.

Sirovich, B. E., L. M. Schwartz, and S. Woloshin. 2003. Screening men for prostate and colorectal cancer in the United States: Does practice reflect the evidence? *Journal of the American Medical Association* 289:1414–20.

Smith, J. P. 1999. Healthy bodies and thick wallets. *Journal of Economic Perspectives* 13 (2): 108–32.

———. 2004. Unraveling the SES health connection. *Population and Development Review. Aging, Health, and Public Policy: Demographic and Economic Perspectives* 30:133–50.

Steptoe, A., and M. Marmot. 2004. Socioeconomic status and coronary heart disease: A psychobiological perspective. *Population and Development Review. Aging, Health, and Public Policy: Demographic and Economic Perspectives* 30:133–50.

Wilkinson, R. G. 1996. *Unhealthy societies: The afflictions of inequality.* London: Routledge.

Contributors

James Banks
Department of Economics
University College London
Gower Street
London WC1E 6BT England

Jay Bhattacharya
117 Encina Commons
Center for Primary Care and Outcomes
  Research
Stanford University
Stanford, CA 94305-6019

Axel Börsch-Supan
Mannheim Research Institute for the
  Economics of Aging
University of Mannheim
Building L13, 17
D-68131 Mannheim Germany

Anne Case
Woodrow Wilson School
367 Wallace Hall
Princeton University
Princeton, NJ 08544-1022

Amitabh Chandra
John F. Kennedy School of
  Government
Harvard University
79 JFK Street
Cambridge MA 02138

James J. Choi
Yale School of Management
135 Prospect Street
P.O. Box 208200
New Haven, CT 06520-8200

Courtney Coile
Department of Economics
Wellesley College
106 Central Street
Wellesley, MA 02481

David M. Cutler
Department of Economics
Harvard University
1875 Cambridge Street
Cambridge, MA 02138

Angus Deaton
Woodrow Wilson School
328 Wallace Hall
Princeton University
Princeton, NJ 08544-1013

Alan M. Garber
Center for Primary Care and Outcomes
  Research/Center for Health Policy
  (PCOR/CHP)
Stanford University
117 Encina Commons
Stanford, CA 94305-6019

Edward L. Glaeser
Department of Economics
315A Littauer Center
Harvard University
Cambridge, MA 02138

Michael D. Hurd
RAND Corporation
1776 Main Street
Santa Monica, CA 90407

Hendrik Jürges
Mannheim Research Institute for the
  Economics of Aging
University of Mannheim
Building L13, 17
D-68131 Mannheim, Germany

Mun-Sim Lai
Business and Public Administration
California State University
9001 Stockdale Highway
Bakersfield, CA 93311

David Laibson
Department of Economics
Littauer M-14
Harvard University
Cambridge, MA 02138

Mary Beth Landrum
Department of Health Care Policy
Harvard Medical School
180 Longwood Avenue
Boston, MA 02115

Ronald Lee
Departments of Demography and
  Economics
University of California, Berkeley
2232 Piedmont Avenue
Berkeley, CA 94720

Thomas MaCurdy
Department of Economics
Stanford University
Stanford, CA 94305-6072

Brigitte C. Madrian
John F. Kennedy School of
  Government
Harvard University
79 JFK Street
Cambridge, MA 02138

Michael Marmot
Dept of Epidemiology and Public
  Health
University College London
Gower Street
London WC1E 6BT England

Andrew Mason
Department of Economics
University of Hawaii at Manoa
Room 543, Saunders Hall
2424 Maile Way
Honolulu, HI 96822

Tim Miller
Department of Demography
University of California, Berkeley
2232 Piedmont Avenue # 2120
Berkeley, CA 94720-2120

Zoe Oldfield
Institute for Fiscal Studies
7 Ridgmount Street
London WC1E 7AE England

James M. Poterba
Department of Economics
MIT, E52-373A
50 Memorial Drive
Cambridge, MA 02142-1347

Joshua Rauh
Graduate School of Business
University of Chicago
5807 South Woodlawn Avenue
Chicago, IL 60637

Monika Reti
RAND Corporation
1776 Main Street
Santa Monica, CA 90407

Susann Rohwedder
RAND Corporation
1776 Main Street
Santa Monica, CA 90407

Andrew Samwick
6106 Rockefeller Hall
Department of Economics
Dartmouth College
Hanover, NH 03755-3514

Jonathan Skinner
Department of Economics
6106 Rockefeller Hall
Dartmouth College
Hanover, NH 03755

James P. Smith
RAND Corporation
1776 Main Street
Santa Monica, CA 90407

Kate A. Stewart
Mathematica Policy Research, Inc.
600 Maryland Ave, SW, Suite 550
Washington, DC 20024-2512

An-Chi Tung
Institute of Economics
Academia Sinica
Taipei 11529, Taiwan

Steven F. Venti
Department of Economics
6106 Rockefeller Center
Dartmouth College
Hanover, NH 03755

Robert J. Willis
Survey Research Center
University of Michigan
3048 ISR Building
PO Box 1248
Ann Arbor, MI 48106

David A. Wise
John F. Kennedy School of
    Government
Harvard University
79 John F. Kennedy Street
Cambridge, MA 02138-5398

Author Index

Subject Index